Adrift in the Old World

Adrift in the Old World
The Psychological Pilgrimage
of Washington Irving

JEFFREY RUBIN-DORSKY

The University of Chicago Press   Chicago and London

JEFFREY RUBIN-DORSKY is assistant professor of English
at the University of California, Los Angeles.

The University of Chicago Press, Chicago 60637
The University of Chicago Press, Ltd., London
© 1988 by The University of Chicago
All rights reserved. Published 1988
Printed in the United States of America
97 96 95 94 93 92 91 90 89 88   54321

Library of Congress Cataloging-in-Publication Data

Rubin-Dorsky, Jeffrey.
  Adrift in the Old World.

  Bibliography: p.
  Includes index.
  1. Irving, Washington, 1783–1859—Fictional works.
2. National characteristics, American, in literature.
3. Homelessness in literature. 4. Europe in
literature. 5. Psychology in literature. I. Title.
PS2092.F53R83 1988   813'.54   87-25468
ISBN 0-226-73094-8

For Roberta

This spur which is ever in our sides, . . . this desire for travelling: the passion is no way bad,——. . . order it rightly the advantages are worth the pursuit; the chief of which are——to learn the languages, the laws and customs, and understand the government and interest of other nations,——. . . to take us out of the company of our aunts and grandmothers, and from the track of nursery mistakes; and by shewing us new objects, or old ones in new lights, to reform our judgments——by tasting perpetually the varieties of nature, to know what *is good*——by observing the address and arts of men, to conceive what *is sincere*,——and by seeing the difference of so many various humours and manners,——to look into ourselves and form our own.

Sterne, *The Sermons of Mr. Yorick*

CONTENTS

ACKNOWLEDGMENTS

Research and writing, I was warned in graduate school, are lonely occupations, and so they have proven. Yet when I consider the number of persons who have supported and encouraged me in this project, and who have aided in its completion, I realize the extent to which I belong to a vital community of scholars and friends. Perhaps more than anything else, it is this sense of connectedness that makes the isolation endurable.

Robert Streeter and James E. Miller, Jr., provided guidance at the genesis of my research and then commented on the first version of the manuscript. No matter what I turned up in the far corners of the University of Chicago's Regenstein Library, Bob Streeter had already read it. Jim Miller served as my model critic; it was and still remains my desire to emulate his achievements. Wayne Franklin, Norman Grabo, and Larzer Ziff all read the manuscript at a later stage in its development, and each offered valuable recommendations for its improvement. In my wisdom I incorporated most of what they proffered; in my stubbornness I failed to accept all their wisdom. My UCLA colleague (now emeritus), great friend and mentor, Blake Nevius, gave me the benefit of his vast editorial expertise; his careful scrutiny of the entire book saved me from errors both large and small. I consider myself fortunate to have begun my career while he was still active in the profession.

Several of my fellow Americanists at UCLA—Martha Banta, Michael Colacurcio, Richard Lehan, Kenneth Lincoln, and Barbara Packer—read my work either in article or chapter form and made useful suggestions. Each added a unique and essential perspective. In addition to offering substantive revisions, Richard Yarborough also encouraged me to streamline my prose. Beyond precept, he taught by the example of his own clean style. Maximillan Novak confirmed the scholarly direction I had chosen at a particularly important moment in the manuscript's history. Albert Hutter provided valuable advice on psychological issues, especially the subject of anxiety. Through conversation and the quality of his own research, Gary Nash intensified my interest in American history; later he challenged me to be as precise as possible about Irving's political orientation. But of all the colleagues who lent assistance to my project, Susan Brienza assumed true yeoman duties: during two careful readings of my manuscript, she helped me to clarify ideas, improve structural flaws, and correct stylistic infelicities. Her unacknowledged presence graces almost every page.

My network of academic support extends beyond institutional boundaries. Jack Salzman imparted his love for the study of American culture at a time when I was searching for values; his intellectual passion has become my own. Donald Weber's views on American texts have informed and broadened my thinking. Judith Sensibar and Alan Golding, who have remained my steadfast friends long after our graduate school days at Chicago, continue to enrich my understanding of American literature. William Hedges has willingly shared his ideas and knowledge. As all Americanists know, his writing constitutes the foundation of modern Irving criticism. Terence Martin's favorable evaluation of my scholarship has been a great source of encouragement. Arthur Golden gave invaluable advice when I needed it; he will always have my gratitude. Irene Williams, my scholarly "aunt from Brooklyn" (as she likes to call herself), listened and questioned; I welcome the opportunity to play a similar role for her. Marjorie Perloff's generosity of spirit is unequalled in academia; I am only one of a number of younger scholars whom she has nurtured.

Friends outside the academy were as important as those within. Les and Linda Silverman and Ken Ash and Teri Rojna always opened their homes and their hearts to me, recognizing that scholars need affection as well as books. This was especially true of my brother, Howard, and his wife, Elaine. My parents have been exactly what parents are supposed to be: they believed in me although they did not understand my compulsions. Roberta Rubin-Dorsky's faith in this project remained constant, even when I spent more time in the library than at the dinner table. I dedicate this book to her in recognition of her own dedication and devotion to me.

Many other institutions and individuals lent support to this undertaking. The Mrs. Giles M. Whiting Foundation and the UCLA Academic Senate provided grants that facilitated my research and writing. The staffs of the Regenstein Library at the University of Chicago, the University Research Library at UCLA, the Houghton Library at Harvard University, the New York Public Library, the Huntington Library, and Sleepy Hollow Restorations helped me make the most efficient use of much valuable material. My research assistants during the years I worked on this project—Amy Zheutlin, Sandra Gunning, Stan Yogi, Laura Ferguson, and Tom Burkdall—performed their duties zealously. Jeanette Gilkison and Renee Pickering contributed their word processing skills. Finally, without the scholarship produced by the editors of the Twayne edition of Irving's works, I could not have written this study.

Earlier, condensed versions of chapters 1, 2, 3, and 6 have been published as follows: "Washington Irving: Sketches of Anxiety, *American Literature* 58 (1986):499–522; "A Crisis of Identity: *The Sketch Book* and Nineteenth-Century American Culture," *Prospects* 12 (1987): 255–91; "The Value of Storytelling: 'Rip Van Winkle' and 'The Legend of Sleepy Hollow' in the Context of *The Sketch Book*," *Modern Philology* 82 (1985):393–406; and "*The Alhambra*: Washington Irving's House of Fiction," *Studies in American Fiction* 11 (1983):171–88. I wish to express my appreciation to the editors and publishers of these journals—and to their referees—for the careful readings they gave my work.

PREFACE
National Crisis / Personal Trauma

Washington Irving has been stereotyped primarily as the last significant
American writer who aspired to and achieved a classic English style, and as
the conservator of aristocratic values in a rapidly changing republic. *Adrift in
the Old World* is dedicated to overturning this notion of Irving as an An-
glicized writer by establishing his "Americanness," meaning, by that elusive
term, that he was shaped by, and came to identify himself with, his country
and its particular heritage. More than twenty years ago, in *Washington Irving:
An American Study, 1802–1832*, William Hedges demonstrated that he was a
forerunner of the great renaissance in American prose fiction (stylistically he
precedes Hawthorne and James; narratively and thematically he anticipates
Poe and Melville); nevertheless, Irving has yet to be historicized, to be connected to the milieu that produced him and yet disappointed him for most of
his adult life. In order to accomplish this end, and thus to fix Irving's place in
our literary and cultural history, I have concentrated on how he became an
emblem for his generation: Irving's fictional writings between 1815 and 1832
present us with a history of his search for order and literary sustenance in the
Old World; and in a wonderfully paradoxical fashion, this history recapitu-
lates America's own as the American people sought to accept and then embrace the overwhelming growth and prosperity of the first half of the nineteenth century.

Yet these years—from, approximately, the end of the War of 1812 to the
foreshadowings of Civil War—also defined an era of national anxiety, which
centered on the worry that the furiously developing nation would lose touch
with the spirit of the patriot age. Correspondingly, numerous documentary
sources suggest a general apprehension for the future of the Republic, the fear
that an unprecedented prosperity would deprive America of its self-proclaimed
role as a redeemer nation, and that it already had, in fact, distracted loyal but

unsuspecting citizens from the virtuous path of their heroic predecessors. Coming of age during these years of extraordinary change and amidst an unstable environment, a second generation had to grapple with the belief that they were not shaping the nation, the nation was shaping them, and with the great fear that American success had demeaned the country's spiritual heritage. Significantly, this generation made Washington Irving the most popular and respected writer of his time.

Since, clearly, the life and writings of our first professional author spread across a much larger segment of the formative decades of American literature and culture than the 1815–32 period on which I focus, it is necessary to say a few words about this choice. I would not, first of all, wish it to be misconstrued as reflecting either a belief that Irving's earlier and later years are without significant interest or an acceptance of previous interpretations of these phases of his career as definitive. As I see it, fresh readings are in order for both the 1783–1815 span, when, in his youthful burlesque writings, Irving was outrightly critical of republican culture and mores, and the 1832–59 range, during which, after returning in triumph to his native land, the prodigal became an American celebrity/celebrant (or so it seemed on the surface). Yet beyond the primary difference in orientation, and other unique defining characteristics, these eras are linked to each other, and connected to the central one of 1815–32, which was spent exclusively in Europe, by the feeling of homelessness continually haunting Irving. Whether settled in New York, traveling on the Continent, or exploring the western frontier, he belonged to no real place in time. Nor did he share the Americans' love of space. Only in the realm of the imagination, the world of timelessness, could the pilgrim find the order and continuity, wholeness and harmony, that had become his grail. Nowhere is this as foregrounded as in the European fictions which, paradoxically, also reveal more about the expectations and desires of his native audience than any of the books he wrote in America before or after this seventeen-year sojourn. To a greater extent than the celebrated style, charm, humor, or narrative ease of Irving's writings, it was his story of dispossession, told in various fictional forms and through different personae, that affected (and I would maintain, still touches) the hearts and minds of his countrymen.

I have limited my study to the fiction because it is far richer in meaning and implication than the histories Irving also wrote during these years abroad. Though he was not an "original" writer in the way we might apply the term to Poe or Hawthorne, nevertheless it was in his fiction that, to the extent he was able, he permitted his imagination to follow its own dictates and impulses; yet, at the same time, that fiction strongly reflects his American origins. Irving's romantic retelling of the stories of Columbus's four voyages to the New World and the Spaniards' conquest of the Moors and Granada, especially the way in which he turns both into emblems of loss and unfulfilled possibilities, deserve attention and analysis. I will offer new readings of the *Life and Voyages of Columbus* and the *Conquest of Granada* in the future. But for the present, they fall outside the scope of this work which, finally, may be understood as a history of Irving's imagination as it manifested itself in the most creative and vital phase of his long career.

I am arguing, therefore, that Irving held his American readers in thrall (for example, "Rip Van Winkle" was probably the most popular and reprinted piece of the nineteenth century) because the tale he had to tell essentially re-enacted their doubts about identity and their fantasies about escape. In this respect he was a truly representative American author; almost all his productions from this period directly or indirectly chronicle his reaction to the failure of America to embody the principles and live up to the expectations of the Founding Fathers. Like so many of his fellow citizens, he could never quite transcend his despair over the decline of American ideals. His consequent search, then, in which Americans eagerly and vicariously joined, was for a home where the impoverished spirit, cut off from its primary source of nurture, could resettle. This tracing of America's failure, occurring even at the level of style, has eluded most of his readers, since they have approached Irving with too many preconceptions about his fabled "geniality," usually finding little more than confirmation of this image. (In fact, he suffered through an extended period of depression which, brought on by a series of losses—including the death of his betrothed in 1809 and the death of his mother in 1817—and exacerbated by the bankruptcy of the family business in 1818, shaped the production of *The Sketch Book* in 1819–20. There is, of course, no necessary opposition between public geniality and private depression; it could even be argued that they are linked.) Moreover, in a remarkable way, Irving's most compelling subject as a writer—the displaced self adrift in a mutable world—which was, of course, autobiographical in substance, coincided with the uneasiness and uncertainty of the American people as they contemplated the fate of the nation in the early decades of the nineteenth century. The conflicts, anxieties, and needs of the new republic were reflected in

Irving's profound sense of homelessness and his acute longing for stability; and it was, above all, the operation of this mirroring effect that subliminally captivated his audience. That is, in the tales of his wanderings and "adventures," the American public found a configuration of its own inner life. Personal trauma paralleled national crisis: for both Irving and America, loss was at the very center of experience.

The present study, therefore, views Irving's "representativeness" primarily in psychological terms; that is, his wrestling with cultural pressures and personal problems parallels nineteenth-century America's struggle with its new self-conception. Thus, for each major work of fiction he published between 1815 and 1832, I examine first its autobiographical dimension and then its connections to the collective social, political, and intellectual consciousness of his countrymen. What did Irving's American audience see in his writings? If he was simply the greatest in a long line of imitators of English models, why did Americans find him so compelling and elevate him to such a revered place as a literary founding father? Since in the pages that follow these questions become constant points of reference, and since I am seeking to link personal psychology and communal politics, two points of clarification must be made at the outset.

Throughout this work I use the word "anxiety" in full awareness of the fact that it is a vexed term, as those who are familiar with the many complex debates surrounding it can attest. No one, of course, has yet derived a precise definition of anxiety, and, clearly, no global definition could possibly satisfy every psychoanalytic paradigm. As Freud wrote in a late work entitled *Inhibitions, Symptoms and Anxiety* (1926), "[a]nxiety is not so simple a matter."[1] Generally speaking, however—and especially when referring to Irving's responses to what he perceives as a threatening environment—I follow Erik Erikson's explanation in the conclusion to *Childhood and Society*:

> [M]an remains ready to expect from some enemy, force, or event in the outer world that which, in fact, endangers him from within: from his own angry drives, from his own sense of smallness, and from his own split inner world. Thus he is always irrationally ready to fear invasion by vast and vague forces which are other than himself; strangling encirclement by everything that is not safely clarified as allied; and devastating loss of face before all-surrounding, mocking audiences. These, not the animal's fears, characterize human anxiety, and this in world affairs as well as in personal affairs.[2]

Both Freud and Erikson apparently agree that anxiety is associated with—indeed, is a reaction to—some form of outer danger; for Erikson, a diffuse state of tension accompanies this reaction. Interestingly, the term as it is defined here would not be alien to Irving's understanding; in fact, he employs the word anxiety (or one of its variants) as a normal part of his diction when writing about the strained days of his early years in England.

The second clarification concerns Irving's political orientation and the set of values that orientation would necessarily imply. For the most part scholars agree that, except for a ten-year period from about 1830 to 1840 when he openly embraced the ideas espoused by Andrew Jackson and the Democratic party, Irving remained a staunch Federalist (later a Whig). I do not wish to challenge this notion, nor do I desire to dispute the belief that Irving's temperament and sensibility (perhaps his "gentility") naturally kept him from championing the cause of the common man. The picture Sean Wilentz paints in *Chants Democratic* (with the help of a few passages from *Salmagundi*, written by Irving, his brother, William, and James Kirke Paulding in 1807) of the young man looking on aghast at a political rally "while 'old cartmen, cobblers, and tailors' clambered onto the hustings, as if a set of demotic lunatics had been turned loose to arouse 'that awful despot, the people,'" vividly captures a public attitude that, while it may have mellowed over the years, never quite disappeared (again, except for the decade of the 1830s).[3] I would insist, however, that in this respect a distinction must be made not only between the early and middle phases of Irving's career, but more especially between the man who formed political allegiances and the author who expressed an imaginative commitment to the conception of the Republic, a formulation that transcended class boundaries. Irving may not have walked among the masses, but he did not exclude them from his vision of America. Every important fiction of his during the years 1815–32 transposes, in personal terms, the tension recognizable to all Americans between a vanishing ideal and a diminished reality.

Yet it might be argued by a populist historian that when I pursue the idea of a "crisis of identity" in early-nineteenth-century America and stress the consequent fear on the part of many citizens that the moral underpinnings of their society were collapsing, what I am actually highlighting is a crisis of authority for the Federalist (later Whig) party and for the ideology it promulgated. Certainly the various types of artisans and workers whose rise to class status Wilentz chronicles in *Chants Democratic* would not have responded with the same fervor to the jeremiads being issued in the 1820s and 30s as those who belonged, say, to the upper middle class. In fact, according to Wilentz, the former "came at various points to interpret social disorder and the decline of the Republic at least partly in terms of class divisions between capitalist employers and employees."[4] Nevertheless—and Wilentz certainly makes this clear about the subjects of his book—Americans from all classes gravitated toward the "language of the Republic" to articulate their concerns and explain their views. Faced with profound changes that affected the stability of their lives, Americans reinterpreted the meaning of the Republic— "their shared ideals of commonwealth, virtue, independence, citzenship, and equality."[5] While on the level of intellectual evaluation of republican concepts Irving spoke primarily to those with a cultured background, on the lower frequency of emotional response to disorder and diffusion he touched Americans everywhere.

Adrift in the Old World has been conceived then as an act of historical recovery and critical revision. Some scholars have rightly acknowledged Irving as a literary pioneer: he was among the initial group of writers and artists to journey back to the civilization of the Old World and ahead to the frontier of the New, as well as venturing into the underside of the American psyche before Poe, Hawthorne, and Melville would stake it out as their particular terrain. Others have recognized him as an innovator in the commercial aspects of authorship: he was the first to devise a way of securing simultaneous British and American copyright in the days before an international agreement had been reached. We have, nevertheless, lost sight of just how central a figure he was to Americans in the early decades of the nineteenth century. In many respects his story was theirs, and when, in print, they accompanied him on his psychological pilgrimage in search of a secure, safe haven from the tensions of American life, they too were escaping the disappointments of early American dreams. The sense of "boundlessness" that defined the period, coupled with the uneasiness of the "postheroic generation" in light of its inability to emulate the unswerving integrity of the Founding Fathers, left Americans fearing that the character of the Republic had altered forever. Consequently, the imaginative life of the time, expressed in the writings of such authors as James Fenimore Cooper, Sarah J. Hale, and Irving himself, was preoccupied with the loss of the nation-as-home, a loss that was not yet viewed as permanent. Following Irving to Europe and, finally, to that great pleasure palace of the fancy, the Alhambra, Americans sought along with him not only a release from the oppressive realities of a materialist society but, as well, a source of continuity to replace the one that was fast becoming historically obsolete. It might in fact be argued that he subconsciously gave them exactly what they subconsciously wanted. It is equally true, however, that neither he nor they were ready to accept the order provided by the imaginative process of Washington Irving's fictional world as a substitute for the political order of George Washington's republican vision.

The American Writer and the Loss of Home

The year 1815 signifies a point of demarcation for the youthful American nation. With the War of 1812 brought to a successful conclusion, the new Republic was finally legitimized; though culturally it would continue to wince under the verbal attacks of its estranged parent, politically it had secured itself from further intervention. The Old World could no longer willfully impose its desires upon the New. As a result of this triumph, Americans envisioned a peaceful and prosperous future, in effect the culmination of the efforts of the Founding Fathers. Soon enough, however, shadows appeared on the new horizon, and the "era of good feelings" gave way to an "age of anxiety."[1] Not cohesiveness but diffusion, not certainty but doubt, not harmony but discord characterized the two decades following America's second victory over England.

Anxiety, in fact, frames the period. Even at the outset there were those who feared that the glory days of the Republic had already passed. John Adams, for one, perceived a movement toward "disaggregation," which signaled a decline in the character of the nation. Writing to Thomas Jefferson in 1815, he had expressed this point of view interrogatively: "Is the Nineteenth Century to be a Contrast to the Eighteenth? Is it to extinguish all the Lights of its Predecessor?" The usually sanguine Jefferson was loath to agree with his friend, preferring to "steer [his] bark with Hope in the head."[2] Nevertheless, he had earlier admitted that the "public spirit" motivating the American people during the War for Independence had dissipated; a fervor that was once directed toward Revolutionary goals now served abjectly nonRevolutionary ends. "From the conclusion of this war," he wrote in *Notes on the State of Virginia* (1787), "we shall be going down hill. . . . [The people] will forget themselves, but in the sole faculty of making money, and will never think of uniting to effect a due respect for their rights."[3] In 1814 he confirmed that prediction: "I have overlived the generation with which mutual labors & perils begat mutual confidence and influence."[4] By 1830 the currents of uneasiness ran deeper. Defending the "virtues" of New England while arguing for a protective tariff and against the doctrine of nullification, Daniel Webster ended the first half of one of his most famous Senate speeches with a plea for renewed republican feeling: "Would to God," he cried out, "that harmony might again return!" He then closed his remarks with a horrific vision of disunion: "When my eyes shall be turned to behold for the last time the sun in heaven, may I not see him shining on the broken and dishonored fragments of a once glorious Union; on States dissevered, discordant, belligerent; on a land rent with civil feuds, or drenched, it may be, in fraternal blood!"[5] This political fragmentation and disharmony is reflected in the literary work of James Fenimore Cooper, Sarah J. Hale, and Washington Irving.

The year 1815 also marks a point of departure in the life of the most revered and most popular writer of the early Republic. Along with hordes of his fellow Americans, Washington Irving set sail for England, and like many of these travelers he turned his European voyage into an Old World pilgrimage. The end of the Napoleonic wars had made the Continent once again safe for travel, and Americans were eager to explore the land of their forefathers in order to view for themselves the famous monuments and institutions that had excited their childhood imaginations. Irving, however, had already done the Grand Tour in 1804 and 1805, so the motivation for his travels lay elsewhere. Peripatetic and aimless since 1809, the year his fiancée, Matilda Hoffman, had died of tuberculosis, Irving had produced no substantial piece of writing after the publication of *Knickerbocker's History of New York* (1809). He needed to shake loose from his torpor; he hungered for creative stimulus. "Unsettled and almost joyless as has been my life for some time past," he wrote to his friend Henry Brevoort on the eve of his journey, "I am satisfied that a little absence will be greatly to my advantage."[6] Judging from his initial response to England, his prediction was accurate. "I am like another being from what I was in that listless period of existence that preceded my departure from America," he told Brevoort shortly after landing. "It seems as if my whole nature had changed—. . . my very blood seems to flow more warm and sprightly." His spirits were high, for he had located, literally at the house of his sister and brother-in-law and more generally in England overall, what was unavailable to him in America: "Never before did I find myself more completely at home."[7] Or so it seemed in those early halcyon days.

Though he wandered through Europe from 1815 to 1832, Washington

Irving never relinquished the dream of finding a home; and, somewhat para-doxically, during those years of travel (and the production of several "travel books"), "home" became the central concern of all his writings. Not home as a physical place, however, for that always remained America and, even more specifically, New York. But home as a spiritual and emotional entity, where trusted values—the values of the Fathers—were inculcated, nurtured, and protected, where the feeling of belonging, based upon the harmonious reci-procity between individual mind and collective consciousness, prevailed—this was the object of Irving's quest. The idea of home was also of profound concern to most nineteenth-century Americans; the near-obsession with the values of the Fathers and the domestic metaphors that were applied again and again to the country reveal the general preoccupation with the distance Amer-ica had traveled from its spiritual source in the Revolution. Later, in the 1850s, domesticity would be used politically as a way of harnessing the rheto-ric and attitudes accompanying "woman's sphere" to the cause of saving the Union. But in the 1820s and 1830s, the configuration reminded Americans of their proper relationship to the Fathers and of their duty to preserve the house that they had built. The deepest connection between the celebrated au-thor and his generation occurs precisely at the point where Irving's home-lessness intersects with America's anxiety that the home the Founding Fathers had established was lost forever.[8]

I

The idea of "boundlessness" exerted a controlling force on American life dur-ing the years Washington Irving sojourned in Europe.[9] From 1815 through the early 1840s, Americans envisioned endless possibilities for the physical, intellectual, and moral development of the nation. Just as the acquisition of new territories expanded the borders of the Republic, the development of new modes of perception stretched man's potentialities beyond their former boundaries. The limits that the eighteenth century had respected, and which had been threatened but not deposed by the American Revolution, receded before the onslaught of the nineteenth. The restraints of reason, rank, and rev-erence for the past, for example, could no longer hold in check democratic man's zeal for self-aggrandizement. This was the age, after all, of transcenden-talism, romanticism, and Jacksonianism; of perfectionism, communialism, and millennialism; of technological advancement, reform movements, and the "woman question." In an 1841 lecture, William Ellery Channing labeled the "commanding characteristic" of the time as its "tendency . . . to expansion, to

3

diffusion, to universality." This movement was "directly opposed to the spirit of exclusiveness, restriction, narrowness, monopoly, which has prevailed in past ages. . . . Thought [had] free[d] the old bounds to which men used to confine themselves."[10]

Like others far more conservative than he, Channing doubted the efficacy of these tendencies in the sphere of human action. Troubled by man's unwillingness to recognize the inherent limitations of his powers, he criticized the questioning of "the infinite, the unsearchable, with an audacious self-reliance." A more tangible sign of the disturbing "centrifugal" quality of American society, however, was the rapid migration of large parts of the population. A restless, unsettled feeling pervaded American life: for those who were aggressive and mobile enough there were land to be had and fortunes to be made. Communities were left behind, new ones begun and then abandoned for the promise of still greater opportunities. Personal success and national expansion had "displaced considerations of the coherence and stability of the social order."[11] Risk taking was the mode of the day. From his European perspective Irving was able to perceive and assess these changes occurring in America, and in a notebook he kept during his first years abroad he wrote that

> the impatience of restraint, the neglect and almost contempt for minor observances, the restless spirit[,] speculative turn and proneness to hyperbole, with which Americans are charged, may be traced to the unsettled mode of their life—the rapid changes that are continually taking place in the state of society and the face of the country around them—to the frequent shiftings of place and occupation—the vast migrations they undertake—. . . . [He] who beholds every thing around him changing as if by enchantment—what was once a wilderness becoming a busy hive of population—what in childhood he saw a village grown into a city before he arrives at manhood—every where reality outstripping imagination—surely it is no wonder that such a one should be speculative and hyperbolical.[12]

Fueling this frenzy of speculation was, of course, the American creed of "individualism," which provided an intellectual rationale for the push outward toward the promise of self-fulfillment. Certainly there were locales where the Revolutionary spirit of cooperation had not been eradicated and where a cautious view of the present still persisted.[13] Yet, for the most part, as Tocqueville had observed, the American saw his destiny as shaped by himself alone: "The woof of time is every instant broken and the track of generations effaced. Those who went before are soon forgotten; of those who will come after, no one has any idea: the interest of man is confined to those in close propinquity to himself. . . . Aristocracy had made a chain of all the members of the community, from the peasant to the king; democracy breaks that chain and severs every link of it."[14] However, because Tocqueville took Americans at their face value, he highlighted only a professed creed; below the surface bravado—deeper even than the new selfishness he had correctly perceived—there existed an undertow of anxiety about the breakdown and loss of community.

Thus, at the same time that his comment underscores the buoyant spirit of self-reliance, it also points to a less joyous result of the "age of boundlessness": as much as declarations of selfhood and acts of dispersion were affirmed, a feeling of spiritual homelessness began to grip the American psyche. "Mere physical propinquity" did not bind people into a community; the gains achieved in material production and acquisition could not offset the loss of social cohesion that had characterized earlier settlements. According to Rowland Berthoff, after 1825 neither the local community nor the state could exert control over, or give direction to, the "rush of economic change."[15] Americans were painfully aware that the society their ancestors had bequeathed them was being ineradicably altered; the continuity of cherished values that makes a culture whole, that creates the deepest point of identification between a citizen and his country, was in the process of being shattered. The communalism of the Founding Fathers, dedicated not to the fulfillment of the individual but to the collective welfare of the burgeoning nation, championing principles of liberty and equal rights rather than the free pursuit of wealth and power, became a troubling memory instead of a cheerful reality. Such a dramatic shift in orientation would be disrupting at any point, but the beginning of a society crystallizes a crucial moment in its history, with a power to evoke an emotional response far greater than any other; and, as George Forgie convincingly argues, "to American adults living in the middle of the nineteenth century that power was doubly strong, for—if we may fix its boundaries generously—the national beginning was simultaneous with their own." Thus, what Abraham Lincoln claimed for Henry Clay (born 1777) was true for an entire generation, including Washington Irving: "The infant nation, and the infant child began the race of life together."[16]

The "heroic" generation of the Founders had forged a new republic and, simultaneously, given birth to a second generation. These Americans were the "sons of those heroes"; for them, the fathers/Fathers were one and the same.

The identification had been stressed from the outset, so that the fortunes of this "postheroic" generation and the fate of the "infant nation" were indissolubly linked.[17] Therefore, Noah Webster argued, it was necessary to "implant in the minds of the American youth the principles of virtue and of liberty and inspire them with just and liberal ideas of government and with an inviolable attachment to their own country." Furthermore, Webster added, "every child in America . . . as soon as he opens his lips . . . should rehearse the history of his own country; he should lisp the praise of liberty and of those illustrious heroes and statesmen who have wrought a revolution in her favor."[18] Nurtured, therefore, on the belief that as their characters developed so would the character of the nation, this generation could not avoid acknowledging the responsibility that had been placed upon them (though they might, in the end, deny its validity). The Fathers had sacrificed for the Republic, so must they. In 1824, the *United States Literary Gazette* issued but one of the era's numerous reminders of the nature of that sacrifice and what it had wrought: "We look back to the earliest struggles of our fathers; we follow their records down to the establishment of our country, and see them brought out from bondage, and led through the desolations of famine, pestilence and war, to this, the promised land. We look around and find the nation which they planted, multiplied with unprecedented rapidity, and now enjoying an accumulation—we had almost said an intensity, of blessing, which no other nation has known."[19]

A nation rapidly multiplying and materially prospering, and yet one that was inexorably moving away from the harmony of republican cooperation and toward the disorder of civil strife, burdened the conscience of the postheroic generation. There was no denying that the Fathers had bestowed an extraordinary gift, and at a great cost to themselves: "Our existing prosperity and happiness," claimed one writer who typified this view, "and the whole of our present magnificent possessions, are based upon the heroic darings and endurances, the gigantic struggles and equally gigantic achievements of those who have preceded us."[20] The task of the sons, pronounced everywhere—in newspapers, magazines, literary journals, Fourth-of-July orations—was to preserve that inheritance intact. "We take our pure liberty . . . by descent," said the *United States Literary Gazette* in language reminiscent of Noah's covenant with God; "it is, not our right, but our *first national duty*, to feel that the ark of freedom and of truth, is, and is to be, committed to our hands, for ourselves and for our children."[21] Addressing the crowd which had gathered at Faneuil Hall on August 2, 1826, to hear his speech in commemoration of

6

the passing of Adams and Jefferson, Daniel Webster said that "this lovely land, this glorious liberty, these benign institutions, the dear purchase of our fathers, are ours; ours to enjoy, ours to preserve, ours to transmit." But the Fathers' bestowal brought with it a moral imperative (which Webster puts, interestingly, in terms of financial responsibility): "Generations past and generations to come hold us responsible for this sacred trust. . . . We can never, indeed, pay the debt which is upon us; but by virtue, by morality, by religion, by the cultivation of every good principle and every good habit, we may hope to enjoy the blessing, through our day, and to leave it unimpaired to our children." [22] Reminding them at every turn of their obligations, posterity spoke loudly to the postheroic generation.

So, too, did the progenitors. "Our fathers, from behind, admonish us, with their anxious paternal voices," Webster told his Boston audience. Like the patriarchs Adams and Jefferson (of whom Webster was speaking particularly), "they live in their example; and they live, emphatically, and will live, in the influence which their lives and efforts, their principles and opinions, now exercise, and will continue to exercise, on the affairs of men." This affecting presence of the founders was nowhere more obviously felt in the mid–1820s than in the recurring reference to their legacy, the Union, as the "house" the Fathers had built to secure the republican ideals for which they had gone to war. Not only did the image help to literalize an abstract concept, making it emotionally available for both children and adults, but it encouraged the extension of feelings and attitudes toward the nation that were generally reserved for the home. Having referred to the Union on one occasion as the "holy and beautiful house of our fathers," Rufus Choate on another linked the strong emotions evoked by familial associations with surging patriotic feeling; all that we cherish in private life, from "the faces of brothers and sisters, and the loved father and mother," to "the laugh of playmates, the old willow-tree, and well, and school-house," inculcates in us a love for the country that makes these scenes possible. Patriotism comes alive as soon as we awaken to "love and the *sense of home* and of security and of property under law." [23] What better way to validate the idea than by evoking Washington, the Republic's most devoted patriarch, whose thoughts never wandered from its cause while serving it selflessly. As the Union's faithful servant, Daniel Webster said in his centennial oration, our first president had regarded it, "less as one of our blessings than as the great treasure-house which contained them all." For Washington, the Union was "the great magazine of all our means of prosperity; here, as he thought, and as every true American still thinks, are deposited all our animating prospects, all our solid hopes for future greatness."[24]

Protecting the family home and preserving the Union, therefore, were mutually reinforcing acts. In part, this identification may be traced back to the revolutionary period, when the question of what form the new state would take was being debated. Primarily the great uncertainty lay in where moral authority should reside; the solution, however temporary, fixed upon the idea of the family. But now, in the increasingly open society of nineteenth-century America, where men pursued private, rather than public, ends, and where the forces of competition and greed were daily rending the social fabric, the idea of the nation-as-home suggested an overarching security that could not be shaken by random events. The Union, "this great palladium of our security and happiness," would shelter the American people. Like a family, it created an unbreakable bond: "Born to a common inheritance, purchased by the toils, the sacrifices, and the blood of their common ancestors," the citizens of the Republic "should be united, not less by the ties of common sympathy and kindred feeling."[25] Thus, the nurturing function of the home was easily transferrable to that of the nation; one prepared the child for adult social and economic reality, the other taught him the ethics of citizenship and admiration for democratic values and institutions. Parental authority, which was based upon love and affection, and which encouraged the child to develop self-control, was precisely the correct analogy for the voluntary respect due the Republic from its citizen-sons.[26]

In a period when economic and geographic expansion was beginning to disrupt the stability of domestic life and relocate the center of meaningful activity from a rural, agricultural environment to an urban, commercial one (which was further accompanied by a realignment in the locus of authority and control from the home to the marketplace), the house metaphor called forth visions in the nineteenth-century imagination of an older, more traditional world—the village of pre–1815 America—where, as they saw it, communitarian practices had been the standard. The organicism of that earlier time maintained its strong appeal: "home," characterized by a self-sufficient domestic economy dependent upon "cooperation, trust, and a spirit of mutuality," was the center of the community and "community" was the heart of the nation. Americans may have consciously eschewed the authority of history, yet there were aspects of the Revolutionary past, most immediately the Founding Fathers who were still alive, that directed their minds. In this context it is important to note that Irving's most popular works of the 1820s, especially *The Sketch Book* and *Bracebridge Hall*, illustrate his attraction to England as both a cohesive nation and a united people held together by respect for fundamental social and political principles. Later in the century, the American Romantics would celebrate the Constitution (not the Revolution) as a symbol of unity and the Union, "generalized and lifted above a narrowly political context," as an incarnation of "natural wholeness" and spiritual bonding.[27] For these writers, the idea of America as a "united states" took precedence over proclamations of liberty and freedom; the nation as an integrated culture—essentially the quality of familial harmony implied in the house metaphor—captured their imaginations. By the 1850s, the issues surrounding "home" became charged with political significance. For example, Harriet Beecher Stowe, who was deeply concerned about the integrity of the traditional home, used domesticity to arouse popular sentiment for the cause of abolition.[28]

Given the writings of recent historians like Stephen Innes and William Cronon, who have demonstrated that, contrary to the earlier studies of Lockridge, Greven, Demos, and Zuckerman, many New England colonial towns were not subsistence communities at all but significant participators in the commercial economy of the North Atlantic (and, moreover, as Cronon puts it, treated "land and property as commodities traded at market"), the objection might easily be raised that the organic unity of the past celebrated by the nineteenth century was vastly overrated.[29] Indeed, Innes forcefully demonstrates that in at least one Early American agricultural center, Springfield, Massachusetts (and undoubtedly in many others, since it was surely more typical of farming communities than either Dedham or Andover), self-assertiveness was the dominant spirit, and that by "all measures Springfield was a more individualistic, less communal and egalitarian place than early New England is thought to have been." Rather than a "common and coherent system of values" and cooperation, economic competition and social conflict prevailed.[30] Clearly, Americans had experienced social instability, personal unrest, and, because of another heinous commercial practice—land speculation—painful uprootedness long before Irving's day.

But under the pressure of an advancing industrialism that was rapidly changing the texture of their society and eroding the cherished values of the Founders, the postheroic generation created in the early nineteenth century a myth of America's colonial simplicity, a myth which Irving himself helped construct (with the formulation of a legendary community like Sleepy Hollow), but which he also mocked in his earlier burlesque comedies and, to a degree, in "Rip Van Winkle." (Later he would explode the myth in some of his essays.) Accompanying this vision of a time of simple harmony was an exaggerated sense of the disinterested benevolence of those who fought the struggle for America's independence. Such extraordinary selflessness contrasted markedly with their own self-aggrandizement, and served as a reminder of what they were sacrificing. The psychology was a complex and disturbing one—surely anger provided one component along with the operative guilt of not measuring up to the Fathers—and it kept Americans on the periphery of a spiritual void, confronting a sense of themselves as outcasts and failures, much as, in the mid–1820s, Irving would be forced to examine his lack of direction.

It is hardly surprising, then, that for Irving's generation, and for the later Romantics as well, the image of the "house divided" was a terrifying one, since it signified, on a conscious level, the dissolution of the Union (followed by civil war and the demolition of families) and, on a subconscious one, the collapse of the protective environment of a national home. "A house divided against itself cannot stand"—by the time Lincoln uttered the biblical phrase in his famous speech of 1858, setting himself up as the defender of the Fathers' estate, Americans were accustomed to hearing the Union described in the language of domesticity. Lincoln himself had frequently applied house imagery to matters of national concern; and he would continue to use it, as in his first debate with Douglas, where he referred to slavery as "an element of division in the house." Daniel Webster was only one of many who had previously employed the house-divided metaphor: "If a house be divided against itself, it will fall, and crush every body in it."[31] Nevertheless, the dramatic formulation of a house "besieged" from within its own walls affected Americans deeply. They had, after all, been charged with the task of preventing such a threat.

Between 1815 and 1832, Americans told themselves repeatedly that the only way they could ensure the continuity of the virtuous Republic was to emulate the personal and domestic character of the founders: the nation had inherited its sacred quality from that character and only through its imitation could the nation's identity be maintained.[32] There was no more important prerequisite for public achievement than private rectitude, and no better example of this than the life of George Washington, the preeminent Father. He perfectly illustrated his own maxim, set down so compactly in the First Inaugural Address, that the "foundation of our national policy will be laid in the pure and immutable principles of private morality."[33] According to Mason

10

Locke Weems, whose *Life of Washington* became a nineteenth-century moral guidebook, "it was to those *old-fashioned virtues* that our hero owed every thing." "For they in fact were the food of the great actions of him, whom men call Washington. It was they that enabled him, first to triumph over *himself*, then over the *British*."[34] Early in his life Washington knew that he was destined to play a major role in a great historical event and he prepared himself by developing a "system of moral discipline by which he trained himself to greatness and virtue." We should, said the *Southern Literary Messenger*, "mould ourselves by his precepts and example."[35] "The best eulogy" to the Fathers "would be for Americans to study his character . . . and then bow their hearts before Heaven, and in a spirit of pious patriotism fervently ask 'make me like Washington.'"[36]

In speech after speech, essay after essay, the connections were carefully drawn between the spotless character of Washington and the righteous quality of the Republic. Significantly, Washington's morality was most often linked to his love of domesticity; in fact, the virtues that had led Washington to victory in the American Revolution—"unselfish devotion and patient self-respect"—were just as equally "the great reconciling principles of . . . social and domestic life."[37] Thus, as one writer put it, the "character of George Washington, pre-eminent as it is for those civil and military talents which were peculiarly his . . . , was not less exalted in the private walks of life, and distinguished for all those domestic endearments which were daily exemplified in the bosom of his family."[38] Another was even more explicit: "There can be no doubt that a love of home and native soil, and of the shade of retirement was one of the master passions of his mind. And it is very probable that this passion for home actually had much to do . . . with that grandeur of more than Grecian or Roman civic virtue by which he [unlike King George] gave freedom, instead of despotism, to a continent."[39] "From beneath that humble roof went forth the intrepid and unselfish warrior," Edward Everett said; "to that he returned happiest when his work was done."[40] Domestic harmony was so valuable to him that, in Weems's portrait, military triumph meant he could project his love of household employments onto the nation: "With a father's joy he could look around on the thick settled-country, with all their *little ones*, and flocks, and herds, now no longer exposed to danger."[41] In effect, by securing the Republic Washington transformed it into a home. (It can hardly be accidental that the seat of the executive branch of government in Washington is called the White House.)[42] For Weems's nineteenth-century readers the message was not hard to fathom: failure to protect the nation's integrity

11

would be the equivalent of defiling Washington's memory; worse, it would be like desecrating his house.[43] Thus, it is not surprising to learn that just as this generation of Americans let the Republic die, they permitted Washington's home at Mount Vernon to deteriorate.

The more personal ambition undermined private morality, the greater the jeopardy to the Republic. However, as long as the Revolutionary generation was still living, and men who had participated in that struggle were holding the government's highest office, anxiety was held in check. The visibility of the Fathers alone ensured the continued vitality of the institutions they had established. "The presence of these few Revolutionary patriots and heroes among us seems to give a peculiar character to this generation," Edward Everett declared in 1824. "It binds us by an affecting association to the momentous days, the searching trials, the sacrifices, and dangers, to which they were called. The feeble hands and gray hairs of those who, before we were living, faced death, that we, their children, might be born free, are a sight which this generation ought not to behold without emotion."[44] Assessing this period thirty years later, *Putnam's Monthly* said that it was "still the heroic age of the Republic": "The heroes . . . were still walking among the people; lingering a little as if to give their farewell benediction to the nation whose infancy they had baptized with blood. Still the golden age of the sentiments of the people continued, still the brazen age of the commerce of the people had not opened."[45] The repetition of the word "still" four times here in the space of three sentences suggests how soon the "heroic age" would vanish. In fact, it could be argued that the "brazen age" already had begun; nevertheless, while the founders were alive the sons enjoyed the benefit of a continuous present, what Lincoln called a *"living history."*[46] "Dead" history—history as a chronicle of loss—had no immediate relevance, since America as yet had no acknowledged "past," no irrecoverable self to mourn. The failure to preserve the Republic had not yet been written.

However, in 1825 John Quincy Adams, the first president who was (literally) a son, not a Father, began his Inaugural Address by acknowledging that the founding generation "has passed away."[47] As if to prove him prophetic, exactly sixteen months to the day later John Adams and Thomas Jefferson died, taking with them to their graves America's youthful innocence. Even though the Fathers would continue to inhabit a psychological present, the "revolutionary age of America" was "closed up" by their deaths.[48] Just a short while previously, Daniel Webster told his Faneuil Hall audience, "the drama was ready to be closed." Now, "it has closed." "Our patriots have fallen"; with

12

their demise a "great link, connecting us with former times, was broken." The sons were alone. Americans "had lost something more . . . of the presence of the Revolution itself, and of the act of independence, and were driven on, by another great remove from the days of our country's early distinction, to meet posterity, and to mix with the future." Finally, there was a history the nation could not disavow, a past from which it might not rebel. In spite of various mechanisms of denial, what was heretofore unconscious now became an indelible part of the sons' consciousness. Only one of the signers of the Declaration of Independence survived the simultaneous passing of Adams and Jefferson. He was Charles Carroll of Carrollton, and from 1826 to his death in 1832 he was often spoken of, not as if he were a meaningful part of the present but, as Webster put it, a "venerable object," a "relic of the past."[49] "Carroll is alone," the *Casket* announced in 1830, "[t]he last relic of a noble band": "He is the link which connects us with the past. When he departs, the Declaration of Independence will be a monument of the dead."[50] Samuel L. Knapp summed up the feeling of his generation that the historical process had finally been put in motion when he said that "we are no longer the new men of the new world."[51]

When the first generation died, the second, like Rip Van Winkle on returning to his native village, fell into time. And time, as Washington Irving would show again and again, meant loss—loss of expectation, loss of identity, and the loss that had a special poignancy for his generation, loss of home. "They *were* the pillars of the temple of liberty," Lincoln said of the Fathers almost twelve years after Adams and Jefferson died, using, as he often did, a structural image to enhance his rhetoric, "and now, that they have crumbled away, that temple must fall, unless we, their descendants, supply their places with other pillars."[52] That was not to be, and thus what had been but a muffled whisper in the Fathers' presence gradually became, once they were gone, a loud proclamation: the Republic was dying. In October 1831, seven months before Washington Irving again touched native soil, the *New-England Magazine* sounded its death knell in an essay appropriately titled "The Perilous Condition of the Republic." "An epoch has been reached," it warned, "from whence the ruin or regeneration of our republican institutions must be dated." The future, depending entirely upon "the virtues and intelligence of the people," did not look propitious, since during the past ten years "the standard of public morals ha[d] been reduced, and an unwarrantable distraction countenanced, between popular and private virtue." The illustration offered was the practice of partisan politics, which encouraged the "sacrifice" of "principle to policy, duty to expediency," and which "compromise[d] the great interests of the country for sectional objects, and party aggrandizement." Selfishness, prejudice, and factionalism, rather than "the glory of their country, and the reguerdon of patriotism," now motivated men's actions. Building to a climax of denunciation, the essay asked its readers: "Could you have anticipated such a sudden and wide deviation from the virtuous course of your forefathers, such an entire abandonment of the fundamental principles of a republican confederacy, such an alarming aberration from the prescribed orbit of national glory?"

How could this have happened? "Was there an original and radical defect in the organization of the government" which has led to such dire consequences? No, the *New-England Magazine* firmly stated, the "age" is responsible: "there has been a lamentable degeneration from that sublime political morality, which characterized our ancestors; . . . we must go back to the days of primitive purity and excellence, and be imbued with that holy spirit of independence, by which the adventurous founders . . . were inspired." Yet, even though it offered political, educational, and moral prescriptions for bolstering the Republic in its present state, the essay still ended on a note of despair as it envisioned the consequences of electing public officials devoid of "talents, experience or moral rectitude": "We might behold that proud national spirit, which had never brooked insult, quail in the presence of royalty, and stoop to arrogant dictation; and the glory of the country,—that priceless gem of all governments,—might be ignominiously tarnished, by the recreant guardians to whom it had been confided." All Americans "are bound, by the most solemn obligations, to maintain, unimpaired, the rich inheritance bequeathed to them by their fathers," it reminded its readers. If they fail in their duty, "the ultimate ruin of the republic is certain."[53] Interestingly, many American paintings from this era used architectural ruins to suggest the collapse of American society (though others were referring to the larger context of Western civilization), and Irving would eventually pursue this idea of a ruined civilization in *The Conquest of Granada*.

"Of our Great Fathers we may say with truth, what was said of the Romans in their golden age," Attorney General William Wirt intoned in his 1826 "discourse" on Jefferson and Adams; "'with them the Republic was all in all; for that alone they consulted: the only faction they formed was against the common enemy: their minds, their bodies were exerted, sincerely, and greatly and nobly exerted, not for personal power, but for the liberties, the honor, the glory of their country.'"[54] No such epitaph would be pronounced for the postheroic generation; having chosen private ends over public duty, sectional affiliation over national loyalty, they witnessed the end of America's golden age. The Republic the Fathers had birthed the sons buried, but not without consequences to the national psyche. The careless stance toward the past that Americans were fond of parading was more a self-conscious posture than a genuine psychological attitude. Beneath the official rhetoric—rhetoric which claimed that America had "thrown off its allegiance to the past," that "the things of the past have but little interest or value for us"[55]—the memory of the Fathers plagued the sons. Paradoxically, in a country devoted to the future, the past had taken hold of the collective imagination. The age was indeed "retrospective." Emerson understood that, ten years after the deaths of Adams and Jefferson, it was still "build[ing] the sepulchres of the fathers." In fact, when American literature first began to attract critical attention in the 1820s, it was already haunted by a sense of loss. The vanishing of "home" was the primary concern of both the greatest novelist of the era and of the most important "women's" writer of the early nineteenth century, and, as well, the means by which a generation identified with Washington Irving.

II

When the call for a truly "American" literature was issued in the years following 1815, James Fenimore Cooper answered with a series of novels that wove native scenes and historical incidents into a revealing pattern of American consciousness. At the heart of these works—from *The Pioneers* (1823) through *The Wept of Wish-ton-Wish* (1829) to *Wyandotté* (1843) and *The Crater* (1847)—lies the theme of "dispossession," the loss of a pristine world that had once been home to Cooper's characters.[56] Again and again these books illustrate that despite the settlers' struggle to protect and fortify their civilization, something dark, mysterious, and powerful lurks just beyond its boundaries, threatening to disrupt and overturn the order of things within. But it is *The Spy* (1821), Cooper's first successful American production, and perhaps the most enduring and popular novel of the 1820s,[57] which demonstrates even more effectively than his later works how compelling a subject the besieged house was for the early nineteenth century. In an era when Americans were seeking affirmation and literature was being put to the service of recapturing the heroic past, Cooper transcended the demands of patriotism placed upon the American writer to make a complex statement about the origins of discord in the Republic and the possibilities for the reemergence of a unifying spirit.[58]

Set in the Revolutionary era, *The Spy* pertains as much or more to the America of the 1820s than it does to its historical time-frame. In addition to an extended discussion of the inconsistency (and injustice) of slaveholding in a land dedicated to liberty, Cooper takes up the related issues of what constitutes virtuous behavior in postheroic America and how the sense of "home" can be restored to a troubled nation. These problems are examined and, to a certain extent, resolved within the symbolic structure of the novel, which centers on the Wharton family and the patriarch's attempt to preserve the sanctuary of his home in a time of crisis. Cooper does not criticize this desire (though it turns out to be a futile one), only the degree to which Mr. Wharton translates it into purely material terms. Loyalist in sympathy, Wharton has instead declared his neutrality, acting not out of deep conviction but in the selfish hope of safeguarding his property. Cowardly and ineffectual, he "dread[s] victory by either [side], as a source of certain private misfortune."[59] Motivated, therefore, by personal gain, and eschewing public duty, he has removed his family from New York and settled them in Westchester County, a "neutral ground" between the two opposing camps, where he believes he can avoid the war. But just as, in *The Wept of Wish-ton-Wish*, the "forest moves in" on the Heathcotes because they try too hard to keep it out, the Revolution overtakes Mr. Wharton because he wants to escape what it signifies about his own moral failure. Trying "to insure the safety of his large estate, whichever party succeeded" (p. 17), he has in the meantime jeopardized the family he originally had hoped to shelter.

In the way in which he tries to secure his property through manipulation and dealing, Mr. Wharton resembles the figure who would come to prominence in nineteenth-century society, the businessman. Money is his bottom line, dictating relationships as well as physical movement. Because his son, Henry, is a captain in the British army, his estates were almost confiscated, and were saved only through the intervention of a relative holding high rank in the state government. As a consequence of this fright, he has permitted his youngest daughter to become engaged to the American Major Peyton Dunwoodie, primarily so that he can secure republican support. In the course of the novel's early action, Henry, in disguise, passes through the American lines in order to see his sisters and pay filial respect to his father. When he is subsequently captured as a spy, the elder Wharton experiences a dilemma: if the British prevail in the battle soon to be fought outside his door, his son will be freed but his neutrality will be undermined, for, he fears, in the public mind he will be aligned with Henry as a "plotter against the freedom of the

States" (p. 76); however, should the Americans gain victory, his son will remain captive and subsequently undergo trial, which might very well mean death (as in the highly publicized case of Major André). Mr. Wharton's internal conflict, basically the result of his moral flaccidity, drives him to imbecility. His saving grace, though, and the reason we finally accept him as a character worthy of empathy, is that as "much as he loved his wealth," he "loved his children better" (pp. 76–77). Indeed, in line with his deeper thematic purposes, Cooper clearly establishes that Wharton has placed his family in a dangerous situation not because he is evil, but rather because he has refused to accept the moral responsibilities of citizenship.

Much of our concern for the Wharton household, therefore, involves their attempts to remain a family unit in spite of the surrounding circumstances. They share warmth and affection for each other and, in the beginning, they also manage to maintain a semblance of order and decorum. Washington, who has taken refuge from a storm in the Wharton home in the guise of the traveler Harper, notices and approves of the family feeling which surrounds him. Yet underneath the surface solidarity the family is divided by conflicting political affiliations, with each of Wharton's daughters acting as spokeswoman for the opposing side. The division is intensified once Wharton's son and son-in-law are quartered in the house. And the novel enters an even more richly suggestive terrain when Dunwoodie is charged with apprehending the escaped Henry and bringing him to trial. Sister set against sister, brother versus brother (and countryman opposed to countryman, since both Henry Wharton and Peyton Dunwoodie are Americans), with the morally vapid financier/father overseeing but incapable of redirecting the action: surely Cooper's audience recognized in this scenario an almost literal depiction of the "house divided" motif. True to his sources, and perhaps desiring to issue a prophetic warning himself, Cooper shows that such a structure cannot stand.

Symbolically, the house is vulnerable from without because a genuine communal spirit has disappeared from within. Literally, representatives from both sides of the conflict invade the domicile, transforming it into fort, hospital, and prison.[60] But it ultimately collapses because of its precarious position in the "neutral ground," the territory which, as it comes to dominate the novel's symbolic structure, represents postheroic America, with its divided loyalties and shifting values. No safe haven from conflicting passions and points of view, it operates strictly by wilderness codes. As Colonel Singleton informs Henry during his trial, "its name, as a neutral ground, is unauthorized by law; it is an appellation that originates with the condition of the country" (p. 316).

Patrolled by the Skinners, the American irregulars whose savagery and treacherousness are directed toward the helpless on either side of the conflict, the neutral ground is characterized by violence and disorder; "the law was momentarily extinct in that particular district," Cooper writes at the novel's outset, "and justice was administered subject to the bias of personal interests and the passions of the strongest" (p. 3). Even more than lawlessness, moral indifference defines this terrain; the behavior of the Skinners, "fellows whose mouths are filled with liberty and equality, and whose hearts are overflowing with cupidity and gall" (p. 302), is but a gross exaggeration of Wharton's greed and duplicity. "The time must arrive," Captain Lawton says later, "when America will learn to distinguish between a patriot and a robber" (p. 288). But where the gratification of selfish desire is the norm, the two sometimes appear conjoined. Seeking to pillage and plunder in the name of freedom, the partisans invade, then destroy the Wharton house by fire. As the regulars finally rout the irregulars—again, Americans fighting Americans heightens the theme of internal tensions—the house burns until all that remain are the blackened walls, "dreary memorials of the content and security that had so lately reigned within" (p. 280). The Whartons learn from painful experience that, in a republic, there can be no "neutral" ground when it comes to moral choice.

Even the benevolence of Washington cannot save the Whartons' house which, symbolically speaking, is beyond redemption. However, as the archetypal father (as well as Founding Father) who possesses both virtue and authority, Washington accomplishes the greater task of setting his lands in order by healing the divisions that have threatened their internal security. As the only legitimate paternal figure in the novel, he projects a sense of control that the other characters find reassuring. Toward the end of the story he tells the younger Wharton daughter, Frances, that "all who dwell in this broad land are my children, and my care" (pp. 380–81). Accordingly, while he directs the American campaign against the British forces, he does not neglect Henry Wharton, whom he knows to be innocent of the charge of spying. Ever the trusted father, Washington would not betray the helpless son, yet he knows that by exercising his powers as commander-in-chief he would subvert the military tribunal that has condemned him. The situation facing him represents, in still another form, the major issue of *The Spy*: the conflict between public duty and private desire. Since Washington must remain anonymous to be most effective, he entrusts the task of rescuing Henry to his spy, Harvey Birch, who, by his disinterested deeds, extends the Father's virtue to the neutral ground.[61] Scorned and condemned by his fellow countrymen as a traitor to their cause, Birch is, ironically, the true agent of selfless action in the novel. Rescuing the Tory Henry from the Americans who are about to execute him, Harvey performs this and other duties with the knowledge that he will never receive just recognition for his daring acts. Moreover, even those who, like the Wharton family, do not despise him as the enemy, view him in his Yankee-peddler garb as little better than a mercenary: "I am afraid," Henry Wharton says at one point (believing Harvey to be a royalist), his "love of money is a stronger passion than love of his king" (p. 52).

Of course, just the opposite is true (though it is the American George whom Harvey loves), and in the penultimate chapter of the novel, and the climactic moment in the symbolic structure, Harvey proves himself a man of transcendent virtue. Toward the close of the war Washington sends for Birch, informing him that from now on their "connection must cease." Praising his trustworthiness and loyalty, Washington belatedly offers his spy gold as compensation for his past risks and deprivations. Harvey, offended by the gesture of payment for his services, responds angrily, "Does your excellency think that I have exposed my life, and blasted my character, for money?" The incredulous Washington asks, "If not for money, what then?" Whereupon Harvey reveals, rhetorically, his true character: "What has brought your excellency into the field? For what do you daily and hourly expose your precious life to battle and the halter?" (pp. 418–19). Though Washington still does not comprehend, Birch's motives are clear: patriotism, not profit, has led him to sacrifice comfort, reputation, and future prospects of happiness for his country. Harvey's self-renunciation, far more than Captain Jack Lawton's conventional (and unnecessary) death on the battlefield, becomes the real heroic act of the novel.[62] As if to underscore this truth, Washington smiles upon him benevolently as he finally sees the meaning in Birch's rejection of the gold.

For Cooper, Harvey's selfless devotion to the nation was the single most important virtue Americans needed to practice if the Republic was to survive. In 1821, it seems, he believed this was possible, and in his (rather unconvincing) final chapter he indicates his faith by reuniting the divided family, and duplicating Harvey's patriotism, in the person of Wharton Dunwoodie. However, in a rather ironic footnote to Cooper's tale, Susan Fenimore Cooper wrote that soon after the book was published her father was approached by an acquaintance, a prominent Wall Street merchant, who, though he praised the novel highly, pointed out the one significant flaw in the rendering of Harvey's character. Cooper, it seems, "'ha[d] given the man no motive!'"

"'Just look at the facts [said the merchant]: here is a man getting into all kinds of scrapes, running his neck into the noose of his own accord; and where, pray, was his motive? Of course I thought, until the last page, that he would be well paid for his services; but just as I expected to see it all settled he refuses the gold. There was your great mistake; you should have given Harvey some motive.'"[63] Whether Cooper was amused by the incident, or despaired over its implications, his daughter does not say. Surely, though, his optimism about the fate of the Republic must have been dampened when the representative of America's future could not recognize the genuine lack of self-interest on the part of the representative of America's past. Washington would not have smiled on Cooper's Wall Street critic.

III

The sanctuary of "home" and the threat posed to it by the shifting mores of the 1820s also figured prominently in the writings of another important spokesperson of the era. During the fifty years that Sarah Hale edited first the *Ladies' Magazine* (1827–36) and then *Godey's Lady's Book* (1837–77) she became an American cultural institution, recognized for her authoritative comments on domestic issues and celebrated for her promotion of women as "*the* moral guardians*" of society.[64] But Sarah Hale was also a true daughter of the Republic: while her imagination ran along an entirely different track from Cooper's, she shared his concern that America was drifting further and further away from its origins. As a result, she was fierce in her promulgation of republican manners and values. In the series "Sketches of American Character," which she published anonymously in the *Ladies' Magazine* and other journals and then collected as *Sketches of American Character* (1829) and *Traits of American Life* (1835), she illustrated what she believed were the fundamental American attitudes and characteristics "originated by our free institutions."[65] Recognizing that a "spirit of restlessness" pervaded contemporary America, severing households and destroying familial bonds—"Let no man, while planning his lofty dwelling, flatter himself he is building for his own posterity—the son of his enemy may inhabit there" ("Ann Ellsworth," pp. 99–100)—she re-created a world of republican balance and simplicity in order to persuade her readers that basic American beliefs had not vanished. In her books and, furthermore, in the political rhetoric of the time, present stability and future order are often discussed in terms of architectural metaphors. In the previous citation, for example, both the nouns and the verbs refer to constructing a house.

20

In the moral landscape of her sketches, "merit and talents, in whatever station, if rightly exerted, will command respect, and ensure success"; this, she insisted, was "the blessing of our happy institutions" ("Walter Wilson," p. 24). For Hale, the pursuit and acquisition of riches bring anxiety rather than enjoyment; however, prosperity, though in general a corrupting force, is not necessarily anathema. In fact, she follows her Puritan ancestors in holding to the idea that wealth and comfort are often the reward for leading a disciplined life, for, that is, embracing such tested New England virtues as "industry, enterprise, intelligence and perseverance" ("A Winter in the Country," p. 279). On the other hand, "deviations from morality and integrity are punished either with the loss of fame, fortune, or public confidence" ("The Wedding and the Funeral," p. 68). Indeed, Hale understood what she called the "bank-note world" of 1820s America: many of her characters are merchants or the sons of merchants, and when they permit their hunger for money to distort their better judgment they suffer bankruptcy as punishment.

Again and again in her sketches Hale champions the principle of self-control, by which she means "not the suppression of our feelings, but their right *direction*." Her purpose is not to "censure passion, or its expression," but rather to guide it "to worthy objects, and incite it to great sacrifices." The "gratification of [one's] own wishes and whims" is secondary ("The Village Schoolmistress," pp. 119, 118; original italics). Her most successful sketch, "The Soldier of the Revolution," builds on this premise to articulate the crucial difference between the heroic and postheroic generations: the former did not hesitate to "sacrifice . . . all selfish and private feelings" for the benefit of the new nation. "In these days of peace and plenty," much to America's detriment, "the generous, devoted, self-denying spirit that was exhibited during the revolution" has disappeared. Clearly, the sons fare poorly in comparison to the Fathers: "The thirst for private gain, that is now so engrossing, was then a feeble passion, compared with the ardor to promote the public good; and the final success of our arms is mainly to be attributed to the virtue and patriotism of the people" (pp. 37, 38). Hale's language here is curiously appropriate to the sexual realm: in stressing virtue she (and others) equated self-denial in all ways with patriotism. One should be passionate about the country to the exclusion of all others. Thus, in those glory days the soldiers never lost sight of the fact that they were also citizens, and they equated the love of their country with the protection of their homes. Having "fought the battles of freedom," they "gladly relinquished their weapons and returned to the firesides their valor had preserved from insult and spoilation" (p. 28). Eager for posterity to understand what the Revolutionary struggle demanded, Hale's old soldier repeatedly mentions his beloved home: how painful it was to leave, how much he missed it, and the strength and comfort he derived from knowing that it was to his family he could return at war's end.

In "The Soldier of the Revolution" Hale insists that the old-fashioned virtues the founding generation valued—"good sense, industry, economy and piety"—accompanied a devotion to home, whereas in the America of her own time the hunger for wealth has destroyed this sacred feeling. And, says Hale, wealth can never confer happiness; only within a family "united by the confidence of affection towards each other" can an individual secure peace of mind ("Ann Ellsworth," p. 92). The closing sketch of her collection, "A Winter in the Country," stresses this point as Owen Ashley, a city gentleman given to music, theater, and "good society" (and whose father has gone into bankruptcy), travels west of the Green Mountains to discover the "generous hospitality" and "cheerfulness of feeling" which exist among the country folk (p. 277). In the long letter he writes to his friend Edward back in Boston he celebrates the "New England character of industry, enterprise, intelligence and perseverance" and speaks glowingly of the wonderful home of his host and "the Eden-like love and happiness that pervade th[e] good family" with whom he is quartered (p. 284). Once believing that the American interior was rude both in physical appearance and in the character of its inhabitants, Owen now praises its beauty and the disciplined self-reliance of the yeomanry, "lords of the soil and the laws." Having learned to appreciate the simplicity of rural living and to respect those who "labor for themselves," he has been converted from a man of fashion to a true citizen of the Republic. "Luxury may enervate our cities," he says by way of marking his passage, "but through our wide spread country, the healthful tide of liberty will still flow uncorrupted." His final words make manifest the connection between a nurturing home and a stable nation: "I am a patriot," he declares; "I love my country" (pp. 285, 287).

"There is for me no place like *home*," says one of of Sarah Hale's characters at the conclusion of "The Belle and the Bleu" (p. 146; original italics), words that might have been pronounced by Hale herself and used as an epigraph to her life's work. Yet though they are simple, they avoid being trite since, for Hale, America's salvation lay in maintaining the qualities fostered by the traditional New England home, chief of which, as the citations show, was "industry" (also called "usefulness"); this trait, above all, tended to stabilize character.[66] She dedicated her most sustained piece of imaginative writing, published before she had achieved national prominence, to fully articulating this point of view and, equally as important, to illustrating how even in their prosperity Americans will never experience contentment unless they inculcate the virtues of the Founding Fathers into their own society. In *Northwood* (1827), Hale does not deny that fortune confers "advantages" (her hero, though he must lose his wealth in order to gain a proper sense of his priorities, eventually has his fortune restored); rather, her point, and the foundation upon which she constructs her entire imaginative edifice, is that "men are seldom qualified to improve or enjoy them rationally, without that moral, intellectual, and physical discipline, to which the inheritors of wealth will not readily submit."[67] Restraint, self-control, and a wise and judicious apportioning of his energies—these, among others, are the character traits Sidney Romilly must develop before he can safely assume his place in the morally debilitated America of the 1820s. The tale *Northwood* tells, therefore, involves a decent, but misguided, son learning to adopt his father's values in order to become the ideal republican of the postheroic generation, one who uses his money and influence to support and extend the Fathers' heritage. Thus the novel is a microcosm of the national family.

Hale's story of Sidney Romilly's education has primarily two locales, the New England village of Northwood, New Hampshire, and the southern city of Charleston, South Carolina. But in 1827, Sarah Hale was far less interested in the North and South as territorial entities than she would be in 1852 when she republished her novel as a response to *Uncle Tom's Cabin*; her dominant concern at the outset of her career was the difference in moral stature between the heroic and postheroic generations, and it is according to a temporal, rather than spatial, geography that she develops her tale. Northwood, and especially James Romilly's home, represents the "peace, plenty, and security" which characterize the life of a first-generation American farmer, one who believes in "usefulness," not rank or wealth, as the chief criterion for men's esteem. "To be actively useful, as far as our ability permits, is the law of our being, the debt we owe for the enjoyment of life," Hale wrote in "The Village Schoolmistress" (p. 115).[68] In *Northwood*, Squire Romilly practices "temperance" and "industry," and depends upon his own labor for domestic needs and luxuries, since the "exertion to procure them cherishes a spirit of patriotism, independence, and devotion" (p. 95). The virtuous yeoman—husbanding his resources, cultivating only what he needs, eschewing excess—is also the ideal republican: "Living in all the simplicity of retirement," Squire Romilly "inur[es] his children to habits of prudence and laborious industry;

yet cultivat[es] in them a taste for the refinements of literature and the love of science, and cherish[es] in their minds hopes of obtaining the highest honors and privileges their country could bestow" (pp. 133–34). For Romilly, a spiritual Father, "the dear domestic affections and tranquil happiness of home" are "more inestimable than the treasures of Ophir" (p. 294).

Charleston, and Horace Brainard's plantation, are indicative of the moral climate of postheroic America, with its emphasis on fashion, refinement, elegance, and sophisticated manners. Having inherited his wealth, Brainard devotes himself to gamesmanship and the theater. Society, not home, is the center of his life. However, like Cooper, Hale did not see evil in such a character; rather, Brainard's dissipations are the result of a degenerated sense of duty and a severe lack of self-control. When as an adolescent Sidney becomes his uncle's heir and goes to live on the plantation, the relaxed moral climate temporarily undermines the sturdiness of his New England upbringing; with too much leisure and without proper guidance, he abandons his father's principles and, adopting his uncle's manners, he squanders his energies in "frivolous and pernicious pleasures" until luxury, gaiety, and sensuality nearly undo him. Fortunately, the "early lessons of sobriety and virtue which he had, as it were, drawn in with his mother's milk" save him from profligacy (p. 180). Ironically, his pursuit of pleasure takes him everywhere but the one place where it is to be found—"in a virtuous home" (p. 73).

Like America, Sidney is basically decent; he has just lost his direction. Accordingly, the way to health leads back to the Fathers. Once Sidney is reimmersed in Northwood, the original spirit of the Republic, in the person of his father, heals his soul. On the same site where he had previously rescued his son from physically drowning, James Romilly now saves him from spiritually sinking. In despair over his own meaningless existence, Sidney generalizes about the futility of life and wonders if it were not better to have died knowing only childhood innocence. "To those who improve it as they ought," Squire Romilly advises his son, life "is undoubtedly a blessing" (pp. 123–24). Sidney's experience of the world has not brought him happiness because he has not lived usefully. Taking his father's words to heart, he transforms himself into a virtuous republican, climaxed by a great redemptive act involving Ephraim Skinner, Connecticut Yankee par excellence—merchant, moneylender, and miser. "Steady in the pursuit of his own interest," Skinner has taken advantage of the difficult economic times to prey upon his customers and amass a fortune (pp. 154–55). The only truly contemptible character in the book, the man who places economic gain above spiritual goals and communal ties, Skinner undoubtedly takes his name from Cooper's rogues who, during the stress of Revolutionary times, seek to gratify their own passions by plundering the neutral ground. With the aid of his father (since he still needs to draw on the source of moral power) Sidney devises a plan that eventually removes the blight from the New England landscape. In Northwood, duty and charity triumph over rapacity and greed. For his selfless act, Sidney receives his father's blessing: "How I rejoice," James Romilly tells his son, "that wealth has not made you selfish, nor prosperity hardened your heart" (p. 257).

Given Hale's instructive purpose, it remains only for Sidney's virtue to be tried, and the moment conveniently arises when his uncle forfeits what would have been Sidney's inheritance. Not quite a moral bankrupt since, like his nephew, Horace Brainard had been led into extravagance by his companions, he nevertheless dies a financial one. Sidney now faces the great challenge: was his act of "disinterested benevolence" possible only because his fortune was intact? to what extent can he, like his father, be truly self-reliant? "Those who have never experienced reverses," Sidney is counseled by one of his teachers, "are but halfschooled in the discipline of the world, and know not the resources of their own minds." "Dare to appear what you are," urges his father (pp. 267, 270). Having thus prepared Sidney both by lesson and example to meet the future, James Romilly, like Adams and Jefferson, dies; the son is alone, yet he has received a legacy far more valuable than gold. And by physical labor and moral forthrightness he shows that he is worthy of it. "Were I now to recover my fortune," he thinks near the story's conclusion, "how differently should I enjoy it from what I did in my prosperity!" (p. 341), by which he means he would dispose of it usefully. Whereupon his wealth is restored to him since, plot manipulations notwithstanding, Providence (and Hale) rewards virtue.

Didactic to the end, Hale had one more move to make in order to complete her design. Rich once again, Sidney redeems his uncle's estate and, with labor in New Hampshire no longer necessary, he returns to Charleston. Naturally so, says Hale, since "it was in Charleston his habits had been formed, opinions imbibed, and friends selected; and though he had yielded to necessity with philosophical firmness, and had labored with his hands without much repining, yet but few voluntarily subject themselves to the penalty of Adam; and I confess my hero felt very willing to lay down the spade when he found to dig was no longer necessary" (p. 368). A son, not a Father, Sidney belongs to postheroic America where yeoman tasks are part of a symbolic past rather than a living presence. Once again, Sarah Hale knew her audience: in Charleston, the America of her own day, Sidney can enjoy independence, domestic bliss, *and* the "pleasures of elegant society." Even more than Cooper, Hale held out hope for the second generation.

In 1827, Hale subtitled her novel "A Tale of New England"; upon reissuing it in 1852 she changed this to "Life North and South: Showing the Character of Both." For the most part, she weakened what was already an overburdened structure with tutorials on the proper use of charity and on the responsibilities of slaveholding (as opposed to abolitionism). She even added a final, offensive chapter which dealt with emancipation-in-time and the colonization of Africa as the ultimate solution to the slave problem. However, she did manage to strengthen her original conception in two instances by bringing to the forefront a connection that had been lingering in the background. In the new conclusion, when Sidney and his wife enter Charleston, Hale exclaims: "And now they are at home;—Sidney and Annie Romilly are at *home*! To them the word is full of meaning—significant of Love, of Hope, and of Happiness" (p. 389; original italics). But there could be no individual home, no happiness, unless Americans salvaged their collective home, the Union. Thus, she wrote in the Foreword to the new edition that "from the glorious old Granite State, where the scenes of this novel begin, have come forth those great men, 'Defenders of the Constitution,'—who 'know no North and no South,'—but wherever the sacred Charter of Union stretches its cordon of brotherhood, and the Eagle and the Stars keep guard, is their country." "In the same spirit our book goes forth" (p. iv). The Union was a family;[69] home and nation are one. Sarah Hale's book, written with the ardor of this familial spirit, insists that selfless action could protect both. Like *The Spy*, therefore, *Northwood* was a product of the moral and imaginative climate of 1820s America. "We depend for decency, sobriety, order, and economy, on the good sense, cultivated reason, and enlightened patriotism of our citizens," Squire Romilly had lectured. "Excessive luxury and rational liberty were never yet found compatible" (p. 93). If the former prevailed, the latter would be lost. So, too, would home.

IV

"Why should I go home," Washington Irving wrote in an 1817 notebook, "what home have I—I carry my home with me, it is the wrld of my thoughts, it is peopled with the memories of those I loved—it is filled with faces of loveones[?] & looks of friendship—with friends that have sunk into the grave & lovliness [sic] that has passed to heaven."[70] In the same notebook, in the midst of a meditation on the transience of life and the futility of longings and desires, Irving wonders, "Why erect such mighty fabricks of expectation & confidence upon such unsteady sands[.] Why dress we up then our Inns as if they were our homes & are as careful about a few nights['] lodgings here as if we designed an everlasting abode. For we are but sojourners & pilgrims here, and have no fixed habitation upon earth."[71] These, and other sentiments like them, while not profoundly original, nevertheless reveal Irving's state of mind once the foundation of his hopes for a career as a gentleman author had collapsed. When he lost the security of his brothers' financial backing he was set adrift in foreign waters; for the first time in his life he would have to steer his own course. He was alone, and he was homeless. Like one of Sarah Hale's characters, he had to locate other sources of protection, to create new meanings for home: "It has pleased heaven," reads another of his personal jottings, "that I should be driven on upon my own strength—and resort to the citadel within me."[72] Once again, a structural metaphor images a desire for safety, for a sanctuary. Washington Irving experienced personally what Americans in the 1820s underwent collectively.

But despite his metaphysical recognition that as "sojourners" and "pilgrims" on earth we are all bereft of a spiritual home, and his personal determination to build an interior fortress that would shield him from life's "vicissitudes," from the "blows of fate & fortune thickening around him,"[73] he was continually preoccupied with the idea of home during his seventeen years of self-imposed exile. "The solid, permanent happiness for life must spring from some settled *home*," Irving wrote to Henry Brevoort in 1816, and while he addressed his friend directly, he appears to be unconsciously prescient about his own future: "All those vagabond, roving propensities . . . are the offspring of idleness of mind and a want of something to fix the feelings. You are like a bark without an anchor, that drifts about at the mercy of every vagrant breeze or trifling eddy."[74] Only a few years later he began to wander the Continent, seeking literal and figurative houses—places of comfort, nurture, and creative freedom—where, if he could not find the domestic happiness that Charles Stuart enjoyed in *Northwood*—"the quiet consciousness of peace, the calm security of reciprocated affection" (p. 239)—he might at least escape from the trials of his current existence: "an empty home[,] no blazing hearth—no door thrown open to receive [me]—no voice of affection to hail [me]."[75] Ironically, it was not the future for which he searched, but the past, hence his gravitation in *The Sketch Book* to old buildings like Westminster Abbey and Bracebridge Hall. His celebrated love of antiquity was, in one respect, a surface manifestation of a deeper psychological need. He yearned not for England's "shadowy grandeurs," but his own: "I dreamt that I was once more in my native home[—]every thing around me looked as in my happier days. The mother that had so fondly cherished my childhood was hanging over me with looks of fondness—I awoke—in a strange land—poor[—]sick—solitary—desolate."[76] Unlike ordinary homesickness (the desire to return to a place that is), this was a sickness for "home" (the yearning for a time and condition that was).

Like his countrymen, Irving was haunted by the memory of the home he had once possessed, by the thought that somewhere back in his youth in New York existed a golden age of uncircumscribed and untrammeled emotional freedom. What lay behind the phrases of lament—"In the days of early youth before I had lost a friend or experienced a disaster"; "when I look back for a few short years what changes of all kinds have taken place[,] what wrecks of time & fortune are strewn around me"; "I can remember the day when the least joy would move me"—was a profound longing for an original idea of himself, when life was all promise and expectation, as yet unsullied by failure, moral and otherwise. Not only had his brothers' importing firm gone under; the entire present was bankrupt. "I have seen the world," he confided to his journal, "I have tasted its plasures [sic] I have explored its recess & what have I gaind[,] what but a distaste for life and distrust for mankind." "Oh that I had never strayed beyond the Solitudes of my native Alleghanys." His notebooks and journals from his first years in England, therefore, show him recalling and attempting to recover the era before he, too, fell into time, before he lost what could not be retrieved. Most often this vision (which occasionally lapsed into self-indulgence) took the form of Matilda Hoffman, whose untimely death had brought an end to innocence:

> The reccollection [sic] of Matilda—ever allied in my mind to all that is pure[,] spiritual & seraphic in woman came stealing over my soul—I recalled . . . her gentleness—her purity—. . . She was now in heaven—. . . while I—lonely—desolate—humiliatd—was grovelling[,] a miserable worm upon earth—Oh Matilda where was the soul-felt devotion—the buoyancy—the consciousness of worth & happiness that once seemd to lift me from the earth when our eyes interchanged silent but eloquent vows of affection and I seemed to imbibe a degree of virtue & purity by associating with all that was virtuous & pure—How innocent . . . was then my life—How has it changed since—what scenes have I

gone through since thou hast left me—. . . what sordid pursuits—what gross associations—what rude struggles—. . . . I feel
like one witherd up & blighted.[77]

In spite of what he accomplished, no matter how much prosperity he enjoyed, Irving, like America, was unable to regain a sense of himself as virtuous. Though *The Sketch Book*'s success repaid his strenuous labor and erased
much of his literary self-doubt, it could not undo time, could not, that is, as
R. A. Yoder has said of the Union's achievement, restore "natural wholeness."
When James Kirke Paulding chided Irving for not fully appreciating his fame,
he misunderstood the source of his old friend's despair: "The only man I ever
yet envied was yourself [Paulding wrote], and when I tell you this, in God's
name let us hear no more complaints on the score of fortune and future prospects. With youth, health, talents, and reputation—with all the noble means
of pursuing noble ends still within your power, let me entreat you to contemplate yourself and future fortunes through a brighter medium."[78] All the "fortune and future prospects" in the Old World, however, could not cleanse what
Irving believed to be the stain on his soul: he had lost his youthful demeanor;
he had lost his beloved; he had lost his financial security; and he had lost
his home.

When Irving left America in 1815, he believed that with a change of scene
and the liveliness of travel he would again be able to write. Having produced
no original work after *Knickerbocker's History*—in six years he managed only a
revised (and weakened) version of this book and another edition of *Salmagundi*—he was becoming nervous over his inability to settle down to serious
literary pursuits. But more than just personal malaise kept him from putting
pen to paper. Since in the years following Matilda Hoffman's death he had
retreated from the intellectual circles in New York, spending a good deal of
time in the country houses of friends, representing the family business interests in Washington, and editing the *Analectic Magazine* (which was composed
almost entirely of articles reprinted from foreign publications); and, moreover, since he no longer enjoyed the frame of mind in which he had conceived
and then executed the burlesque comedy and wicked satire of his *History*,
he found himself increasingly alienated from the self-conscious and often
strident calls for an indigenous literature. Men of letters were expected to be
alive to the hum of American enterprise and prosperity, to be, said the *New-
York Review*, "excited to zeal in their vocation by the happy circumstances surrounding us." More significantly, the *Review* testified to a tendency that would

grow stronger during Irving's European years: American writers were to assume responsible roles in the public sphere. "The highest honours belong to those men," said the *Review*, "who have united active talents to the power of fine writing. . . . The lessons which teach the wisest conduct of life, come with best effect from those who have passed through its busy scenes." According to the *Review*, then, not only were politics and literature compatible, but the American writer must instruct the American people in virtue. "We will respect the politician who serves the purposes of the moment with fidelity," it claimed, "but deeper gratitude is due to him, who, besides labouring faithfully for the national prosperity, extends this influence beyond limits by committing just thoughts to eloquent language." Recognition in letters, therefore, is dependent upon patriotic duty: "Every man in a free country owes his best service to the state, and may feel honoured on being called to public employments by the will of an intelligent people. . . . Many of the names which are mentioned with most esteem in our literature, are those of men who were distinguished in public life." [79]

From 1815 through 1832 Irving was incapable of becoming the writer that the official spokesmen for a national literature were championing. There were at least two reasons for this: for one, he had no desire to affirm American values, uphold American ideals, or inculcate American morality; and for another, he was equally uninterested in putting his creative energies to the task of seriously invoking the American past. Cooper and Hale, on the other hand, were much closer in spirit to this model, and while Irving shared some of their political and social concerns, his point of view was far more ambivalent. (In "Rip Van Winkle" and "The Legend of Sleepy Hollow," for example, he could be quite ironic about the issue of leading a "useful" life.) In addition, even though he made notes and gathered materials about America, and contemplated producing an "American Sketch Book" (an effort which never reached fruition), his imaginative life during these years was not centered on his native land.[80] His writings, therefore, with the exception of his two famous stories and a few other pieces in *The Sketch Book*, do not, as William Hedges has said, "reveal any great concern with American themes—at least not on the surface." [81] But the disclaimer is significant for, in fact, as Irving himself understood, he wrote with the sensibility of an American. "Whatever I have written," he told Brevoort, "has been written with the feelings and published as the writing of an American." [82]

The literature that Washington Irving created during his seventeen years abroad was almost completely subjective in its rendering of experience, even when that experience was historical in its orientation. Though he traveled widely, his imaginative terrain became increasingly interior. But he was first and foremost a son of the Republic, and Washington, whose "character" was a "national property," whose "example" was as "valuable as his services," was his spiritual father.[83] As his journals illustrate, while he may have drifted away from America physically, he never left it psychically. "England so richly dight with palaces," reads one entry, "so embroiderd with parks & gardens[—]So storied—so wrought up with pictures.—Let me wander along the streams of beautiful England & dream of my native rivers[—]of my beautiful native country."[84] However subliminally, his American audience perceived this, recognizing that whether his focus was Geoffrey Crayon, the English landed gentry, Columbus, or the Moors, he filtered everything through an American consciousness. It is not surprising, therefore, that his writings are permeated with feelings of anxiety and loss.

ONE

A Persona Is Born

The popular image of *The Sketch Book*'s creator as a "genial" though diffident tourist indulging his fancy for aristocratic culture amidst the finery of the Old World lingers on. Washington Irving himself must bear some of the blame for this misconception, since in his introduction to that widely read miscellany he pictured its author as a sophisticated traveler "following the bent of his vagrant inclination" and dashing off a few sketches "for the entertainment" of his "friends."[1] Perhaps, too, because Irving wrote as well as the eighteenth-century Englishmen (Addison, Goldsmith, Sterne) whose prose served as models for his unconvoluted style—"so elegant and so simple" that it earned for him the distinction (in British eyes) of being "the first literate American"[2]—his readers have imagined him a gentleman of letters in the stately English tradition. Distortion also has resulted from the fact that too often Irving's life has been sentimentalized out of all proportion to what a critical interpretation of the documents available will allow.[3] While these notions have helped to situate Irving pleasantly in the collective national mind, they have at the same time obscured the real achievement of his struggle to compose his masterpiece. In addition, preconceived ideas about Irving's life have tended to govern readings of his work, to the extent that the pervasiveness of this polite spirit has come to be mistaken for the essence of *The Sketch Book*.[4]

The life and work, in fact, do mirror each other, but the reflection is one that few readers have caught. The truth is that the famous collection of sketches, essays, and stories, which lifted American literature out from the cultural backwater and into the mainstream, was conceived and produced in a time of great anxiety for its author. The ultimate collapse in 1818 of the business of P. and E. Irving, which had been slowly dying for two years, brought the youngest Irving to the brink of emotional exhaustion; moreover, by stripping away his brothers' financial protection it forced him to confront the issue he had been avoiding since the publication of *Knickerbocker's History of New York* in 1809: could he risk declaring himself a professional author and succeed where no American previously had? Yet once this obstacle was overcome he faced, as an American in England seeking literary sustenance and "values" in a tradition not his own,[5] the enmity of the British reviewers and their scorn for the general inferiority of American letters. *The Sketch Book's* prenatal period was, therefore, a trial of nerve, fortitude, and faith for Irving; approached with this knowledge in mind, the book reveals itself as a work of personality different from the congenial mask. The transformation of anxiety into successful literary endeavor was accomplished through the creation of Geoffrey Crayon, the persona who functions as a surrogate for Irving in the autobiographical sketches that form a large part of the collection.[6] Like Thoreau, he had to avoid the danger of writing self-indulgent personal anecdote—a "pitiful story reflecting [him]self"[7]—and just as Thoreau did, he conquered that impulse in penning *The Sketch Book* which, in its layered emotional complexity, is itself a testament to his triumph over plaguing self-doubt and crippling cultural insecurity.

As a result of the misconceptions that surround both the man and his book, readers have tended to see his work as a casual collection of disjointed sketches. While they have enjoyed the evocation of English scenes, embraced the sentimental rendering of various tales and characters, laughed at the humor of Crayon's (mis)adventures, and applauded the occasional expression of American patriotism, they have not detected the web holding these disparate pieces together. The "miscellany" does possess a genuine coherence: it is anxiety, displayed in the undertones, themes, and motifs, that forms the hidden links. Paradoxically, *The Sketch Book's* very harmony derives from the working out of this anxiety—the process of re-creation, examination, and release that takes place in the interstices of its tranquil, and therefore more easily recognizable, emotions.

I

In his chapter entitled "First Years in England" (1815–19), Stanley Williams chronicles the difficult months during which Irving decided to resume authorship, when all of his efforts to extricate himself from the morass of the family business ended only in increased frustration and failure.[8] But Irving's biographer adopts a curious attitude toward his subject: on the one hand, he sympathizes with the "lacerated" Irving as he suffers through (in Irving's words)

33

"the horrible ordeal of Bankruptcy," including the "bitterness & humiliation" of financial ruin,[9] the ensuing hardship for his brothers, and his doubts about his own future; on the other hand, however, Williams takes him to task for overreacting, for failing to maintain a proper perspective on both present misfortunes and past crises. For Williams, Irving is "neurasthenic, close to hypochondria"; "he [can]not remember that he ever had a normal moment."[10] Unlike Emerson, Williams laments, Irving is incapable of turning worldly grief into "revelations of essential questioning": "His decisions concerning the conduct of life lack the dignity of a subversive spiritual experience. . . . His doubts compassed not the total meaning of existence but merely his own inadequacy in certain exacting circumstances."[11] Thus, when he finally does acknowledge Irving's reliance upon his own "inner strength" to turn misfortune into success, it occurs in such a mixed context of praise and scorn that the achievement is muted almost beyond recognition. In response to Irving's resolve to "return to my pen . . . to reinstate myself in the world's thoughts—to raise myself from the degradation into which I considered myself fallen," Williams writes that Thomas Carlyle (who tried to contact Irving in Paris in 1824) "might have applauded this defiance from a whimpering biped."[12] Intentionally or not, Williams's ironic deflation here almost equals the best mock-heroic moments in Irving's fiction.

Though he may not have turned to metaphysical speculation for release (as Williams's logic would have dictated), "the horrible ordeal of bankruptcy" did traumatize Irving. In particular, while his assumption of failure and his loss of self-respect must not be minimized, nor his concern for the welfare of his family discounted—"My heart," he wrote, "is torn every way by anxiety for my relatives"[13]—Irving's greatest trial centered on the question of his own stability. With the crumbling of his economic foundation he would, at thirty-three, for the first time in his life, have to depend solely on his own resources. Besides the burden of the pending financial crisis, therefore, he was also laboring under the weight of tremendous psychological pressure. He was "so harrassed & hagridden by the cares & anxieties of business," he told his friend Henry Brevoort in July 1816, that he "at times felt almost broken down in health and spirits." "Anxiety" (or one of its variants) thus had become a normal part of Irving's diction when writing about these strained days, as in this line sent to an unknown correspondent in January 1816: "I would not again experience the anxious days and sleepless nights which have been my lot since I have taken hold of business to possess the wealth of Croesus."[14]

Irving's repeated images are as revealing as his reiterated words: again and again in his correspondence with Brevoort during this period he likened his state of mind to a ship lost at sea. "Brooding over the hardships of these disordered times" and the "uncertainty" of his "future prospects" in 1816, he sees himself as "temptest [sic] tossed and weather beaten."[15] Italicizing the prophecy of Ecclesiastes (11 : 1), he writes in this 1816 letter that "'my bread is indeed *cast upon the waters*.'" Still in the same letter, as if obsessed by his loss of the firm ground of his brothers' support, he responds to Brevoort's inquiry about returning to America by insisting: "I will make no promises or resolutions at present, as I know they would be like those formed at Sea in a storm, which are forgotten as soon as we tread the shore, or the weather grows propitious." Unfortunately, "propitious weather" would be long in coming; months later, having promised Brevoort in one paragraph that he "shall not let present difficulties give [him] any uneasiness," he immediately writes in another that he longs for the time when he may "be able to return home . . . and have wherewithal to shelter [him] from the storms and buffetings of this uncertain world."[16] In July 1817, having already formulated his plan for *The Sketch Book*, which he believes will provide him "a scanty but sufficient means of support," he tells his friend—his desperation barely hidden beneath the momentary respite from worry his new idea has brought— that though "you would probably consider it precarious, & inadequate to my subsistence . . . a small matter will float a drowning man": "I have dwelt so much of late on the prospect of being *cast* homeless & pennyless upon the world; that I feel relieved in having even a straw to catch at."[17] Moreover, in a notebook from that same year, which contains the material for several sketches, he continues to think of himself as "a shipwrecked mariner . . . look[ing] out upon the tranquil bosom of that deep in which my hopes have been overwhelmed."[18]

In recounting the agony of these events to Mrs. Amelia Foster seven years later, Irving again chose the word "cast," in a similar semantic context, to express his sense of loss and disorientation: "I felt cast down—abased—I had lost my *cast*—I had always been proud of Spirit, and in my own country had been, as it were, a being of the air—I felt the force of the text 'a wounded spirit who can bear?'"[19] His entire psychological frame of reference having shifted, Irving plummeted (was "cast down") from the height of a carefree, unexamined gliding to the depths of a painful, deliberate self-scrutiny; in addition, "cast" also implies "castaway" or "cast out to sea," and therefore connects to his fear of being "shipwrecked." Buffeted about by the storm of economic disaster, Irving had lost his safe moorings. Years later he told Edward

Everett that "it was my lot, almost on landing in Europe, to experience a reverse of fortune, which cast me down in spirit, and altered the whole tenor of
my life."[20] "Cast," in all of its emotional ramifications of meaning, had become his script for this drastic upheaval.

With the loss of his financial underpinnings, the days of undisciplined wandering reached an abrupt end; Irving could no longer afford, either economically or psychologically, to assume the role of gentleman-author. This last
"jarring collision with the world"[21] shook his complacency: the question of
vocation finally had been called, and though the resolution to "return to [his]
pen" may have been a noble one, it was carried out with much hardship.
"Darkness . . . lower[s] upon my mind," he wrote dramatically a few months
before attempting to resume writing, "and the times are so hard that they
sicken my very soul."[22]

In fact, in March 1816, in response to Brevoort's request for "anecdotes of
characters" that he has met with in his "rovings," Irving confessed that he had
nothing to offer his friend; his notebooks were empty. His "last stay in London," he writes, "was a period of great anxiety," so that instead of participat-
ing in the life of the town by discovering new people and scenes, which or-
dinarily would have engendered some type of literary activity, he has colored
the cityscape with his own somber mood. "I seemed to have lost my *cast*," he
says once again, "and to have lost also all relish and aptitude for my usual
pursuits."[23] Interestingly, Irving italicized the noun "cast" here, just as he
would seven years later when remembering this time. In addition, his use of
the word "cast" in this context suggests that he was concerned not only about
his depressed feelings but, more significantly, about the consequent loss of
stimulation to his creative faculties. His "cast," therefore, is directly related to
"the literary feeling" which, he bemoaned to Brevoort a few months later, he
could not "revive."[24] His fear that his imagination was "blighted" generated
even more anxiety, since his orientation had shifted away from literature as
youthful passion to one of professional commitment. The "throng of worldly
cares hurrying backward & forward through my mind," he writes in yet another letter to Brevoort, have made it "as bare as a market place: and when I
do take hold of my pen, I feel so poverty struck, such mental sterility, that I
throw it down again in despair of writing any thing that should give you gratification."[25] Bereft of inspiration, and weighed down by the gravity of his decision, Irving struggled to regain his literary composure.

Fortunately, with the crucial issue of vocation pending, he was strong in his
resolve: the letters from 1816 through 1819 contain a history of his conquest

of despair and self-doubt. Though he may not have exemplified an Emersonian ideal, nevertheless a determined self-reliance, coupled with "the horrors of destitution" and "the more galling mortifications of dependence," drove him on.[26] Aware that, as he wrote to his brother William, his "future career must depend very much upon [him]self," Irving created, out of "adversity," "loneliness," and "painful economy," the emotionally complex work known as *The Sketch Book of Geoffrey Crayon, Gent.*[27] Reading like a map of his psychological pilgrimage, the sketches show him, through his persona, trying alternate paths of expression, discovering different outlets for his frustrations. Yet in their scope and variety they also indicate how successful he was in transforming these raw feelings into a multivalent finished product.

As if the problems of self-respect and vocation were not producing enough anxiety, Irving suffered from the gnawing need to justify his continued absence from America. Though he assured Brevoort (and others) that all his "ideas of home and settled life centre in New York," and that he had enjoyed "too little pleasure or even comfort in England to wean [him] from that delightful little spot of earth," he also emphasized that he would only "return home at a proper season, and under favourable circumstances: not to be driven to [his] native shores like a mere wreck."[28] Nevertheless, he was besieged by accusations that he had been "lingering in Europe" because of an "indifference" to the welfare of both his friends and his country. On the contrary, he declared to his brother Ebenezer in 1819, touching upon the three areas of greatest concern to him—personal pride, economic necessity, and national loyalty—that his efforts to establish "a legitimate literary reputation" and "form a stock of copyright property," which would keep him in "bread and cheese" and repay him for "a world of care and privation," have been made in the hope of "win[ning] the affections" of Americans: "My greatest desire is to make myself worthy of the good-will of my country. . . . I am determined not to return home until I have sent some writings before me that shall, if they have merit, make me return to the smiles, rather than skulk back to the pity of my friends."[29] Clearly, Irving's letters reveal his need to be in control of his life, with literature as the balancing weight to set the scales straight. But no matter what reasons he offered, the longer he remained in Europe the more he was taunted with having abandoned loved ones. Even after *The Sketch Book*'s initial success had earned for him a much-appreciated measure of fame and support, Irving was still justifying his strategies. Proud of his resourcefulness and determined to capitalize on the displaced situation, yet frustrated by the continued challenges to his patriotism, he told Brevoort that he wished "to have done with" the troublesome subject: "My return home must depend upon circumstances, not upon inclinations. I have, by patient & persevering labour of my most uncertain pen, . . . managed to open to myself an avenue to some degree of profit & reputation—I value it the more highly because it is entirely independent and self created. . . . In remaining therefore abroad, I do it with the idea that I can best exert my talents, for the present, where I am." [30]

To be sure, these personal complaints are both disconcerting and tedious, yet beyond these qualities there is something rather pathetic about Irving's continually having to answer the charge of defection. That the man who brought America its first glimmer of literary recognition should be deemed a betrayer of his country for delaying his return, especially after he stated that his art depended on continued European travel, reveals in its absurdity an aspect of early American defensiveness (to be discussed in literary terms below) and one of the most severe extrinsic pressures operating on Irving. How deeply disturbing he found the questioning of his loyalty may be seen from his angry response to Brevoort's urging him "to return to New York" by way of saying that "many ask whether" he intends to "renounce" his country: "I feel that even with [my pen] I can do very little, but if I do that little, and do it as an american [sic] I think my exertions ought to guarantee me from so unkind a question as that which you say is generally made." [31] The salient point here is not merely that he overcame the obstacles strewn in the path of mental ease and emotional comfort to produce one of the classic works in the American canon; rather, it is that Irving derived the techniques, tone, and texture of *The Sketch Book* from the very traumas that threatened to debilitate him. His creative energies, even the impulses that led to his artistic choices, originated in these anxieties—as a man, as a writer, and as an American.

II

Besides being personally anxious, Irving was also culturally insecure: the issue of justification extended beyond satisfying the inquiries about domicile and loyalties from solicitous friends and relatives. He had the eyes of both the Old World and the New World upon him; with the publication of *The Sketch Book* in America in 1819–20, and in England in 1820, Irving placed himself squarely between the two in their debate over when (and in more hostile moments, if) the instruments of American culture would reach maturity. Irving was well aware that since the reopening of travel between England and the United States after the War of 1812, American society had been repeatedly abused by British travelers. Again and again accounts appeared in English journals and magazines describing the raw and uncouth manners of the Americans, the lack of nobility and sophistication in their democratic institutions, and the almost complete absence of refinement in their growing frontier cities. Not only the British, but other European visitors as well, wrote travel books which lambasted American culture, so much so that Americans came to feel themselves to be on trial before the bar of European and British opinion. Sydney Smith's remark in the *Edinburgh Review* (1820) about the obscurity of all modes of American art is but the most notorious of such critiques: "In the four quarters of the globe, who reads an American book? or goes to an American play? or looks at an American picture or statue?"[32] By the time Americans read Mrs. Trollope's scathing attack in *Domestic Manners of the Americans* (1832), they had become somewhat accustomed to, though no less indignant over, such diatribes. In the years between Smith's comment and Mrs. Trollope's book, Americans entered this verbal warfare and found means of retaliation through their chauvinistic journalists. But when Irving sat down in 1817 to write the sketches and essays that would become *The Sketch Book*, they had barely begun to declare themselves.

Fierce as they were, these attacks compose only the background to understanding the chance Irving took by daring, as an American, to write on English scenes and manners. The real risk involved the response of the British literary establishment, which had been merciless in its criticism of American writers, chastising them for their defective taste and brutish manner. Irving had every right to be apprehensive about making his professional debut before such a hostile audience; in fact, he had already felt the sting of the British reviewers in 1811 when the *Monthly Review* had criticized *Salmagundi*'s "hyperbolical" excesses and its "want of a good style."[33] Exactly what Irving had to contend with is evident in their comments on *The Sketch Book*. Even the comparatively gentle Francis Jeffrey was quick to point out that although *The Sketch Book* was "a very pleasing book in itself," it is a "remarkable publication" precisely because "it is the work of an American, entirely bred and trained in that country." And, continues Jeffrey, "the most remarkable thing in a work so circumstanced certainly is, that it should be written throughout with the greatest care and accuracy, and worked up to great purity and beauty of diction. . . . It is the first American work . . . to which we could give this praise."[34]

More typical of the contemporary English attitude, however, was the *Quarterly Review* (1821) which, at the same time it was praising *The Sketch*

Book for its "delicacy of feeling" and "refinement of taste," chided America for a lack of "cultivation of mind." Though it sent up a cheer for "English Writers on America," the *Review* simultaneously attacked the American character: it is "written for the most part in a spirit of good sense and moderation which could scarcely be expected from an American,—even when intended for publication on this side of the water."[35] The *Edinburgh Magazine and Literary Miscellany* (1819) said that *The Sketch Book* "shows, in many passages, an aspiration after an excellence which is by no means unattained." "It proves to us distinctly," it went on, "that there is *mind* working in America, and that there are materials, too, for it to work upon, of a very singular and romantic kind."[36] The general purport of these remarks, much to Irving's irritation, was to profess surprise that a citizen of America should be able to express himself intelligently, articulately, and, most of all, in decent English. In Stanley Williams's phrase, "the paradox of an elegant book from an aborigine" was in fact one of the important factors in its success.[37] (An amusing corollary is that the *Retrospective Review* [1824], while acknowledging Irving as a "very agreeable writer" with a "pleasant amicable vein running through his writings," referred to him as a "native of the woods and savannahs.")[38] Perhaps the final indignity was the oft-stated comment that the primary reason for the success of Irving's work was that it is "exclusively English."[39] Not content merely to degrade his country, these Englishmen could make Irving acceptable only by stripping his prose of its national origins.

As if the specter of the English critics was not enough to traumatize an aspiring writer, Irving also heard the echoing voices of their American counterparts: he had the misfortune to be publishing *The Sketch Book* at a time of escalating demands on American authors to produce recognizably "American" works. The responses to *The Sketch Book* of two respected American critics reveal not only another reason for Irving's uneasiness, but the insecurity that ran through American letters as well. Writing in the *North American Review* in 1822, Edward Everett began by acknowledging that Irving's essays and sketches on English rural life and manners could be favorably compared to "anything else of the kind in English literature, for accuracy and fidelity of observation, for spirit of description, for a certain peculiar sly pleasantry."[40] Nevertheless, he was compelled to register his disappointment that Irving's writings were almost totally without "that peculiar interest, which the author's position enabled him to give them"; it was Irving's responsibility, Everett argued, to have presented to the British public "topics purely American," and to have expressed "those judgments, which are formed in an American's mind, as he treads the soil where his fathers repose." At this crucial juncture in the history of American letters, Irving had not written an American book: "Mr. Irving need not have abated a whit of his courtesy and benevolence, he need not have omitted one nice trait in character or manners, above all he need not have employed one Americanism, and yet have written a book, which . . . should have revealed itself at once as an American production."[41] Exactly what an "American production" was, or was supposed to be (beyond merely focusing upon native scenes), remained a mystery, but Everett was expressing a culturally sanctioned demand made upon the American writer in the second decade of the nineteenth century.

The pressure was extended as well to matters of style. Reviewing the first two numbers of *The Sketch Book* in the *North American Review* (1819), R. H. Dana, Sr., complained that Irving writes "as if his mother English had been sent abroad to be improved, and in attempting to become accomplished, had lost too many of her home qualities."[42] Unfortunately, like Everett, Dana does not quite articulate what these "home qualities" are or ought to be (in fact, he retreats to Addison as a model of perfect control and modulation), but since he specifically categorized Irving's style as "feminine, *dressy*, elegant and languid," we can guess what he has in mind.[43] Dana clearly prefers what he classifies as Irving's former style—that of *Salmagundi* and *Knickerbocker's History*—but had he looked as closely at all three works as some modern Irving critics have, he would have seen that *The Sketch Book*'s diction, syntax, and prose rhythms were consistent with the earlier productions.[44] Probably the real cause of Dana's disapproval was the shift in Irving's subject matter and the fact that he had abandoned the satiric mode;[45] but what his critique shows above all is that neither he, nor Everett (nor for that matter any other American commentator of the time), was able to bypass accepted norms of criticism or transcend a recurring paradox: American anxiety and solicitude to establish a national literature made it impossible for these critics to recognize that the source from which the literature would emanate was that anxiety itself. Thus, they failed to see that Irving had combined the same cultural insecurity they shared with his own personal tensions and projected them onto Geoffrey Crayon, and that this displacement created a persona to narrate a very American book.

III

Economic, artistic, and other forms of personal and cultural anxiety pervade *The Sketch Book*. "The Voyage," the first sketch following Crayon's introduc-

CHAPTER ONE

tory "account" of himself, sets the tenor for the entire trip and presages his
future, more extensive forays into the domain of an antiquarian England.
Caught between the instability of the New World and the intransigency of the
Old, Crayon is a tentative man for whom the fixed points of social reference
continually dissolve. As he sees it, an ocean voyage is an excellent means by
which to commence a journey of adventure, since it separates one from
"worldly scenes and employments" and arouses "a state of mind peculiarly
fitted to receive new and vivid impressions" (p. 11). Yet no sooner does he
signal his role as romantic observer than he sounds the opposite note as well,
one that will reverberate throughout the sketches: a "wide sea voyage severs us
at once.—It makes us conscious of being cast loose from the secure anchorage
of settled life and sent adrift upon a doubtful world. It interposes a gulph, not
merely imaginary, but real, between us and our homes—a gulph subject to
tempest and fear and uncertainty, rendering distance palpable and return precarious." Thus, right from the outset—and using the idea of "cast off"
again—Irving delineates the dual nature of experience (mirrored narratively
in the Crayon/Irving duality) in *The Sketch Book*: a surface layer of anticipated
satisfaction camouflages a subterranean level of gnawing doubt.

As America disappears, Crayon attempts to set his mind in tune with the
still vacancy of the scene, seeking harmony in a richer realm of consciousness:
to "gaze upon the piles of golden clouds just peering above the horizon; fancy
them some fairy realms and people them with a creation" of his own (p. 12).
As his distance from concrete particulars widens, his mental activity increases,
so that he is able to perceive, in effect, what he desires to perceive; that is, his
emotional responses to his environment, rather than being shaped by his perceptions, are in fact determining those very perceptions. This is the Crayonesque ideal—the imaginative agenda that the pilgrim in search of the Old
World of his youthful reading and daydreaming has established for himself—
but it cannot be sustained. A delicious stimulation of the fancy as, perched
atop the mainmast, Crayon delights in the sensuous accord of his imagination
with the sea below yields to the fear of detachment. Separation from emotional ties and a familiar way of life—the very condition that stimulates his
creativity—induces a sense of alienation that informs all Crayon's activities.

From the "giddy height" of the quarterdeck Crayon surveys the watery
world, conjuring up "wild phantasms that swell the tales of fishermen and
sailors." Though they may appear ominous at first, these images are benign,
merely themes of "idle speculation," as is a "distant sail, gliding along the edge
of the ocean." But the object that precipitates a rejoicing in man's achievement

42

in one paragraph engenders reflections on death in the next when Crayon notices the floating mast from a wrecked ship and, tied to it, "the remains of handkerchiefs, by which some of the crew had fastened themselves to the spar to prevent their being washed off by the waves." These images of disaster recall his previous worry that the "uncertain currents of existence" may prevent him from ever returning to his homeland. Crayon's self-conscious meditation on the fate of the lost crew—"their bones . . . whitening among the caverns of the deep"—and on the trials of those left behind—"prayers offered up at the deserted fireside of home," "expectation darkened into anxiety[,] anxiety into dread and dread into despair"—reveals Irving's own terror of being, both realistically and metaphorically, lost forever between two shores. In addition, this musing on human misfortune and the sudden shift from triumph to tragedy—a very mirror of Irving's distraught mind during the bankruptcy crisis—give rise to the captain's tale of another shipwreck, which reinforces the mood of uneasiness that pervades the sketch. The fury of an ensuing storm raging all about him, which pursues him even as he escapes, literally "tempest tossed and weather beaten," to his cabin suggests the troubled state of Crayon's soul (and signals, in the echoed phrases from his letters, Irving's haunting fear that he may never have an opportunity to redeem himself from the state of bankruptcy). Though a subsequent fine day chases all "dismal reflections," it only temporarily alleviates his inner burden.

Upon arrival at the coast of England, Crayon's expectations inflate—at long last his dream of encountering the Past is about to be realized. Surveying the shore with a telescope, he finds the landscape just as he had envisioned it: "My eye dwelt with delight on neat cottages with their trim shrubberies and green grass plots. I saw the mouldering ruin of an abbey over run with ivy, and the taper spire of a village church rising from the brow of a neighbouring hill—all were characteristic of England" (p. 15). He appears ready to project himself imaginatively into that landscape, to assimilate the glories of the past, but like the earlier view from the quarterdeck, the panorama of England does not produce the intellectual/emotional union he anticipated. The scene of "hurry and bustle," with its variety of expressed and shared emotion, increases Crayon's consciousness of his own isolation as he recognizes his fundamental separateness: "I alone was solitary and idle. I had no friend to meet, no cheering to receive." His debarkation, instead of freeing him from self-preoccupation by connecting him to the collective history of his ancestors, only intensifies it: "I stepped upon the land of my forefathers—but felt that I was a stranger in the land."

The pattern established here, with some variation, holds throughout *The Sketch Book*. Crayon's "fine fancies" continually give way under the pressure of fact. His yearning for a transcendent moment or a participatory experience ultimately brings him face to face with prosaic reality. Though his responses (as in "The Voyage") sometimes appear to be not much more than the customary apprehensions of the newly arrived visitor entering a foreign land, they emanate from the feeling of being dispossessed ("castaway"), from a man who, estranged at home, now finds himself a stranger in the mother country. Embedded in no secure traditions, attached to no nurturing culture, Crayon epitomizes the very derivation of the term "un-settled." Moreover, since the main objective of his travels is to penetrate the timelessness of England via an emotional extension into the very fiber of its spiritual heritage, it is especially significant that upon sighting the desired landscape his status as an American prevents him from imaginatively grasping hold of it. Despite the fact that England is the "land" of his "forefathers," he remains an exile, barred from the stability conferred by the conservative, aristocratic order.

Much of *The Sketch Book*, therefore, involves Crayon's generally futile attempt to internalize the unifying principle of British society. From the comfortable solidity of John Bull's house ("John Bull"), to the pastoral beauty of the English rural landscape ("Rural Life in England," "The Country Church," "Rural Funerals"), to the recognizable artifacts of the London cityscape ("The Boar's Head Tavern, East Cheap," "London Antiques," "Little Britain"), to the "ancient and festive honours" of a Christmas celebration on Squire Bracebridge's estate (the "Christmas" sequence), there appears to be a genuine cohesiveness in English life that elicits Crayon's admiration and respect. Yet, as the displaced pilgrim from the New World, he cannot help tinging his portraits of these characteristic English scenes with mild irony: John Bull has landed deeply in debt because he remains outrightly intractable on the subject of change; the countryside has been infiltrated by the pretentious and vulgar nouveaux riches; London has metamorphosed into a city reflecting a garish modernism and political unrest in the nature of reform conspiracies; Squire Bracebridge's fierce antiquarianism threatens a future of decay. On the whole, Crayon seems not quite sure how to react to the English. Emotionally incapable of either unmitigated reverence or blatant satire, he most often channels his nervous insecurity into self-mockery. Or he retreats to a shameless sentimentality.

"Let me not indulge in this mawkish feeling and sentiment," Irving wrote in an 1817 notebook, "which has produced a morbid sensibility and sustain all the melancholy tendencies &c."[46] Yet despite his self-warning, sentimentality, with its substitution of a flaccid, unexamined sympathy for a rigorous, unmediated introspection, becomes Crayon's favorite technique in *The Sketch Book* for avoiding the recognition of painful truths. Seeking communion on a Sunday in an English rural village with its ceremonial church service ("The Widow and Her Son"), Crayon anticipates "holy repose" and "hallowed calm," but instead finds himself "continually thrown back upon the world by the frigidity and pomp" of the fashionable society in attendance (p. 83). The one "true christian" in the congregation, a "poor, decrepid old woman," attracts Crayon's notice because of her piety. When he learns of her bereavement over an only son (in whose death chance, interestingly enough, plays a significant part), he attends the funeral and, in the manner of Sterne's sentimental traveler, empathetically participates in the mother's grief: "I could see no more—my heart swelled into my throat—my eyes filled with tears—I felt as if I were acting a barbarous part in standing by and gazing idly on this scene of maternal anguish." His subsequent meditation on the sorrows of the aged widow deflects attention from his isolation at the same time that it enables Irving to direct the pain of his own losses into an acceptable literary vehicle. And while it is impossible to take seriously Crayon's bathetic confession in "The Broken Heart"—"I believe in broken hearts and the possibility of dying of disappointed love!" (p. 56)—his sympathetic rendering of the story of the young widow's "devouring melancholy" and "hopeless decline . . . into the grave" after her lover's execution serves Irving as a means of release from the loneliness of bachelorhood and, therefore, a partial consolation for the diminished choices of a life of emotional impoverishment. Since the death of his betrothed, Matilda Hoffmann, in 1809 he too had known "widowhood."

Obviously, Crayon is no Addisonian "spectator": he neither observes nor records his perceptions with anything like reportorial distance. In fact, objectivity is hardly his aim; rather, he gravitates toward characters, places, and stories that are intimately connected to Irving's recent emotional history— hence, the tone and the order of the varied pieces. These sketches function as metaphorical revelations of his longings, hopes, and fears. "Roscoe," which immediately and naturally follows "The Voyage" and therefore offers the first prolonged view of England in the collection, provides an excellent example of this process while illustrating once again the layered quality of *The Sketch Book*. The sketch highlights William Roscoe, respected banker, renowned author of Italian histories, and purveyor of culture in commercial Liverpool (where Irving spent his first trying years in England). Crayon's capsule summary of Roscoe's achievement could very well stand for Irving's up to the time of his European sojourn: "Born in a place apparently ungenial to the growth of literary talent; in the very market place of trade; without fortune, family connexions or patronage; [and] self prompted, self sustained and almost self taught, he has conquered every obstacle, [and] achieved his way to eminence." Moreover, also like Irving, he has suffered financial setbacks. Crayon, in what amounts to a self-reflexive act, celebrates Roscoe's refusal to be "*cast down* by the frowns of adversity" (p. 18; my italics). Having lost his security, his home, and his beloved library (which has been sold at auction), Roscoe is "bowed"; yet his dependence "upon the resources of his own mind" and "the superior society of his own thoughts" in meeting the crisis manifests a heroism worthy of emulation. The world cannot violate him. Thus, for Crayon, Roscoe is a man for all time, "the literary land mark" of Liverpool. The obvious parallels here reveal Irving's determination not to let economic disaster overwhelm his ambitions, and further indicate his hope that literature would be the source of retrieved dignity.

Yet in spite of the encomium, there is something undeniably disturbing about the portrait of Liverpool's most honorable citizen.[47] For all of his efforts on behalf of his city—among other projects, he has promoted "institutions for literary and scientific purposes"—when his need was greatest his townsmen deserted him. Painfully aware of this, Crayon gives his words an uncharacteristic bite: "Surely if the people of Liverpool had been properly sensible of what was due to Mr. Roscoe and themselves, his library would never have been sold. . . . It certainly appears to me such an opportunity as seldom occurs, of cheering a noble mind, struggling under misfortunes, by one of the most delicate but most expressive tokens of public sympathy." No such benevolence was forthcoming; in fact, Roscoe's neighbors "thronged like wreckers" to purchase his books.[48] In Crayon's imagination they are "pigmies rummaging the armoury of a giant, and contending for the possessions of weapons which they could not wield." Perhaps an allusion to Gulliver among the Lilliputians, the metaphor indicates suppressed anger, a feeling which may account for Crayon's inability to see that Roscoe's sonnet upon parting with his books, rather than displaying "pure feeling and elevated thought," strikes instead a deeply pathetic note. Consciously, Crayon acknowledges and applauds Roscoe's grandeur, the moral firmness inherent in the stoic acceptance of his fate; unconsciously, however, his identification with the abandoned and homeless man of letters bespeaks Irving's continued uneasiness over his own disconnectedness, and the inchoate fear that his literary endeavors were little more than disguised self-pity.

The following sketch, "The Wife," ostensibly a hymn to filial devotion and its spiritual healing power, provides another example of how Crayon's unexpressed anxieties can be detected below the surface of his sentimental pieties and, in this case, can belie the homiletic vision of marriage central to the sketch. Clearly, the connubial state is the preferred one, with a "world of love at home," where the husband is "monarch"; the single life promises only "waste and self neglect," loneliness and abandonment. This is especially true in times of trouble, when more than ever a man needs support and succor, which happens to be the precise situation of Crayon's friend C. R. Leslie who, after only a few months of marital bliss, has suffered severe financial misfortune. His great agony, however, centers on his belief that the news will destroy his bride; her heart, he thinks, "will be weighed down like mine by the cares and miseries of the world." But rather than wilt, his wife Mary responds with "sweetness and good humour"; she is "all love and tenderness and comfort." Still, Leslie agonizes: having been forced to retreat to a humble country dwelling, he imagines Mary "exhausted and spiritless, brooding over a prospect of future poverty." But again, his fears fail to materialize; arriving at the cottage with Crayon, Leslie is greeted by a vision of pastoral beauty: Mary, decked out in a pure white dress, with "wild flowers" twined through her hair, leads her husband to the patio where she has prepared a dessert of fresh strawberries and cream. The sketch closes with the couple in rapturous embrace, yet the symbol of marital bonding also reminds us that in such instances Crayon acts the part of voyeur, that although he would like to know the pleasures and comforts of such union—to experience Leslie's moment of "exquisite felicity"—he is but an itinerant wanderer, excluded from domestic harmony. Since Irving had suffered both financial ruin and the loss of his fiancée, he was without the security of marriage or home; he faced bankruptcy, and the bleak future, alone. Unlike Leslie, therefore, he is the monarch of nothing—or of nothing but words, which sometimes bring succor, but at other times merely fill up the blank page.

Even with his expectations of a "genial" book, the fact that sadness and regret accompany a portrait of joy is, by the third sketch in the collection, not terribly surprising to the reader. The really troubling element in "The Wife" involves Crayon's re-creation of his extended dialogue with Leslie, as he tries to convince his friend, first, that to protect his wife by hiding the news of economic disaster from her will only exacerbate matters and may make her feel "undervalued," and second, that her ability to handle the reduced circumstances of country living may very well exceed his expectations. In both instances, Leslie exhibits near-hysterical behavior; his "transport[s] of grief and tenderness" are the sounds of man in the throes of an anxiety attack. To Crayon's words of encouragement and his expression of confidence in Mary's fortitude Leslie behaves as if he were listening to an inner, not an outer, voice: "How can she bear poverty!—she has been brought up in all the refinements of opulence.—How can she bear neglect!—she has been the idol of society— oh, it will break her heart!—it will break her heart!" Once this "paroxysm" subsides, he then cries out "convulsively" and rather inarticulately: "I could be happy with her in a hovel!—I could go down with her into poverty and the dust!—I could—I could—God bless her!—God bless her!" And later, after he has led his friend to believe that Mary is in poor spirits, Leslie responds impatiently to Crayon's inquiry about her health by totally exaggerating the circumstances that now prevail in the country; he envisions her "reduced to [a] paltry situation," "caged in a miserable cottage," "obliged to toil almost in the menial concerns of her wretched habitation" (pp. 24–26).

Leslie's rantings—and they amount to just that, since there is nothing in either Mary's attitude or behavior to justify them (in fact, she expresses relief over the mildness of his news)—are the barely coherent statements of a man suffering intense doubt and fear. Part of what drives him to extremes—his other mode of response borders on gushing sentimentality—is witnessing his prosperous home suddenly collapsing into ruin. Surely it is he, and not Mary, who may fall apart because of the sacrifices demanded of them; the fragile heart about to break is Leslie's own. Unable to locate the true source of his trauma, he projects his worries about facing a life of "sordid cares . . . paltry wants . . . petty humiliations" onto his wife. While Crayon counsels that "it is not poverty so much as pretence, that harrasses a ruined man," it looks as if the specter of poverty carries quite a sting after all. And Crayon knows this only too well; as Irving's letters reveal, the image of privation has been haunting him (and will continue to plague him long past *The Sketch Book*'s success) since his earliest days in England. Yet because he has firsthand knowledge of this level of Leslie's experience, and because Crayon's counseling of his friend is a form of self-communion, though easier and therefore more immediately satisfying than undistracted self-scrutiny, Crayon appears fairly calm and controlled (especially in relation to Leslie). Even when he acknowledges feeling some "trepidation," the conscious uneasiness lasts but a moment.

But a life of diminished prospects is not the most profound cause of Leslie's distress. As Hedges puts it, "what frightens him most is the idea that his bride will be unable to live without the house, clothes, and furniture to which she is accustomed."[49] The key word here is "idea"—Leslie's idea—that these accouterments define happiness for Mary; without them she will be miserable. A woman wants "the elegancies of life," "the pleasures of society," and Leslie apparently believes it a man's duty to secure them for her. The operative equation for him in regard to marriage, therefore, looks something like this: no possessions for Mary = his failure = loss of Mary's love. (Interestingly, that Mary might care more about security, continuity, and faithfulness in affections never crosses his mind.) Beneath the bourgeois concern for material goods, however, lies Leslie's far greater fear of his own inadequacy—that he cannot provide his wife with what *he thinks* she needs or requires for satisfaction, be it in terms of status, physical comfort, or, perhaps (and this is quite unstated in the sketch), sexual gratification. It is revealing, therefore, that even after he tells her the news and she reacts well, he *still* dreads her sadness. Mary makes no demands whatsoever, yet Leslie responds as if each day he awakes to an ultimatum.

Although Crayon refers to Leslie as "manly," ultimately he leaves the impression of pitiful weakness. At the beginning of the sketch, in a sentence interesting for its unconscious revelation of Leslie's character, Crayon portrays his friend in a position of power in relation to his wife: "The fond confiding air with which she looked up to him, seemed to call forth a flush of triumphant pride and cherishing tenderness; as if he doted on his lovely burthen, for its very helplessness." Leslie, in other words, feels "triumphant pride" when Mary idolizes him in a childlike manner; he "dotes on his lovely burthen" precisely because she needs his love and approval. It appears as if his own strength can be measured only in relation to the proper degree of her "helplessness." "Never," Crayon writes, "did a couple set forward on the flowery path of early and well suited marriage, with a fairer prospect of felicity" (p. 23). The lurking suggestion here is that if Mary were too strong or independent (or the opposite, too weak and dependent) the marriage would not be "well suited" at all; "felicity" is possible to the extent that she remains in a state of blissful ignorance, never having to face, and therefore neither overcoming nor succumbing to, the tensions and cares of the world. Continually panicked that Mary will fall into nervous collapse, Leslie never acknowledges her capacity to handle adversity: when she reacts well to his disclosure of their new financial position, he claims that she "has no idea of poverty but in the abstract"; when she shows herself undaunted by the threat of a bleak future, he counters that she has no "real experience." Reality is colored by what he secretly fears will be the claims made upon him; whether Mary grows firm and self-reliant or sinks into debilitating despair he is petrified that he could not handle it. In fact, since it would be far worse for him if Mary exhibited genuine fortitude, he completely denies this possibility. He acts like a man who has a great deal invested in the image of his wife's passivity, since he clings to it even in the face of its falsity.

So, too, does Crayon. His vicarious participation in Leslie's drama—at one point he confesses that his "feelings had become strongly interested in the progress of this family story"—reveals the extent to which he identifies with his fellow artist's dilemma. Only Crayon is more deceptive about his worry that Mary may come apart under the strain. Although he has solaced and advised his friend, his reassurances are no more than nineteenth-century platitudes about the mysterious way a woman overcomes her natural timidity in a crisis: the "latent energies and fervent sympathies of her nature" which are "call[ed] forth" so that she can prove that she loves a man for himself; the miraculous power that transforms the "wife of his bosom" into a "ministering angel" as she passes with a man "through the fiery trials of this world." It sounds suspiciously as if, like Leslie, he harbors the fear that in their "weakness" women require constant attention and tremendous emotional energy. Indeed, Crayon confirms this when he confesses to the reader, as if he were on a stage speaking an aside to the audience, that he does not quite believe his own words. Privately, he doubts that Mary has the capacity to adjust to a different mode of living: "Who can calculate on the *fortitude* of one whose whole life has been a round of pleasures?—Her gay spirits might revolt at the dark downward path of low humility" (p. 25; my italics). This, too, sounds like the projection of a disturbed psyche, especially given the fact that Crayon opened the sketch with the opposite generalization about how often he has witnessed "the *fortitude* with which women sustain the most overwhelming reverses of fortune" (my italics). The same word "fortitude" services both positive and negative belief. In addition, even though he learns from Leslie that she bore the truth "like an angel," he later refuses, again only to his readers, to controvert his friend's mental picture of Mary's abject state in the humble country abode. At the outset of "The Wife," Crayon compared the woman who supports the bent frame of a man in his "calamity" by "winding herself into the rugged recesses of his nature" to the "caressing tendrils" of the vine that "clings round" and binds the "shattered boughs" of the thunder-

rifted oak. In the end, however, the oak of manhood, less "hardy" than Crayon would have us believe, appears to have had its strength sapped, rather than replenished, by those "caressing tendrils" of womanhood.

Not surprisingly, ineffectual, inadequate men dominate the two most famous stories in Irving's collection, "Rip Van Winkle" and "The Legend of Sleepy Hollow." Both Rip and Ichabod long for comfortable homes, to be settled in a pastoral community and let time pass them by, yet neither takes the necessary steps to secure this: both men waste their lives in dream and inaction. Insistently conventional as she may be, Dame Van Winkle nevertheless has a point: "ready to attend to any body's business but his own," to gather with his friends in front of the inn rather than "doing family duty, and keeping his farm in order" (p. 30), Rip may be American literature's first total failure as a husband. His farm in ruin, his children ragged, and yet his mind continually scattered in other pursuits, he is at least partly responsible for his spouse's sharp-tongued and mean-spirited outbursts. After all, given his "habits of idleness," he does not provide for her. While it is true that she makes demands, it is equally true that he has neglected his responsibilities. Ichabod, too, makes no gestures that would indicate his fitness as Katrina Van Tassel's mate. An indifferent schoolmaster making his steady rounds among the local farmers on whom he depends for board, and flattering the country women in the hopes of securing a "dish of cakes or sweetmeats," he contributes nothing of any permanent value to the life of the Hollow. In fact, as the "genius of famine descending upon the earth," he offers only his lean, hungry self in return for the ample charms of Katrina Van Tassel (and the abundance of the Van Tassel farm). She is right to reject him, moreover, since he shows little interest in her personally; possession of her father's property turns out to be his real goal, and then only for its cash value. Furthermore, Ichabod's sexuality is severely in doubt; the pedagogue channels all his erotic energy into the act of eating. Rip manifests problems in this area as well: though he escapes to a sexualized landscape, he chooses to curl up on the bosom of a "green knoll" and sleep away twenty years of potency, awakening when he is incapable of any further (re-)productivity.[50] Both protagonists behave as if the last thing they wanted was a healthy relationship with a woman. Surely one of the most powerfully appealing aspects of these stories to the American man is that Rip and Ichabod are overgrown versions of children, seeking to gratify boyish impulses for a carefree life devoid of adult male responsibilities.

Whether you have an angel or a shrew for a wife—or, as in Ichabod's case, hope to win a coquette—marriage and commitment are too frightening. They engender deep feelings of inadequacy or threaten to engulf our heroes in a world of domesticity that would force them to abandon their self-preoccupations—which means, essentially, that they would have to stop dreaming and start paying attention to the territory beyond their own fantasies. How much more preferable to live one's life in rural retirement, like "the angler," completely "independent of external circumstances," whose circumscribed pursuit of piscatorial pleasure brings him great contentment. "The whole tenor of his life," Crayon writes, "was quiet and inoffensive, being principally passed about the neighbouring streams when the weather and season were favourable; at other times he employed himself at home, preparing his fishing tackle for the next campaign" (p. 270). His most striking characteristic, however, is his utter lack of anxiety: "he was satisfied that the world, in itself, was good and beautiful." While Crayon marvels at the old angler's peacefulness, and would like to share in his sense of security—to be "safely moored in a snug and quiet harbour in the evening of his days"—he is much closer in spirit to the male figures of "The Wife," "Rip Van Winkle," and "Sleepy Hollow," who are all men of some imagination and creativity (Leslie is a genre painter, Rip and Ichabod are variations of the storyteller). In *The Sketch Book*, these pathetic, though likable, characters function as surrogates for Geoffrey Crayon and, in turn, for Irving: their doubts, fears, and anxieties are his, and he shares, as well, their most meaningful way of handling the demands of a not-so-"beautiful" world—escaping into the realm of imagination. Moreover, the impotent, weak male protagonists represent Irving's projections of failure as a writer, and his own deeply felt sense of insignificance as a cultural figure.

On the positive side, however, Irving also tends to see something of himself in poets whose art aided them in overcoming personal misfortune. The most obvious example of this mirroring effect in *The Sketch Book* is Crayon's depiction of Shakespeare's youth in Stratford, where the bard suffered humiliation when caught poaching on the estate of Sir Thomas Lucy. Then, after further arousing Lucy's ire by burlesquing him in a "rough pasquinade," Shakespeare fled Avon to London, eventually writing for the stage. In *The Merry Wives of Windsor*, he "confer[red] immortality on his oppressor" by caricaturing him as the pompous, "puissant" Justice Shallow (p. 222). Shakespeare, therefore, having once "wander[ed] forth in disgrace upon a doubtful world," elicits Crayon's greatest admiration because he transformed the painful realities of his life into "fancied beings" and poeticized landscapes. Moreover, having Crayon dwell on the problems of young Shakespeare enables Irving to reflect on his own vocational crisis.[51] In Shakespeare's being cast out upon the world, and in the contrast between his humble beginnings and ultimate fame, Irving was reminded of his own recent plight and his hopes for literary success. For similar reasons, Irving has Crayon celebrate James I of Scotland who, as a prisoner of state in the tower of Windsor Castle, composed "King's Quair" directly in response to the melancholy events of his youth. But Crayon's sketch deals with James in a more complex fashion, for unlike Shakespeare (and, for that matter, Irving), he did not begin his poetic career in humble, deprived, penurious, or even ignominious circumstances. James, of noble birth, was heir to the throne of Scotland.

In "A Royal Poet," Crayon pilgrimages to James's dungeon in Windsor Castle, for it was within these walls that James first sighted his beloved Lady Jane, strolling in the garden below his window, and it was here that he wrote "King's Quair," which Crayon describes as "another of those beautiful breakings forth of the soul from the restraint and gloom of the prison house" (p. 69). Since he wants to identify with James's experience, he is only interested in those parts of the poem "which breathe his immediate thoughts concerning his situation . . . in the tower." These sections have "such circumstantial truth" that Crayon feels he can be "present with the captive in his prison" and become "the companion of his meditations." Thus, Crayon lauds James as a poet triumphing over the actual scene of his pain and humiliation; but this becomes problematic since James, as a monarch, "was treated with the respect due to his rank," which meant that he had the opportunity to develop his intellectual and artistic tastes. To maintain the illusion of James as a deprived, suffering artist, Crayon claims that he "had learnt to be a poet before he was a king," and insists that his primary interest in writing was to communicate, purely as an author to his audience, his "true feelings, and the story of his real loves and fortunes." The "Quair" therefore reveals, much to the reader's satisfaction, "the simple affections of human nature throbbing under the ermine." Suspiciously, James's psychological relationship to literature resembles Washington Irving's.

Crayon's reading of the "Quair" as an account of the poet's intense love for Lady Jane and his bitter afflictions in the tower suffers from the fact that the entire scene, and much of its descriptive manner, bears a strong resemblance to Chaucer's "Knight's Tale," which suggests that, rather than a truly original composition, "King's Quair" embodies the poetic conventions of its day. Quite aware of this, Crayon nevertheless eschews critical judgment in order to preserve the authenticity of James's experience. Looking for literary forebears whose art also originated in self-conscious deprivation (the obverse, perhaps,

53

of Harold Bloom's "anxiety of influence"), Irving has Crayon deliberately misread "King's Quair," accepting the heightened sentiments and "poetic fiction[s]" as true history. "Let us not," he declares in support of his interpretation, "reject every romantic incident as incompatible with real life; but let us sometimes take a poet at his word."

Unlike other sketches in which Crayon's excesses of feeling and susceptibility are undercut by comic deflation, turning him into a mock-heroic, quixotic figure, "A Royal Poet" does not shift its tone as it chronicles the rest of James's unfortunate life and applauds his artistic achievements. Irving indulges Crayon's sentimentality here because he needs to reflect on James in a particular way: having been victimized by misfortune, James rose above his persecution and turned adversity into creative accomplishment. Despondent but resolute during *The Sketch Book* days, Irving aspired to the same goal. Moreover, James serves as an inspirational symbol of the ability of the imagination to create its own world. In the "loneliness of confinement" James's mind did not "corrode and grow inactive," but became "tender and imaginative." As a poet, James envisioned an order of experience full of the passion and beauty that his earthly one lacked: "it is the divine attribute of the imagination, that . . . when the real world is shut out, it can . . . conjure up glorious shapes and forms, and brilliant visions, to make solitude populous, and irradiate the gloom of the dungeon." Once again, Crayon also speaks metaphorically; Irving has, in effect, sketched James in the image of his own captivity. Devastated by his losses, and psychologically imprisoned by his need for nurturing traditions, Irving depended upon his art to channel disruptive feelings, and at times to create an alternate dreamlike world, a territory in which all the feeling and meaning he sought temporarily existed.

However, while the art served both a compensatory and a redemptive function, it became, paradoxically, yet another source of anxiety. Irving's primary means of shading his writings with romantic nuance, and embossing Crayon's experience with the color of antiquity, was to rework the moods of some of his favorite English authors. In fact, books had so shaped his sensibility that the cast of mind from which Crayon viewed the world was fraught with literary association. Seeing Irving as an "anachronism," William Hazlitt rudely noted that the British were quite familiar with the prevailing spirit of these sketches;[52] echoes could be heard, for instance, of Thomson's *Seasons*, Goldsmith's *Deserted Village*, Cowper's *The Task*, and Crabbe's *The Village*. "The Broken Heart" reminded readers of *The Vicar of Wakefield*; "Westminster Abbey" sounded a similar note to Browne's *Urn-Burial* and James Hervey's

Meditations and Contemplations.[53] Every sketch, essay, or tale in the collection bore an epigraph derived either from some antiquated English lyric, ballad, song, or essay, or from the writings of major British authors, including Milton, Lyly, Burton, Marlowe, Herrick, Nashe, and Chaucer. Although the elaborate framework of allusion, the use of direct quotation and indirect reference, and the melding of the sentiments of previous writers into the texture of *The Sketch Book* were all part of a deliberate, compelling strategy—to place his book within time-honored traditions in English literature—Irving worried that he would be perceived as an American impersonation of the revered English writers who had focused on native scenes.[54] Uncertain about publishing his first new work in ten years, Irving compounded the tensions by poaching on the hostile, closely guarded territory of British literary conventions.

Actually, more than just professional realignment motivated Irving's authorial choices. Because he saw literary culture as enhancing the stability of English life—passed on from one generation to the next, it tied the past to the present, thus providing continuity and meaning through a shared heritage— books were for him an inherent part of England's spiritual grandeur. The great English prose writers had always represented the noblest and most enduring values of the society, and their wisdom and moral vision lived on in their writings. Therefore, even though he had tried to view the past through the eyes of a citizen, only to discover that he was doomed to be a stranger in the present, his book would link him to the great chain of an English prose tradition—Browne, Bacon, Addison, Swift, Sterne, Smollet, Goldsmith, and Johnson. In a sense, Irving attempted to gather this heritage into himself, filling up an American cultural void with hundreds of years of literary achievement. He was not simply trying to embellish his writing by ornamenting it with bits and pieces from classical authors; rather, on a larger scale, he was attempting to interpolate his random wanderings and observations into the continuous flow of a valued inheritance. He was, in other words, adopting a prestigious family. In this complex manner, the network of allusion exerted a controlling force over the atmosphere of *The Sketch Book*, not, however, without Irving running the risk that his professional debut would be marred by cries of "literary posturing" from the reviewers.

That he would be labeled an impostor was only the most extreme form of Irving's general fear of public disapproval; in addition, he believed that the energy required for sustained creative activity would fail him. And even though he fathered a new literary genre, the fictional sketch,[55] by calling his writings "sketches" he could, at the same time he desired respectability, evade the demands of a more venerable prose form. Indeed, the word "sketch" implies a preliminary study or a representation of a work of art intended for elaboration; and while a sketch may have line, shading, and color, it connotes hastiness and incompleteness. "His very title, 'The Sketch Book,' has apology in it," Fred Lewis Pattee has written, "for a sketch book is a random receptacle for first impressions, materials collected *for* work and not the work itself." [56]

In fact, Irving sounded an apologetic note both early and late in the collection. The "Prospectus" to the first number has Crayon informing his audience that his writings "will partake of the fluctuations of his own thoughts and feelings" and that he "will not be able to give them that tranquil attention necessary to finished composition" (p. 300), self-disparaging remarks that reveal not only Irving's insecurity about reappearing in print, but his anxiety over the originality and permanence of his work.[57] "L'Envoy," the closing piece of *The Sketch Book* (which first appeared in the second volume of the British edition of 1820), shows Crayon again assuming the pose he had struck in the "Prospectus"; though his friends had counseled him about what to include and what to exclude in this second volume, Crayon has decided to "ramble on even as he had begun." Openly playful here, he turns "serious" in his final words, as he confesses his anxiety about being an American writer in England: he has been so "full of solicitude to deserve" British "approbation" that he has discovered "that very solicitude continually embarrassing his powers, and depriving him of that ease and confidence which are necessary to successful exertion" (pp. 298–99). Hoping ultimately to achieve a "steadier footing," he has, in the meantime, doubly protected himself from the sting of his audience's ridicule: the self-effacing tone ("surprized at his own good fortune, and wondering at his own temerity") bespeaks his contriteness for presuming to write on British subjects while the slight, but still discernible, irony indicates a stubborn if undemonstrative belief in his own abilities; after all, as he says, he will "proceed," though it be in a "half venturing, half shrinking" fashion. Irving's original plan of irregular publication, resembling that of the English essayists,[58] accords perfectly with Crayon's self-assessment of unpredictable energy and undisciplined talent and accommodates as well the desire to shield himself from the worldly "cares and vicissitudes" that had so recently victimized "him." For a moment, Crayon and Irving converge into one being.

It is not surprising that a mind like Irving's, capable of joining conflicting points of view in some creative tension (an unwillingness for commitment,

for example, coexisting with a hunger for success), could be absolutely rever-
ent about a literary calling and yet at the same time mock his ambitions and
denigrate his very achievement. The fruits of authorship and the exalted profession of letters could be just as much the subject for ironic humor as they
could be for high seriousness, which is precisely what occurs in "The Mutability of Literature," where Crayon's fantastic confrontation with forgotten
books signifies Irving's skepticism about the worth of his own aspirations.
The sketch begins with a familiar pattern: after "loitering about the old gray
cloisters of Westminster Abbey," Crayon makes his way into the recesses of the
building where the library lies "shut up from the tumult of the world." The
secluded place, usually for Crayon a scene of anticipated discovery, becomes
instead the setting for his symbolic projections of anxiety over the oblivion to
which authors are doomed: buried "in the solitude of cells and cloisters," devoted "to painful research and intense reflection," their reward is "to have the
title of their works read now and then in a future age" and "in another age
to be lost, even to remembrance." The "boasted immortality" of literature
amounts to a "mere temporary rumour, a local sound, like the tone of that
bell which has just tolled among these towers, filling the ear for a moment—
lingering transiently in echo—and then passing away, like a thing that was
not!" (p. 101). While the metaphor reaches for philosophic expansiveness,
the tone is elegiac. Crayon appears to know for whom the bell tolls.

As he sits in the library in this deprecating mood, he begins to thumb
through an old quarto; when he accidentally loosens the clasps, the book mi-
raculously comes to life and the remainder of the piece turns into a seriocomic
quarrel. In this fantasy of verbal exchange with the ancient tome, Crayon confronts his unconscious apprehensions (and Irving his conscious ones) that he
has committed himself to a medium that must by necessity perish. Since the
English language does not spring "from a well or fountain head," but is a
"mere confluence of various tongues, perpetually subject to changes and
intermixtures," age will sweep away everything in print. "Subject to the dilapidations of time and the caprice of fashion," the language falls into decay.
Thus, Crayon laments the mutability of English literature and the instability
of the reputations built upon it: old writers are supplanted by modern ones,
who in their turn will be supplanted by their successors. An elaborate form of
self-communion, Crayon's "colloquy" with the quarto appears to be unconsciously prescient about Irving's celebrated book: "however it may be admired
in its day, and held up as a model of purity, [it] will in the course of years
grow antiquated and obsolete."

But as these gloomy ponderings begin to weigh on Crayon, he attempts to turn "this mutability of language" into a providential benefit for all mankind by seeing it as a preventative against the "alarming" possibility of the world being "drowned in the deluge" of print: "The stream of literature has swoln [sic] into a torrent—augmented into a river—expanded into a sea. . . . Unless some unforeseen mortality should break out among the progeny of the muse, now that she has become so prolific, I tremble for posterity." Where Crayon was previously so eloquent in his metaphorical depiction of the fate of all literary endeavor, including Irving's own, his backtracking here—an instance of comic exaggeration—does not persuade, which is evinced rather humorously in the boredom of the little quarto. Yawning in his face, the book tells him that he is "rather given to prose." Self-directed irony resolves the inner tensions of the sketch, as Irving expresses his personal uncertainties through the mildly ludicrous figure of Crayon.

Part of Crayon's comic appeal, of course, derives from his pretense that the quarto is alive and from his willingness to quarrel with it. However, neither his guise of credulity nor the condescending attitude of the quarto mitigates the one substantial argument that Crayon offers in opposition to the idea of mutability—his passionate defense of Shakespeare, who embodies the fundamental law of permanence itself. Shakespeare is "proof against the mutability of language" because he has rooted himself in the "unchanging principles of human nature." He has defied the "encroachments of time, retaining in modern use the language and literature of his day." The one absolute representative of the world of the imagination superseding the world of time, he symbolizes the continuity of the creative impulse, becomes the source of Crayon's wonder over the enduring potency of the imagination—a lesson Irving needed to reaffirm (which may account for the multiple use of Shakespearean allusion in the sketches).[59] The world did not undo Shakespeare; rather, Shakespeare "spread the magic of his mind over the very face of nature" (p. 223). But as Crayon, Irving, and everyone else knows, in the long history of English literature there has been only one Shakespeare.

Whether the author of *The Sketch Book* believed in 1820 that he could inhabit the realm of the enduring English writers is doubtful; his strategy of indirection—that is, his muffled expression of pain, frustration, and insecurity—certainly suggests otherwise. Reverence for the bard notwithstanding, his book testifies to the fact that although authorship became his salvation from personal despair, he did not trust it enough to declare the world well lost. Too many fears about his own legitimacy still persisted: of what did his credentials consist, after all, but a few youthful burlesques and now a miscellany of sketches, essays, and stories, most of which merely reframe his experiences and perceptions in a new fictional matrix? Beyond this, from both inside and out, voices nagged at him about the proper pursuits for an American man; like Rip and Ichabod, he understood that one day there would be a price to pay for "following the bent of his vagrant inclination." (In fact, the emotional cost of wandering and writing becomes his major preoccupation while composing *Tales of a Traveller*.) Yet, to his credit—and the good fortune of American literature—he persisted in actively writing about inactive, unaggressive men. Perhaps, too, because he had experienced anxiety on so many different levels, he intuited that the only way out of its stasis-producing web was through the struggles of the self, through, that is, an exertion of effort and will beyond what he believed were his capacities. *The Sketch Book*, an American classic wrought out of American anxiety, resulted from just the right combination of these many factors and, consequently, transformed the man who suffered into the persona who narrated.

IV

"Geoffrey Crayon," Washington Irving's most significant creation of this era, was the vehicle through which he released personal, cultural, and artistic anxiety, metamorphosing it into humorous irony and lighthearted self-mockery. By making Crayon his spokesman, his persona,[60] Irving freed himself (temporarily, if not wholly) from the oppressive insecurities of his personal life, from the troubling instability of his perspective as an American commenting on English scenes and manners, from the overwhelming burden of representing American letters in a country that had heaped scorn and abuse on his native culture, and from his debilitating doubts about both the immediate propriety and ultimate value of authorship. By re-creating his own experiences in the guise of his persona, he is at once emotionally involved in and yet psychologically detached from Crayon's activities, perceptions, and judgments. Geoffrey Crayon becomes responsible for everything, while behind the mask Washington Irving simultaneously participates and observes, determining the meaning and significance of the events of his recent life. Irving completely controls the dynamics of the author-persona relationship; thus, as the need arises, he is either disjunct from, overlapped with, or superimposed upon, Crayon. That is, while he shares Crayon's outlook and attitudes, intellectual and emotional qualities, longings and fears, he also recognizes that at certain moments Crayon's stance toward the world is excessively romantic or sentimental, indulgent or foolish, and in these instances he disengages himself from his persona. The sketches, therefore, enable Irving to define his *own* vision by measuring the extent of his identification with Crayon's. Laughter, mild ridicule, and (at times) amused self-recognition are some of the ways he widens the gap (or occasionally narrows it) between Crayon's fantasies and the facts as he comprehended them, between the illusions Geoffrey Crayon pursues and the reality Washington Irving experienced.

But, like the mask of drama, especially in its primitive, ritualized form, which "reveal[s] more than it hides," "affirm[s] more than it obscures,"[61] Irving's use of a persona does not cloud the truth of his inner life; on the contrary, it highlights aspects of the man that would otherwise have remained undisclosed. Rather than being removed from *The Sketch Book*, Irving becomes, paradoxically, more intriguing to his readers. Thackeray provides an excellent gloss on the nature of the persona in a letter to friends about the writing of *The Newcomes*: "Mr. Pendennis is the author of the book, and he has taken a great weight off my mind, for under that mask and acting, as it were, I can afford to say and think many things that I couldn't venture on in my own person."[62] So, too, for Irving: though he was not as forcefully satiric as Swift, Pope, or even Addison, he could point, in Crayon's diplomatic fashion, to failures and shortcomings in the English character ("English Writers on America," "John Bull") or to the slow decline of the hierarchic social order ("Little Britain," "The Country Church"). But far more important was the latitude Crayon provided Irving in terms of personal exploration: through his persona Irving confronted his romantic visions and youthful expectations of a Past filled with wonder, mystery, and hidden meaning and, also via Crayon, he reexperienced and silenced his great disappointment in discovering that his dreams of participation in a transcendent order had failed. Having felt the absence of a home, Irving has Crayon searching for one among the monuments, artifacts, and traditions of the Old World; when "home" proves unattainable, Irving absorbs the loss through Crayon's sentimentality.

Since Crayon becomes, therefore, the primary factor in Irving's elaborate ritual of self-examination, the sketches concentrate on the frustrations and (occasionally) joys he extracts from his journeys into the dark recesses of the city or the rarely traversed areas of the country. Thus, as he seeks inner fulfillment, Irving tested his responses to the exterior landscape. The real emotion, whether it be disappointment, suffering, or even satisfaction, lies underneath the words, filtered through the persona-Crayon, assimilated by the creator-Irving.[63] To reach that emotion—and to differentiate truly between mask and man—we need to read *The Sketch Book* more closely than has been done be-fore, even applying detailed stylistic and rhetorical analyses to seemingly simple sketches and tales.

Crayon's comic uncertainty accounts for his gullibility and thus for a good deal of *The Sketch Book*'s charm. Each time he ventures forth to uncover the mystery of community lurking somewhere in the heart of the city he encoun-ters another aspect of the mundane, which he then furiously tries to invest with transporting significance. When he finally must admit that his "re-searches" have yielded little in the way of meaningful discoveries, Irving can laugh along with the reader at Crayon's foolish preoccupations. The form of these London pieces approaches parody of gothic suspense, but personal dis-appointment and failure compose the subtext; yet because Crayon is the fool—the fall guy, so to speak—the sketches rarely, if ever, descend into pa-thos. (They also never reach anything like the emotional sublimity of Chap-lin, or the sublime absurdity of Kafka; Irving's range, though wider than has been acknowledged, was nevertheless circumscribed.) But Crayon is never dull or simple, and therefore the humor avoids sinking into the burlesque of Irving's earlier works. *The Sketch Book* marks a definite change in comic mode, as Irving amplifies his technique while purposely suspending critical judg-ment: though prompted by anxiety, the effects are disciplined and far more sophisticated than in his youthful productions. For example, in "London An-tiques" Crayon sets out in search of "reliques of a 'foregone world' locked up in the heart of the city." Passing through a "gothic gate way of mouldering antiquity" and stepping into a building beyond, he pauses to loiter about the great hall where he kindles his imagination by meditating upon the possible "ancient uses of this edifice." When a line of "grey headed old men, clad in long black cloaks" files past him, each one staring at him with a pale face while uttering not a word, he convinces himself that he is lost in a "realm of shad-ows, existing in the very centre of substantial realities." Hoping to discover the truly magical, the quintessentially romantic, Crayon enters the inner re-cesses of this "most venerable and mysterious pile." The old grey men in black mantles—to Crayon the "pervading genii of the place"—are everywhere, leading him to believe that he has stumbled into a medieval college of magical sciences, with black-cloaked old men as "professors of the black art."

Irving builds gothic suspense as Crayon attempts to lose himself in the shadowy grandeurs of his own speculations. In a chamber hung round with all kinds of weird and "uncouth objects," including "strange idols and stuffed alligators," "bottled serpents and monsters," Crayon encounters a small, shriveled old man. "His quaint physiognomy, his obsolete garb, and the hide-ous and sinister objects by which he [is] surrounded," persuade Crayon that he is the "Arch Mago" who rules over this "magical fraternity." However, the discovery punctures his expectations about the "antiquated pile" and its in-habitants, for he learns that the building is none other than the Charter House, a hospital providing provisions and shelter for workers in their dot-age. The black-cloaked magi are no more than "pensioners returning from morning service in the chapel"; the arch magician of curiosities is actually one John Hallum, a garrulous old man who has decorated the "final nestling place of his old age with reliques and rarities picked up in the course of his life." After all his peregrinations, suppositions, and reveries, Crayon winds up the dupe of his own desires for something divine hidden under the mundane, at once arcane and mystical, at the heart of old England.

Engaging John Hallum in conversation, Crayon discovers that the sus-pected conjurer is anything but a magical personage: a rather doughty old fellow, his pretensions to gentility are betrayed by his ignorance of Latin and Greek and his opinion that the ability to squander an enormous sum of money is an "indubitable sign of gentle blood." In addition, fancying himself a man of the world, Hallum, "according to his own account," had once been in France and very nearly made a trip to Holland. "He regretted not having visited the latter country," Crayon tells us, "'as then he might have said he had been there'" (p. 195). Crayon tinges his opinion of such a meager view of travel—"He was evidently a traveller of the simple kind"—with disdain, be-cause as far as "travellers" are concerned, he is proud of being one of the more complex sort. Being "there" in London or the English countryside, at a rural funeral or in the library of Westminster Abbey, is an experience molded by many variables, since Crayon amalgamates the scene of his activities with as-sociations from his vast literary heritage and his romantic projections in an attempt to envision a world that functions according to his quixotic illusions. Because Irving indulges in the fiction, the comedy he uses to separate himself from it preserves Crayon's integrity at the same time that it underlines the flaws and inconsistencies in his point of view. Humor may not resolve all the tensions in the sketch, but it does mitigate their power to frustrate Crayon while psychologically immobilizing Irving.

The conclusion to "London Antiques" illustrates how, in a variety of sketches, Irving as author participates in the emotional life of his persona only up to a certain point; by shifting the focus away from Crayon's fantasies back onto the "real world"—that is, the original setting in which he loitered until his imagination took flight—he signals the reader to be wary of too easily identifying Crayon with his creator. The sketch proper concludes with the revelation of Hallum's character, but Irving then changes modes and appends a note that elucidates the functions of the Charter House. Written in rather prosaic language, its factual nature starkly opposes Crayon's romantic and visionary effusions:

> It [the Charter House] was founded in 1611 on the remains of an ancient convent by Sir Thomas Sutton, being one of those noble charities set on foot by individual munificence, and kept up with the quaintness and sanctity of ancient times amidst the modern changes and innovations of London. Here eighty broken down men, who have seen better days, are provided, in their old age, with food, clothing, fuel and a yearly allowance for private expenses.

The voice of this paragraph (and the remainder of the note) is Irving's own, more sober one, indicating that while there is nothing terribly romantic or mysterious about the Charter House, it does possess, if viewed in its concreteness, the "sanctity of ancient times," a bit of the old style "amidst the modern changes and innovations of London." But such a structure would never satisfy Crayon, nor could he ever see it as Irving describes the building. Not only is the Charter House unpoetical, but without simultaneously imbuing it with a sense of the occult, without attributing to it a capacity to yield mythic lore, Crayon would lose the hope of fathoming the undisclosed significance of Old World institutions. (He had been previously self-deluded by the arcanum in such sketches as "The Boar's Head Tavern, East Cheap" and "Westminster Abbey.") The abrupt shift in tone from the sketch to the note confirms that Crayon has committed himself to an imaginative endeavor the thrust of which Irving approved, though he also recognized its futility. Thus, by comically undercutting his persona, Irving achieved a necessary perspective on the rather less than glamorous reality surrounding him. And even more important to the success of his psychological pilgrimage, he deflected attention away from the covertly expressed anxiety lying below the smooth surface of so many of his sketches.

While at the literal level Geoffrey Crayon was telling stories with the genial tone and romantic tenor for which *The Sketch Book* became celebrated, in the subtext Washington Irving was overcoming the traumas of his life through artistic creation. "Survey[ing] the landscape through the prism of poetry"

(p. 223), Crayon wove a fabric of illusion around all of his experience, glorifying "commonplace realities of the present" into "shadowy grandeurs of the past" (p. 9).[64] Written in the aura of Walter Scott, when the cult of the Middle Ages predominated and the spirit of romanticism was beginning to overwhelm England as well as America, *The Sketch Book* convinced its audience that Crayon's sentiments and sensations were the bedrock emotions of Irving's book. In addition (as we return to where this chapter began), Irving's "musical, rhythmical style," which according to Van Wyck Brooks bespoke "his cheerful good nature and transparent good taste," also beguiled readers into believing that persona and author were one.[65] The narrative strategy returned many dividends, since Irving earned commercial and critical success while setting right the balance after an emotional as well as financial bankruptcy. How much of the personal anxiety present in *The Sketch Book* he actually acknowledged is difficult to say, but, to shift images, he did shake himself loose from immobilizing despair and gained, through Crayon, the emotional leverage that permitted just the release necessary for the sustained flow of creative energy. Thus, while he had not quite expected such results, the development of a persona led him to synthesize and arrange what was left of a shattered past. Though in future productions he failed to maintain a consistent personification,[66] it was absolutely crucial that it be achieved here, in the first of his European works, since it gave him the confidence and impetus to proceed with his career. Moreover, besides the individual order achieved through the Crayon persona, *The Sketch Book* also expressed and diffused national anxiety.

A Crisis of Identity: *The Sketch Book*

It is one of the commonplaces of our literary history that Washington Irving's *Sketch Book* put America firmly and finally on the cultural map by pleasing the British reviewers. For the English, rigid in their aesthetic demands and expectations, Irving fulfilled the requirements for literary approval, namely, he wrote a formal, smooth, dignified prose. His style, though richly adorned, remained unconvoluted. In fact, writes William Hedges, "his very sound has affinities with the language of Addison and Goldsmith."[1] Moreover, his outwardly romantic idealization of the realm of everyday experience—the life, manners, and customs of ordinary people—coincided with a tendency still alive in English literature and satisfied popular and revered canons of taste. But as Francis Jeffrey noted, even before Irving's sketches had charmed the British they had been "extensively circulated, and very much admired" among his own countrymen, so much so that two of our literary historians have claimed a place for *The Sketch Book* on the all-time American "best seller" list.[2]

Unlike the British reaction, the nature of the American response is much more elusive and complex, encompassing several levels of cultural meaning. The most commonly proferred explanation is that to Americans, not yet liberated from a dependency on the established English forms in writing, and consequently suffering from a deep sense of literary inferiority, Irving was, at last, an American who could write like a gentleman. The emphasis here is on a genteel audience's need for sweetness of sentiment clothed in the stately and refined apparel of a fashionable prose style. Given this conception of the American reading public, Irving's biographer insists that "to understand Irving's hold upon his generation is to understand a dominating tendency of American literature prior to the Civil War, which, beginning only two years after Irving's death, helped to destroy the cult of elegance and made comprehensible the voices of a Whitman or a Clemens."[3] The problem with this judgment is not that it is wrong, but rather that it is superficial; it neither explains America's passionate regard for Irving's famous miscellany of sketches, stories, and essays, nor accounts for its continued and sustaining interest in his subsequent productions.

To a certain extent, Irving's contemporary reputation does reveal "the literary principles of the age for which he wrote," but if this were all, we long ago would have exhausted his usefulness for American cultural studies. Of course, just the opposite is true, which is why the other commonly held view, summed up in James D. Hart's statement that "the dreamily poetic mood, quiet antiquarian interest, and picturesque legendry appealed to a public accustomed to Scott and searching for an interpreter of its own past," also minimizes the issue.[4] America indeed may have been desperate for such an "interpreter," but the qualities of Irving's writing outlined here—which again amount to little more than "the patina of romanticism cherished by the public"—hardly could be put to the service of such a noble enterprise. If this is what Irving meant to his generation—and in turn ours—he would have been indistinguishable from the countless American writers like Nathaniel Parker Willis and Donald G. Mitchell who, though extremely popular in their own time, were little more than pale imitations of their English predecessors, and like them he long since would have faded from memory. Irving's famous book touched his American readers on a deep, subconscious level because the nation was in crisis, and because Irving himself was an acute register of the anxieties of his age.

I

It was Irving in the guise of Geoffrey Crayon, then, rambling through the English countryside and exploring the nooks and crannies of London in quest of some element of sensibility not to be found in the New World, who appealed so enormously to his countrymen. But what did he seek, and why in England? The usual assessment is that along with so many other Americans in the early years of the nineteenth century, Irving expressed a passionate feeling for European antiquity. The justification for this view derives from his own oft-quoted words in "The Author's Account of Himself" in *The Sketch Book*, where he declared that while America was "full of youthful promise," "Europe held forth the charms of storied and poetical association." For the "sublime and beautiful of natural scenery" no country could surpass America, but in Europe "were to be seen the masterpieces of art, the refinements of highly cultivated society, the quaint peculiarities of ancient and local custom." "Rich in the accumulated treasures of age," the Old World was history and chronicle come to life. The pleasure it offered could not be re-created in America—an opportunity "to lose [one]self among the shadowy grandeurs of the past."[5] But even though this answer substantiates a definite attraction to the older, richer civilization, it does not solve the potential disruption inherent in the fact that Irving and his fellow Americans were, in Cushing Strout's words, so "deeply responsive to the authority and appeal of an officially alien culture."[6]

Strout himself offers two possible ways of accounting for the affinity of the American mind for the images and products of European society, both of which accommodate cultural differences and therefore preserve native loyalties. On one level, American interest in Europe was stimulated by the Romantic movement, with its emphasis on medieval artifacts, folklore, and ancient customs. What greater source of "romance" could Americans find than the European landscape, dotted with castles and fortresses, ivied halls and towers, quaint and picturesque villages, as well as the ruins on which poets and painters loved to meditate? As Strout points out, "on these terms the contrast between the Old World and the New could be accented without tension." As long as the past was remote and its "opposition" to the present perceived as aesthetic and stylistic rather than philosophical and political, it offered no impending threat. In this way, "the New World remained unquestioned as the land of the free, the home of virtue, and the hope of the future," he writes, "but its undecorated simplicity and bustling practicality stifled conventional romantic impulses." For Strout, England became useful to the American symbolizing imagination precisely because it maintained its "antithetical charm." Irving, in this view, makes no political or social use of the antithesis, but harmlessly restates it through the filter of romantic imagery.[7]

The theory that American longing for a European "Past" was promulgated on "romantic impulse" has the virtue of completely diffusing the "alien cultures" issue. Strout's second explanation, however, while it follows in the same general direction, nevertheless hints at an aspect of American cultural uneasiness denied by his first premise. According to this latter paradigm of New World experience, through a "compensating irony" the Old World, especially as it was envisioned by American romantic traveler-writers such as Irving and Longfellow, became attractive because of the extraordinary American push to shape a democratic future. The immigrants who labored to build this new nation felt and acted upon, for reasons which they little understood, a need to turn backward and imaginatively embrace the life they had left behind. Since the images of this European world were viewed through the prism of romanticism and, says Strout, "drained of nearly all contemporary social significance,"[8] they "did not challenge native pieties, but complemented them." Escaping from the pressures and demands and drudgeries of their own New World existence, Americans immersed themselves in an idealized Old World, "vicariously enjoy[ing] the forbidden fruits of the past." It would have been intellectually and politically treasonous, of course, to project such a feudal order onto the American landscape, violating the commitment to a "republican destiny." But Europe as an incarnation of the past was a permissible vision which soothed American tensions and "appease[d]" a hunger for "values alien to the national mythology" without corrupting or invalidating it.[9]

What Strout's second argument anticipates but leaves undeveloped is that the intensity of Americans' participation in the imaginative exploration of the Old World manifested a deep anxiety about their own culture, an anxiety for which a rational explanation of this attraction/participation—Europe as an object of Romantic aspiration—cannot account. In fact, this issue of national anxiety, and the level of psychic experience suggested by it, actually informs *The Sketch Book* and is largely responsible for its subconscious appeal to an American audience. By "psychic experience" I am referring to what some scholars have called an American identity crisis, and to what Fred Somkin labels "the American essay at self-definition," a period in our history of great turbulence, spanning—and extending beyond—the years of Irving's European sojourn.[10] Since this "crisis" (which has been preliminarily sketched in the Introduction) bears directly upon an appreciation of the depth and meaning of the American response to Irving's famous book, it is necessary to delineate its parameters further and to suggest the extent to which it permeated American life in the first half of the nineteenth century.

During this time some old questions took on a new immediacy: "What is America?" and "Who are the Americans?" had been asked before, but not with the same intensity, and not with quite the same compulsion for a satisfying answer. Americans were suddenly becoming unrecognizable to themselves; the extraordinary economic growth and territorial expansion of the twenties, which most approved of, brought with it the open pursuit of such previously un-"American" goals as power, prestige, and pleasure, without even the pretense of being linked to moral ends. Many Americans began to fear that the forces of artificiality, which they associated with European aristocracy, were corrupting republican simplicity, and they repeatedly expressed this anxiety in the form of a warning that an unparalleled prosperity would "rob the American experiment of its exemplary and missionary character" while at the same time severing Americans from their connection to a "virtuous past";[11] this development was not only dangerous, but fatal, since the destiny of the nation depended on its maintaining high standards of virtue. As Montesquieu had said and many others echoed, "the principle of democracy is virtue."[12] Failure to achieve it was both a denigration of the Fathers' principles and an act of self-violation: "Republicanism [Gordon Wood has written] meant more for Americans than simply the elimination of a king and the institution of an elective system. It added a moral dimension, a utopian depth, to the political separation from England—a depth that involved the very character of their society."[13] The sense of responsibility burdening this generation was, therefore, especially great; if, as George Santayana had suggested, "to be an American is of itself almost a moral condition, an education, and a career," then nothing less than the definition of America and the identity of its people were at stake.[14]

The signs of prosperity—primarily, the continual westward movement of the frontier, rapid industrialization and the rise of urban centers, the development of more sophisticated means of transportation and communication, and an ever-expanding population—were in fact taken by some to be an indication that America was indeed still virtuous, for virtue, in the old Puritan scheme of things, undoubtedly manifested itself in prosperity. Along with Benjamin Franklin, who had expressed the idea in 1782 while discussing religious toleration, these Americans believed that God "manifested his Approbation . . . by the remarkable Prosperity with which He has been pleased to favour the whole Country." They shared, as well, Thomas Jefferson's faith, embraced toward the end of his life, that moral and material progress were not antithetical.[15] But the majority thought that the benefits accompanying material gain—greater social fluidity, a period of uninterrupted peace, expanded educational opportunities, to name but the most important—were offset by the shift toward recognizably non-"virtuous" behavior, especially the hunger for wealth and the desire to avoid strenuous labor. American success, it was believed, had transgressed all moral boundaries: within a relatively short period of time it had reshaped a nation of essentially decent, religious-minded, democratic individualists into an unrestrained mob of self-centered (and ultimately, self-consuming) materialists. In spite of the attempt by manufacturers to equate the profit incentive with a moral pursuit, Americans remained skeptical about the efficacy of such "progress." "In those great republics, which have fallen of themselves," Emma Willard told the New York State legislature in 1819, "the loss of republican manners and virtues has been the invariable precursor of their loss of the republican form of government. . . . [and it] may be said, that the depravation [sic] of morals and manners, can be traced to the introduction of wealth, as its cause."[16] "Increasing wealth rolls the tide of fashionable vice over the land," Elihu W. Baldwin declared in a Thanksgiving sermon in 1827 on considerations for the American patriot. "Who that reflects, but must tremble for the consequences?"[17] Lyman Beecher, whose voice was continually raised against the evils of a prosperity which, he worried, would invade even the most revered and protected areas of American life, and thus actively cause "national corruption and ruin," preached in 1829 that

> All which is done to stimulate agriculture, commerce, and the arts, is, therefore, without some self-preserving moral power, but providing fuel for the fire which is destined to consume us. The greater our prosperity the shorter its duration, and the more tremendous our downfall, unless the moral power of the Gospel shall be exerted to arrest those causes which have destroyed other nations.[18]

For Beecher, the great ill was unbridled passion leading to anarchy; the cure was the "blessed influence" of the Gospel. Nevertheless, he expressed the deep concern of the American people that the moral center of the new Republic had failed to hold.

Although he did not register his responses directly in *The Sketch Book*, Irving shared the foreboding that accompanied American prosperity. In an 1818 notebook, after copying several passages in French from Montesquieu's *De l'esprit des lois*, he translated, as if to underscore its prophetic warning, the final sentence from book 7, chapter 4 of that work: "Republics end by luxury[,] Monarchies by poverty."[19] Indeed, while he toured Europe in the 1820s, this perplexing issue was very much on his mind. He filled one of his journals with passages from, among others, Plato, Cicero, Milton, and Burke, containing discussions of virtue; these contrast sharply with notations on "the more sordid passion of Gain" and the weakness that besets a society when "luxury [is] introduced."[20] The conflict played out in these notes is between riches, selfishness, and profit on the one hand and virtue, happiness, and freedom on the other. His further ruminations on this disturbing topic— "Nothing so ominous as a time of *unexampled prosperity*"; "Speculation is the romance of trade—it turns it all into poetry"[21]—became the core of an essay he eventually published in the *Knickerbocker Magazine* in 1840. In Irving's view a "time of unexampled prosperity" signals danger, since it tempts "designing men" to build an air castle known as "'the credit system'" based upon promissory notes, which are nothing more than mere words. These "promissory notes, interchanged between scheming individuals, are liberally discounted at the banks, which become so many mints to coin words into cash; and as the supply of words is inexhaustible, it may readily be supposed what a vast amount of promissory capital is soon in circulation." The result is that "speculation rises on speculation" just the way "bubble rises on bubble." The "stock-jobber" turns into a "magician"; the merchant becomes a "commercial Quixotte" [sic]. "Sober realities" are lost amidst schemes for wealth. But let one doubt arise and the entire delusory edifice collapses, bringing the "'season of unexampled prosperity'" to an abrupt end: "The coinage of words is suddenly curtailed; the promissory capital begins to vanish into smoke; a panic succeeds, and the whole superstructure, built upon credit, and reared by speculation, crumbles to the ground, leaving scarce a wreck behind."[22] Irving envisions nothing less than the American commercial world falling in upon itself, a house in ruins.

Protest and recoil came from other cultural spokesmen as well: in the succeeding years such eminent literary New Englanders as Emerson and Thoreau would deplore the materialism that was fast becoming an American secular religion. *Walden*, of course, stands as a repudiation of the American way of wealth, but Emerson, too, expressed both his distaste for an economic system built upon false principles and, more forcefully, his scorn for a money-mad people bereft of genuine values (though it is true that his most virulent responses were confined to his private journals). America, he feared, had grown into a nation without character, desperately in need of judicious—and just— leadership. "In a former age," he wrote in 1834, "the men of might were men of will[,] now [they are] the men of wealth."[23] That era, not so far distant from his own, was a time when men could be admired for what they thought and believed. But that age was gone. "O what a wailing tragedy is this world considered in reference to money-matters," he declared in his journal, and then, addressing himself in the second person (perhaps as a distancing technique), he revealed his despair over the spiritual state of his country, where the voice of truth had gone unheeded: "[You are] rather melancholy after asking the opinion of all living to find no more receivers of your doctrine than your own three or four & [you] sit down to wait until it shall please God to create some more men before your school can expect increase."[24]

Emerson did not despise all businessmen or reject legitimate business as a profession.[25] Rather, like Irving, it was unsound and unchecked speculation—the mindless pursuit of wealth—which repelled him, and he expressed his disgust in similar imagery: "The most powerful men in our community have no theory of business that can stand scrutiny but only bubble built on bubble without end. They skate so fast over a film of ice that it does not break under them. It seems[,] when you see their dexterity in particulars[,] as if you could not overestimate the resources of good sense & when you find how utterly void they are of all remote aims, as if you could not underestimate their philosophy."[26] He was discouraged to see the majority of the middle class—a "puny & fickle folk"—following suit, heralding a "progress" whose dangerous consequences they little understood. For Emerson, such voraciousness had transformed America into "the country of small adventures, of short plans, of daring risks, not of patience, not of great combinations, not of long, persistent, close woven schemes, demanding the utmost fortitude, temper, faith, & poverty."[27] Cut off from a nurturing connection to the "virtuous" past, and as a consequence deprived of an overarching, comprehensive vision of its destiny, commercial America was destroying the Republic, in the process transforming it into its very antithesis: "This invasion of Nature by Trade with its Money, its Credit, its Steam, its Railroad, threatens to upset the balance of man, & establish a new Universal Monarchy more tyrannical than Babylon or Rome."[28] "Bankrupt of principles & hope," the New World citizen was not what he should have been: "He is the treadle of a wheel. He is a tassel at the apron string of Society. He is a money chest."[29]

The passion for wealth had destroyed the eagerness for great deeds that distinguished the Founders. "Prosperity," wrote James Russell Lowell, "is the forcing-house of mediocrity; . . . our position as a people has been such as to turn our energy, capacity, and accomplishment into prosaic channels."[30] Worse, said *Putnam's Monthly*, it produced "men of small ambitions and cold hearts." By 1855, the magazine was linking prosperity to a dangerous moral corruption which had led, in general, to a disrespect for law, principle, and human suffering, and, in particular, to the repeal of the Missouri Compromise and the threatened spread of slavery to the Western territories. This was, in part, the fault of the country's political parties having lost "the stringency and sternness of conviction, the nobleness and purity of purpose, in which they began." In its earliest stages of development, America had produced magnificent statesmen; now, in its "opulence," it mustered only "second-rate" administrators. But final blame rested with the people for allowing the civil life of the nation to become utterly demoralized, for permitting the spirit of American society to degenerate: "A gross materialism, the success of trade, the progress of gain, an external expediency, is preferred to lofty ideal aspirations and spiritual truth." A jeremiad comparable to the Puritan originals, "The Kansas Question" charted the loss of America's integrity while chastising its citizens for having abandoned "the foundation-principle" upon which national greatness relied:

> We speculate how to get rich; we build railroads and ships, to increase our stores; we spy out the neighboring lands which promise us luxurious harvests hereafter; . . . but the heroic values, the chivalric sentiments . . . we lay aside[;] . . . the fair dreams of our youth we despise. The dream that this young land . . ., unpolluted by the stains of time, should be the home of freedom and a race of men so manly that they would lift the earth by the whole breadth of its orbit nearer heaven . . .—and supplanting the despotism under which mankind had withered, by a rich, and noble, and free republican civilization, has passed away from the most of us as nothing but a dream. We yield ourselves, instead, to calculation, money-making, and moral indifference. The prophet of the Lord might again cry in our streets, "How is the gold become dim, how is the most fine gold changed!"[31]

It was in this extended age of anxiety, an era of incomprehensible and unprecedented change, that the story of "Rip Van Winkle" captured the American imagination. Though Irving's readers could appreciate the mystery of Rip's encounter with the odd-looking Dutch sailors, Hendrik Hudson and his crew of the *Half-Moon,* and his subsequent twenty-year sleep, their most heartfelt response, if we can take as one indication the several artistic renderings of the scene, occurred when Rip, "with a heart full of trouble and anxiety," made his way down from the mountains to his home, only to find that both the village and its inhabitants had undergone a metamorphosis. Political events had transformed the soothing world of "drowsy tranquility" into a "bustling" and "disputatious" one; a burgeoning (and crass) commercialism had displaced the mild agrarianism of former years. "Larger and more populous," the expanding village is a reflection of an advancing America. Rip views it with horror: "There were rows of houses which he had never seen before, and those which had been his familiar haunts had disappeared. Strange names were over the doors—strange faces at the windows—every thing was strange" (pp. 36, 37). A generation of beleaguered, confused Americans recognized its

"The Return of Rip Van Winkle," by John Quidor. (National Gallery of Art, Washington, D.C.; Mellon Collection.)

own plight in Rip's, and despite the fact that Irving's hero awakened in 1789, his longing for pastoral innocence, for a regression to the security of nature and an unrecapturable past, mirrored the desires of an 1820s sensibility. Moreover, this "lost" generation of Americans symbolically could trace the source of its spiritual anxiety to the birth of the nation—a "moment of cultural upheaval and psychic dislocation"[32]—represented in the story by the two significant events of that very year 1789: the ratification of the Constitution and the election of the president. In fact, Rip happens upon "*the first* election day in the new state."[33] Anyone who has viewed John Quidor's portrayal of Rip Van Winkle's return, with its haunting evocation of Rip's distress in the face of a disorienting present, will have some idea of the cultural and psychological milieu of *The Sketch Book*'s first American audience. Frozen on Quidor's canvas in a shock of nonrecognition, dread and confusion over his own identity etched into his features, Rip reflects the nation's anxiety. His words also spoke movingly to and for the populace in Irving's text: "'Every thing's changed—and I'm changed—and I can't tell what's my name, or who I am!'" (pp. 38–39).

Earlier in the story, after Rip has escaped the "clamour" of Dame Van Winkle, who represents the shrill and incessant demands of the present, by climbing "to one of the highest parts of the Kaatskill mountains," he comes to rest on a lush green mound that "crowned the brow of a precipice." At that solitary and transcendent point, and before he descends the mountain—a descent that, as we know, is about to be postponed for many years—he pauses for a visionary moment to gaze upon the panoramic scene below him. To the east he sees the known world, peaceful, serene, and light, represented by rich wooded countryside and the "lordly" Hudson moving on its "silent but majestic course," reflecting purple clouds and sailing ships on its "glassy bosom." To the west he perceives the unknown wilderness, hostile, frightening, and dark, characterized by "a deep mountain glen, wild, lonely and shagged, the bottom filled with fragments from the impending cliffs and scarcely lighted by the reflected rays of the setting sun" (p. 33). In one direction, then, lies the past, plotted, cultivated, and safe; in the other awaits the future, uncharted, coarse, and terrifying. Rip is not alone on that precipice between two worlds; alongside him stands his creator and behind him his country. When Irving wrote "Rip Van Winkle" in June 1818, youth and several failed careers were past; middle age and the precipitous road of professional authorship lay ahead. America, too, was moving forward, yet aching to retreat to some golden moment of uncorrupted innocence: in the time of the story, the colonies are verging on nationhood; in Irving's day, the (relatively) unified society is about to yield to the multiplicity of the industrial era. Like Rip, for whom twenty years is but twenty-four hours, the country seemingly had shifted overnight from a communal organization based on mutual dependence to a fragmented body of opposing self-interests. How apt that the stranger's voice that calls out Rip Van Winkle's name and fills him with "vague apprehension" comes not from the idyllic woodland to the east, but from the threatening glen to the west. Though Rip looks "anxiously" in that direction, he is given a twenty-year reprieve before meeting the future. But for Irving and his countrymen the suspension of time was a fiction in which they could only participate vicariously.

"For some time," Irving wrote, "Rip lay musing on this scene" in the Catskills. Afternoon shades into evening, the mountains cast deep blue shadows across the valleys, and Rip, who knows that when he arrives home long after dark he will encounter "the terrors of Dame Van Winkle," sighs heavily. It is not surprising, therefore, that the voice Rip hears staying his downward course has been interpreted as his own,[34] an unconscious signal to himself that of the definite options available to him at that moment—down to the present, west to the future, or motionless to suspension (the past being only an imaginative possibility)—the least painful choice is to do nothing at all. Thus, the long hiatus in the action fulfills Rip's wish for avoidance, but the present he meets on his delayed arrival in the village is the future he escaped twenty years before. Time can be fabulously halted, not obliterated. Rip may be free of petticoat "tyranny," but in the new United States he is a nonentity. To a bewildered Van Winkle, the American election-day rituals are "babylonish jargon"; worse, since his entire orientation and allegiance are to what is by now the "distant" past, he is taken for a traitor. When asked "'on which side he voted?'" and "'whether he was Federal or Democrat?'" he responds with stupid silence. When confronted by a member of the community demanding to know "'what brought him to the election with a gun on his shoulder and a mob at his heels, and whether he meant to breed a riot in the village?'" Rip replies with dismay that he is "'a loyal subject of the King—God bless him!'" Thereupon he is threatened by the mob who cry for his head with shouts of "'A tory! a tory! a spy! a Refugee! hustle him! away with him!'" Given such a rude welcome, Rip naturally might have about-faced and marched back into the mountains; realistically, of course, the only choice is to accommodate himself to the inevitable. Thus, Irving ends his tale comically with the vision of Rip settled as "one of the patriarchs of the village and a chronicle of the old times 'before the war.'" This was psychologically satisfying, since now he can continuously relive the past through his story. Such a smoothed transition from one era to another could be appreciated by Irving's readers as fantasy, perhaps their own form of escape from the harsh uncertainties of the unpromising future.

Indeed, despite all the surface optimism of their society, Americans were quite tentative about that future, and the extent of their feeling may be gauged from contemporary responses to some startling events which occurred in the second decade of the nineteenth century. Undoubtedly a legacy from their Puritan ancestors, their penchant of looking for signs and symbols to prove, or in more optimistic moments to disprove, their fears and anxieties about their own spiritual condition or the state of the nation led them, in 1811, to interpret the appearance of the steamboat *New Orleans* on the Mississippi River at the same time that a fiery comet was sighted in the sky and a great earthquake shook the entire valley as having apocalyptic meaning. Later that same year the leveling of the Richmond Theater by fire, killing more than sixty patrons, substantiated this conviction. The burning of Washington by British troops in 1814 was also perceived by some in a cosmic framework: the destruction of the nation's capital indicated God's displeasure with Americans for claiming to have built the "temple of freedom" while enslaving several hundred thousand blacks. Divine wrath, in fact, extended in all directions; the explosion of the steamboat *Washington* in 1816, for example, even though it was man-made and not, like an earthquake, an act of God, was nevertheless taken as a symbol of His anger and, in addition, as a portent of future disasters. Moreover, because the vessel was named the *Washington*, this catastrophe was linked to the national destiny. In 1819, the year *The Sketch Book* was first published, economic panic, causing severe financial distress and loss of property, and the Missouri question, which threatened both the Union (literally) and the nation's "reforming sense of mission" (symbolically), and led to the troubled "compromise" of 1820, were additional sources of apprehension for the Republic.[35]

In an 1817 notebook, Washington Irving brooded over some of these strange happenings, trying to assess their significance in a cultural context. As he jotted notes for a story never completed, he saw a connection between recent calamities and "the diseased state of the public mind": "Various circumstances had occasioned to give a melancholy tone to the public mind & to excite the public imagination—This Dreadful conflagration of the Theatre of Richmond which had wrapped beauty & talents in flames—Tornado which had swept the southern coasts & desolated the country &c[—]The continual succession of earthquakes—all had produced a feverish excitement & filld the imagination with dreams of horror & apprehensions of sinister & dreadful events." Irving knew that his countrymen would view such disasters as God's judgment on a wayward people; thus, a sense of doom prevails as he ends the brief meditation with one of his characters "run[ning] frantically about the street foaming at the mouth—& crying Woe Woe Woe—the destruction of Columbia is at hand &c—prepare for the presence of the Lord."[36] Although generally not given to prophetic utterances, Irving here echoes the jeremiad rhetoric of the day.

It is hardly surprising, therefore, that Americans seized upon what is surely the most extraordinary coincidence in their history, the deaths of Thomas Jefferson and John Adams on July 4, 1826, as events of special revelatory meaning. Was this dual loss a warning that the "spirit of the republic" had vanished utterly, or was God once again reassuring Americans that they were a chosen people?[37] John Quincy Adams, for one, believed the occurrence was providential, commenting in his diary on the meaning of his father's death that "the time, the manner, the coincidence with the decease of Jefferson, are visible and palpable marks of Divine favor, for which I would humble myself in grateful and silent adoration before the Ruler of the Universe."[38] Most of the eulogies delivered in honor of America's "political parents" echoed the younger Adams's sentiments, manifesting a faith that such an extraordinary "spectacle" on the fiftieth anniversary of independence was, as Daniel Webster said in Boston, "a special dispensation" from God: "who is not willing to recognize in their happy termination, as well as in their long continuance, proofs that our country and its benefactors are objects of His care?"[39] One eulogist, however, took the occasion to caution Americans that the political factionalism of the present times was antithetical to true republican principles. Speaking in Washington on October 19, 1826, William Wirt told his audience that the correspondence between Adams and Jefferson in their "declining years . . . reads a lesson of wisdom on the bitterness of party spirit, by which the wise and the good will not fail to profit."[40] The arguments thus moved in both directions, but in either case were motivated by the anxiety that something fundamental to American identity had passed away.

Another opportunity for self-assessment, which quickly turned into a self-conscious attempt to undo the present by reestablishing the basic values of the society, occurred before the end of the decade when the United States Congress invited the elderly Lafayette to visit America. Their hope was that after seeing the country for whose freedom he had fought he would bestow his approval on the course it had taken. A representative of the heroic age, Lafayette symbolized the best of the national past as one of the Fathers of the Republic, so much so, in fact, that he was identified in the public mind with— indeed, he was virtually a "surrogate" for—Washington.[41] He "brings . . . our revolution nearer to us," George Ticknor wrote, "with all the highminded patriotism and selfdenying virtues of our forefathers."[42] Thus, to literally millions of Americans, his return in 1824–25 was a sign that such virtue could be reclaimed, that liberty had not perished. His gentle affirmations were taken to mean that the Republic was thriving; his fatherly presence, in other words, reassured the anxious sons. The countless receptions on his behalf provided them with the opportunity to praise what in their view was Lafayette's most esteemed quality—"disinterested benevolence"—and therefore to recommit themselves, in the most strained and exalted rhetoric, to fundamental republican ideals. Or, as George Ticknor said in retrospect, because Lafayette was "so free from all alloy of doubt and human imperfection," he permitted Americans, "in recognising his merit, to reassert the principles to which his life had been consecrated."[43] The need for continuity with the uncompromised moral passion of the Fathers was so great that, interestingly enough, few noticed that the champion of democratic freedom was being welcomed throughout the United States with an aristocratic and ceremonial formality that Washington himself would have disdained. One who did, however, was the newspaper editor Hezekiah Niles, who warned his readers that they must not behave toward Lafayette as vassals to a lord: "Let the trumpet to the cannon speak, the cannon to the heavens, and the ardent prayers of free millions ascend to the throne of the OMNIPOTENT, that blessings may be heaped upon him; but, in all this, let us remember that we are *men* like unto himself, and *republicans*."[44] Ironically, they *were* acting as republicans, and their extreme response, which manifested the hope that "elaborated form might induce that sense of the living past which was fast slipping away," was but another sign of a generation's anxiety.[45]

Consciously apprehensive of radical changes and yet dissatisfied with their vague self-image, and unconsciously fearful that the definition of their democratic society as egalitarian and virtuous had eroded, this generation of Americans responded to Europe in a symbolically complex way. On one level, through the poetization of the Old World, with its quaint and archaic customs, values, and traditions, Americans attempted to reemphasize the essential differences between the two worlds, but in such a way that the highly sophisticated and developed European culture was neither hostile nor threatening to their sense of themselves. By looking back at their European origins, and at the Revolution, they sought to determine who they once were, and reassure themselves about who they had become and, moreover, what they could become. At the same time, however, in a deeper, far more psychically charged way, the European "Past" and, ironically, those alien aristocratic values inherent in it that had survived for centuries, became to the besieged Americans an image of balance and stability.

No longer, therefore, was the Old World the menacing presence that it had been for the Fathers. Writing from England in 1775, Benjamin Franklin, for example, had repudiated the vices of European civilization: "when I consider the extream Corruption prevalent among all Orders of Men in this old rotten State, and the glorious publick Virtue so predominant in our rising Country, I cannot but apprehend more Mischief than Benefit from a closer Union. I fear They will drag us after them in all the plundering Wars their desperate

Circumstances, Injustice, and Rapacity, may prompt them to undertake." Jefferson, too, had warned of an uncomfortably close association to "the ancient world"; his first inaugural address was only one of several occasions where he expressed a sense of gratitude that America, "a chosen country," was "kindly separated by nature and a wide ocean from the exterminating havoc of one quarter of the globe."[46] For the Founders, there was little to be learned from Europe; morally and politically, its civilization was anathema.

But less than fifty years later it was an entirely different story. Europe—and especially England—now offered a vision of order, not "havoc," since it represented the fact that a way of life had endured, that a society and its beliefs could remain intact through all the destruction wrought by time. As long as Americans did not actively relocate their allegiance from a democratic to an aristocratic system—in other words, as long as they understood that, however attractive the durable and solid European institutions were, they necessarily had to remain beyond cultural reach—then the American image of the Old World could serve a psychologically healing function. At this historical juncture, Irving's use of England and his rendering of the past in *The Sketch Book* offered his countrymen precisely what they needed. Thus, paradoxically, America's gravitation toward its ancestral home encouraged, rather than denied, the hope that the growth and progress stimulated by industrialization would not efface the new society created by its ancestors. The "Past," therefore, was of far greater importance to Americans as a context for self-scrutiny than as a source of romantic images, since what was ultimately at stake was the preservation of virtue rather than the satisfaction of genteel expectations.

II

How many of these psychological undercurrents of political thought Irving understood well enough to articulate is not clear, but surely something of the Americans' fear of the loss of stability and the collapse of the moral underpinnings of their society is behind Geoffrey Crayon's imaginative formulation of England in *The Sketch Book*. Even when he is most blatantly nationalistic, when, for example, in "English Writers on America" he proclaims that "all the writers of England united . . . could not conceal our rapidly growing importance and matchless prosperity," Crayon still exudes those "hallowed feeling[s] of tenderness and veneration" with which Americans look to "the land of [their] forefathers" (pp. 45, 47). Although the essay's ostensible aim is to defend America against its British detractors by emphasizing the significance of its democratic principles and its unprecedented and "singular state of moral and physical development," Crayon winds up cautioning his countrymen that as a young nation, and therefore in some ways an unsure one, they should view England as a cultural model. Boasting of America's "sound moral and religious principles" and lauding "one of the greatest political experiments in the history of the world" now being performed there, he still concludes that England is worth studying: by drawing on its "wisdom," garnered from "ages of experience," Americans may "strengthen" and "embellish" their "national character" (pp. 45, 44, 49). While Crayon may crow about "political liberty" and "the general diffusion of knowledge" in America, his tone changes to one of quiet reverence when he remarks that

> it is in the moral feeling of the people that the deep foundations of British prosperity are laid; and however the superstructure may be time worn, or over run by abuses, there must be something solid in the basis, admirable in the materials, and stable in the structure of an edifice that so long has towered unshaken amidst the tempests of the world. (p. 49)

The voice is that of a younger generation's praise for parental fortitude and endurance; set against such admiration, Crayon's patriotic maxims sound hollow and strained. Indeed, the analogy to architecture transcends even his tone in its glorification of the "idea of England": England is a fortress that has withstood the onslaught of the ages. As a man who has spent his youth and early maturity in a nation not yet fifty years old and, moreover, devoid of a meaningfully articulated history, Crayon has hit upon the primary value of the mother country for the New World imagination.

In *The Sketch Book*, the most striking visual image of this value, of the cohesiveness and durability of English society, is John Bull's "family mansion"—for Crayon, a true domestic establishment. Here, in the sketch which bears the name of the popular allegorization of England, Irving fashions the edifice figure into a metaphor for the very qualities Americans had yet to establish in their own society: stability, continuity, and order. It is, writes Crayon, an "old castellated manor house" that "has been built upon no regular plan," yet is nevertheless of such harmonious constitution that each part is essential to the cohesiveness of the whole. Though Crayon goes on to depict the various ways England has overextended itself, especially because of its "great disposition to protect and patronize," and twice alludes to the severe financial troubles the country suffered at the end of the Napoleonic Wars—the national deficit had grown to a staggering seven hundred million pounds, and Bank of England notes were not redeemable in gold (p. 255)—he makes it clear that John Bull's house is only temporarily in disrepair. Repeating the image from "English Writers on America" of an edifice "unshaken amidst the tempests of the world," Crayon emphasizes that since it "has stood for several hundred years," it is, despite the plight at present, "not likely to tumble down now." Its "centre" is "as solid as ponderous stone and old English oak can make it" (pp. 252, 251). Although he was a thoroughly New World man, Irving nevertheless wanted John Bull's mansion to remain intact; he had no desire to see it meddled with by agitating "levellers" devoted to democratic progress. This was not, as critics have claimed, a case of divided loyalties; rather, on the level where individual psychic pattern and cultural archetype merge, Irving perceived the powerful symbolic import for America of the indestructibility of English society.

"John Bull" emerges as a pivotal sketch in Crayon's collection because it helps define the word that he inevitably reaches for when characterizing the English: "moral." Crayon genuinely appreciates the way in which each succeeding generation respects the accomplishments of its predecessors and seeks to build upon them as it goes about the business of shaping society. Though he teases John Bull for a whimsical adherence to "family usages," which leads to occasional embarrassment and inconvenience (John "will not hear even of abuses being reformed, because they are good old family abuses" [p. 253]), and adopts a playfully ironic tone in discussing John's intractable attitude toward improvement of his house (John "grows testy" when "advised to have the old edifice thoroughly overhauled, and to have some of the useless parts pulled down" [p. 252]), he nevertheless admires how the "wisdom of every generation" is incorporated into the present structure—improving, not encumbering it. The remnants of antiquity that were vital to the daily existence of the people are not destroyed; they nourish and enrich contemporary life, serving as an active link between past and future. What Irving means, therefore, by "moral feeling" in the English is that they unswervingly accept the obligation of passing on to their progeny the beliefs, the values, and the institutions they have inherited from their ancestors. In "English Writers on America," Crayon declared his own nation's moral worth, but offered no evidence to support the claim; when he speaks of America's "matchless prosperity," he undoubtedly is referring to its economic good fortune. In "John Bull," however, he illustrates again and again that rural England's copious virtues—"all plain, homebred, and unaffected" (compared, for example, to the affectations of the French court)—are outgrowths of its "rich and liberal character." John Bull's family mansion thus provides a permanent home for its inhabitants; like the sturdy English oak, it is "rough without, but sound and solid within" (p. 256).

In "Rural Life in England" Crayon turns to the countryside, where an Englishman is his truest, most "joyous and free-hearted" self, to deepen his sense of the harmony, order, and peace which result from a belief in the interconnectedness of the generations. The stability of English society derives from a dedication to the preservation of that which has undisputed value; this is manifested in the temporal dimension of the rural landscape, which "is associated in the mind with ideas of order, of quiet, of sober, well established principles, of hoary usage and reverend custom." "Every thing seems to be the growth of ages of regular, and peaceful existence" (p. 54). All the signs of human civilization which dot the landscape—the church, with its tower, windows, monuments, and tombstones; the parsonage; the stile and footpath leading from the churchyard; the village, with its peasant cottages and public green; the antique family mansion looking down on the surrounding countryside—are symbols of the "moral character" of a nation committed to a "hereditary transmission of home bred virtues and local attachments." The language Crayon employs to describe the effects of this scene—"calm and settled security," "sheltered quiet," "settled repose," "sweet home feeling"—indicates not only its impact on him, but more importantly how transcendently domestic the English are: they steadfastly refuse to violate the fundamental principles or abandon the traditional values that have given their society its meaning. While America would betray the convictions of its Founding Fathers, the English remain loyal to their origins.

"Rural Life in England" also extends Crayon's definition of "moral" to include the idea of control, by which he means the process whereby a nation determines and forges its own destiny. Critics who are content to see Crayon's long descriptions of nature in this sketch as merely realistic detail and local color miss their strong metaphorical import. Primarily his imagination is captivated by the deliberate way in which the English cultivate the land, so much so that he transforms their careful reshaping of nature's unstructured beauty, represented by a devotion to landscape gardening, into a metaphor for the way they control their world. The relationship of the gardener to the landscape parallels the relationship of the Englishman to his country; that is, the English preserve the same stability in their society that they maintain in their gardens. Where nature remains free in other cultures to lavish her charms in "wild solitudes," in England these same charms are "assembled round the haunts of domestic life." Wildness may have been preferred by those Americans for whom it was equated with the joy of unfettered flight (like Henry Thoreau), yet most of Irving's countrymen were attracted to the particular order that the "Jardin Anglais" represented: the irregularity of line, suggesting freedom rather than restraint, has been *designed* to produce just such an effect. In addition, though the sensitive observer describes "the magnificence of English park scenery" in the stylized "manner of the Flemish colorists whom he admired,"[47] he nevertheless captures the spirit that infuses it and that "gives an air of classic sanctity" (as opposed to novelty) to the surroundings. The subdued terrain of the English countryside has been created purposefully: the once free-flowing brook is "taught" to wind in seemingly "natural meanderings," or made to "expand into a glassy lake—[t]he sequestered pool reflecting the quivering trees, with the yellow leaf sleeping on its bosom" (p. 51). The secluded scene produces a deep, sustaining emotion, a serenity— a "settled security"—that elevates the soul. This is precisely what the English intended and achieved.

Crayon delights in the fact that such "creative talent" does not confine itself exclusively to parks and gardens; on the contrary, "the rudest habitation; the most unpromising and scanty portion of land, in the hands of an Englishman of taste, becomes a little paradise." Crayon also admires the shaping principle and the sublime logic at work in the movement from problem to solution: the Englishman, knowing precisely what he wants from his environment, "seizes at once upon [the earth's] capabilities, and pictures in his mind the future landscape," the result being that the "sterile spot grows into loveliness under his hand." Nothing, of course, has been left to chance, "yet the operations of art which produce the effect are scarcely to be perceived":

> The cherishing and training of some trees; the cautious pruning of others; the nice distribution of flowers and plants of tender and graceful foliage; the introduction of a green slope of velvet turf; the partial opening to a peep of blue distance or silver gleam of water—all these are managed with a delicate tact, a pervading yet quiet assiduity, like the magic touchings with which a painter finishes up a favourite picture. (p. 52)

Significantly, Irving derives his metaphor from painting: art is nothing less than perfect control, and perfect control appears natural when it is in the service of moral purpose. Moreover, the sensibility responsible for such ordered beauty has "diffused" from the higher to the lower classes, so that "taste and

elegance in rural economy" pervade even the "lowest levels of public mind."
When these artistic metaphors are translated into social and political terms
and the definition of "nature" is expanded to include the human terrain as
well, it becomes clear that in order to preserve and protect the special quality
of their society, the English have exerted a necessary control over all the potentially disruptive forces in their midst; not unrestrained desire, but reasoned
action prevails. While it is true that wealth and power in an aristocratic social
system remain inherently stable, there is a cohesiveness to English society that
extends beyond the class structure. In fact, despite clear *divisions* among them,
the various orders of English society—nobility, gentry, independent farmers, and laboring peasants—were united in their loyalty to those traditions and principles that, for them, define the essence of England. Unlike
their offspring on the other side of the Atlantic, the English are secure in their
identity.

Neither "John Bull" nor "Rural Life" makes an explicit statement about the
difference in cultural values between England and America; in fact, Crayon's
homeland is mentioned nowhere in the two sketches. But given that early on
he calls attention to himself as a wanderer from the New World and that
"Rural Life" directly follows "English Writers on America," the comparison
looms in the background, if not stated outrightly, then certainly implied.
While Irving's elegant style and figuratively heightened language lift the
sketches above the prosaic world of American travel writing and give them a
hue and radiance all their own, the highly finished productions are no mere
"poetization" of the Old World. Concealed beneath the carefully selected
words are the uncertain emotions of the displaced American. Moreover, if the
favorable images Crayon presents us with are supposed to be taken as examples of England's "antithetical charm" (Strout's term again), then it is
charm with a vengeance. Yet as long as he can remain the passive observer of
England's virtues—that is, the chronicler of its appeal rather than an active
celebrant/participant in its institutional life—he can avoid transgressing the
boundaries of national loyalty. In these sketches, however, we feel Crayon's
engagement with his subject, witness his admiration for the design and structure of English society, and sense his spiritual gravitation toward the forms of
its culture. His passion for order and his hunger for a nurturing home will not
permit him to remain detached.

In the opening paragraph of "Rural Life in England," Crayon declared that
"the stranger who would form a correct opinion of the English character"
must not concentrate solely on the London metropolis; he must travel through

the country with its parks and gardens, "sojourn in villages and hamlets," "visit castles, villas, farm houses, cottages," wander through the back lanes, "loiter about country churches, attend wakes and fairs and other rural festivals," and mingle with the people in all their "habits and humours" (p. 50). Faithfully adhering to his own advice, Crayon journeys to both familiar places (where he proceeds to establish an unfamiliar relationship with them) and obscure sights, each new experience revealing the intensity of his longing for a deeper, more personal involvement in England's cultural institutions. For example, in a rural village he visits a churchyard, where, according to William Hedges, in "the floral imagery of English funerals and burials" he senses "how naturally and deeply rooted in a culture poetry and symbolism can be."[48] On a Sunday in a different rural village, he attends a customary and cereonial church service, hoping to achieve some form of communion with the village's inhabitants; on another Sunday, this time "in the very heart" of London (p. 89), he again approaches the mystery of shared spiritual union as he observes a congregating community in the midst of worship. Though on occasion overwhelmed by picturesque beauty, and often bathing in lavish sentiment, Crayon's selected images of characteristic and immortal parts of Old England gradually coalesce into a pattern of reverence and discovery. Beyond his assumed posture as the "sketcher," standing at an emotional distance from and filling in the spaces between himself and his environment, Crayon is the pilgrim, in search of an original source of wonder. His shrine is the spirit of the English character itself, the fountainhead of Britain's cohesive and enduring society. Attempting to touch, and to imbibe, that intangible and ineffable "something" that distinguishes the English and gives their society its special quality, Crayon symbolically poses the question that so many of his generation had unconsciously formulated and subsequently sought to answer in their own pilgrimages, both real and imagined, to the Old World: Could an American participate in the accumulated and extended English cultural tradition? Could he grasp and gather into himself their internalized communal history? Was the invulnerable essence of the world's longest uninterrupted continuous society able to be appropriated by the New World imagination?

The Sketch Book's answer, of course, is no, as every American, somewhere in his inner recesses, must have known. Despite the fact that Irving's sentimentalism tends to obscure the gap between anticipation and satisfaction, beguiling the reader at first into believing that the actual scenarios of Crayon's experience accord with his expectations and desires, the truth is that England's past had long ago been subsumed into the primarily verbal forms of history, legend, and myth, beyond the emotional reach of the cultural outsider. *The Sketch Book* illustrates that, *as an American*, Crayon is permanently estranged from the moral order of the Old World, implying that the only way to secure a comparable stability is to create it at home, to redefine and realize it in specifically American terms. Even more than this, and not coincidentally accounting for much of the book's lasting charm, Irving diffuses the manifest tension of the Anglo-American ideological conflict, and undermines the danger inherent in the intense attraction of the Old World society for the New World man, by making Geoffrey Crayon the foolish victim of his own (and America's) obsessions. Each new quest ends not in the witnessing of timeless order, but rather in comic futility; unable to distinguish between fact and fancy, between mundane reality and transporting epiphany, Crayon becomes the butt of Irving's humor. Yet, even though his fanciful adventures are presented in mock-heroic fashion, his failure is treated tenderly. In this case, if Crayon had accomplished his goal, it would have meant that Old World traditions could have nurtured an American, and therefore obviated the need for new, American values. Thus, paradoxically, success would have reinforced American anxiety and discredited the still viable belief in a republican destiny.

The clearest instances of this comic deflation occur in the sketches of London scenes, where Crayon wanders into several hidden corners of the city in search of cultural artifacts which, upon contemplation, will reveal the "true," or perhaps the "mythic," England to him.[49] In East cheap, for example, Crayon sets out on a "pilgrimage" to find the old Boar's head Tavern so that he may have the pleasure of "treading the halls once vocal with [Dame Quickly's] mirth." Fully aware that "no such knot of merry roysters" as Falstaff and his friends "ever enlivened the dull neighborhood of East cheap," Crayon nevertheless resolves to locate the heart of English wit and good humor which Falstaff represents. What the reader realizes, though Crayon does not, is that he is searching for an intangible. Not surprisingly, the Boar's head has vanished, the only physical remains being its former site and sign; more significantly, East cheap, "that ancient region of wit and wassail, where the very names of the streets relished of good cheer," has undergone a metamorphosis from the "roaring days" of Falstaff: "the mad cap royster has given place to the plodding tradesman—the clattering of pots and the sound of 'harp and sawtry' to the din of carts and the accursed dinging of the dustman's bell; and no song is heard save haply the strain of some syren from Billingsgate chaunting the eulogy of deceased mackrel" (pp. 92–93). Somewhat like Rip upon reentering his village, Geoffrey is frustrated in his hunt for a comfortably recognizable past; the obvious difference here, however, is that Geoffrey tries to locate what he never possessed while Rip desperately searches for what he has lost.

This helps to account for the ironic humor, which continues throughout the remainder of the sketch, and though Crayon at first shares in it, it does ultimately betray him as a victim of his own fantasies as he embarks on an odyssey through "Crooked Lane and divers little alleys and elbows and dark passages" in pursuit of a remnant of the Boar's head. The common people he meets are more than willing to accommodate his expectations; his enthusiastic though undiscriminating responses to their distorted information and bogus antiques, however, make him their dupe. In a setting which presupposes the imminence of a great discovery or an important revelation, Crayon is presented with an "august and venerable relic," an iron tobacco box, on the lid of which is engraved a picture of Falstaff and his cronies. Receiving the object with "becoming reverence," Crayon questions "whether the learned Scriblerius contemplated his Roman shield, or the Knights of the Round Table the long sought san-greal with more exultation" (p. 98). The disparity between Crayon's exaggerated responses and the meager stimulus highlights the comedy, which in turn points to the impossibility of attaining the worldly reward: a consciousness of tradition—which is the equivalent of possessing an immutable past—and the secure feeling of being rooted to a place in time exist only in the minds and hearts of Englishmen. Although the resulting humor may not meet Crayon's psychic needs or repay his emotional investment, it does, however (just as in "London Antiques"), help console the "spectator of other men's fortunes."[50]

In addition to showing the inaccessibility of an internalized cultural heritage, *The Sketch Book* also demonstrates that the Past has disappeared because the British, too, are susceptible to the follies of human nature. While the English may be secure in their knowledge of national identity—questions such as "What is England?" and "Who are the English?" never arise—they have not always been as responsible in preserving the living remnants of that heritage as Crayon would like to believe. "Little Britain," in its cumulative survey of the life of a historical neighborhood, represents an aspect of Old England from which something irretrievable has been lost. The piece is referred to by Crayon (in a transitional paragraph from the previous sketch) as a "modicum of local history" for all those "who may wish to know a little more about the mysteries of London" (p. 196). But it soon becomes apparent why the "history" of this neighborhood, a community "shut up within itself," appeals so powerfully to him:

> Little Britain may truly be called the heart's core of the city; the strong hold of true John Bullism. It is a fragment of London as it was in its better days, with its antiquated folks and fashions. Here flourish in great preservation many of the holyday games and customs of yore. The inhabitants most religiously eat pan cakes on Shrove Tuesday; hot cross buns on Good Friday, and roast goose at Michaelmas: they send love letters on Valentine's Day; burn the Pope on the Fifth of November, and kiss all the girls under the misletoe at Christmas. Roast beef and plum pudding are also held in superstitious veneration, and port and sherry maintain their grounds as the only true English wines; all others being considered vile outlandish beverages. (p. 199)

Moreover, Little Britain has its share of burial societies and drinking clubs, and festivities such as St. Bartholomew's Fair and the Lord Mayor's day keep up the good old ways. Superstitions and ghost stories abound; the community also possesses its "sages and great men" and its tellers of tales, all "originals." The overwhelming effect of these trappings is the equivalent of having stepped through a time warp into the past.

Like the antiquated folks and fashions that thrive here, the "general spirit of harmony" prevailing at the outset of the history is destined to change. The tranquillity of Little Britain is disturbed and its "golden simplicity of manners threatened with total subversion by the aspiring family of a retired butcher" (p. 205). The light, whimsical tone, by this time a familiar one, does not obscure the fact that Crayon, a sincere advocate of the eccentric character of the neighborhood, is genuinely disappointed when the community is thrown into confusion by the overreaching family. Worse, the entire sense of order and tradition is disrupted as the members of the family go outside the boundaries of what is known, accepted, and trusted for their new manners and social habits. The community at first is in an uproar over this display of social ambition, but gradually the hostility ceases and the people begin to imitate the pretenders to worldly sophistication and rank. A rival faction develops, led by the family of a rich oil man; when confronted by the gaucheries of money and fashion, the genuine manners, customs, and games deteriorate. Venerable "cockney" (by which Irving means authentically London) pastimes thrive no more: the demise of all the old ways (and thus the charm of the neighborhood) signals the end of Little Britain as a repository of true English character and antiquity. While this may be a laughable exception in England, it did, however, become a problematic norm in America. The comic example of "Little Britain" is thus a microcosm of the larger pattern of American social disruption.

The little "history," an amalgam of fact and fabrication, is a parable about changes wrought in this protected area of the city by the process of mutability aided, to a large extent, by the ignorance and willful neglect of its inhabitants. Crayon here is only the indirect target of the humorous satire, implicated primarily because of his indiscriminate acceptance of all Englishmen as apostles of John Bullism. Having exaggerated the depths to which the moral quality of the English character extends, Crayon is forced to revise his estimations.[51] More significant, however, especially in terms of the efficacy of English institutions to create stability for an American, is Crayon's direct confrontation with Westminster Abbey, the glorification of the English spirit itself and, in *The Sketch Book*, the most important symbol of the ordering forces of tradition and culture. At first the abbey, housing as it does the remains of the custodians of English culture, elicits Crayon's most elegant hymn of praise. But deep inside the abbey's walls the New World man grows uneasy as he slowly comes to understand that, both realistically and symbolically, the representative of living tradition is also a monument to the dead. As befitting his American character, he now fears that the past may engulf the present; moreover, staring continually at the "vestiges" of that "past," his intellect is forced to recognize (and his imagination to succumb to) the inevitability of decay.[52] Eventually, the "dilapidations of time" prevail; sooner or later, the "emblems of living and aspiring ambition" terminate in "dust and oblivion" (pp. 134, 139). Stability metamorphoses into mutability when the emphasis shifts from the abstract concept of memory to the felt presence of mortality.

The artist in Irving is nowhere more apparent in *The Sketch Book* than in "Westminster Abbey," which effectively conveys Crayon's agitation and stress in the midst of this monument to tradition through the modulation of light and darkness. As Crayon gradually proceeds through the abbey, a shift occurs in the pattern of light from the daytime world outside, through a gradual dimming in the "monastic remains" of the approach, to a nearly total, enveloping gloom within.[53] The first stages of the building are already filled with images of bleakness and contain in their shadows a potential threat to the visitor: the realization that death is not the final oblivion. In the cloisters, which "still retain something of the quiet and seclusion of former days," the walls are crumbling and "hoary moss has gathered over the inscriptions of the mural monuments, and obscured the death's heads, and other funereal emblems." Signs of moldering antiquity are everywhere, and as Crayon descends into the vaults the atmosphere becomes more oppressive; the abbey as a symbol of the preservation of English society yields to the weight of time, the eternity of death, and the revelation that a monument ceases to be a memorial once an inscription or a record has been obliterated. Attempting to "kindle" his imagination, Crayon instead finds that the past is unavailable: the tombs are "reliques of times utterly gone by; of beings passed from recollection; of customs and manners with which ours have no affinity." They appear to him "like objects from some strange and distant land, of which we have no certain knowledge, and about which all our conceptions are vague and visionary." Here, the customary poetic rapture gives way to a solemn recognition of the formidable barriers that separate one civilization from another. As he wanders from "tomb to tomb, and from chapel to chapel," the mood of the sketch shifts even more drastically: with the onset of evening and the ceasing of all activity, the noise from above diminishes until he is surrounded by only "desertion and obscurity." In the prevailing silence, the shadows of evening "gradually [thicken] around" him, confining and enclosing him like a coffin. Amidst the "wilderness of tombs" his sojourn among the dead takes on a nightmarish quality: "the marble figures of the monuments [assume] strange shapes in the uncertain light"; the crypts themselves "cast [a] deeper and deeper gloom"; and all about him he sees "'beds of darkness.'" At the tomb of Edward the Confessor he is shocked to discover that the coffin has been violated and the "remains despoiled of their funeral ornaments." "Even the grave is here no longer a sanctuary" (pp. 140, 141).

Crayon experiences a moment of profound disturbance in Westminster Abbey. By the time he is ready to emerge from the dreariness of the abbey, the light, which at first had shone in the square of the cloisters and gilded the "pinnacles of the abbey towering into the azure heaven," and which had then "struggle[d] dimly through windows darkened by dust" where Mary, Queen of Scots, lay buried, has entirely faded, leaving him obscured by darkness. The deepening shadows at the end suggest the fate of all living things, and imply that, in any way that could be meaningful to an American, the past cannot be preserved. Crayon verges on just such a declaration in his closing meditation on the inevitable demise of the abbey:

What then is to insure this pile which now towers above me from sharing the fate of mightier mausoleums? The time must come when its gilded vaults, which now spring so loftily, shall lie in rubbish beneath the feet; when, instead of the sound of melody and praise, the wind shall whistle through the broken arches, and the owl hoot from the shattered tower—when the garish sun beam shall break into those gloomy mansions of death; and the ivy twine round the fallen column; and the fox glove hang its blossoms about the nameless urn, as if in mockery of the dead. Thus man passes away; his name perishes from record and recollection; his history is a tale that is told, and his very monument becomes a ruin. (p. 142)

For Crayon and, as Irving means to suggest, for all Americans, the "past" is basically ungraspable: it is but a memory, doomed to be obliterated. For the British, conversely, the past is preserved in their internalized sense of identity, not in any one cathedral. Change in this respect matters less to them because it does not alter the fundamental character of the nation. Thus, nowhere is Crayon more emotionally distant from his English subject (and, as a consequence, more *recognizably* American) than in his response to the abbey, especially when he declares that "each age is a volume thrown aside to be speedily forgotten," the monument erected to preserve it nothing more than a "vast assemblage of sepulchres," "a treasury of humiliation," "a huge pile of reiterated homilies on the emptiness of renown, and the certainty of oblivion!" Whatever was once alive with feeling has now taken its place among the dead, which is why Crayon appropriately delivers this final peroration from beyond the abbey's walls. In describing his departure, he creates the impression that he has emerged from the imprisonment of a tomb:

> the evening breeze crept through the aisles like the cold breath of the grave; and even the distant footfall of a verger, traversing the Poets' Corner, had something strange and dreary in its sound. I slowly retraced my morning's walk, and as I passed out at the portal of the cloisters, the door, closing with a jarring noise behind me, filled the whole building with echoes. (p. 141)

Once outside the abbey, Crayon can breathe again, symbolically having put the fear of entombment behind him. At the monument of a crusader he may have made a momentary connection between factual history and fictional exploit, but in the process of his escape he has intuited a much greater truth: the past may very well be the sepulcher of the American imagination. For Americans, officially dedicated to the future, to newness, the past will not free the mind; instead, memory functions as a prison, encumbering it with symbols radically opposed to its primary orientation.[54] Crayon's fear—inherent in the paradox of the abbey as a symbol of England's virtuous heritage—is that once inside, the reality of the present, of the outside world, may vanish altogether. Immersed in the great mausoleum—metaphorically buried in the past—Crayon experiences a living oblivion. On the other hand, the sketch goes even further by implying that despite the palpable presence of the abbey, Crayon is left at its conclusion only with his contemplation of it. All that the abbey represents—the inheritance of tradition, the preservation of culture, the eternal past—has no real emotional impetus for Crayon (and thus no transcendent meaning for his American audience) outside of his imaginative projections. If, as he has insisted, "history fades into fable; fact becomes clouded with doubt and controversy; the inscription moulders from the tablet; [and] the statue falls from the pedestal"; and if "columns, arches, pyramids" are "but heaps of sand; and their epitaphs, but characters written in the dust"; and if "a tomb" guarantees no "security," nor "an embalmment" no "perpetuity"; and if the abbey, finally, is just "the empire of death," itself fated to become a ruin, what possible significance is there to an American in the "durability" of English institutions? What permanent shaping force can Old World forms really exert upon a New World imagination? Where, then, is America to find a source of "American" virtue?

III

Crayon's withdrawal from the black void of the past in "Westminster Abbey" neither denies the moral quality of English society nor negates the powerful hold that society has on the American mind. It does, however, put these truths into proper perspective, a perspective Irving's countrymen needed and, if their response to his book is an accurate indication, one they recognized. In this respect, *The Sketch Book* implied that while England could be acknowledged as a cultural tower of strength and the Old World verified as a source of romantic wonder and beauty, Americans have to remain loyal to democratic ideals and republican principles; ultimately, these defining characteristics of American society were the only ones with which they could be comfortable. Geoffrey Crayon's inability to penetrate beyond physical exteriors into the depths of moral and emotional interiors has everything to do with the fact that he approaches and assimilates his surroundings as an American; the consciousness with which he perceives and comprehends events, for all its desire to extend beyond its own boundaries, is quintessentially an American one. Thus, beneath the aesthetic appeal of formalized cultural institutions, and in spite of the splendor of ceremonial pomp and the glory of aristocratic circumstance, the essence of the Old World troubles Crayon because it violates the American commitment to the newness of experience and the revitalization of the spirit; above all, it contradicts the fundamental American belief in the ability of the self to shape its own destiny. Though in practice such an ideology might (and did) lead to amorphousness and formlessness, its opposite was understood as imprisonment—a shackling of the mind. Geoffrey Crayon's response to Westminster Abbey constitutes the American's fear of the absorption of the self by society, a relinquishing of individual personality to the forces of tradition, which amounts, finally, in American terms, to nothing less than self-obliteration. (While it might seem as if Americans desire contradictory things—stability yet newness—this is not actually the case; what they want is an anchor for the self, something, that is, that will act as a ballast as the self navigates wild and uncharted territory—literally and figuratively. For example, we dare to develop and institute wholly new political systems, and precisely because of this we have a greater need for other fixed cultural landmarks.) Symbolically, the abbey does not set him free; it engulfs him. Like Rip Van Winkle, Crayon knows when his soul is threatened. And just like Rip, he flees.

Geoffrey's loss, however, is America's gain. Through his Crayon persona, Irving's readers could sympathetically entertain a view of England filled with achieved intensity and meaning, while at the same time, because of the way Geoffrey is ironically (though humorously) mocked, they could maintain an amused perspective on its less glamorous and satisfactory reality. That is, as they shared in his emotions, the humor forced them to distance themselves from those emotions. Laughing at Geoffrey, whose obsessions blind him to critical truths, Americans were in effect making fun of their own desires to experience the moral order of the European social system. In the portrait of Crayon as the outsider, they were forced to recognize their otherness, their Americanness. Inevitably, it came down to a question (which was really a crisis) of identity. The tension between the way things are and the way Crayon would like them to be thus duplicates Americans' uneasiness that their society was developing along lines that had little relationship to the vision of the Founding Fathers. This straying from the source could not be laughed away, but it could be rechanneled. The flow of change, no matter how fast, fierce, and rampant, nevertheless could be halted. Or, to address the problem in psychological terms, the first step in controlling anxiety is to locate its origins.

The value of England in *The Sketch Book* ultimately lies in its ability to provide an inspiration for this process. As a model of spiritual fortitude, as an example of moral sturdiness—this is the only kind of affirmative power England can exercise over the American imagination. In retrospect, when in "English Writers on America" Crayon said that Americans must not "shut [their] eyes to the perception of what is really excellent and amiable in the English character," the deeper meaning of those words lay in precisely what America could learn from England's constancy. Despite all the pressures and attacks from outside its realm, and despite whatever internal divisions and disharmonies were occurring within its borders, despite, even, the unconquerable forces of mutability, England has persevered as a cohesive and unified nation. Even though as a "young people" Americans are by necessity "imitative," Crayon urges his countrymen *not* to imitate England, but to emulate her. By placing England before them as "a perpetual volume of reference" (p. 49), Crayon does not expect his American readers to derive specific formulas or guidelines for success; rather, he hopes they will achieve a profound understanding of just what constitutes the foundations of national greatness. Thus, England teaches that such greatness—such solidity and unity as a nation—can be achieved only to the extent that Americans rely upon fundamental American resources and strengths. "Our only chance for character," Irving wrote in his journal, "must arise from self dependance."[55]

In a book primarily about England, it is not easy to find clues to the nature of these strengths and resources. Aside from the bombast of "English Writers on America," Crayon has little to say about particular American values. Moreover, though the miscellany contains Irving's two most famous American stories, "Rip Van Winkle" and "The Legend of Sleepy Hollow," which some critics have read in relation to ideas about American character and the American imagination,[56] it is not to these, finally, that we must turn for an answer. Irving's conception of the core of the national character comes, instead, in the two other "American" pieces he included in Geoffrey's collection of sketches, "Traits of Indian Character" and "Philip of Pokanoket." Both had been published several years before in the *Analectic* during Irving's editorship of the magazine and therefore have been regarded as mere "filler" for *The Sketch Book*. But this attitude is a mistaken one, since the essays contain trenchant observations about what might prove to be an available source of American virtue.[57]

95

It is a terrible irony, of course, that Irving would find qualities in the Indian character to recommend to his American audience, for in both "Traits" and "Philip" he clearly blames white civilization for the cruel hostilities and excessive punishment it meted out to its Indian adversaries. In fact, Irving suggests that the tribes he is concerned with in his essays—the Pequods, the Narragansets, and the Wampanoags—although they were angered by the incursion of the whites into their territory, had no active desire to war against them, and finally took up arms only because white treachery and oppression left them with no other choice. "They cannot but be sensible that the white men," Irving writes in "Traits of Indian Character," "are the usurpers of their ancient dominion, the cause of their degradation, and the gradual destroyers of their race" (p. 229). Yet as Irving chronicles the undeserved fate of the North American Indians, and celebrates the moral tenacity they exhibited in trying to preserve their community, it appears as if he wants to see them as ur-Americans: the native who preceded the colonist, the savage "linked to his fellow man of civilized life by more of those sympathies and affections than are usually ascribed to him" (p. 225). Americans would profit from studying accounts of the Indians in which they would witness "the native growth of moral sentiment"; in the Indian character they would perceive those "generous" qualities necessary to the development of a society "vegetating in spontaneous hardihood and rude magnificence." As the "aborigines of America," these original settlers may bequeath to their vanquishers a primal relationship to the land—the land as family, tribe, nation—a relationship at whose core was an unbreakable bond of commitment.[58] "Prefer[ring] death to submission," they "made the most generous struggle of which human nature is capable; fighting to the last gasp in the cause of their country, without a hope of victory or a thought of renown" (pp. 232, 235).

There is a complex mythology operating here: England, as the parent country having given birth to her offspring, America, must in the end be kept at a safe emotional distance; the Indians, as the cultural infants who depend upon their white fathers for "civilized" life, may be embraced more fully as a paradigm of character and virtue because they are much less psychologically threatening. Clearly, Americans occupy a position of strength in relation to them. Interestingly enough, the qualities of Indian character that emerge in the two sketches echo the earlier praised virtues of the English—communal spirit, steadfastness of purpose, and fidelity to country and cause being particularly prominent. Yet the one Irving most often singles out and applauds is "resolution." Under the pressure of ominous circumstances—namely, the concerted effort of the white man to eradicate their culture—the Indians do not give ground morally or collapse spiritually. Faced with an adversary of superior might and far greater material resources, the Indian chieftains persevere, not only in their military efforts, but even more emphatically in their duties and responsibilities to family and tribe. The one thing they will not relinquish, even in utter defeat, is their identity. Given the opportunity to lay down their arms and eventually be assimilated into white society (except for the leaders, the "Sachem," who must be destroyed), they steadfastly refuse to comply, partly because they have seen their fellow Indians, "who have lingered in the vicinity of settlements," become "mere wrecks and remnants of [their] once powerful tribes," sinking "into precarious and vagabond existence," but mostly because they are absolutely loyal to the "spirits" of their "fathers." Irving's Indian hero, Philip of Pokanoket, perfectly illustrates this "unconquerable resolution" to live authentically. A man of princely nature, a "patriot attached to his native soil," Philip suffers and perishes in defense of all he holds dear. Rather than betray his heritage by becoming a "servant to the English," he chooses to live as a fugitive in his own land and dies unmourned. Irving's penultimate sentence indicates his unmitigated approval of this virtuous champion: "Proud of heart, and with an untameable love of natural liberty, he preferred to enjoy it among the beasts of the forests, or in the dismal and famished recesses of swamps and morasses, rather than bow his haughty spirit to submission, and live dependent and despised in the ease and luxury of the settlements" (pp. 246–47).

As a "unity of interest and feeling" develops in *The Sketch Book*,[59] there is a strong impulse to locate within its pages Irving's answer to the dilemma of national identity. "Traits of Indian Character" and "Philip of Pokanoket" satisfy this desire since, above all, they illustrate Irving's admiration for the Indians' resolve to safeguard their traditions. Given America's inability to halt the breakdown of fundamental "American" values and to impede the transformation of their society from a communal and agrarian to an urban and industrial one, Irving's Indians provide heroic examples of fealty to origin and purpose. But *The Sketch Book* is not a didactic work: Irving makes no apparent connections between the Indian essays and the other sketches in the volume; he offers no polemic nor does he issue any warning to his countrymen. *The Sketch Book* is primarily a work of personality and emotion; whatever concern it expresses for the moral well-being of its audience lies far below the surface of its literal meaning and presentation. Yet it is precisely on this level where Irving has never been understood and where all the varied images, impressions, thoughts, feelings, and pictures of *The Sketch Book* coalesce into a co-herent whole. Now it becomes clear how significant are the choice and order-ing of the sketches. An added advantage of my argument, therefore, is that it explains the odd juxtaposition of the disparate pieces in Irving's collection. And the two Indian sketches provide the best example: though Irving may not consciously be holding up his American Indians as exemplary figures, the subterranean movement of the book as a whole points in this direction. This is why, finally, *The Sketch Book*, though it expresses the anxiety of a generation, does not terminate in despair. By first perceiving the deeper issue of anxiety in selected sketches, and then tracing the larger pattern of loss in the entire text, we are able to see that *The Sketch Book* is structured in terms of problem/ solution, and that the solution to America's crisis of identity can be found through the English and through the Indians. From the distance of foreign shores Irving, in the guise of his persona Geoffrey Crayon, and in his own more sober voice, affirmed the hope that America could preserve the ideals of its Fathers.

Irving, whose life (1783–1859) spans the years from the birth to the col-lapse of the American dream of republican order, may not have been aware of the erosion of belief that would underscore the events of the middle 1820s. He may not, in 1819 and 1820, have felt the tremors that would tear the nation apart in the succeeding decades. But there can be little doubt that, however vaguely, as a representative American he did sense these tensions, and thus his words and images touched the collective psyche of his troubled countrymen. In fact, that so early in the century he was an accurate register of the undercurrents of American feeling, and that he had intuited the deeper meaning of England for his compatriots, is reinforced by the experience of one of his literary admirers. More than forty years after Irving penned *The Sketch Book*, a dispirited and distraught Nathaniel Hawthorne, after his own home had been rent in two, turned also to England for images of sturdiness, strength, and moral fiber. Of England he would write: "we may expect it to sink sooner than sunder."[60]

Although America never actually "sundered," its moral underpinnings be-gan to give way in the 1820s, eventually to become forever lost and un-recoverable. Irving, who would spend his last years furiously composing a val-idation of his country in the form of a biography of its *first* representative American, George Washington, did not want to acknowledge this truth. But despite his refusal, and without his knowing it, he was a perfect barometer of its fall. Because the images of homelessness embedded in his writings are deeply American in origin, and because he possessed the ability to seize upon what was psychologically meaningful for his countrymen in the symbols of a foreign culture, the pattern of his European sojourn illustrated the profound depths of an American anxiety not easily discerned at home. Yet *The Sketch Book* also records the pilgrimages of two of American literature's most memorable characters, and these fictions show that the teller of tales found some compensation for the emotional trial of having witnessed the passing of the Old order and the failure of the New.

T H R E E
The Crisis Resolved(?): "Rip Van Winkle" and "The Legend of Sleepy Hollow"

In the more than a century and a half of their existence, Washington Irving's two most famous stories, "Rip Van Winkle" and "The Legend of Sleepy Hollow," have taken on a life of their own. They have been read, listened to, and, from the time of Joseph Jefferson's first staging of "Rip" to our own age of mass media, watched in various productions, by generations of adults and children alike. Yet relatively few people are aware of the fact that they are part of *The Sketch Book of Geoffrey Crayon, Gent.*, and therefore fully resonate only when read in that context. An apparently miscellaneous but, as we have seen, actually quite coherent and unified collection of sketches, essays, and stories, *The Sketch Book* provided Irving with an opportunity for transmuting personal anxiety into literary expression at the same time that it afforded Americans the vehicle for moving from national anxiety into awareness and resolution. But whether this was only an immediate, temporary release from crippling tensions on both levels, or whether the book's conclusions were permanently viable (especially for Irving himself), requires further examination. It is at precisely this point that the two stories enter the internal/external drama since, in order to answer the question, it is necessary to put the pieces back together again and to explore what possible significance there might be in the fact that "Rip Van Winkle" and "The Legend of Sleepy Hollow" first made their entry into the world as leaves of Geoffrey Crayon's *Sketch Book*.

These two stories stand out from the collection because neither of them is about, nor is narrated by, Irving's persona, Geoffrey Crayon.[1] They are, presumably, the results of Diedrich Knickerbocker's antiquarian researches among the old Dutch families of New York: "Rip" is subtitled "a posthumous writing of Diedrich Knickerbocker," while "Sleepy Hollow" was supposedly "found among the papers of the late Diedrich Knickerbocker." Both tales in-

100

clude postscripts—"Rip" has an introductory headnote as well—that sustain this guise by tracing the stories back to their origins and accounting for the ways in which they initially came to the attention of Knickerbocker. Irving, it seems, has gone to considerable lengths to make it explicit that Crayon is not passing off these stories as his own or claiming to have seen or witnessed in any way the events related within them; in other words, they are of a quite different order from the sketches and essays that form the rest of the collection. "It is a technical inconsistency," William Hedges has declared, "for Crayon to include in *his* sketch book stories ostensibly told by Diedrich Knickerbocker."[2] Indeed, the inconsistency appears more than just "technical" if we consider that Knickerbocker, the fictional Dutch historian who narrated the raucous *History of New York* (1809), the final work of the first phase of Irving's career that he had muted for republication in 1819, was almost always comic and irreverent while Crayon is often sentimental and respectful. But Crayon himself does not have to provide the source of narrative consciousness in the tales in order for them to be a meaningful part of his sketchbook or for *The Sketch Book* to be unified. Their ultimate significance lies in the fact that they tend to reflect back on him (and Irving) in multifaceted ways; when considered in the aggregate of *The Sketch Book*, they function in much the same way that the individual sketches do: they are part of the collection of impressions, thoughts, feelings, ideas, pictures, and portraits that reveal aspects of Geoffrey Crayon's personality. Like so many of Crayon's views and notions, the tales have been picked up along the route of his incessant travels, and like the finished sketches, they assume importance in *The Sketch Book* because they are fundamentally expressive of Crayon's concerns. Above all, they address the question of what role the imagination is to play in the life of an early-nineteenth-century American author.

In *The Sketch Book*, Irving uses his Crayonesque persona to affirm the emotional and psychological value of storytelling. As a dupe of his own desires, Crayon is a humorous, sometimes mildly ridiculous figure, and in this way Irving points to the differences between himself (as author) and his persona, making the reader aware of their disjunctions in consciousness: Crayon, he reminds us, lives only inside Irving's fiction. As a narrative technique, this allowed Irving to achieve a perspective on his own experience; while he could share in Crayon's emotions, he could also separate himself from them. Since it was this sense of "separation" that provided a measure of ease and comfort for Irving by freeing him from the pain of exploded dreams, he created even more distance in these highly personal tales by sustaining the guise of multiple narrators. Moreover, having gained control over his psychic/imaginative life, he included the two stories in his *Sketch Book* primarily because they also commented on this process: "Rip" emphasizes the need for true storytelling in a mysterious, unfathomable world, while "Sleepy Hollow" insists that, where experience is unthreatening (and therefore comic), stories need bear no more truth than legends.

I

Before analyzing the differences in "Rip Van Winkle" and "The Legend of Sleepy Hollow" as fictions, we ought to notice the resemblances Rip and Ichabod bear to Irving and his *Sketch Book* persona. Like Geoffrey Crayon, apparently, both Rip and Ichabod desire nothing more than to live tranquil lives, primarily by inhabiting a safe, ordered, unchanging environment. Ironically, the opportunities are there but not grasped: Rip possesses a "patrimonial estate" which, up to the time of his inheritance, consisted of a fully functioning farm in a quiet village at the foot of the Catskill Mountains; Ichabod resides or, as he would have put it, "tarries" in the peaceful little valley known as "Sleepy Hollow," the proverbial retreat from the "world and its distractions."[3] Yet neither character has managed to create a home for himself; like Crayon, neither one will, literally, "settle down."[4] Rip refuses to work his land, and though he claims that everything goes wrong in spite of his efforts to set it right, the truth is, as the narrator tells us, he cannot focus his mind on his own affairs. Instead, he drifts about the town, gossiping with the "good wives," assisting the children at their sports, or gathering with the "sages, philosophers, and other idle personages" in front of the village inn. Ichabod, whose claim to authority as a schoolmaster is based almost solely upon his effective handling of the birch, and whose schoolhouse remains continually unkempt, is even more itinerant than Rip, since he "boarded and lodged at the houses of the farmers, whose children he instructed" (p. 275). As he makes the "rounds of the neighborhood," he carries, like a vagrant, all his "worldly effects tied up in a cotton handkerchief." Yet, interestingly, neither of them can rest easily, and without anxiety, in his chosen mode of behavior: Dame Van Winkle continually hounds Rip and routs him from all his leisurely pastimes; the farmers consider housing the schoolmaster a burden, and therefore Ichabod must find ways of ingratiating himself with them.

What keeps these men from achieving a sense of continuity and harmony in their lives? Oddly enough, while they both enjoy idleness and love to daydream, neither one is truly lazy. Rip willingly assists his neighbors "even in

102

the roughest toil," and on festive occasions proves his prowess by "husking Indian corn, or building stone fences." Ichabod also shares in the many "labours of [the] farm," though clearly, like Rip, he has no interest in caring for a place of his own. Neither man loves the land or the rhythms of working it: ploughing, sowing, harvesting. Both characters, in other words, are physically capable of fulfilling the legitimate requirements of communal participation, but both avoid the means of doing so; that is, they refuse to engage in a life of husbandry with its clearly defined roles and properly designated tasks. Not only Rip, of whom it is said, but Ichabod, too, has "an insuperable aversion to all kinds of profitable labour" (p. 30). In one sense this is positive, as neither seeks mere monetary reward. But in another, far more troubling one it is negative, since neither Rip nor Ichabod can establish permanence or achieve respectability in his village. While (as previously indicated) such a denial of adult responsibility has definite sexual overtones, embedded in their behavior is a negation of the American belief in the principle of usefulness. A nineteenth-century credo, this doctrine claimed that each man contributes to the welfare of his community (and therefore his nation)—and in turn reaps the supreme benefit of being in harmony with his society—by establishing a strong, stable home, one that upholds, instead of challenges, meaningful norms. "Usefulness" was such an important concept in national life that, along with individualism, it constituted the core of an American secular religion.

As a result, Americans found the "idea of leisure" an uncomfortable and, in extreme cases, a disturbing prospect.[5] This was especially true for Sarah Hale, who expressed some of her strongest views on the topic through Mr. Chapman, her version of a Connecticut Yankee (though quite unlike Ichabod), in "The Springs." Set in Saratoga, the sketch shows Chapman attempting to accustom himself to the fashionable life of a spa but thoroughly detesting the experience. Speaking for his creator, he asserts that to be happy a man must be useful, and that leisure (like idleness) was a form of uselessness. For once, Hale's republican point of view coincided with the purposes of an increasingly commercialized society:

> "I don't think [says Mr. Chapman] those gentlemen and ladies there are so happy as the persons I left at work in my factory. They do not look half as cheerful and gay. Indeed, the observations I have made, have convinced me that employment, some kind of business, is absolutely necessary to make men, or at least our citizens, happy and respectable. This trifling away of time when there

is so much to be done, so many improvements necessary in our country, is inconsistent with that principle of being useful, which every republican ought to cherish."[6]

While both "Rip Van Winkle" (at least before Rip's twenty-year sleep) and "The Legend of Sleepy Hollow" may take place "in a remote period of American history" (with a play on "remote"), the need for appropriate, contributory labor and, in opposition, the fantasy of escape from this burden were issues of uppermost importance to Irving's American audience. Thus, his tales make manifest a primary tension in their lives, and though the stories resolve that tension differently, each reinforces the primacy of reality (usefulness) over dream (escape). At the same time, in parallel fashion, they also reveal Irving's grappling with his choice of profession. On the one hand, he believed in the value of fiction and hoped that American society might come to recognize the importance of the man of imagination; in 1818, for example, he wrote the Philadelphia bookseller Moses Thomas that his "literary reputation" was "very dear" to him and that he would not "risk it by making up books for mere profit." On the other, however, he worried at times that telling tales was just a substitute for (and a way of avoiding) more adult concerns; several letters to Brevoort indicate a desire to return home to a settled way of life, and even after *The Sketch Book*'s initial success Irving wished that he "may yet do something more worthy of the approbation lavished" on him.[7]

Not surprisingly, then, given that they have no real desire to fulfill their communal obligations, neither Rip nor Ichabod has any relationship with the working men among his neighbors; both are appreciated primarily by women and children. Rip functions as the village messenger and handyman for everyone's wife except his, and, like him, Ichabod also performs household chores for the farmers' spouses. However, the fact that youngsters enjoy Rip's company, that the village wives take "his part in all family squabbles," and that the "junto" (which is, after all, an "assemblage" of gossiping men) welcomes him among its members counts for little since, literally, Rip must flee society's incessant demands for responsibility, embodied in the wrath of Dame Van Winkle, and take refuge in the Catskills. Nor does it really matter that Ichabod finds favor as "the companion and playmate of the larger boys," the instructor of psalmody to the younger ones, and, in general, as "a man of some importance in the female circle of [the] rural neighborhood" (not least because he delivers the "local gossip from house to house"), since he fails to win over the farmers. The latter, who consider schoolmasters "mere drones" and frown upon their easy lives, tolerate him only to the extent that he willingly helps in the field. Of the two who are mentioned by name, one, Baltus Van Tassel, father of Ichabod's inamorata, is completely indifferent to his presence, since, in Irving's wry version (here) of the yeoman tradition, he "seldom . . . sent either his eyes or his thoughts beyond the boundaries of his own farm"; the other, Hans Van Ripper, astride whose horse Ichabod sits on his fateful midnight gallop, manifests outright hostility for the pedagogue by burning his books and poems after his disappearance and then declaring that his own children will no longer attend school. In other words, the patriarchs do not take Ichabod seriously; like Crayon in England and Rip in his native village, he is an entirely peripheral character. His gullibility and his impracticality notwithstanding, his naïveté defines him most clearly: he never realizes that, in spite of his attempts to be both charming and entertaining, Sleepy Hollow society regards him as superfluous.

Had Ichabod succeeded in gaining the hand of Katrina Van Tassel, social acceptability would have been his, since the community confers its approval on outsiders through marriage to one of its daughters.[8] However, Katrina clearly prefers Ichabod's rival, Brom Bones, "the hero of the country round" (p. 281)—and, on the night of the Van Tassel party, "the hero of the scene" (p. 286)—whose "feats of strength and hardihood" are legion. Yet while Brom represents the quintessential manly figure—"Herculean" in frame, excelling in horsemanship, rough but good-humored—it might be argued that he, too, contributes little of positive value to the rural society. A prankster who specializes in mischief and rustic brawls, Brom nevertheless enjoys the "awe, admiration, and good will" of his neighbors; ultimately, they recognize and love him as one of their own. His sowing of wild oats is just that for, eventually, he will "settle down" and assume his place as one of the sturdy citizens of the village. His "uncouth gallantries" please Katrina—and by extension all the Hollow women—far more than Ichabod's stealthy "advances," which are made "in a quiet and gently insinuating manner." Indeed, shortly after the schoolmaster's departure, Brom "conducted the blooming Katrina in triumph to the altar." One piece of evidence that Brom belongs to the Hollow (and Ichabod does not) is his (supposed) daring response to the Headless Hessian: the apparition from whom Ichabod flees in utter terror Brom challenges to a race. Of course he knows the truth of the phantom's (non)existence, which only makes it easier for him to exploit the gullible Ichabod, who lives so much within his imagination that he is absolutely vulnerable to its promptings. Although in the beginning pages of "Sleepy Hollow" we are told that Ichabod's appearance was "apt to occasion some little stir at the tea table of a farm house" (p. 276), in the end he is lightly dismissed and easily replaced: "As he was a bachelor, and in nobody's debt, nobody troubled his head any more about him, the school was removed to a different quarter of the hollow, and another pedagogue reigned in his stead" (p. 295). Interestingly enough, Rip's situation follows suit: when he suddenly returns twenty years after his departure, no one recognizes him and, apparently, no one has really missed him. Upon concluding their investigation and listening to his explanation, most townspeople simply shift their attention back to "the more important concerns of the election" (p. 40). Only later, as a storyteller and a chronicler of the town, does Rip become an important and integral part of the community.

"Rip Van Winkle" and "The Legend of Sleepy Hollow" belong in Geoffrey Crayon's sketchbook, therefore, since Rip and Ichabod reflect Crayon's sense of impermanence and his fear of irrelevance. Geoffrey's despair over his own cultural obscurity might easily have led him to read something of himself into the behavior of these social miscreants. Furthermore, Crayon could very likely have seen another parallel between his own experience and Ichabod's: like Crane, who cannot make a place for himself in the community of Sleepy Hollow but is nevertheless the central figure in its "legend," Crayon cannot fit into English society and its traditions, becoming instead the focus of fictional sketches which illustrate that failure. (Crayon also has a fondness for legends that approaches Ichabod's gullible belief in magic and superstition.) Yet beyond this achievement of *The Sketch Book*'s unity, the tales also tell us something important about Washington Irving. Quite clearly, Irving did not possess the same "aversion" to "profitable labour" as either of his characters; in fact, though (as stated before) he would not write solely for pecuniary gain, he repeatedly worried that his writings would not bring him a subsistence. The specter of financial embarrassment haunted him; he feared becoming a "burthen" to his "friends" or, worse, an object of their "pity."[9] But he believed that, like Rip and Ichabod, he had no talent for continuous and useful (in the specified definition) work. When he refused Walter Scott's offer to edit an Edinburgh magazine, he based his decision on a judicious assessment of his habits and inclinations: "My whole course of life has been desultory and I am unfitted for any periodically recurring task, or any stipulated labour of body or mind. . . . Practice & training may bring me more into rule, but at present I am as unfit for Service in the ranks as one of my own country Indians or a Don Cossack."[10] Irving acknowledges here that his behavior is far from the norm, that, in fact, he has crossed the bounds of the culturally acceptable; and that eventually, perhaps, he may be brought "into rule." Moreover, by comparing himself to the exiles and the true disinherited of American society, the Indians, he makes it clear that he considers himself an anomaly among his countrymen. Yet the sense of helplessness in his statement ("I can't help it, that's the way I am") conceals a covert protest: like Rip, Ichabod, and Crayon, Irving *will* not abide by the rules of prosaic American society. Participation simply costs too much; the price was nothing less than the life of his imagination.

Had he desired, of course, Irving could just as easily have said that he was as incapable of regular employment as either his persona or his two most celebrated characters. In effect, he did just that when, in 1848, he reserved a permanent place in *The Sketch Book* for these comments by including them in the "Preface to the Revised Edition" (which recounts the history of the book's first publication). Thus, almost immediately after encountering the self-deprecating Washington Irving, the reader engages the self-mocking Geoffrey Crayon. A wanderer who began his travels by making forays into the "unknown regions" of his "native city" and "rambles about the surrounding country" (p. 8), Crayon offers his "account of himself" in the same bemused tone that the narrator Knickerbocker adopts in delineating the personalities of Rip and Ichabod. In fact, at least part of the reason Crayon interests us is that, like them, he chooses to gratify his "roving passion." Eschewing the path of "every regular traveller who would make a book," he heeds the call of his "idle humour." Unlike the majority of Americans devoted to useful pursuits, but exceedingly like his undutiful heroes, Crayon (and behind him Irving, since mask and man are one here) "follow[s] the bent of his vagrant inclination."[11]

No matter what deeply moral purpose lay behind Irving's tour in England, such an open declaration of "imaginative indulgence" violated the fundamental orientation of America toward "fact and doctrine." Or to take a different social perspective, in childhood a boy may pursue the pleasures of the fancy but, as Terence Martin has written, upon reaching adulthood, a man "must assume his place in the actual, and practical, world."[12] To fail at this or, worse, to refuse it often meant being relegated to cultural marginality. This is just the position that Irving occupied in America (and another reason why he withdraws behind a persona). Like Crayon, Rip, and (sometimes) Ichabod, he may be an amusing, likable person, but up until the time of his departure for England he performed no necessary function and thus had secured no permanent place in his native community of New York. The way he understood it, his hometown had little regard for a man of his talents: "As to the idea you hold out of being provided for *sooner or later* in our *fortunate* city," he told his friend Brevoort, "I can only say that I see no way in which I could be provided for, not being a man of business, a man of Science, or in fact any thing but a mere belles lettres writer—And as to the fortunate character of our city—To me & mine it has been a very disasterous [sic] one." [13] "This world is usurped by the plodder & the moneymaker and the labourer," he wrote in his notebook; "so Scarce a quiet corner left in it for the poet." [14] Irving's restless, unsettled state, therefore, metamorphosed into Crayon's peripatetic seeking after something lastingly substantial, which in turn yielded a release of creative energy: the freedom of imaginative exploration attended, and was dependent on, the search for a secure, safe mooring in a life of continual flux.

In this light, and remembering Irving's language of loss, the outcasts Rip and Ichabod (who are literally "cast out" of their respective societies) emerge as distorted mirror images of the author of *The Sketch Book*. Fictionally, they occupy the same territory that Irving associated with the beginning of his imaginative life: "I trace [he wrote in a notebook entry] many of my best feelings and best thots to their first burst while wandering on the banks of the Hudson. It was there the world dawned upon me as a fairy land; and though checquerd and sad experience have [sic] thrown many a cloud on it, yet still I look back beyond these all to the sunny realm of boyish imagination." [15] It was Irving's manifest aim to recapture that "realm," and to a certain extent he accomplished that goal by shaping his protagonists in his own image and then locating them amidst the setting of his treasured memories. However, while he may contain them, he ultimately diverges from the path of their flight; Irving, it should be remembered, voyaged toward imaginative repossession. Like Crayon, Rip and Ichabod constitute *his* fictional creations.

Thus, the most important aspect of this skewed identification between author and characters involves the fact that Rip and Ichabod are men of some imagination. Both, of course, are dreamers; like Crayon, they "loiter about"—Rip in the midst of the gathered "sages" and in the Catskills, Ichabod among the old Dutch wives and in the hills of the Hollow—extending their imaginations either to the communities' tale-tellers or in sympathetic harmony with the surrounding landscape. And those imaginations are powerful—so strong, in fact, that for both these characters the wide border between the recognizably common and the fantastically grotesque dissolves completely: Rip never questions the existence of the Dutchmen whom he meets in the mountains because, even if he did conjure them up, they are real to him; Ichabod believes so firmly in occult phenomena that when, on his last dark night in the valley, he sees "something huge, misshapen, black and towering" in his path, he *knows* in his bones that the ghost of the galloping Hessian has descended upon him. These confrontations with fearful specters result directly from the way both characters have imaginatively reconstructed the superstitions and legends of their environments. Fictions, therefore, generate more fictions and thus animate, and even determine the course of, their lives, though with opposite effects. Rip's creative energy proves to be an asset, since it enables him to shape his mysterious encounter with Hendrick Hudson's crew into an identity-creating product—both for himself and "all henpecked husbands in the neighbourhood." Having "got his neck out of the yoke of matrimony," and safely domiciled in his daughter's house, he finds the home he always wanted, one with no adult responsibilities—no wife, children, or farm to look after. Ichabod's creativity, however, undoes him; coupled with his extensive reading in Cotton Mather's *History of New England Witchcraft* (that is, *Wonders of the Invisible World*), it causes him to take the figure of a hooded horseman as confirming the validity of the "marvellous tales" he has heard in the Hollow. Like Crayon, he becomes the dupe of his own imaginative propensities (and the victim of Brom's practical joke), losing the trappings and luxuries of a home he foolishly believed he could possess. The farmer rightfully ousts the pedant from a world whose values he does not share.

"The Legend of Sleepy Hollow" comically exaggerates Irving's projection of himself as artist-parasite, feeding on a society (just as he fed off his brothers) that, at best, regards his peculiar talent with suspicion. Ichabod's voracious appetite suggests the extent to which he devours the resources of the community without ever replenishing what he consumes. Yet in spite of his tremendous capacity he remains thin, almost gaunt: such ravenous hunger cannot be satisfied. His only creative offering—his tales and "anecdotes of witchcraft"—the people do not really need, since they are by nature imaginative and visionary and, as a result, plentifully endowed with "wild and wonderful legends." Though he twice refers to Ichabod as "my hero" (pp. 284, 287), the narrator (ostensibly Knickerbocker, actually Crayon/Irving) still mocks him for his pretensions to a position of some importance in Sleepy Hollow. Ironically comparing him to a "knight errant," he knows what an inflated sense of self Ichabod has; moreover, it is patently absurd that someone of such meager stature should have such great ambition: Ichabod "could not help, too, rolling his large eyes round him as he ate, and chuckling with the possibility that he might one day be lord of all this scene of almost unimaginable luxury and splendor. Then, he thought, how soon he'd turn his back upon the old school house; snap his fingers in the face of Hans Van Ripper, and every other niggardly patron, and kick any itinerant pedagogue out of doors that should dare to call him comrade!" (p. 287). Once again Ichabod assumes an antagonistic stance toward his society: his dream of being "lord" of the manor is an aristocratic, not a democratic, one. Tired of accommodating the demanding farmers and desiring far more than the portion he has been allotted, he forgets his place, overreaches his limits, and poaches on Brom Bones's territory. In the end, forced to flee, he mut adopt a new identity: he has no more tales to tell. Thus, with its burlesque treatment of the man of letters, "Sleepy Hollow" diffuses Irving's fear of the artist as freeloader into the apparatus of legend.

"Rip Van Winkle," on the other hand, represents Irving's dream of returning to an American society that has finally made a place for him. Like his fictional counterpart after a twenty-year absence, he longed for the familiar terrain of his boyhood rambles. "Oh my dear Brevoort[,] how my heart warms toward you all, when I get talking and thinking of past times and past scenes," Irving wrote five years into his European sojourn. "What would I not give for a few days among the highlands of the Hudson with the little knot that was once assembled there." Yet twelve more years would pass before he chanced that homecoming. Economic security, though obviously crucial, was not the only issue that concerned him. He did not want to reexperience, like Rip entering his village after "enormous lapses of time" (p. 38), that accustomed but dreaded alienation: "I am continually picturing to myself," he told Brevoort in that same letter, "the dreary state of a poor devil like myself who after wandering about the world among strangers returns to find himself a still greater stranger in his native place."[16] In Irving's fantasy, however, Rip makes a success out of his own inadequacy: he is ultimately recognized, welcomed, and, once it is understood that he wants nothing more than to be allowed to relate his adventure to all who will listen, accepted. Totally unaggressive, he poses no threat to the business of postRevolutionary America. In fact, he becomes a great favorite with "the rising generation," since he has something to tell them about the past which, contrary to the America Irving knew, they apparently value. Thus, with its depiction of the anxiety of estrangement transformed into the ease of acceptance, "Rip Van Winkle" weaves Irving's desire for a settled life (as chronicler) into the fabric of story.

The Sketch Book demonstrates that, for Irving, authorship offers a possible compensation for the experience of alienation and loss. In "The Boar's Head

Tavern" sketch, the counterparts to Crayon are the neighbors about East cheap who "believe that Falstaff and his merry crew actually lived and revelled there" (p. 98). As with their dubious relics, their understanding of history, fact, and truth is distorted, commingled as it is with legend and anecdote. They live, in a sense, inside a fiction of their own creation, which Crayon cannot fathom; destined to play the role of observer, the best he can do in this regard is fabricate an emotion, devise an illusion, or create his own fiction. The latter activity proved, at least temporarily, to be the most satisfying. It was not an entirely imaginary world that Irving was creating but, rather, a coloring of the one he knew; his experience, fleshed-out by moods, tones, and, occasionally, methods of presentation borrowed from older authors, was related to the reader by the age-old technique of telling a story. Having been excluded from participation in the continuous flow of an ordered society, Washington Irving discovered that storytelling itself was an uncircumscribed, timeless activity that could satisfy his hunger for cultural continuity.

Having explored the correspondences and connections among Irving, Crayon, Rip, and Ichabod, we may now examine the two famous tales in terms of their relevance to Irving's understanding, as exemplified in *The Sketch Book*, of the place of fiction in his life. Set within the context of these identities, and when regarded as particular kinds of fiction—story and legend— they show Irving's discovery of the imagination as the only solution to real-world crises.

II

In a headnote that serves as an introduction to the story of "Rip Van Winkle," Crayon attests to the "scrupulous accuracy" of Diedrich Knickerbocker's work (p. 28). Then, at the conclusion of the narrative, Crayon intrudes just briefly—one might say almost compulsively—to inform the reader that the tale he has just read "is an absolute fact, narrated with [Knickerbocker's] usual fidelity," fidelity in this instance meaning that Knickerbocker has presented the tale exactly as he heard it. To support these assertions, Crayon subjoins a note that Knickerbocker himself had originally appended to the tale in which he affirms the verifiability, indeed, the value of the story: "The story of Rip Van Winkle may seem incredible to many, but nevertheless I give it my full belief, for I know the vicinity of our old Dutch settlements to have been very subject to marvellous events and appearances. . . . The story . . . is beyond the possibility of doubt" (p. 41). These mechanics, by which Crayon insists on the truthfulness of the story, seem heavy-handed, contrived, ironic, espe-

111

cially when one considers that the central events of "Rip Van Winkle" (a meeting with Hendrik Hudson's crew and a sleep of twenty years' duration) are inexplicable in logical terms. It is possible that Irving is engaging here in what Haskell Springer calls a "technique of self-contradiction"—the "story proper and the comments upon the tale" exert pressures in "opposite directions," so that together they wind up asserting the "reality" of seemingly unreal events—to alert the reader to the essentially fictional character of this world.[17] Yet, while this may satisfy as an explanation of Irving's literary posturing, it hardly provides an adequate gloss on Crayon's psychology, for in the urgency with which he expresses his belief in the story, Crayon reveals that there is something else at stake here. If "Rip Van Winkle" is "true," then perhaps that truth is to be found not within its own borders, but in its relationship to the pattern of Crayon's experience (and therefore Irving's) as it is delineated in *The Sketch Book*.[18]

It is usually assumed that the central, most significant event in "Rip Van Winkle" is Rip's encounter with the odd-looking Dutch sailors, Hendrik Hudson and his crew of the *Half-Moon*, and his subsequent twenty year sleep. But these events are not the most troubling for the protagonist of the story, nor are they really disturbing to the reader, who tends to accept them as a given mystery. The real "what happened," and as Hedges describes it, "the closest thing to terror" in the story, occurs when Rip awakens to a world he does not recognize.[19] It is at this point that he becomes disoriented: faced with an incomprehensible reality, he feels overwhelmingly lost and utterly alone. Returning to the village, he finds that his house has "gone to decay," and when he calls for his family, his voice is met only with "silence." His despair intensifies when he realizes that he is completely out of sync with contemporary America: the political climate of the town is sharp, factional, and unfriendly. The harsh tone disturbs Rip; the "sad changes in his home and friends" bewilder him. In fact, the alterations affect him to the extent that he believes both he and his surroundings must be "bewitched." Nothing of the predictable, comfortable world remains—even Rip's loyalty to George III is outdated. Most frightening of all, Rip perceives that he himself has been supplanted; his son, a "precise counterpart of himself" when younger, is the Rip Van Winkle everyone knows. (In Freudian terms, the impotent father yields to his offspring.) In the face of this enormity, Rip is confused, confounded, bewildered.

As critics have previously noted, the latter part of the story centers around Rip's identity crisis.[20] On his return to the village, Rip expected to locate something soothing, something recognizable but, instead, discovers that he has lost pace with time, that the familiar terrain of his younger days is gone forever. In a mysterious, irrational world, in which the only constant factor is change, Rip undergoes a privileged rebirth into the storyteller.[21] The "true" nature of the experience is of secondary importance in the larger scheme of the tale. This is implied in the suggestion that Rip may not have actually entered the womblike "amphitheatre" in the Catskills but may simply have fallen asleep and dreamed of his encounter with the old men, whose images, we are told, were the exact duplicates of "the figures in an old Flemish painting" that Rip had seen hanging in the parlor of the village parson (p. 34). In this respect, the fact that the "dream" occurs during a sleep of twenty years makes the state of events in the story almost completely ungraspable: as Hedges has explained, "to see the experience as a dream is to have its unreality emphasized."[22] However, we as readers do not share the doubts of some of Rip's auditors, who maintain that he was clearly "out of his head" for twenty years. To them, the story becomes nonsense. But their commonsense approach, their skepticism, is naïve in comparison to our understanding of the story. It is a blunder on their part not to acknowledge that doubt and belief combine to form the listening/reading experience.[23] The story exists precisely because there is a quality about experience that must be conveyed—call it magic, mystery, incomprehensibility, or whatever—and we as readers, as important an audience as Rip's pals, realize that common sense is unnecessary. The story prevails on a level far removed from such logic. It is true, even if it never happened.

As a result of having a story to tell, Rip is accepted into the community, and although he has trouble comprehending "the strange events that had taken place during his torpor" (p. 40), he is reconciled to them by the very fact of his new identity. His story, in this respect, is a palliative, alleviating the anxiety of his loss; even more, it is a compensation for unsettling changes. Having been freed from his role as henpecked husband, the story/plot awards him another reality, so palpable to him, and eventually to others, that it becomes part of the collective consciousness of the old Dutch inhabitants. The new reality is also the story itself (what Crayon meant by insisting on its "truth"), in that it has a timeless, imaginative existence of its own. Knickerbocker corroborates this, for the tale that he has left behind among his papers is Rip's very own, heard directly from his lips: "He used to tell his story to every stranger that arrived at Mr. Doolittle's hotel. He was observed at first to vary on some points, every time he told it, which was doubtless owing to his having so recently awaked. It at last settled down precisely to the tale I have related and not a man woman or child in the neighbourhood but knew it by heart" (p. 41). Moreover, in his appended note, Knickerbocker further states that he talked with Rip himself and on that occasion he was perfectly "rational and consistent." Thus a life has been generated that transcends the confines of such sets of terms as "real and imaginary," "fact and fiction." From Rip Van Winkle's tale through Diedrich Knickerbocker's writings to Geoffrey Crayon's sketchbook: the story is "beyond the possibility of doubt."

The value of the story, however, is even greater than the fact of its existence or the reconciliation it allows Rip. All the changes that Rip perceived were the work of history, whose ability to bring these about is, as John Lynen has said, "summed up in the great political event [of] revolution."[24] Yet the reader may legitimately wonder on which level of reality the alterations occurred; in what stream of human time-consciousness do the changes register? Prerevolutionary politics was confined to the perusal of an antiquated newspaper and the leisurely discussions this activity engendered, while postrevolutionary politics involves the thunder of an election-day debate. Contented farmers are giving way to aggressive businessmen. But beneath these cultural shifts there is still an unexamined loyalty to the village patriarch and a fundamental need to engage in work. Irving suggests that the apparent enormity of the changes is just that—apparent, that is, on the surface. While the Union Hotel has supplanted the old inn, the sign at the door has only been transformed so that George Washington emerges out of George III—some form of political leadership/authority will always be in order. The old Dutch worthy Nicholaus Vedder is gone, as is the giant tree that provided such lovely shade for the inn; in their place we find the unappealing Yankee and a bare liberty pole, yet Rip and his friends have as little trouble accommodating themselves to this environment as their predecessors did to the prerevolutionary scene. In fact, the townspeople now take their cue from the gestures of the self-important man with the cocked hat much the same way as Rip's cronies used to gather Vedder's opinions from the variations in his manner of pipe smoking. The real, profound changes are the ongoing, perpetual ones, those of mortality, "growing up and growing old."[25] This type of alteration is the result of neither historical nor political processes, but rather of the natural ones of birth and death, growth and decay, which never cease and, in effect, make one period of time the equivalent of any other. The variations in the exterior of Rip's society, then, when viewed against these eternal patterns, are only modifications of appearance or form, while the deepest structures remain permanent, everlasting truths of existence. Thus, much as Vedder once was, Rip is now "reverenced" as a village worthy, and Rip, Jr., assumes his father's ragged image from twenty years ago.

Rip is a storyteller, and his tale—a fable about the nature of experience—poses the question of whether or not there is such a thing as true perception/knowledge. As a coherent sequence, a concatenation of events moving from a beginning to an end, Rip's story has its immediate, temporal order. But storytelling itself is a timeless, eternal activity. It exists on the same plane, and is part of the same time-consciousness, as those immutable natural patterns. People have always constructed stories to explain their experience. This process, this myth-making, allows one to participate in, and to reflect, the unalterable rhythms and sequences that form the nucleus of all existence. Irving's discovery of this "truth," mirrored here in "Rip," was crucial, for it enabled him to believe that a second principle of time exists wherein change is circumscribed and ordered in terms of a cyclical development in man and nature. This is the principle of continuity, which, as Donald Ringe has phrased it, affirms that some idea of permanence "transcends the apparent flux of life," and that mutability is therefore not the ultimate meaning of experience.[26] Without this realization, his imagination would have faltered. No wonder, then, that Geoffrey Crayon included "Rip Van Winkle" in his sketchbook (and Washington Irving in his *Sketch Book*, where he also became a storyteller), since it absolutely attests to the necessity and value of "story." Ultimately, Irving hoped that the nation would expand its idea of "usefulness" and accept him—just as the village finally welcomed Rip—as chronicler.

III

That "The Legend of Sleepy Hollow" bears the description "legend" rather than "story" is neither whimsical nor accidental, but a significant ploy on Irving's part, both in terms of the type of community portrayed there and in the context of the argument just presented. Unlike a story, a legend does not try to approximate or re-create worldly experience but, according to Haskell Springer, is a "waking use of dream concepts that combines the real and the unreal to create a new, distinct imaginative reality properly existing on the frontier of consciousness."[27] The world of a legend inhabits neither the plane of pure fantasy nor that of history; its terrain is not a complete and totally unrecognizable fairyland, nor is it the world of our daily lives. A legend is not a story: although it may be told and retold, shaped and reshaped, it does not embody or reflect on the patterns of human endeavor. Its pictures, its images, are not those of our conscious experience; rather, they are similar to those of "unauthenticated narratives, folk-embroidered from historical material."[28] Thus, the world of a legend, and the figures portrayed within it, may have enjoyed, once upon a time, a historical reality, but, having ascended to the plateau of legend, they now bear only a slight resemblance to their former selves. Here, Irving's insistence on legend is supported by his epigraph, which re-creates the indolent mood of the Hollow itself—neither that of the real world of fact nor the mimetically real world of story:

> A pleasing land of drowsy head it was,
> Of dreams that wave before the half-shut eye;
> And of gay castles in the clouds that pass,
> Forever flushing round a summer sky. (p. 272)

The outstanding feature of the community of Sleepy Hollow is that it is a self-contained world, where "population, manners, and customs, remain fixed, while the great torrent of migration and improvement, which is making such incessant changes in other parts of this restless country, sweeps by [it] unobserved" (p. 274). In this valley of "uniform tranquility," "one of the quietest places in the whole world," a healthy, reciprocal balance with nature is maintained. The characters of the tale, who "live in an organic time, ruled by the seasons,"[29] are content and completely resistant to progress. There is no internal conflict in Sleepy Hollow, and the only tensions that exist are those introduced by Ichabod Crane, the outsider. Even the disturbing aspects of nature here turn out to be no more than harmless titillations of the fancy; such supposedly supernatural occurrences as the Headless Horseman and the often repeated stories of frightening apparitions inhabiting every part of the landscape are only tales told for amusement on a winter's night.

The people of Sleepy Hollow are as much a part of the landscape as the natural growth of the valley; indeed, they are imagined by the narrator to be "still . . . vegetating in its sheltered bosom." But this is not surprising, since the Hollow amply provides for all their needs. Baltus Van Tassel, the representative farmer of the region, is pictured as a "thriving, contented, liberal hearted farmer" (p. 278). He does not seek to extend his domain beyond the "boundaries of his own farm," for "within those every thing was snug, happy, and well conditioned." Such farmers as Van Tassel enjoy the full gifts of nature—the "treasures of the farm" which Irving, in a justly famous passage, describes with glee—because they appreciate nature's abundance and desire to live only in harmonious intimacy with it.

Given this presentation of the "sleepy," "dreamy" community as a land of plenty, Ichabod Crane is clearly cast in the role of the despoiler although, as I have indicated, he may also be characterized as "imaginative," and (according to Terence Martin) his routing by Brom Bones as a "victory for common sense and hard-headed practicality over imaginative indulgence."[30] From the first time that he comes on this scene of nature's munificence, where he is described as "the genius of famine descending upon the earth" (p. 274), Ichabod is seen as an intruder. As Herbert Smith has noted, images of "eating, consumption, destruction" are closely associated with all his actions.[31] While his pursuit of Katrina Van Tassel's affections may be likened humorously to a man carving "his way to the centre of a Christmas pie," he is in fact guilty of a serious offense: he neither values nor desires to preserve the plenty that surrounds him. In another famous passage Irving shows that, contrary to the farmers who embrace them as part of an organic whole, Ichabod appreciates the barnyard animals only as luscious edibles:

> In his devouring mind's eye, he pictured to himself every roasting pig running about with a pudding in his belly, and an apple in his mouth; the pigeons were snugly put to bed in a comfortable pie, and tucked in with a coverlet of crust; the geese were swimming in their own gravy; and the ducks pairing cosily in dishes, like snug married couples, with a decent competency of onion sauce; in the porkers he saw carved out the future sleek side of bacon, and juicy relishing ham; not a turkey, but he beheld daintily trussed up, with its gizzard under its wing, and, peradventure, a necklace of savoury sausages; and even bright chanticleer himself lay sprawling on his back, in a side dish, with uplifted claws, as if craving that quarter, which his chivalrous spirit disdained to ask while living. (p. 279)

Although the felicity of Irving's description again points to the humor in Ichabod's vision, he is nevertheless a threat to the life of natural harmony.[32] Given the opportunity, he would neither husband the resources nor conserve the riches of Sleepy Hollow but exploit them by turning the self-sustaining farm of Van Tassel into a capitalistic enterprise: "His heart yearned after the damsel who was to inherit these domains, and his imagination expanded with the idea, how they might be readily turned into cash, and the money invested in immense tracts of wild land, and shingle palaces in the wilderness" (p. 280). Here Ichabod resembles the farmers' greatest enemy—and a recognizable villain in the early Republic—the land speculator.

That these actions generate no great anxiety either in the people of the tale or in the reader attests to the basic legendary quality of the fiction. (For the reader, there is nothing that approaches Rip's moment of fear in the Catskills or his despair on reentering the village.) Sleepy Hollow is not an imitation of the real world; thus, a disturbing presence such as Ichabod may be treated comically, for he is easily eliminated with a practical joke. Though he would like to possess the land and enjoy a "well-fed repose in the drowsy hollow,"[33] this dream is denied to him because he is an alien force: a greedy entrepreneur and a destroyer of nature; such particularly human traits have no place in this world. He is routed by what we as readers know to be only Brom Bones and a pumpkin. Yet the headless ghost he sees on his midnight ride is, perhaps, the consequence of more than just his belief in supernatural stories; it could very well represent, on a deeper level, the guilt and fear of a betrayer, the violator of the agrarian principles and dreamy atmosphere of Sleepy Hollow. Katrina Van Tassel's rejection of Ichabod as suitor and his subsequent flight signify the triumph of the pastoral community over its potential exploiter. It is thus a fitting conclusion to Ichabod's career that he should have found his way to New York, the archetypal center of big-city greed and corruption, where he "kept school and studied law at the same time," was "admitted to the bar, turned politician, electioneered," wrote "for the newspapers, and finally [was] made a Justice of the Ten Pound Court" (p. 296).

Although Ichabod acts as a force of destruction, he is an anomaly in his environment. Primarily, Sleepy Hollow is a safe place. When the supernatural, so often discussed and debated, finally appears, we are not frightened; when the potentially dangerous, but more, the inexplicable, occurs, we are not troubled or disrupted. In "The Legend of Sleepy Hollow," we know what really happened to Ichabod Crane. But in "Rip Van Winkle," we can never be sure that we understand what took place in the Catskill Mountains; we will always be awed, mystified, and continually disturbed by Rip's expression of overwhelming loss on returning to his native village. The story reinforces the idea that experience is often an incomprehensible and complex mystery, compelling yet baffling. The eternal appeal of "Rip" has everything to do with this sense of anxiety, but in "Sleepy Hollow" there are no unsolved mysteries or psychological complexities, for all its actions are clearly explainable in rational terms. It seems odd, then, and somewhat paradoxical, that "Rip Van Winkle" is a "story," insisting on its own truthfulness and actuality, and "Sleepy Hollow" a "legend," existing on the borderline of the conscious and the unconscious mind.

Several interpretations have been offered for what the word "legend" in the title "The Legend of Sleepy Hollow" actually means in relationship to the tale itself. Springer summarizes these: it may refer to "the misadventures of Ichabod Crane"; it can also be considered as "alluding to the fact that no matter how rationally accountable Ichabod's experience appears to us, it is legendary to the drowsy people of Sleepy Hollow"; in addition, the title may refer "not at all to Ichabod's exploits, but to the old legend of the Headless Hessian [who was supposed to have lived and flourished in this area at one time] which the schoolmaster heard from the residents of the Hollow." Each view is acceptable, and each in its turn supports the ultimate assertion of "the power of . . . fictional literature" to enhance the value of life for imaginative people.[34] However, it is also possible to insist that the "legend" is Sleepy Hollow itself. As an actual geographic entity, as a community, Sleepy Hollow never could have existed, for its harmony, its somnolence, its peaceful coexistence with the forces of nature, are, if anything, prelapsarian. Our enjoyment of the tale is, to a certain extent, based on this recognition, which is one reason why the "Postscript," in which the "truthfulness" of the tale is attacked by a rather decrepit old man, is presented in a bemused, mockingly humorous tone, so contrary to the earnestness of Knickerbocker's note at the conclusion of "Rip." The pompous old fool, unable to accept the tale as amusement, is confounded by the storyteller who, in exaggerated motions of deference, offers this grave listener a purposely ridiculous accounting of the tale. "Sorely puzzled by the ratiocination of the syllogism," the latter has missed the whole implication of both the "legend" and the storyteller's joke, which is repeated in the final line of the "Postscript" as he mockingly responds to the dry old man's doubts about its validity: "Faith, sir, . . . I don't believe one half of it myself" (p. 297). Truthfulness, applicability, or psychological precision is neither to be demanded of nor even expected from the world of "Sleepy Hollow."[35] In addition, the old man badgering the narrator might very well be Ichabod himself, many years in the future. Having turned into a curmudgeon, and disturbed to learn both the real events of that fateful night and that he has now become a figure of comic derision, he insists that the portrait of himself must be a fiction. Ironically, having once believed in magic and the imagination, he now insists on law and logic. Yet he is still the victim of a joke.[36]

In "The Legend of Sleepy Hollow," the storyteller, from whom Diedrich Knickerbocker heard the tale, is not dependent on his story for anything more than entertainment; indeed, at the "corporation meeting of the ancient city of Manhattoes," where it was first related, there was a great deal of

119

"laughter and approbation." The "legend" need not be true in the way that Rip's story has to be, for nothing discernible has happened to the storyteller, while in Rip's case, the whole question of his identity was involved. For Rip, then, the story lends form and coherence to the experience, thereby making it psychologically acceptable. In the legendary world of Sleepy Hollow, thought, effort, and experience culminate organically in farming, whose natural rhythms (sowing and reaping) become the ideal metaphor for all human activity. But in the fictional world of Rip Van Winkle—and the real world of Washington Irving—this was not the situation. The failure of mind and landscape to merge in harmonious conjunction, and the world's indifference to all longing and desire, made the efficacy of experience doubtful, and not infrequently caused pain and despair; it also posed the problem of whether there was some way to counteract the acute sense of loss that accompanied this recognition. Like Rip, Geoffrey Crayon fashioned a story out of his "adventures" and, paradoxically, by so doing, he was able to make the connections between fact and fiction, between existence in the mutable world and the unchanging foundations of all human endeavor. Experience, therefore, was not lost: it became a story, and the story took its place in the ongoing process of life. And like his alter egos in this sense, Washington Irving also constructed little fictions out of his own experience and quite cleverly made it seem as if they were just a series of sketches that one might come across as he casually flipped through the pages of an artist's sketch pad.

IV

"Rip Van Winkle" and "The Legend of Sleepy Hollow" taken together reinforce the belief that it was fiction itself, rather than any of the illusions that Crayon invented and then sought to perpetuate, that served as Irving's compensation for the loss of, and the failure to make connections to, the past. *The Sketch Book* verifies that Irving did find a measure of aesthetic satisfaction and that he did glimpse the meaning and value of storytelling. Yet one still must wonder how firmly Irving trusted in the ways of the imagination. Although a few years later he would write in a notebook entry that "the muse . . . serves outward[ly] to be my only comfort,"[37] he continued to doubt the efficacy of creative activity to bring order and control to his life. On occasion, in fact, his ambivalence yielded to outright hostility: "The imagination [he wrote in "Mountjoy"] is alternately a cheat and a dupe; nay more, it is the most subtle of cheats, for it cheats itself, and becomes the dupe of its own delusions. It conjures up 'airy nothings,' gives to them a 'local habitation and a name,' and then bows to their control as implicitly as if they were realities."[38] While the bitterness would pass, the changing tone measures his inability to rest securely with his discoveries.

In *The Sketch Book*, Irving dramatized his anxieties about fiction and authorship—and thereby testified to the fact that he could not embrace these absolutely—in "The Art of Book Making." The sketch begins as Crayon, on a peregrination about "the great metropolis" of London, wanders into the reading room of the British Museum. Comparing himself (like Ichabod) to a "Knight errant" about to enter the "portal" of an "enchanted castle," and the black-clothed men he spies about the place to a "body of Magi, deeply engaged in the study of occult sciences," Crayon believes he has stumbled upon an "enchanted library." But the "pale, studious personages, poring intently over dusty volumes, rummaging among mouldy manuscripts, and taking copious notes of their contents" are nothing more than a group of modern authors principally occupied in manufacturing books by borrowing thoughts and sentiments—"classic lore, or 'pure English undefiled'"—from the literature of the past. Crayon's humor turns into revulsion at this instance of shabby pilfering. Subsequently, he falls asleep and dreams that these literary pretenders are metamorphosed into a "ragged, thread bare throng," garmented in leaves of ancient books and manuscripts. Outraged at the plunderers for their scandalous behavior, the nearby hanging portraits of eminent writers suddenly come alive and dispel the parasites. Crayon laughs out loud at these fleeing bookworms, which wakes him from his uneasy dream at the same time that it alerts the librarian, who thereupon dismisses *him* for failing to present the necessary identification for admission (pp. 61–66). In effect, Crayon's imagination self-reflexively expresses Irving's doubts and anxieties about his literary position, as it transforms, in a humorously exaggerated fashion, what he [Crayon] has seen in the reading room into what Irving fears: that the fictional sketches of his experiences, fleshed out by his reworking of the moods, descriptions, and nuances of feeling of his favorite writers (in fact, he himself prefaces at least two-thirds of the sketches with an epigraph from one of these revered authors) were only another form of imitation, similar to the productions of the seedy ragpickers Crayon had envisioned.[39]

Burdened by insecurity over his professional commitment to literature and troubled about the validity of the sketch form he had developed, Irving worried that like the patchwork productions of the "scholars" in the British Museum reading room, his creations did not have a life and meaning of their own. He feared, too, that his process of composing was just one more in-

121

stance of "book making" and that he was a mediocre copy of one of the long line of writers who had described the British scene. And as an American ostensibly commenting upon English manners and customs, Irving could not help but speculate whether he would be viewed as an imposter or a fraud by the British, and as an affected snob by the Americans. The conflict in this particular sketch, however, is temporarily resolved in the same way as many of the other personal problems Irving dealt with in *The Sketch Book*, through comedy and the good-natured mockery of his persona. Once again, the importance of Geoffrey Crayon cannot be overstated: even though he has no "card of admission" to the British Museum reading room, as an original creation he gives to Irving, who heretofore felt that he had no legitimacy as an author, admission to the world of professional letters.

Nevertheless, as an American writer in 1820, Irving was not capable of fully resolving his (or America's) crisis of identity through fiction, since his creations could not provide the sustenance that he sought from the principle of continuity operative in the world. While *The Sketch Book* shows the development of a form that permitted Irving to tell stories about himself and his losses, and illustrates the verification of that process in "Rip" and "Sleepy Hollow," the psychological satisfaction that it brought seemed to him not much more than a small pocket of stability and order, constantly threatened by the large forces of change that surrounded him. As he eventually understood and experienced it, the fight would have to be fought—and the battle would have to be won—again with each book. The solution in *The Sketch Book* to the dilemma of mutability is imaginative, but nagging doubts persisted as to whether there was not yet the possibility of achieving this order through a political or historical solution. Given Irving's particular psychology and American skepticism concerning fiction in the early nineteenth century, one can see why he was not yet willing to declare the world lost and place his trust solely in the imagination. He had not yet exhausted all the constructs that a conservative society like England had to offer.

F O U R

Something Is Lost in the Past
Bracebridge Hall

The search for "home," and the ideological distinctions between a republic and an aristocracy—issues crucial to *The Sketch Book* though diffused—come to the forefront in *Bracebridge Hall*. Once they do, the republican in Irving takes priority, but not, unfortunately, with enough satiric thrust to make *Bracebridge Hall* a genuinely ironic work. Always aware of both his dual British and American audience and current literary taste, Irving tried to divert attention from what might be perceived as the "political" content of his new book. In "The Author," he claims that although he is curious about "the ordinary circumstances incident to an aristocratical state of society," and although at times he might "amuse" himself by "pointing out" some of its "eccentricities," he does not wish to be misconstrued as "pretending to decide upon its political merits." "I am," he declares, "no politician." [1] True enough—nevertheless, one has the distinct feeling that he protests too much. No contemporary reader of *The Sketch Book*—not even the most careful and discriminating of its reviewers—had spotted a political allusion, let alone discovered a hint of political controversy, in the first of Irving's European writings. Why should anyone suspect him of such a motive here? Geoffrey Crayon's inappropriate and unexpected comment suggests Washington Irving's self-consciousness over the fact that his picture of traditional aristocratic society expressed a point of view incongruous with a celebration of its "poetical characteristics." *Bracebridge Hall*, unlike its predecessor, does not express artistic or cultural anxiety, but does hint at political dis-ease.

To be sure, Irving's imagination was genuinely attracted by England's scenery and landscape and stirred by its ancient and venerable institutions. In fact, one could argue along with Allen Guttmann that the ancestral estate, representative of a "Conservative society with a sense of the past," was an "image of value" for him. [2] In "English Country Gentlemen," Crayon says that he appreciates the "rural establishments of the nobility" and the "lesser establishments of the gentry," but only to the extent that they promote and preserve "freedom" and the "virtue and welfare of the nation" (pp. 160, 161). As Hedges has pointed out, Irving was capable of justifying the English "system in theory . . . by appealing to the Burkean and Montesquieuvian conception of the suitability of different social and governmental institutions to different peoples."[3] However, even though he may have intellectually embraced this idea, it is a mistake to assume that he also formed an emotional and imaginative attachment to the hierarchical society or, worse, that he desired to conserve aristocratic values in a rapidly changing American republic. Guttmann misreads the tone and texture of both books when he claims that Irving made a "political commitment" to Old World institutions, that he unequivocally championed the "orderly world of settled society as [he] found it in England."[4] Political commitment encompasses belief, loyalty, and active support, and Irving's veered in the opposite direction. By demonstrating how Squire Bracebridge's moral authority disintegrates as a "growing freedom and activity of opinion" from within his community and an advancing industrialization from without undermine his attempt to preserve order, Irving indicates that the world the Squire tries so desperately to keep alive is distinctly finite. What he shows his American readers, not through the Squire but through the yeoman farmer character, is that they must look not to an English, but to an American, model for an ideal of the stable society.

According to Irving's biographer, the Irish poet Thomas Moore supplied him with the idea for *Bracebridge Hall* by suggesting that he expand *The Sketch Book*'s Christmas sequence, with its delineation of the traditional customs and manners of an English squire firmly established on his country estate in Yorkshire.[5] Now, the story goes, Irving could proceed with his plan to compile another collection—thereby bolstering his reputation and ensuring his continued popularity—since he would have a suitable subject "reminiscent of [*The Sketch Book*] yet sufficiently varied in form and development," one that would enable him to produce an equally substantial volume, but less miscellaneous.[6] However, both the documentary and imaginative evidence fail to support these assumptions. For one, the notebooks from the period, coupled with the fact that some of the sketches and stories were either finished or begun at the time of Moore's inquiry, indicate that Irving had previously fixed upon the life of the ancestral mansion as the focus of his next book.[7] For the other, in *The Sketch Book*, Bracebridge Hall is unique among Geoffrey Crayon's Old World shrines; here, the past truly did live on to nurture and enrich the present. With its "strong rich peculiarities of ancient rural life,"[8] Squire Bracebridge's home promised to satisfy the pilgrim's need for transcendent order and continuity. Since he could not leave England behind until he had imaginatively exhausted its possibilities, Irving places Crayon there as an extended guest, with ample opportunity to sketch every facet that attracts his eye.

I

Context is crucial for understanding the significance of the Bracebridge Hall episode in *The Sketch Book*. Certainly the Squire's example of celebrated English hospitality and his strict adherence to "old rural games and holyday observances" delighted Irving's American audience; like Crayon, they had been reading since childhood of the "traditionary customs of golden hearted antiquity, its feudal hospitalities, and lordly wassailings" (pp. 159, 151). In the three sketches that conclude the series—"Christmas Eve," "Christmas Day," and "The Christmas Dinner"—Crayon witnesses (as Irving fabricates) the England of his dreams. Christmas eve at the Squire's house is celebrated by the burning of the Yule clog (a great log lighted with the residue of last year's clog) and Christmas candle, the hanging of the mistletoe, the singing of old Christmas songs, the dancing of "the heel and toe, rigadoon, and other graces of the ancient school," and the calling upon the waits (bands of local musicians) from the neighboring village to deliver the soft strains of music which conclude the festivities. Christmas Day brings more carols, a breakfast of "old English fare," and a church service in the nearby village, complete with orchestra and choir. The sketch ends with an exuberant dance by the village rustics, a "fanciful exhibition" which the Squire eyes with great interest and delight. Good cheer and affability fill the air, and the merriment carries over to the Christmas dinner. In front of a "blazing crackling fire" and a sideboard set out with a sumptuous display of dishes, Crayon watches as the feast turns into a pageant: the traditional meal, which begins with the appearance of a pig's head (supposed to represent the boar's head, "a dish formerly served up with much ceremony and the sound of minstrelsy and song, at great tables on Christmas day" [p. 182]) and ends with the disappearance of the Wassail Bowl, yields to a "burlesque imitation of an ancient masque," climaxing the evening in high frolic. Excited by the "scenes of whim and innocent gayety passing before [him]," Crayon clearly appreciates the re-creation of an old-fashioned tradition and identifies with the Squire, who oversees the activities "with the simple relish of childish delight." Interestingly, the word "childish" harks back to the order of the previous generation and suggests that the Squire (perhaps anachronistically) extends into the present what pleased him about the past.

But underneath the surface revelry a subtle and far more serious development is taking place, one that concerns both Crayon's status as Old World pilgrim and the implications of his attraction to life at the ancestral mansion. In "Christmas," the first piece of the series, despite the prevailing conviviality, an air of melancholy descends upon Crayon, which derives only in part from his disappointment over the passing away of the "ancient and festive honours" that once universally accompanied the celebration of Christmas. Mostly, Crayon suffers from loneliness, from the fact that he shares only vicariously in the pleasures of the season. While he values the "home feeling . . . which holds so powerful a place in every English bosom," no home awaits him: "stranger and sojourner as I am in the land—. . . for me no social hearth may blaze, no hospitable roof throw open its doors, nor the warm grasp of friendship welcome me at the threshold." Though he tries to salvage a measure of holiday feeling for himself by claiming that "happiness is reflective," it is a mere fragment to shore against his ruined spirit. He possesses but the "*idea* of home, fraught with the fragrance of home dwelling joys" (p. 152; my italics). The word "home" may appear often as both noun and adjective yet, once again, imagination provides his only comfort.

Thus, in the following sketch, when Crayon is rescued from his solitary fate by Frank Bracebridge's invitation to spend the holidays at his father's country seat, *The Sketch Book*'s reader feels a great sense of relief. This paves the way for stronger emotions, primarily admiration and respect for Squire Bracebridge. An active, vital figure, a source of productivity and growth, the Squire husbands his resources, raises and provides for his family, and cultivates venerable traditions because he believes that his sons will grow to be better men and truer Englishmen in an atmosphere reminiscent of ancient rural life. As they were maturing, he "ma[d]e his children feel that home was the happiest place in the world"; indeed, it is precisely the Squire's ability to create this "delicious home feeling"—"one of the choicest gifts a parent could bestow," according to young Frank Bracebridge (p. 161)—that endears him to Crayon more than any of his other accomplishments. Comparing him to the "sun of a system, beaming warmth and gladness to every heart," Crayon confesses that he "had not been seated many minutes by the comfortable hearth of the worthy old cavalier, before I found myself as much at home as if I had been one of the family" (p. 164). Nowhere else in *The Sketch Book* does he make

126

such a claim. Thus, not only does the Bracebridge Hall sequence offer Irving's readers an opportunity to share in Crayon's good fortune; it also invites them, however subliminally and temporarily, to consider the viability of the ancestral mansion as an actual mode of living.

At the end of his introduction to the new book, *Bracebridge Hall*, Crayon declares that he has not discovered the world to be "all that it has been represented by sneering cynics and whining poets"; "I cannot," he adds, "believe this to be so very bad a world as it is represented" (p. 7). But no world was ever an evil place for the optimistic Geoffrey Crayon. In *The Sketch Book*, England is a country whose ordering traditions he perceives but cannot share. By contrast, Bracebridge Hall represents an ideal society whose values are both permanent and available, whose very existence denies the mutability that triumphs everywhere else in *The Sketch Book*. A stable, harmonious home, where even the animals are "confident of kindness and protection," forms the nucleus of the Squire's "system" but, as Irving was well aware, that system exemplifies a purely hierarchical conception of order. He may not have agreed with Thomas Jefferson that privilege breeds corruption;[9] nevertheless, he had to wonder if a republican could accommodate himself to an environment where a member of the gentry, no matter how venerable his family, receives "almost feudal homage" from the neighboring village.

Earlier in *The Sketch Book* Irving had used the metaphor of landscape gardening to indicate the kind of control the English assert over their society; here it serves to highlight the Squire's "proud aristocracy." Since his imagination belongs to the sixteenth and seventeenth centuries, "when England was itself," the Squire has, with proper homage to literary tradition, arranged the grounds about his house with "formal terraces, heavily moulded ballustrades, and clipped yew trees" (p. 171). Moreover, as much as he admires this "obsolete finery" in gardening—"courtly and noble," it has an "air of magnificence . . . befitting good old family style"—he deplores even more the current imitation of nature, the result of "republican notions." Totally unsuited for a monarchical government, this modern form of gardening "smack[s] of the levelling system." While Frank Bracebridge assures Crayon that his father never meddles with politics, the Squire's preferences nevertheless have political import, however submerged it may be in *The Sketch Book*.

The place where such meaning does rise to the surface involves the one aspect of aristocracy Crayon cannot ignore—the subservient role assigned to the peasantry. The Squire may indeed assert a benevolent authority, but part of his reason for promulgating the old-fashioned amusements among the lower orders is to keep the villagers and servants, upon whom he depends for the smooth running of his estate, content with their lot. "'Our old games and local customs,'" he declares, "'had a great effect in making the peasant fond of his home, and the promotion of them by the gentry made him fond of his lord'" (p. 177). Although he believes he has their best interests at heart, more than a little condescension enters his voice—he values and longs to preserve the "simple, true hearted peasantry." Unfortunately, "'[t]he nation is altered'"; the peasants "'have broken asunder from the higher classes, and seem to think their interests are separate.'" It is difficult "'to keep them in good humour in these hard times,'" the Squire bemoans, for "'they have become too knowing, and begin to read newspapers, listen to ale house politicians, and talk of reform.'" (Perhaps subconsciously, Irving in this passages recalls the situation of black slaves on American plantations.) Directly, Crayon neither responds to these lamentations nor passes judgment on the Squire's belief that the status quo could be maintained if the nobility and gentry would spend increased time on their estates, "mingl[ing] more among the country people." Subtly, however, so as not to mar the smooth exterior of his canvas, he undercuts these images by relating how the Squire once tried to put his principles into practice by keeping open house during the holidays, but was undone when the country people thwarted him by refusing to play their roles properly. As a result, "many uncouth circumstances occurred," and "the manor was overrun by all the vagrants of the country." In addition, on Christmas Day when the Squire visits the villagers and is toasted by them, Crayon notices that a few of the younger ones grimace and wink to each other as he turns his back.

Beyond these few instances, however, the possibility of public discontent remains unexamined; since he lives in an isolated part of the country with no "rival gentry" nearby, the Squire's authority remains unchallenged. Nor does Crayon give even so much as a passing nod to the Squire's allusion to "these hard times." Because he wants to preserve the good feeling generated during his brief stay at the Hall, he accepts the Squire's eccentric ways and whimsical pastimes as merely adjuncts to his kind nature. Moreover, as Hedges has pointed out, the two comic characters Irving created as foils to the Squire—Master Simon, his factotum, and the parson, his old school chum at Oxford now living on his estate—are not developed enough to undermine the validity of his purposes. Both are connected to the emphasis on tradition so vital to the Christmas sketches, but neither understands its intrinsic nature or the value it holds for the Squire. The one an amusing functionary, the other a zealous pedant, together they represent the unenlightened attitudes and stagnant mode of thinking which an excessive loyalty to the past produces. In *The Sketch Book*, rather than explore the issues which cluster about these figures, Crayon prefers to wear the holiday mask, perceiving not, in Hedges's words, "the threat of dryness and sterility in the behavior of Simon and the parson,"[10] but instead taking blind refuge in the order and serenity of the Squire's household.

II

At the outset of *Bracebridge Hall*, Crayon reintroduces the Squire before he takes up the questions that were only hinted at in *The Sketch Book*. The prime mover in a patriarchical system, an English gentleman of sound judgment and good feeling, excellent father, master, and landlord, he represents the highest ideals of British character, especially as they are delineated in the sketch "English Country Gentlemen" (pp. 157–62): "considerate in . . . temper," "appreciating whatever is manly and honourable," "methodical and orderly," "fond of established customs" and "long established names." Most of all, he exhibits "that love of order and quiet which characterizes the nation, giv[ing] a vast influence to the descendants of the old families." A "republican by birth, principles, and habits," as Donald Ringe has written, and not one to bow to titled authority by virtue alone of its title (as he says in "Forest Trees"), Crayon nevertheless respects the Squire as a "gentleman landholder" because he possesses "a generous mind" and "selflessly assumes the social responsibility that his rank entails."[11]

The locus of stability in the Squire's domain is the Hall itself; because of his passionate devotion to the ways of antiquity, it has become a "secluded specimen of English housekeeping in something like the genuine old style" (p. 9). The significance of this unfolds as Irving moves easily through the first few expository sketches. Patterned on a tradition that has reconfirmed its essential meaning by providing a sense of harmony for all those who adhere to it, Bracebridge Hall embodies the belief that a stable social structure acts as a means of controlling the inevitable flow of time by affording a proper direction and an appropriate end toward which it is to be channeled. Family history and the manor itself (including the attendant customs and manners) coalesce into an all-encompassing unity: to keep the house going is to preserve the family, and to preserve the family is to protect the values and beliefs on which the tradition and, inevitably, the order, are founded. Achieving this demands an enormous expenditure of psychic energy, since it requires nothing less than the bonding and active loyalty of all the social classes, but it does offer recom-

129

pense: the union of physical entity (Bracebridge Hall) and lineal heritage (though in effect it functions as a spiritual one) serves to seal off family, servants, and, ideally, villagers, from radical and disruptive influences. The ancestral mansion has not survived by accommodating itself to a mutable, dynamic world; rather, it has, in the fundamental sense of the word, "established" itself as a fortress against it. In effect, Bracebridge Hall dominates time.

Continuity depends, therefore, on whether the forces of change can be withstood and whether, under such pressures, the Squire can maintain the special structure he has fashioned within the system he cherishes. Primarily, both the servants and villagers must be willing to play the particular roles he has chosen for them. Most of the former, like the housekeeper, have never traveled more than twenty miles from the Hall, therefore retaining a genuine ignorance of the ways of the larger world and, not surprisingly, fully embracing the Squire's whimsies. But the latter have begun to exhibit some resistance to his demands that they cooperate in the festivities that provide him with "agreeable associations" and transform his surroundings into "a little world of poetry." In "May-Day Customs" (pp. 174–77), for example, Crayon says that although May-Day "is regularly celebrated in the neighboring village, yet it has been merely resuscitated by the worthy squire, and is kept up in a forced state of existence at his expense." Obviously, "a forced state of existence" runs contrary to the spirit of Bracebridge Hall in which Crayon had previously rejoiced. The villagers do not share the Squire's longing for an idealized rural life, nor do they understand his predilection for old games and sports; most certainly, they have no desire to adhere to outmoded means of agriculture and travel. The sense of responsibility the Squire feels to the past, to retrieving what is valuable and worthy of preservation, means little to them. Knowing that the land, its resources, and the fealty to a way of life have passed in unbroken succession from father to son, creating in each generation the belief that it serves as a vital link between past and future, the Squire interprets his duty as the bequeathing of these values to his posterity. His revival of ancient pastimes signifies his commitment to this order and reflects his hereditary state of consciousness. But the peasants do not comprehend his purposes and, for the most part, accommodate his wishes so that they may reap the benefits of his charity.

For these reasons, and because their immediate sphere does not fall within the inner circle of the mansion and the estate, they are susceptible to, and fall prey to, outside influences. Theoretically, the isolation of Bracebridge Hall protects all from the encroachment of the present, but practically the Squire

130

meets with "continual discouragements" because the peasantry have become "too knowing for simple enjoyment." The "happy simplicity" that once supported such customs as the May-Day celebration has vanished. Thus, Crayon agrees with the Squire that a change in English character has occurred, and attempts to account for the loss of joviality, and for the disintegrating authority of the gentry in the face of the upheavals brought by the Industrial Revolution, by reflecting, in "English Gravity" (pp. 166–69), on the "growing hardships of the times" which have forced most people to turn their full attention to securing "the means of subsistence." Once again, contrary to the predominant critical opinion, Irving was conscious of the troubled social conditions of contemporary England. "You have no idea of the distress and misery that prevails in this country," he wrote Brevoort in 1816, "it is beyond the power of description: In America you have financial difficulties, the embarrassments of trade & the distress of merchants but here you have what is far worse, the distress of the poor—not merely mental sufferings—but the absolute miseries of nature—Hunger, nakedness, wretchedness of all kinds that the labouring people in this country are liable to." While here his observations are directed primarily toward the cities, he knew (as we shall soon see) that the country people were also affected. Of course, Irving had no answers— "How this country is to extricate itself from its present embarrassments, how it is to emerge from the poverty that seems to be overwhelming it, and how the government is to quiet the multitudes that are already turbulent & clamorous, and are yet but in the beginning of their real miseries, I cannot conceive"[12]—but in *Bracebridge Hall*, unlike in *The Sketch Book*, these failures of the English system become the covert subject of his text.

Yet in "English Gravity" he also acknowledges that the ancient customs and manners which once animated English life flourished at a time when the common people had relatively few of the comforts and conveniences that they presently enjoy. Perhaps, then, the loss of simplicity and "vivacity" constitutes but one result of the sense of acquisitiveness that has developed in the wake of expanding trade and manufacturing—"the universal spirit of gain, and the calculating habits that commerce has introduced." Neither of these explanations satisfies Crayon, however; nor does he accept the Squire's accusation that the infiltrating mores of the city are to blame, though in "May-Day Customs" he does agree that "the country apes the manners and amusements of the town." Rather, he believes that the changes the Squire perceives are part of a larger and more fundamental alteration in the relation of the social classes to one another—that, in effect, a long-standing decorum and mutual respect among the orders has already begun to deteriorate. Nowhere does he display his fierce regard for free institutions more than when he attributes the change in English character to "the gradual increase of the liberty of the subject." As restrictions on education and mobility diminish, and as the access to information increases, the individual becomes more capable of self-generated thought and desires to act as an independent citizen, which means a willingness to accept a larger share of the responsibility, both for himself and the community. Amusement no longer preoccupies him; as the possibility grows for discussion of "grave" and "lofty" themes, people are less inclined to allow "trifles" to assume the importance they once held, to "occupy the craving activity of intellect." A seriousness of manner and an expanding social consciousness accompany the free exercise of thought. In *Bracebridge Hall*, these ideas operate as a major informing principle; since Irving had witnessed the burgeoning of such attitudes among the lower orders, Crayon carefully sketches into his picture of rural life the peasants' withdrawal of their former, albeit unconscious, acceptance of a prearranged scenario. Their perspective, missing in the Christmas sketches, occupies an important place in the new collection.

In the early views of "The Hall" (pp. 8–10) and "Family Servants" (pp. 15–19), Crayon had implied that the Squire maintains his authority chiefly because the old manor house stood in such a retired part of Yorkshire, away from the decadence of the cities, which he later calls the centers of "political intrigues and heartless dissipations" (p. 161). But in "A Village Politician" (pp. 187–90), he shows that the state of blissful ignorance preferred by the Squire is gone forever. Against the tranquil, indolent setting of the village inn, Crayon introduces the "radical," "a thin, loquacious fellow," who "has but recently found his way into the village, where he threatens to commit fearful devastations with his doctrines." Into an atmosphere thick with gossip, the radical introduces contemporary political and economic issues and "shock[s] several of the stanchest villagers by talking lightly of the squire and his family; and hinting that . . . the [Squire's] park should be cut up into small farms and kitchen-gardens, or feed good mutton instead of worthless deer." His success may be measured by the fact that he has already made some "converts" among the townspeople, shaken the faith of others, and even aroused a few of the oldest ones, "who had never thought about politics, or scarce any thing else during their whole lives." The real threat posed by the radical, and his significance in *Bracebridge Hall*, is that as a champion of reform he has sown doubt among the villagers, hoping they will see that their unthinking devotion to outmoded customs constitutes their political oppression. Undeniably, political consciousness has made its way permanently into the village, an event no republican can regret.

"A Village Politician" clearly indicates that in *Bracebridge Hall* Irving was exposing the failure of the institutions of the past to deal effectively with the dilemmas of the present. Without addressing the issues as an essayist or a social thinker might, he does identify the problems that plagued England in the early 1800s—widespread unemployment, low wages, high prices, and taxes. The "ominous words" the radical spews forth—"'taxes,'" "'poor's rates,'" and "'agricultural distress'"—refer to the two major sources of contention among the English people. The "corn laws," the first of these, were regulations restricting the export and import of grain. Specifically, the corn law of 1815 was designed to maintain high prices and prevent an agricultural depression after the Napoleonic Wars. Consumers and laborers strenuously objected, but to little avail (presumably, of course, agricultural workers would benefit from its maintenance); it was finally the criticism of the manufacturers, that the law hampered industrialization by subsidizing agriculture, that proved most effective for its repeal in 1846. The second great annoyance was the "poor law," a common name for legislation relating to public assistance. From about 1700, workhouses were established where the poor were expected to support themselves by labor; however, because of widespread unemployment and low wages, it became customary in the late eighteenth century to provide home relief. The "poor's rate" assessed the people for this support. The poor laws were extremely unpopular: in 1797, for example, the *Monthly Magazine* was writing about "the exorbitant poor-rates with which the public there have been burthened for some time past."[13]

Appropriately, the village politician alludes to these issues, since discussion of them was widespread in the early 1820s. It is also fitting that he reads newspapers, still considered a rather vulgar source of entertainment and information, and distributes and quotes from pamphlets, a sure sign of political involvement. That in identifying the radical Master Simon should turn to Crayon and exclaim "'That's a radical! he reads Cobbett!'" is also in keeping with the times, for as editor of *Cobbett's Political Register* from 1802–35, William Cobbett was recognized as a political activist and free-speaking man. He discussed, sometimes vehemently, all the major issues of the day, and was actively involved in the heated debates over the "corn laws" and the "poor law"; in several of his "Rural Rides," in fact, he argued strenuously for a repeal of the corn laws.[14]

Crayon's response indicates Irving's reluctant acceptance of the changes presaged by the radical's appearance in the village. His initial description of the agitator—"meagre, but active in his make, with a long, pale, bilious face; a black beard, so ill-shaven as to bloody his shirt-collar, a feverish eye, and a hat sharpened up at the sides into a most pragmatical shape"—is tinged with disdain because he disapproves of the radical's comportment and his lack of a positive program to alleviate the ills he discloses. Basically, he is a force of negativity; yet those who would oppose him appear woefully inadequate for the debate. The Squire is saddened by the introduction of politics into the village, and is fearful that it will be turned into "an unhappy, thinking community." And Master Simon, "who has hitherto been able to sway the political opinions of the place, without much cost of learning or logic," exhibits both awe and horror in the radical's presence. He studiously avoids a confrontation with him and merely puzzles over how to regain the trust and confidence of the peasants and overturn the "heresies" that the radical has implanted in their minds. Thus, the radical's assertions primarily go unanswered. The calm air about the village has been permanently disturbed.

The Squire's program to restore vitality to English life through local participation in the games, sports, and pastimes that he promotes receives another serious threat in "English Gravity," where the forces at work undermining his attempts at renewal are the utilitarian values and pedestrian outlook of the rising middle class. Mr. Faddy represents the expanding commercial element in English society—a retired wealthy manufacturer who, "having accumulated a large fortune by dint of steam-engines and spinning jennies," has moved into the neighborhood and set up for a gentleman. He thwarts the Squire's plans because "he has brought into the country with him all the practical maxims of town, and the bustling habits of business; and is one of those sensible, useful, prosing, troublesome, intolerable old gentlemen that go about wearying and worrying society with excellent plans for public utility."[15] (Of course the Squire never acknowledges what the reader senses: Faddy is "new money" presuming to equal "old money.") Since he believes in profitable and maximizing measures, he has modernized his country seat, enforced the vagrant laws, persecuted the gypsies (whom the Squire favors because they also enjoy his beloved sports), and has even endeavored to suppress country wakes and holiday games. He encourages sober industry in the neighborhood rather than idle frolicking and thus directly challenges the Squire on one of his pet projects, the May-Day revels. Though Faddy has no use for tradition, and though he displays "the ostentation of newly acquired consequence," Crayon recognizes that some of his ideas are worthy of attention. But for the Squire, who believes that progress will engulf whatever richness and imaginativeness rural life still retains, Faddy symbolizes the overwhelming evil of that great monster, the Industrial Revolution. In a long tirade addressed to Crayon, he presents his vision of the urban future as something approaching Milton's description of Hell:

> "I have stood on the ruins of Dudley Castle, and looked round, with an aching heart, on what were once its feudal domains of verdant and beautiful country. Sir, I beheld a mere campus phlegrae; a region of fire; reeking with coal-pits, and furnaces, and smelting-houses, vomiting forth flames and smoke. The pale and ghastly people, toiling among vile exhalations, looked more like demons than human beings; the clanking wheels and engines, seen through the murky atmosphere, looked like instruments of torture in this pandemonium. What is to become of the country with these evils rankling in its very core? Sir, these manufacturers will be the ruin of our rural manners; they will destroy the national character; they will not leave materials for a single line of poetry!" (p. 167)

The Squire's speech approaches incantation: bypassing reason and courting gothic excess, it has little relevance to the particular situation. Crayon dismisses it as a "whimsical lamentation over national industry and public improvement," yet he still sympathizes with the Squire in his grief that "this will soon become a mere matter of fact world, where life will be reduced to a mathematical calculation of conveniences." As Crayon acknowledges, the feasts and festivals, holiday revels and celebrations, are disappearing forever; the gaiety of dress that once prevailed in all ranks of society and made the streets so fine and picturesque has given way to the dull garb of the industrial worker. The Squire rants about this intolerable situation, but as Crayon recognizes, it is one thing to lament the passing of old traditions and quite another to believe you can resist it, that you can stave off the inevitable destruction wrought by time. *Bracebridge Hall* testifies to Irving's having accepted what the Squire refuses to concede: the past cannot be relived in the present.

Crayon's identification with the Squire, therefore, is mitigated by the latter's excesses, which stimulate Irving's talent for various forms of quasi-satirical humor. Whereas in *The Sketch Book* Crayon was often the unwitting dupe of his romantic desires and expectations, and thus was himself the *raison d'être* for the comic mockery, here the wit, irony, and overstatement make him realize the demise of the life he has been sketching. In fact, continuation of the sketch form allows Irving flexibility in shifting point of view and tone. In

"May-Day Customs," to cite one example, the Squire, "like a monarch witnessing the murder of one of his liege subjects," becomes irate over the felling of a beloved tree for a May-pole, yet instead of commiserating with him and sharing the agony he suffers, Crayon describes his reponses in mock-heroic terms: "He could not contemplate the prostrate tree . . . without indulging in lamentation, and making a kind of funeral eulogy, like Mark Anthony over the body of Caesar; and he forbade that any tree should thenceforward be cut down on his estate without a warrant from himself; being determined, he said, to hold the sovereign power of life and death in his own hands" (pp. 174–75). The desire to husband the resources of the forest is certainly a noble one, but as with so many of his loyalties and allegiances, the Squire knows no moderation: he actually sets himself up as a *divine* sovereign. The exaggeration in Crayon's choice of images perfectly matches the more extreme aspects of the Squire's behavior; in addition, he also pokes at royalty with the word "sovereign," since the ironic metaphor cuts both ways. There is, after all, no higher representative of the aristocratic ideal than the king himself.

In fact, the metaphor resonates with even greater meaning when, in "Travelling" (pp. 222–26), Crayon again compares the Squire to a monarch. In this sketch the Squire rails against modern conveniences of transportation such as coaches, which bring, in the persons of enterprising tourists, the follies and fashions of the town to the remotest parts of the country, thus corrupting English rural manners. But Crayon implies that what he really wishes for are the days when, due to the dangers and inconveniences along the road, far less traveling occurred, so that each village was a completely self-contained entity. As a result, "the lord of the manor was then a kind of monarch in the little realm around him." "He held his court in his paternal hall, and was looked up to with almost as much loyalty and deference as the king himself." Thus, the irony extends to yet another level: in the earlier sketch, the Squire's assumption of a kingly posture over trees was humorous because inappropriate to the circumstances, and laughter is the proper response; in the later sketch, however, his presumption turns out to be a serious one, and it is no longer funny. In the first, control over his estate is the issue; in the second, it is power over people's lives. Journeying on aristocratic soil, the good republican Irving treads lightly: only his metaphors and allusions leave the incriminating imprints.

In the final summation, after all the unmanageable projects (like trying to revive the art of falconry, in "Hawking"), and embarrassing mishaps (such as the incarceration—for sheep stealing—and escape of Starlight Tom, leader of the Squire's beloved gypsies, in "The Culprit"), Crayon dismisses the Squire's attempt to maintain the Hall as a "little world within itself" as nothing more serious than the "rid[ing of] his hobby" (pp. 223, 202). The word "hobby," in fact, appears several times—on one occasion Crayon describes the Squire's diversion as a "whimsical, yet harmless hobby" (p. 175)—so that by the time we get to "Travelling" and read of the Squire's obsession with horseback journeys as his "jog-trot hobby" (p. 222), we realize that in a figurative way we are in the ever-delightful but implausible realm of *Tristram Shandy*, with the Squire as an ineffective Uncle Toby, whose efforts at dealing with the present are just so much riding of hobbyhorses.[16] The literary allusion is an apt one, not just because it provides a way for Crayon gently to withdraw his support of the Squire, or because it brings vividly into focus the latter's unrealistic pursuit of ancient pastimes as "the vehement desire to play with a new toy" (p. 75). It also points to the fact that beyond its "humourous" quality, the Squire's domain attracts Crayon because it is eccentric and imaginative. (Interestingly, the word "humour" appears so often in relation to the Squire that its archaic meaning cannot be overlooked, as if he had been victimized by an excess of one of his bodily fluids. This echo, therefore, links him back linguistically and philosophically to the medieval world of Chaucer.) Like the self-absorbed Uncle Toby, the Squire is essentially harmless and basically well-meaning—also creative, fond of lyrical moments, and a source of comic inspiration (much as Uncle Toby was for Tristram). But no matter how long Crayon sojourned at Bracebridge Hall—or Irving remained immersed in the writing of *Bracebridge Hall*—he understood that a real world existed beyond the fictional one, a world necessitating accommodation (something the Squire refuses to consider) to new ideas and disturbing changes that inevitably will occur, one of the lessons of "Rip Van Winkle."

Although the book ends with a wedding, the traditional symbol of harmony and union, the climax occurs earlier, in "May-Day" (pp. 196–202), where furious confusion reigns. As the celebration of the rites of spring breaks down, the structure the Squire has labored mightily to build collapses. Though the festivities have been carefully arranged and all the accouterments gathered, and though the dances and games begin according to plan, forces outside the Squire's control once again exert themselves. Peace is first disrupted by the appearance of the radical and some of his disciples, who decry "these idle nonsensical amusements in times of public distress" when the country is troubled and people are starving. Master Simon and General Harbottle, one of the Squire's guests, attempt to engage him in debate, the General believing that, without doubt, "a look and a word from a gentleman would be sufficient to shut up so shabby an orator." Significantly, the radical merely increases his tirade and neither Simon's "excursive manner," which usually works with the villagers, nor the General's ballooning pomposity can silence him. Insisting on facts instead of overblown rhetoric, the radical dumbfounds his two antagonists, and they are forced into an embarrassing retreat in the presence of several of Simon's followers, "who had always looked up to him as infallible." Crayon openly aligns himself with neither side, but Irving's animated and vibrant language expresses his persona's delight with the proceedings: The General, says Crayon, "found himself betrayed into a more serious action than his dignity could brook; and looked like a mighty Dutch Indiaman grievously peppered by a petty privateer. It was in vain that he swelled and looked big; and talked large, and endeavoured to make up by pomp of manner for poverty of matter; every home-thrust of the radical made him wheeze like a bellows, and seemed to let a volume of wind out of him." While the radical is never praised, his foes become objects of laughter and scorn.

It is quite characteristic of Irving's method that we do not hear the arguments by which the radical overwhelms the two worthies from the Hall, as if the specific issues are in some way beyond the question at hand. The old order is so tenuous, he seems to be saying, that the radical's presence alone can disturb the proceedings. In addition, Irving did not want to issue too strong a political statement. Once the initial agitation occurs, however, it is not long before the entire festival crumbles. After the Queen of the May makes a shambles of the ceremonial highlight of the day, a wrestling match between a villager and an athlete from a rival hamlet erupts into a large-scale brawl, with the festivities thrown into complete chaos. Some of the more important townspeople become embroiled in the battle, but the entire village stands aghast when members of the Squire's household, including some of the higher servants, participate in the fight. The Squire is "grievously scandalized" over the disgrace of his May-Day fete.

The May-Day events represent a culminating moment in *Bracebridge Hall*, for they finally and fully expose a weakness in the Squire's system that has been lurking in the background throughout the series of sketches: the fallibility of the individual—and in turn of his entire class—upon whose character, integrity, and actions the stability of a hierarchical order depends. In this respect the scene may be viewed as the final part of a satiric progression that began about a quarter of the way through the book in the sketch "Forest

Trees" (pp. 57–60). As Crayon walks through the colonnade of stately oaks that leads to the Squire's house, he has an Emersonian vision: "There is a serene and settled majesty in woodland scenery," he writes, "that enters into the soul, and dilates and elevates it, and fills it with noble inclinations." Wondering if, in such an environment, human character could be as noble and sturdy as the oaks that surround him, and "noticing with what taste and discrimination, and [with] what strong, unaffected interest" English gentlemen will speak of rural concerns, he sees a link between this observation and his vision: it is the landed gentry who are capable of fulfilling his dream of human grandeur exerting itself in a simple, pure existence, but one that is nevertheless inherently high-minded. The oak, therefore, becomes "an emblem of what a true nobleman *should be*; a refuge for the weak, a shelter for the oppressed, a defence for the defenceless" (original italics).

Midway through the text (in "English Country Gentlemen"), Crayon pauses to consider the chief duty of the English gentleman living on his hereditary estate, which is to oversee the well-being of his community; that is, "to study the interests, and conciliate the affections, and instruct the opinions and champion the rights" of the lower orders. In this way, those belonging to the well-educated and highly privileged class reciprocate for the advantageous position into which they have been born and for the sustenance they derive from the labor of the common people. But as Crayon realizes, he was merely "indulging in an Utopian dream," since he has found that the "fine estates" are too often "mortgaged," and the owners "exiled from their paternal lands." Rather than "honourable independence and elegant leisure," "extravagance," "lavish expenditure," "senseless competition," and "heedless, joyless dissipation" characterize the upper ranks. Having declared that "the virtue and welfare of the nation" depend on "the rural habits of the English nobility and gentry," Crayon discovers that they have ceased to "discharge their duties on their patrimonial possessions." They have forgotten the "positive nature of their duties" in the midst of their "self-indulgence" in foreign lands, "expending upon thankless strangers the wealth so hardly drained from their laborious peasantry." The seriousness of their responsibility and, therefore, the magnitude of the failure, are shown in the repetition of the word "duties."

About three-quarters of the way into the book, the republican in Irving takes over as Crayon offers another figurative view of the landed gentry, far more devastating than his previous unclouded condemnation. In a sketch entitled "The Rookery" (pp. 191–95), he pokes fun at the upper classes who, as Hedges has pointed out, are "allegorize[d] . . . as little better than scavenger birds, for all their pretensions to dignity."[17] Although the Squire looks upon the rooks as a "very ancient and honourable line of gentry, highly aristocratical in their notions, fond of place, and attached to church and state," Crayon renders the scene of their nest-building with mock-heroic grandeur: "Nor must I avoid mentioning, what, I grieve to say, rather derogates from the grave and honourable character of these ancient gentlefolk, that, during the architectural season, they are subject to great dissensions among themselves; that they make no scruple to defraud and plunder each other; and that sometimes the rookery is a scene of hideous brawl and commotion, in consequence of some delinquency of the kind." Moreover, like the ancient nobility and gentry to whom they are implicitly compared, they have the "true baronial spirit of the good old feudal times," namely, that "they are apt now and then to issue forth from their castles on a foray, and to lay the plebian fields of the neighbouring country under contribution." Despite some attractive qualities and a few ambitious moments in which they display a certain measure of industriousness, the rooks are essentially useless—they have a "happy holiday life of it" for they literally have nothing to do.

The satire reaches its climax when, late each May, the villagers gather about the old church, where a colony of rooks has taken nest, and do their best to kill the young ones who have just begun awkward flight—this, in spite of their awareness of the Squire's regard for the birds. Every now and then someone manages to bag a "squab rook," which "comes to the ground with the emphasis of a squashed apple-dumpling." The delight of Crayon's phrasing mirrors the pleasure the villagers derive from this pastime, and one deliberately has to look the other way to avoid seeing in these actions the peasants' repressed antagonism toward their "betters."

With the shift in metaphor from oak to rook (leading into the "May-Day" fiasco), Crayon diminishes the gentry and therefore destroys the ideal of the English ancestral mansion; all that has been implied by the Squire's belief in old customs is no more than a dream of the past. Moreover, there is something fiercely American about the way he kills off the gentry: the particular zest and exuberance with which he pronounces their demise, and the comic mockery he resorts to as the old order proves unable to maintain itself in the face of onrushing change, are manifestations of his American identity and bias. (Irving's comic tone here anticipates Twain's in *Innocents Abroad*.) This system is doomed to failure, Irving ultimately concludes, because of an inherent weakness in its structure, depending for its survival as it does on the subservience of one class to another. The whole movement of the book, therefore, betrays a predisposition toward American institutions and implies a democratic belief that individuals cannot be held down indefinitely. Having found England's cultural traditions unattainable in *The Sketch Book*, Irving now judges them to be unattractive, unacceptable. In 1822, rejecting Britain's social and political structure as an anachronistic remnant of a feudal past, he still had not located a home for the spirit.

III

Irving had to go to England in order to see America more clearly. That is why, contrary to Hedges's belief, the book does not "simply delight in disorder," although Crayon does find release in the heightened language and exaggerated imagery he uses to characterize the May-Day disruption. But in that sketch, tranquillity is finally restored to the stormy scene by the yeoman farmer, Ready Money Jack Tibbets, who makes his way into the throng and enforces peace through the sheer assertion of his firm, masculine authority. In this respect, he is quite the opposite of a character like Rip. Significantly, when strong leadership becomes necessary, it is not a member of the gentry who acts to reestablish order, but Jack, a small, sturdy, independent, middle-class farmer. In fact, Hedges has argued that Jack is the hero of *Bracebridge Hall*, the true center of "social and political authority."[18] This critical path is not only correct, but can be taken one step further. Indeed, Jack represents the new social order: as the principal stabilizing force in his society, with no aristocratic yearnings, liberal, sensible, and, above all, virtuous, Ready Money Jack is Irving's English version of the yeoman farmer championed by Thomas Jefferson and reclaimed by Andrew Jackson as the source and strength of an American agrarian republic. The historical connections are meaningful, especially because *Bracebridge Hall* highlighted the figure of the yeoman at a time when Americans were becoming conscious of a void in their society and were beginning to exhibit a longing that would grow increasingly more pronounced during Jackson's years: to reaffirm the values of a "golden age in which liberty and progress" were inextricably linked to basic republican virtues.[19] Whereas Jefferson had primarily viewed the enemy as European privilege and sophistication and continually worried about the transplantation to America of a European aristocracy (which he identified with federalism), Jackson saw the threat arising from the privileged monied classes within American society who propagated the evils of acquisition, consumption, promotion, and speculation. Interestingly, the landed gentry of *Bracebridge Hall* manifest many of these negative traits.

While Irving organized his book around Squire Bracebridge, he lavished narrative attention on Ready Money Jack. In a sketch that bears the yeoman's name (pp. 36–39), Crayon emphasizes Jack's many admirable qualities, chief among which is his substantiality, in both prowess and lineage. Like Brom Bones, as a young man he roared about the neighborhood and, athletically gifted, "was the village champion, carried off the prize at all the fairs, and threw his gauntlet at the country round." The old people still talk about his exploits; again like Brom, he remains their hero. Even more importantly, neither tenant nor laborer, Jack is "descended from a line of farmers that had always lived on the same spot, and owned the same property." Thus, equal in some ways to Squire Bracebridge, Ready Money Jack Tibbets represents stability, continuity, and union with the land, but unlike the Squire, he depends upon no man to do his labor. Once he succeeded to his paternal domains, he became an "industrious, thrifty farmer," a veritable Baltus Van Tassel (the liberal-hearted landowner of "Sleepy Hollow") in English dress. Irving knew that his American audience would recognize in his portrait of the English yeoman the virtues celebrated by, among others, Jefferson and Crèvecoeur: not, as Richard Hofstadter has explained, "the capacity to exploit opportunities and make money," but "honest industry," "independence," a "frank spirit of equality," and the "ability to produce and enjoy a simple abundance."[20] Jack "saw to everything himself," Crayon writes; "put his own hand to the plough; worked hard; ate heartily; slept soundly; paid for everything in cash down." (He is "Ready Money" because he refuses to buy on credit, paying cash on the barrel, and despises speculation. Also, utterly dependable, he is ready to assist whenever the occasion arises for his help.) Moreover, his identity is absolutely secure, so that even though he "cherishes a sturdy independence of mind and manner," and makes "candid and impartial" decisions, he remains steadfast in his "disinterested" loyalty to just authority. Any link to the government through private interest would inevitably corrupt civic virtue.[21] As Crayon sketches him, Jack personifies the virtuous citizen, respectful toward (but not burdened by) the past, living prosperously in the present, conscious of the future. His son will succeed him, "both in the labours of the farm, and the exploits of the green."

Like *The Sketch Book*, *Bracebridge Hall* is neither polemical nor didactic. Though it possesses a more obvious (and therefore less complex) unity than its predecessor (Squire Bracebridge's estate being the locus of all activity), like the earlier work it builds no sustained argument. Still—and despite the public disclaimer of the introduction—Irving's political views emerge, especially for the patient reader willing to extrapolate from the mass of antiquarian lore with which he fills out the text, for example, the Squire's preferred methods of educating and disciplining children.[22] Moreover, in addition to the overt criticism of the privileged classes in "English Country Gentlemen," and the covert satire of the gentry in "The Rookery," Irving's notebooks show that his allegiance remained rooted in American soil. Extracts from his reading indicate that the foundation of the new social order was the independent *American* farmer: for example, lines translated from Horace's *Epodes*: "Happy he who shuns business—trade[,] & like the first of men plows his paternal fields [with his own oxen, free from the bonds of credit or of debt]," and passages copied from Jeremy Belknap's *The History of New Hampshire* (1784–92): "Were I to form a picture of a happy society it would be a town consisting of a due mixture of hills, valleys & streams of water. . . . the inhabitants mostly husbandmen; their wives & daughters domestic manufacturers; a suitable proportion of handicraft workmen and two or three traders, a physician & lawyer, each of whom should have a farm for his support. . . . Such a situation may be considered as the most favorable to social happiness of any which this world can afford."[23] In the English yeoman Irving found his mythic archetype: Ready Money Jack's appearance may be British, but his soul is American.

Furthermore, Irving was aware that since the sixteenth century the enclosure movement had been continually reducing the number of independent landowning farmers in England. Commons had been appropriated, the small farmer overrun, tenants evicted. Thus, though the yeoman held a place of respect and importance in Henry VIII's era, his position subsequently deteriorated as a consequence of growing industry and land consolidation. In fact, by the early nineteenth century, the major portion of Britain's agricultural land was held in large units by a comparatively small group of nobility and gentry.[24] In America, however, where land was plentiful and cheap, "freehold tenure" flourished. Under this system the farmer owned the land outright and was under no obligation in either working it or disposing of its harvest. Structured on the belief that everyman has a "natural right" of ownership, freehold tenure guaranteed the fundamental "integrity of private property."[25] Irving fully understood this concept—one of his notebook entries reads, "In America a Farmer is an indpdt [independent] Landholder—not [a] tenant as in Engd. nor [a] serf as in other countries—Most of our Legislators are farmers"[26]—and molded the English yeoman Ready Money Jack in the image of his American cousin to signal his support. Having rejected the Old World's political order, he turned to the central symbol of the New World's, reaffirming his belief in basic American values. So basic, in fact, that the Father of his country was memorialized in the national mind as a transcendent farmer: "if amid all the monuments to [Washington] . . . one could be carved, representing him as he himself evidently preferred to be, it would be the image of a tranquil farmer strolling over his own grounds near even-tide, peacefully meditating with the Roman poet [undoubtedly Horace], what may make the crops rejoice."[27]

In the glory days of the Republic, and beyond, farming was "the American way" primarily because, as a freeholder, the American farmer maintained his independence and controlled his political destiny. Thus, he not only played a vital role in a free society, he was its backbone; in effect, he became a democratic exemplum. Ownership of the land gave him a sense of dignity, since the conditions of his work meant that he was self-reliant and, usually, self-sufficient. And as Thoreau and Emerson would later fashion into an American credo, physical contact with nature and the love of honest labor enabled him to achieve a singularly moral character. In *Letters from an American Farmer* (1782), Crèvecoeur spoke of the spiritual benefits the landscape offered: "it is as we silently till the ground, and muse along the odoriferous furrows of our low lands, uninterrupted either by stones or stumps; it is there that the salubrious effluvia of the earth animate our spirits and serve to inspire us."[28] Having achieved position, economic security, and self-fulfillment as a result of possessing property, the farmer had an investment in the country and would therefore take an active, but unbiased, interest in its affairs.[29] Beholden to no one, he owed no political favors, which is why Benjamin Franklin could write that agriculture is "the most honourable of all employments, being the most independent."[30] Repeatedly, in countless statements about the American farmer, the key word was "independence," the vital equation that of land ownership and democratic values. "The instant I enter on my own land," Farmer James says in a famous passage from Crèvecoeur's *Letters*, "the bright idea of property, of exclusive right, of independence exalt[s] my mind."[31] The citizen's ability to make sound, unforced judgments based on conviction rather than patronage must be nourished and protected, and it was the freehold tenure system that could provide an economically self-sustaining electorate to uphold the principles of an egalitarian government.

Fiercely independent, truly disinterested, Irving's Ready Money Jack exemplifies this American ideal, whose architect, of course, was Thomas Jefferson (though he was not solely responsible for the promulgation of the freehold

144

concept). Although Irving had satirized Jeffersonian schemes and projects in *Knickerbocker's History*, he nevertheless came to agree with him that the yeoman farmer, virtuous because living close to nature where his moral judgment could remain instinctive, was America's only hope for maintaining its republican system. Born to the land himself, Jefferson never lost his love for it, and it formed the foundation of his political thought and democratic belief. "The principles on which I calculate the value of life are entirely in favor of my present course," he told Adams in 1794. "I return to farming with an ardour which I scarcely knew in my youth."[32] In his early writings especially, Jefferson celebrated the marriage of agrarianism and democracy and the "perfect expression" of their union, the family farm.[33] "It is the manners and spirit of a people which preserve a republic in vigour," he wrote in *Notes on the State of Virginia*; "those who labour in the earth are the chosen people of God, if ever he had a chosen people, whose breasts he has made his peculiar deposit for substantial and genuine virtue."[34] "Cultivators of the earth are the most valuable citizens," he told John Jay in 1785, articulating the very principles of the freehold concept: "They are the most vigorous, the most independant [sic], the most virtuous, and they are tied to their country and wedded to it's [sic] liberty and interests by the most lasting bands. . . . I consider the class of artificers [manufacturers] as the panders of vice and the instruments by which the liberties of a country are generally overturned."[35] Again, independence surfaces as a prime concern, since "dependance begets subservience and venality, suffocates the germ of virtue, and prepares fit tools for the designs of ambition." Indeed, those who ploughed other men's land or, worse, worked in factories, would never know the economic stability, the triumphant feeling of possession, or the "wholsome controul over their public affairs" enjoyed by the yeoman farmer.[36]

Throughout his long career Jefferson never changed his mind that the "fundamental right to labour the earth" must be protected, that "small landholders are the most precious part of a state," that government would "remain virtuous" as long as it was "chiefly agricultural," and that industrialization and large cities were corrupting influences; his "vision of a nation of farmers," however, compromised to include other possibilities, and he eventually settled on an "equilibrium of agriculture, manufactures, and commerce" as the national priority. In 1809 he carefully qualified the extent of his flexibility: "Manufactures, sufficient for our own consumption, of what we raise the raw material (and no more). Commerce sufficient to carry the surplus produce of agriculture, beyond our own consumption, to a market for exchanging it for articles we cannot raise (and no more). These are the true limits of manufactures and commerce."[37] But by 1816 he had accepted the inevitable, that a commercial system was "now as necessary to our independence as to our comfort."[38] Still, he remained firmly committed to his original belief that "corruption of morals in the mass of cultivators is a phaenomenon of which no age nor nation has furnished an example," and until his death he championed the farmers' cause. In 1825, for example, he warned that a "government of an aristocracy, founded on banking institutions, and moneyed incorporations under the guise and cloak of their favored branches of manufactures, commerce and navigation, [would be] riding and ruling over the plundered ploughman and the beggared yeomanry."[39]

Six years after the publication of *Bracebridge Hall*, Andrew Jackson was elected the seventh president of the United States and immediately embarked on a campaign to reclaim Jefferson's virtuous republic. For Jackson, of whom Irving had once sincerely written, "I suspect he is as *knowing*, as I believe he is *honest*,"[40] it was government's duty, which he made his personal imperative, "to revive and perpetuate those habits of economy and simplicity which are so congenial to the character of republicans."[41] Farmers held the highest place in his American pantheon, since agriculture constituted "the first and most important occupation of man"; America's "enduring wealth," he said, "is composed of flocks and herds and cultivated farms."[42] To accommodate the changes since Jefferson's time he also made room for planters, mechanics, and laborers who, along with farmers, "all know that their success depends upon their own industry and economy," and that "they must not expect to become suddenly rich by the fruits of their toil." These men "are the bone and sinew of the country—men who love liberty and desire nothing but equal rights and equal laws."[43] As Jackson's exemplars of a "*chaste* republican order," with "their independent spirit" and "their high tone of moral character," they resisted the seductions of risk and novelty, greed and extravagance, rapid migration and complex dealings.[44] To protect them against the disease that was threatening to ruin America and corrupt the Republic beyond cure—the class that lives on "privilege, deceit, and speculation," the "aristocracy" that relies on inherited wealth, unearned prestige, special dispensation—Jackson warred against all forms of concentrated monied power, most recognizably large corporations and the "Monster Bank."

Although his vision may have been alarmist and anachronistic, it appealed to a nation uneasy with its own progress and changing self-image. He palliated their fears because he told them who was to blame for their anxiety: self-

ish financial institutions—banks and corporations—formed a network that had ensnared public officials and "held invisible powers over the life of the community," destroying what was left of the original spirit of the Founders. We must "look to the honor and preservation of the republican system," he said, but the "reformation" and the "restoration," as Marvin Meyers puts it, never took place.[45] Despite his struggle, Jackson could not reconcile yeoman values with burgeoning laissez-faire capitalism, and the two continued to diverge. Along with the Republic which they constituted and symbolized, the independent farmers disappeared.

In *Bracebridge Hall*, Irving echoes Jefferson and anticipates Jackson in locating the sources of vice and virtue in English society. The aristocracy he ultimately repudiates is a combination of the privileged elite Jefferson warned against and the irresponsible opportunists Jackson tried to eradicate. His yeoman farmer, vigorous, practical, patriotic, and, above all, incorruptible, is theirs. Moreover, like these agrarian idealists, he believed that virtue resided in the country, since "our Cities are too exclusively place[s] of trade & bustle."[46] Having illustrated his wariness in *Bracebridge Hall* of the factions and special-interest groups, profiteers and speculators, that swarm about the metropolis, he praised instead the spiritualizing effect of the American landscape. Sounding like Crèvecoeur and Emerson, he wrote in his notebook that "God speaks to us in our forrest [sic]—In our mighty rivers, our great lakes[,] these finer mirrors of nature—It is not that we talk of them and fill our books with tame description but they expand our hearts and fill our minds and call up our enthusiasm." Delighted by "the peopling of our forests," Irving says in another entry, "I look upon the population diffused over the agricultural regions of our country as infinitely more valuable. More national, more virtuous than that congregated and pent up in our cities." Thus, "when the forests are national and a settled people grows up there—we may look for the best part of our nation. More informed, cultivatd—yet simple—removd from the cries of the town—attachd to the soil."[47] Ready Money Jack, who embodies these beliefs, and who resembles the yeoman farmer Jefferson and Jackson envisioned, thus represents one of America's fondest and most enduring myths: that its peculiar virtues resided with the cultivators of the land and with the regenerating powers of nature.

By the time Irving published *Bracebridge Hall* (1822) any real possibility of establishing an agrarian republic composed mainly of yeomen farmers and free from the corruptions of European commercialism had already vanished. As early as 1815 American manufacturers were powerful enough to influence national politics, and as their economic interests expanded they fought large-scale battles over protective tariffs, forming associations in order to plead their cause across the nation. In 1816, for example, a group of these manufacturers founded the American Society in New York, which grew into the much larger and more wide-reaching American Institute, whose stated purpose was "encouraging and promoting [of] domestic industry in this state and the United States."[48] By 1830 America's industrial consciousness had broadened to include a movement for popular education of a practical and technical kind. The issue now disturbing the country was not whether to industrialize, but how to maximize the economic benefits while eliminating the social ills of a manufacturing society. Between 1815 and 1860 the farming enterprise itself was transformed, as native industry created home markets while foreign demand increased for American agricultural products. As early as the 1830s, Hofstadter claims, America had developed an "agricultural society whose real attachment was not to the land but to land values."[49] Still, the country's love affair with the independent farmer persisted; still, America clung to its cherished notions. In 1858 Ralph Waldo Emerson could write with conviction that "every man has an exceptional respect for tillage, and a feeling that this is the original calling of his race. . . . [T]he profession has in all eyes its ancient charm, as standing nearest to God, the first cause."[50]

Clearly, the "agrarian myth" is deeply embedded in the American psyche. Two hundred years of national history has not limited its emotional appeal (for instance, it is still present in Willy Loman's desire for a garden in *Death of a Salesman*), since the complex of ideas surrounding the term "yeoman" delineates how Americans ideally saw themselves (especially as they lived on the frontier).[51] The reality, however, fell somewhat short of the myth. Almost from the beginning, a majority of American farmers were engaged in some form of capitalistic enterprise, especially those involved in wheat and cash-crop farming. Certainly most farms were small, self-sufficient units, with the land providing all necessities, yet even in Jefferson's day commercial necessities and the desire for profit existed. And, as Joyce Appleby has demonstrated, Jefferson himself did not sanctify agriculture "as a venerable form of production giving shelter to a traditional way of life; rather, he was responsive to every possible change in cultivation, processing, and marketing that would enhance its profitability."[52] Yet, by celebrating some aspects of the independent farmer and neglecting others, American writers preserved the values that we still fondly associate today with the concept of the "family farm." Americans have continually needed to believe that their nation was conceived in virtue, and the "yeoman farmer" who fought the Revolution and then returned to freedom and independence on his land has traditionally served as the vehicle for this republican idealism. In his portrait of Ready Money Jack, Irving captured these qualities, and his readers recognized in the English yeoman a kindred spirit.

According to Gordon Wood, the American Revolution had sought to create a Republic based on the classical principle of "the sacrifice of individual interests to the greater good of the whole."[53] The men who believed and acted on this were engaged in a process of cleansing the corruption from within their society as well as resisting subjugation from without.[54] It was a "desperate attempt," Wood says, even in 1776, since the economic and social basis for this belief had "long been disintegrating, if it ever existed" at all.[55] In the 1820s, Americans were involved in a similar desperate attempt to excise the internal cancer that was destroying republican values, and once again (as Jackson's campaign showed) the yeoman farmer became their symbol for self-healing. Nineteenth-century Americans wanted to see themselves, like their ancestors, as "brave patriotic yeomanry, who, with giant strength, met the invaders of our land, and won our independence,"[56] yet could not help recognizing the gap between image and reality. At just this juncture in our history, *Bracebridge Hall* made the yeoman farmer its locus of moral authority, reminding its American readers of the vitality and energy of *American* ideals. In the midst of the Old World Irving evoked a New World archetype to convey his faith in America's civic superiority, which accounts for the popularity of his book.

IV

The yeoman also appealed to Washington Irving on a deeply personal level, far removed from the arena of political ideology. Still disconnected, Irving continued to dream of rootedness. Bonded to the land, the farmer was the most community oriented of people. His "social relationships" and "cultural expectations" kept him closely tied to the inhabitants of the local area, who were often consumers of the foodstuffs he produced. Lineal values prevailed: the basic unit was the family, which encouraged its children not to succeed by venturing out into the world and "rising in the social system," but to remain within the farm community. One generation was naturally linked to the next, and both to the "family land."[57] In addition, family orientation shielded the members from the uncertainties of the mutable world. Farmers, therefore, built and maintained strong, stable homes; Irving only dreamed about them.

A brief but poignant passage in one of his journals reads, "Nature intended me for a husband & an affectionate one—I have all the love of him abide."[58] For the man who would be a husband but remained a bachelor, who wanted a home yet continued to wander, who admired stability while yearning for imaginative freedom, the husbandman provided an image of the simple but profound pleasures life offered to those who were not too driven to appreciate them.

In *Bracebridge Hall*, Irving split these internal divisions into two English characters and then synthesized them harmoniously in an American one, Dolph Heyliger, hero of the longest and richest of the collection's stories framed by the ongoing narrative. In "The Schoolmaster" (pp. 180–83), Irving contrasts the man of "substantial independence," Ready Money Jack, with his old boyhood chum, the schoolmaster Slingsby, an Ichabod Crane look-alike with Rip Van Winkle's disposition. Once such "inseparable friends" that they might have been brothers, the two are complete opposites, and their lives diverged accordingly: Jack took to "ploughing and reaping," Slingsby to books and learning. But in an "unlucky hour," after reading many "voyages and travels," the latter was "smitten with a desire to see the world." When he returns "hungry as well as wayworn" to seek his old friend, Crayon, with a few fine pencil strokes, shows what the intervening years have wrought: "a thin man, somewhat advanced in life, with a coat out at the elbows, a pair of old nankeen gaiters, and a few things tied in a handkerchief, and slung on the end of a stick," Slingsby enters the village a failure. Arriving at Jack's farmhouse, he contemplates a scene reminiscent of the Van Tassel farm: "In the porch of the house sat Ready Money Jack, in his Sunday dress; with his hat upon his head, his pipe in his mouth, and his tankard before him, the monarch of all he surveyed. . . . The varied sounds of poultry were heard from the well-stocked farm-yard; the bees hummed from their hives in the garden; the cattle lowed in the rich meadow; while the crammed barns and ample stacks bore proof of an abundant harvest." Like the two panels of a diptych, the friends face each other, the yeoman who had ploughed the land of his forefathers with little to say, the man of vagabond spirit a source of narrative riches, one poor in words, the other in gold. Like Slingsby, Irving had abandoned home for a glimpse of the world, though in this case he outdistanced his creation by turning his travels into art.

Slingsby, whose name undoubtedly derives from the Shakespearean phrase "the slings and arrows of outrageous fortune," is Irving's projection of himself as he might have been had he returned to New York prior to publishing *The*

Sketch Book. Indeed, the schoolmaster has "come back . . . a wreck to his native place"; Irving, it will be remembered, had said that he would not "be driven to [his] native shores like a mere wreck."[59] What career might he then have pursued but that of an errant pedagogue (or, perhaps, some form of business in which he relied on the benevolence of his friend Brevoort). Like Slingsby, he "was as fit for that as any thing else," meaning, of course, as he had already admitted to Walter Scott, that he was fit for no regular position at all. The entire sketch, in fact, is his self-conscious portrait of misfortune avoided and fortune delayed. Crayon translates Irving's anxieties and fantasies into a symbolic tableau of the yeoman "monarch" and the transient "pilgrim": "Ready Money Jack, seated in lordly state, surrounded by the good things of this life, with golden guineas hanging to his very watch-chain, and the poor pilgrim Slingsby, thin as a weasel, with all his worldly effects, his bundle, hat, and walking-staff, lying on the ground beside him." At the conclusion of the sketch, Crayon says that he has "more than once mused upon the picture presented by [Slingsby] and his schoolmate Ready Money Jack, on their coming together again after so long a separation." How to join the two in fact, not just in fiction; how, in other words, to transform pilgrim into monarch for himself—this dilemma would preoccupy Irving over the next decade. Yet he already knew where the solution lay: "I cannot help thinking," Crayon writes, in "The Schoolmaster," "that the man that stays at home, and cultivates the comforts and pleasures daily springing up around him, stands the best chance for happiness." But a man does not always act on what he knows. Though the Squire, much to the wanderer's delight, has "anchor[ed] Slingsby in his native village" by installing him as schoolmaster, each spring he grows restless and manifests a "disposition to rove abroad again." Here, Crayon merely explains this behavior without judging it: "there is nothing so difficult to conquer as the vagrant humour, when once it has been fully indulged." In "Dolph Heyliger," Irving justifies it by showing that if wanderlust is indulged without anxiety, it may just lead to home.

"Dolph Heyliger" represents Irving's dream of homecoming as a rightful inheritance, prosperity achieved by "following the bent of his vagrant inclination." Dolph is a Slingsby-like character who metamorphoses into a Ready Money Jack because all he ever wanted was to be himself. Hedges has discussed the story in the context of American literature's search for a middle-class hero, and he is surely right in arguing that "Irving aligns himself" with neither the middle class nor rural gentry as a whole, but with "the individual in either class whose spirit is not consumed in the grind of commercial competition or the effort to dignify, or preserve the dignity of, a family name."[60] Yet it is also true that the story has a distinct wish-fulfillment quality to it, which is why it is revealing that of the four full-length tales in the book told by various narrators to a group, "Dolph" is Crayon's own contribution to the entertainment. Moreover, just as Irving did in *The Sketch Book* with his American tales, he puts even greater distance between himself and his story by having Crayon read an excerpt from one of Diedrich Knickerbocker's manuscripts. Here, however, he takes the ruse one step further by prefacing "Dolph Heyliger" with a "prelude," in which we discover that the Dutch historian originally heard the tale from an old gentleman named John Josse Vandermoere (who got it "second hand from the lips of Dolph Heyliger himself") and that he has related it as nearly as possible in the latter's words. In this way, like the final cube in a series of nested Chinese boxes, the inner story apparently is most removed from its outermost container/narrator, yet it represents, in the identical shape, the core of the self. Once again, Irving finds the appropriate narrative strategy for objectifying personal experience, disguising his intimate relationship with the story's psychology. Just as "Dolph," when traced back, is actually a first-person tale, Irving's most interesting and vital fiction is basically autobiography in cipher.

"Dolph Heyliger" is "Rip Van Winkle" minus the anxiety. Another culturally marginal figure, mischievous, wayward, but essentially generous and good-humored, Dolph cannot find his proper place in the city of Manhattoes. First as a "heedless youngster" led away by "idle company" or "play[ing] truant to hunt after birds' nests, to rob orchards, or to swim in the Hudson" (p. 253), then as an adolescent Brom Bones, "the ringleader of all holiday sports, and midnight gambols," he disappoints not a demanding wife but a loving, hopeful mother (much like Irving's own). The difference is crucial, for right from the outset and continuing through the story, and unlike in Sleepy Hollow and Rip's village, there are no unbearable pressures brought on Dolph to conform to some norm. While the townspeople shake their heads and say he will never amount to anything (and pity the poor mother), she never loses faith in her son, though like all mothers of wayward boys, she is "greatly perplexed what to do with him." Even when he fails miserably as a doctor's apprentice (recalling Irving's brief, unsuccessful attempt to practice law) she defends him. The tale has the quality of childish fantasy, so that eventually he repays her steadfast belief: when he finds treasure buried by one of his ancestors, he rescues her from poverty. He accomplishes this by combining Slingsby's adventurous spirit with Jack's moral and physical sturdiness, trusting himself enough to follow his instincts, believing enough in his ability to handle any threatening situation, and remaining relaxed enough to accept his great good fortune.

Dolph, as Hedges noted, is a man of imagination. When he first sees the ghost who will lead him in the end to the hidden gold, whose magical appearance the story never explains beyond identifying it with a distant relation, he neither denies its existence nor flees in terror (though he fears and trembles in its presence). In effect, he has the good sense to permit his unconscious recognition of his true heritage to lead him to self-discovery. The night he sees the apparition of his Dutch ancestor he dreams of an odyssey ending in his return home as a wealthy man. The next day he embarks, "actuated by some irresistible impulse," moving about as if he were "under supernatural influence" (p. 270). In fact, the entire story has a thick, dreamlike atmosphere, so that all Dolph's actions seem fated: he is sleepwalking through life. Untroubled by the past, unconcerned about the future, he allows the present to become his total reality: "he felt himself launched strangely and suddenly on the world, and under full way to explore the regions of wonder that lay up this mighty river [the Hudson], and beyond those blue mountains that had bounded his horizon since childhood." Assisted in his travels by Antony Vander Heyden, a friendly, liberal, independent farmer who looks upon him as a son, Dolph eventually is restored to his proper inheritance and becomes a "rich burgher for life," a "distinguished citizen, and a valuable member of the community," basically a citified version of the yeoman Vander Heyden, who turns out to be another remote family connection. All this has been made possible by Dolph's essentially being in harmony with his fortune (what he calls his "'some how or other'" philosophy) and the proper balance he achieves between his regard for home and his love of spirited adventure.

"Dolph Heyliger" is Washington Irving's projection of himself ten years into the future (when he would in fact return to America content with his achievement) as a man who has assumed his rightful place because he trusted his own instincts to guide him there, even if it meant wandering the Continent for seventeen years. Perhaps for this reason it is a story singularly lacking in tension and overflowing with nocturnal fantasy, despite its hobgoblins and Indians. Not Irving's experience, but rather his dream of experience, composes its texture. In fact, the story reads as if Dolph were the hero of his own legend, as if he were creating himself (just the way Irving had shaped Geoffrey Crayon into his desired persona) as the tale moves along—which is exactly what he is doing. With a deft touch for this mirroring effect where author and character reflect each other, Irving ends the story by revealing that Dolph has most likely fabricated the whole thing, that it is no more than an imaginative history of his origins and his rise to wealth and prestige. Dolph, then, is yeoman turned story-teller, just as Irving was storyteller envisioning himself as yeoman. Finally, a sense of indeterminacy prevails—is Dolph a Slingsby transformed into a Ready Money Jack or a Ready Money Jack romantically conceiving of himself as having begun life a Slingsby?—which meant, for Irving, that anything was possible. The pilgrim Crayon could yet become the monarch Irving.

The yeoman farmer thus had both political and personal significance in *Bracebridge Hall*; once again inner conflicts coincided with national crises. Where in his previous book he had artistically developed Geoffrey Crayon to negotiate this duality—especially through comic mockery—Irving now found that he had little need for his persona. For one, the gentle spoofing and undermining of Squire Bracebridge, and the more spirited send-up of Master Simon, the General, and the other "humourists" of Bracebridge Hall, served as outlets for his frustrations and disappointments with the landed gentry. For another, books, and not his actual lived experience, form the bone and marrow of the sketches. It is not just that he alludes to some thirty English authors, twenty alone from the sixteenth and seventeenth centuries, but that these "antiquarian tomes" provide the sources for the descriptions of manners and dress, sports and pastimes, with which he fleshes out the book.[61] The notebooks which he kept for *The Sketch Book* contain the daily events of his life, reminiscences, confessions of despair and self-doubt; the memoranda for *Bracebridge Hall*, aside from jottings on various halls, are primarily reading lists. Since his second English sketchbook is not a genuine travelogue, although it borrows the form of the travel journal, its vitality derives from his purely imaginative, as opposed to empirical, experience. Thus, having virtually eliminated any engagement with his environment, Irving no longer needed the filter Geoffrey Crayon once provided. Author and persona are now almost indistinguishable, so Crayon fades out at about the midpoint. Though the book loses some warmth and charm because of this, it is still fundamentally autobiographical: Irving would remain his own best subject.

Seven years had passed since his arrival in England in 1815. During that time he had written two books whose general popularity and critical acclaim had made him the most celebrated American writer of the day. Still, Irving did not rest easy. In "The Schoolmaster," he ruminated on the passage of time: "He who has sallied forth into the world like poor Slingsby, full of sunny anticipations, finds too soon how different the distant scene becomes when visited. The smooth place roughens as he approaches; the wild place becomes tame and barren; the fairy tints that beguiled him on still fly to the distant hill, or gather upon the land he has left behind, and every part of the landscape seems greener than the spot he stands on" (p. 183). He might have added that Old World aristocratic traditions and hierarchical order evaporate under the light of scrutiny. By 1822, therefore, he had exhausted England, but he was not yet ready, in spite of what he obviously knew, to give up searching for a "greener" landscape. He had not achieved Dolph's dream, but he nevertheless was determined to give himself more time to search—or to drift. Spain, which would ultimately provide him with the experience he sought, was several years into the future, but Germany now offered new territory. A traveler without a destination, a pilgrim without a holy land, and, apparently, a writer without an ostensible subject, he took to the road.

FIVE

On the Road with Washington Irving: *Tales of a Traveller*

Washington Irving did not want to write the book that became *Tales of a Traveller*. When he left London for Aix-la-Chapelle and its healing waters on July 6, 1822, he fully intended to repeat what by now had become a ritual journey: roaming from place to place, collecting impressions and filling notebooks with anecdotes, observations, and word pictures—a process that his biographer describes as the "cleansing and reclothing" of "his imagination."[1] Then, after he had "*lived into* a great deal of amusing and characteristic information," which, he said, "is perhaps the best way of studying the world,"[2] he would assimilate his experience, filtering it aesthetically and psychologically through Geoffrey Crayon. But this time his creative strategy failed: though the Germans were "full of old customs and usages, which are obsolete in other parts of the world," and though he encountered medieval scenery and a wealth of Teutonic legend and fable—the same romantic gems Scott had recommended to him at Abbotsford in 1817—which he planned to transmute into tales, he produced no German sketchbook.[3] When John Murray wrote in November 1823, asking "what your publisher may be allowed to expect from you in the course of the winter," and adding that "I am perfectly ready for you, and the sooner you take the field the better," an anxious Irving had nothing original to offer; his notebooks, whose veins he customarily mined for precious literary ore, were, for his prsent purposes, dry.[4] His pathetic response, in which he suggested "a brace more of Volumes of the Sketch Book," and the possibility of reworking a manuscript translation of *The Arabian Nights* that Murray had on hand, indicates his desperation.[5] The new year 1824, unfortunately, brought no new inspiration, only a "fit of sterility" and a "sad heartless mood," from which nothing could "rouse" him.[6] His very wording of the composing dilemma hints at yet another problem.

The book he finally published in August 1824, after months of depression and nervousness, like its recent predecessors, revealed the inner man at the same time that it reflected particular American biases and uncertainties, but unlike those other volumes, it possessed no structured or organic arrangement of its four distinct parts. Moreover, since Irving lacked the gift of true invention—that is, he created no pure fictions—and since he made almost no use of any direct, personal experience (as he had done with both *The Sketch Book* and *Bracebridge Hall*), by necessity it was derivative, consisting of bits and pieces of stories and anecdotes that he had picked up on his travels or gleaned from friends, expanded by an imagination that at times appeared to be out of control. The lines copied from *Paradise Regained* in one of his notebooks could easily have served as its epigraph: "But these are false, or little else but dreams,/Conjectures, fancies built on nothing firm" (4:291–92).[7] Or Irving might have prefaced the collection, somewhat more defensively, with another extract, this time from Burke: "It would surprise us[,] if we were to examine the thing critically, how few good original stories there are in the world. The most celebrated borrow from each other, and are content with some new turn; some corrective, addition, or embellishment."[8] But the passage from Ben Jonson that stands at the head of *Tales of a Traveller* more than satisfies, for it suggests the imitative nature of Irving's stories: "I am neither your minotaure, nor your centaure, nor your satyr, nor your hyaena, nor your babion, but your meer traveller believe me."[9] In Renaissance literature the "meer," or pure, traveler was often an object of satire or ridicule, since he was understood to be nothing more than the product of all the disparate information, attitudes, and fashions he had gathered along the route of his wanderings, not one single, definable entity, but an absurd mixture of disunified parts. Like the first three of Jonson's beasts, he was a perversion of a normal person yet, like the last two, he "aped" human behavior. However, the Jonson quotation implies, and quite aptly in this case, not just something conglomerate about the traveler, but something unusually strange and distorted as well.[10] Though he may not, for the American author, metamorphose into a mythological creature, the voyager, cut adrift both literally and imaginatively from any meaningful, anchoring attachment, becomes a more disturbing figure than the "homeless" wanderer Irving previously had projected; here, frighteningly, he assumes an unnatural shape. Despite the claim of Geoffrey Crayon's authorship, *Tales of a Traveller* contains a wildness, a grotesqueness, for which Irving's persona could not have been responsible.

Unlike either *The Sketch Book* or *Bracebridge Hall*, *Tales* consciously asks no vital questions about the physical and emotional terrain Irving had covered since he left his last place of refuge: no encounter with Old World emblems of order and tradition, no confrontation with a cultural or historical past, underlies its pages. Nor could Irving find, nor did he even seek, a correlative through which to express (and presumably plumb) personal traumas. Yet beneath the ghost stories, pictures of literary life, bandit tales, and parables of greed that comprise its four sections lies a realm of psychic experience that he surely did not mean to expose. What *Tales* manifests, beyond the disappointment and despair Irving knew during the time of composing his third European work, is his repressed hostilities and fears of sexuality which disturb the smooth retelling of these hijacked pieces. Like a volcanic pool, they erupt through the surface of the tales, injecting into the book a sense of frustration and violence that reflects, as William Hedges has said, "character in deep conflict with itself."[11] Hedges is speaking here about Irving's fictional protagonists and the violent acts they commit, but these striking moments in the stories reflect not only tensions within the characters, but their creator's turmoil as well.

That conflict, which Irving never truly resolved during these years (though he did eventually achieve distance from it), was his thwarted desire for marriage and home. In fact, it reached a climax in Dresden, where he met and grew intimate with the Fosters, an English family visiting there. The process whereby he gained control over himself following the bankruptcy crisis would not, however, stabilize his life after he parted from them, since they—mother, two older girls, two younger boys—represented everything to which he aspired. Returning to his pen did not enable him to triumph over blasted hope when the elder daughter, Emily, refused his offer of marriage. Again, lines copied from *Paradise Regained* gloss the story cryptically and symbolically:

> —However[,] many books
> Wise men have said are wearisome; who reads
> Incessantly, and to his reading brings not
> A spirit and judgement equal or superior,
> Uncertain & unsettled still remains
> *Deep verst in books & shallow in himself,*
> Crude or intoxicate, collecting toys,
> And trifles [for] choice matters worth a sponge[;]
> As children gath'ring pebbles on the shore. (4:321–30)[12]

The passage reflects, especially in the words he underscored, Irving's sense that he had lost what was truly valuable because he had failed to achieve the proper perspective, or judgment, on himself; like Ichabod, he had pursued literature and flights of fancy, eschewing the practical and mundane, and he had come away empty. Significant by its omission here is the parenthetical line 325: "(And what he brings, what needs he elsewhere seek)?" His fate, he despaired, would remain "uncertain" and "unsettled" because he lacked something fundamentally necessary to secure happiness; unlike Brom Bones, he could neither satisfy nor win his Katrina. Manhood had escaped him: there was a void—a "shallowness"—in himself. He believed, ultimately, that his imagination had betrayed him, since he had traveled its vagrant course until all hope of domestic bliss had vanished. "My life has been, for the greater part, a desultory & unprofitable one," he told his sister in 1822, "owing perhaps to the great ascendancy of my imagination, over the more valuable faculties of the mind."[13] Men married, established homes, amassed profits; children chased illusive dreams, "gath'ring pebbles on the shore."

Not surprisingly, then, *Tales of a Traveller* calls into serious question the efficacy of a life devoted to imaginative pursuits. Built into several of Irving's nested stories and framed tales[14] is a caution about the dangers of imagination, which are primarily ones of dislocation and disorientation, and which are associated with the absence of limits and restraints. During these years, therefore, Irving's view runs parallel to the general skepticism toward imagination (and toward fiction) prevalent in nineteenth-century America, an antipathy based on the belief that it led to the violation of basic American values. *Tales* illustrates a truth Irving's American audience would have had little trouble accepting: if not properly harnessed, imagination could easily undermine both self-discipline and social responsibility.[15] But below the surface of both personal statement and literary meaning there lurks another explanation for Irving's negative attitude: because he could not come to terms with his sexual inadequacy, he blamed imagination for the fact that, at age forty, he had neither wife nor child. Driven to despair, he once again bordered on the edge of nervous collapse. Were he a twentieth-century confessional writer—a Robert Lowell, Adrienne Rich, or Anne Sexton—then he might have written his own version of *Life Studies, Diving into the Wreck,* or *The Awful Rowing toward God,* books which foreground an emotional breakdown, where, in fact, the poet's very experience of that breakdown provides motif, theme, and structure for an entire literary work. Naturally, for an early-nineteenth-century tale-teller such a production was unthinkable; nevertheless, for the reader willing to plunge into the depths of Irving's fiction, as well as his journals and correspondence, *Tales of a Traveller* reveals a man pushed to the edge of sexual hysteria, yet unable to recognize the true source of his pain. Far more complex and interesting than any single tale in the collection, Irving's own story from these years of unhappy wandering—a story of psychological and sexual impotence—becomes the unifying factor in the third chronicle of his Old World odyssey.

I

Writing never came easily for Irving. He often suffered, in addition to the mental stress and emotional strain of actual composition, an extreme physical reaction, a painful inflammation of the ankles which he referred to as his "malady."[16] Usually, however, the completion of a book released the various pressures that had accumulated, and the "lingering cutaneous complaint" (another of his descriptions) disappeared.[17] But not this time: in September 1822, almost four months after the publication of the English edition of *Bracebridge Hall*, the ailment still plagued him. In fact, it troubled him to such an extent that, in several letters written during the summer, he complained of "lameness."[18] At one point near the beginning of his travels, when he was perched "just on the frontiers of Germany, in the vicinity of some of the most beautiful and romantic scenery in Europe," his hobbled condition would not permit him to move on, and he described himself as "fettered and disabled."[19] Such highly charged and suggestive language, implying feelings of inadequacy, helplessness, and imprisonment, points to a psychological disturbance at the root of Irving's discomfort. While it is true that a "cutaneous complaint"—extreme sensitivity and, perhaps, irritation of the skin—could have resulted from the nervousness accompanying creativity, Irving himself seems to have recognized a deeper cause:

> I am now convinced, though reluctantly [he wrote to his sister from Mayence], that this malady has an internal origin. . . . [It] will take me some time, and patience, and care to restore my system to a healthful tone; all these external applications are but palliative; they relieve me from present pain and inconvenience, but it must be by diet, by gentle and slowly operating remedies, by easy recreation and tranquillity, and moderate exercise of mind, that I must gradually bring my constitution once more into vigorous activity, and eradicate every lurking evil.[20]

A change of country and climate temporarily relieved his physical symptoms, but it did not remedy the emotional ache; the "lurking evil" that beset him was not so easily "eradicated."

Since the publication of *The Sketch Book* Irving had been haunted by the ghosts of his bachelorhood and his advancing age, and now, after a little more than two years of submerging the demons under work, they had metamorphosed into his "tormenting malady." [21] In May 1820, he responded to James Kirke Paulding's "picture of domestic enjoyment" by bemoaning his own single state—yearning for a zone he would never be able to "enter"—while at the same time demeaning his profession as mere "scribbling":

> With all my wandering habits, which are the result of circumstances rather than of disposition, I think I was formed for an honest, domestic, uxorious man, and I cannot hear of my old cronies snugly nestled down with good wives and fine children round them, but I feel for the moment desolate and forlorn. Heavens! what a haphazard, schemeless life mine has been, that here I should be, at this time of life, youth slipping away, and scribbling month after month and year after year, far from home, without any means or prospect of entering into matrimony, which I absolutely believe indispensable to the happiness and even comfort of the after part of existence. [22]

On September 8, 1822, nearly twenty-eight months later, he jotted the following entry into his journal, switching at the most painful moment of his confession from prose to poetry:

> My Summer is nearly over—the shadows of autum[n] begin to come—the leaves of past pleasures are strewn around me—the joys of youth how have they passed away—friendships faded—loves untimely fallen—hopes blighted—what fruit is there to repay this ill spent prime[?]
>
> Ah happless [sic] heart how hast thou
> spent
> weep & lament
> for of thy youth no fruit appears
> where are the friends that sportd with me in youth[?] [23]

The answer to his final question was, of course, that they were married, raising families, pursuing carefully planned, useful careers. Their youth had borne the "fruit" that they would enjoy in productive middle age; his advancing years, he feared, would be empty and sterile. In comparison to his friends, Irving saw himself as "a useless being, whose existence was of little moment." His "fate," he tells his friend Thomas Wentworth Storrow, is "to wander," or rather, he adds, "it is my vocation." To Charles Leslie he describes himself as a "vagabond," "driven completely out of [his] course by whim or circumstance." He is "so far adrift from any home," he informs his sister, that her "little tidings of the fireside" are "like the breezes that now and then bring to the sea-beaten sailor the fragrance of the land." [24] Once again the voyager from the New World was shipwrecked in the Old. On September 21, 1822, America's most celebrated writer privately confessed his utter failure in terms that suggest that the "lurking evil" in his body was more than just a physical malady:

> A weight rested upon my mind—there was a soreness of heart as if I had committed some hideous crime & all mankind were justly irritated ag[ain]st me—I went about with a guilty look & sought to hide myself—it was not without some effort that I occasionally threw off this weight & reccollected [sic] that my only crime had been an unsuccessful attempt to please the world. [25]

He "threw off" this guilt by "throwing off" stories (see note 5), as if writing were sometimes a process of unburdening. Something "hideous" that he could not name—and that he never could face—forced him to cover ("hide") himself for fear of exposing his weakness. His "crime," however, was not that he had been unable to "please the world," but rather that he had failed to prove himself a man in its eyes.

One more chance for redemption awaited Washington Irving, and it arrived, oddly enough, in the form of a lost letter. While touring Vienna sometime in late October or early November, 1822, Irving received from German authorities what they believed was a letter of his that had failed to reach its destination. Upon opening the communication he discovered the reason for their mistake: there, on its closing page, stood a long and enthusiastic commentary on his works followed by a transcription from *The Sketch Book*, underneath which, written in bold letters, appeared his name. So much space had been devoted to the American author that the letter writer—Mrs. Amelia Foster, of Bedfordshire, England, but then sojourning with her family in Dresden—had left no room for her own signature. "He told us, afterward," wrote the youngest daughter, Flora Foster Dawson, in 1863, "that no praise had ever seemed to him so sweet, so genuine, as what he so unexpectedly found in those lines." [26] However, in addition to her comments on the family's current reading, Mrs. Foster also included in the letter to her eldest daughter (who had remained behind at their estate in England) descriptions and anecdotes of their Dresden affairs, and these "affectionate details," even more than the glowing tribute to his writing, fired Irving's imagination. They were, he said, "after his own heart," and later confided to the Fosters, almost as if he were a voyeur peering into a private realm that he had no right to enter, that "this little peep behind the curtain at the domestic habits and feelings and events of [their] family circle, pleased and interested him beyond measure, and chimed in with his own tastes, occupations, and pursuits." [27] While it cannot be proven that Irving left Vienna and headed for the Saxon capital solely in order to locate the Fosters—in fact, he told his sister he would winter there because it was a city of "taste, intellect, and literary feeling; and . . . the best place to acquire the German language, which is nowhere so purely spoken as in Saxony" [28]—nevertheless, a few days after arriving in Dresden he sought out this family whose lives, over the next eight months, would become entwined with his own. [29]

Irving's biographer and other scholars have scrutinized his relationship to the Fosters, recording all the details of their shared life: the innumerable dinners and social engagements, the evening readings and conversations, the day trips to the Dresden countryside, the Italian and French lessons several times a week, the participation in amateur theatricals where Irving would often play the male lead opposite Emily. [30] They have shown how immediately comfortable he felt with the mother, Amelia Foster, an intelligent, sympathetic woman of about Irving's own age, who shared his love of literature and languages. They have chronicled his growing fondness for Emily, bright, gentle, and attractive, eighteen years old when Irving met her, nineteen when, apparently, he proposed and was rejected. They have recognized the resemblances between the Fosters and the Hoffmans—the family of Irving's first beloved, Matilda—noticing, quite rightly, that both Mrs. Hoffman (at the time also close to his age) and Mrs. Foster played the same role, that of confidante, while Matilda and Emily were fashioned into the idealized "woman." (In both instances, interestingly enough, the husbands were absent: Judge Josiah O. Hoffman traveled often and for long periods of time; John Foster had remained in England, primarily for business purposes.) In addition, they have correctly determined that in 1822–23 Irving experienced a crisis—during which he again could not work—at least equal to, if not greater than, the previous ones he suffered when Matilda Hoffman died (1809) and the family business collapsed (1818). And, moreover, they have accurately perceived the causal relationship involving his literary stasis: he was unable to compose his German work because he was anxious and depressed, not vice versa. In fact, when Mrs. Foster chastised him for having "tormented" himself "into a nervous fever" over his inability to write, he emphasized that she had misunderstood the source of his despair: "Do you really think me so anxious about literary reputation [he replied]; or so nervous about the fleeting and fallacious popularity of a day? I have not been able to write it is true, because I have been harrassed in mind."[31]

What the commentators have not done, however, is to define the precise nature of the Dresden trauma, which was far more profound than they believed. Within only a few months of that first meeting Irving had become a member of the family's inner circle. He seized every opportunity to be among them, grew dependent on their responses to his stories and anecdotes, and sulked whenever he was forced to share their company with unexpected guests. "Let only one of the many visitors who frequent our house come in," Flora Foster wrote in her memoir, "he immediately buttons himself up, retires to *his recess*, sheltered by curtains and book stands, and there stays, silent and uninterested, till we are again alone, when his animation returns, his countenance, pale and languid, lights up, and he becomes again the most lively and interesting companion."[32] Filled with "homefelt enjoyment," these occasions were, Irving recalled to Mrs. Foster, "the sweetest moments that I have passed in Dresden, though I fear," he added in recognition of his extreme behavior, "I often trespassed on the patience of others." Nevertheless, in spite of his "selfishness," he "would not give up one such evening for all the fashionable parties we were at together." "I felt," he says in a most telling expression of what the Fosters meant to him, "of some consequence in those little domestic scenes."[33] Beyond career-oriented goals—critical recognition, popular acclaim, monetary reward—all of which he had secured, Irving longed for a masculine identity as husband and father. This he achieved in those private moments with the Fosters: for the first time since he was twenty-six years old and courting his beloved Matilda, when in the absence of Judge Hoffman he functioned as the overseer of the family, Irving had assumed the role of man of the house.

"They had made their house absolutely a home to me during my residence in Dresden."[34] In these words to his brother Peter lies encoded the significance of Irving's sojourn in the kingdom of Saxony. The reluctant bachelor with "strong domestic feelings & inclinations," who became "sometimes quite dreary & desolate" when they got "uppermost,"[35] had found in the Fosters a surrogate family—wife, two older daughters, two younger sons—that he sought to borrow. Although he told Mrs. Foster that, in regard to marriage, his "time has now gone by" and that his "means" were too "precarious" to support others besides himself,[36] he nevertheless asked for Emily's hand, risking the pain and humiliation of rebuff in the futile hope of preserving the place he had won. Flora Foster could not have comprehended Irving's motivations, but in her description of his letter of proposal (which has not survived) she reveals how he linked—and merged—feelings for Emily with his need for the family:

> He has written. He has confessed to my mother, as to a true and dear friend, his love for E——, and his conviction of its utter hopelessness. He feels himself unable to combat it. He thinks he must try, by absence, to bring more peace to his mind. Yet he cannot bear to give up our friendship—an intercourse become so dear to him, and so necessary to his daily happiness.[37]

Not anticipated union with Emily, but desire for connection to the Fosters, pushed Irving into an act of "utter hopelessness." It is they upon whom he has become dependent; they are the ones he "cannot bear to give up." Stanley Williams surmised as much, though his thoughts on the matter remained tentative. "Perhaps," he speculated, "the proposal to Emily was a confused expression of Irving's wish to make enduring the happiness he had known in Mrs. Foster's home."[38]

Emphatically, Washington Irving never expressed passion for Emily Foster. While it is true that some of his letters to Mrs. Foster exist only in fragmentary form, and while there may have been correspondence with her daughter that has not been recovered, it still remains safe to say that nowhere does he indicate a regard for Emily beyond that of Platonic admiration. His journal entries reveal nothing that might allow his Dresden experience to be construed as an *affaire de coeur*. No outpourings of emotion even remotely approaching those concerning Matilda Hoffman can be found for Emily Foster.[39] Though he was clearly aware of her charms, and though he never blotted her image from his mind—even as an old man near the end of his life he remembered her beauty, greater, he told her, than Salome's (whose head she had once painted for him in miniature)[40]—he did not pine for her when, in May 1823, he left Dresden in order to settle his nerves. By contrast, during that trip to Silesia and Bohemia he penned a series of letters to Mrs. Foster which manifest feelings of painful separation from the family. (In the space of a month he wrote eight times and received at least seven replies from the mother.) Suffering now from severe headaches and facial neuralgia, he comforted himself by "picturing" the Fosters at their "occupations" in the "little Pavilion," the cottage they had rented for the summer. Like an absent husband and father, he eagerly awaited the post for news of the day's activities; after a little more than a week he was so delighted to have a glimpse of the "dear little circle" that he thanked Mrs. Foster "a thousand times" for her letter:

> I was so impatient to read it [he told her] that I would not wait till I got to my Lodgings which were distant from the post office— yet I would not read it in the bustle & confusion of the Street. I tried to get admitted to Wallensteins garden—it was closed—So I scrambled up to the grassy ramparts, and read it in quiet, with old Prague & the Moldau at my feet. I have since read it over half a dozen times, for whenever I read it, it seems to bring me among you all again.

Irving's response, with the repetition of the word "read" five times, bespeaks an excited state of mind as well as evidencing a spontaneity of thought; he was not in the habit, even in his correspondence, of totally disregarding the niceties of prose style. "I can give you nothing in return for the interesting little pictures you draw in your letters of your family circle," he said a week later. "Do let me have as many of them as you can—and yet they only play the fool with me, and make me wish myself back—and————well—well—well!" Such an uncharacteristic outburst, which at the same time both reveals and conceals desire, expresses and yet checks emotion, betrays a man at war with himself: Irving desperately wants what he knows he cannot have. No wonder he told Mrs. Foster that "at present I am all discomposed."[41]

Irving could not have what he wanted—that is, patriarchal standing in the community—because Emily Foster denied his suit. Why she did so, beyond the obvious reasons that she was not in love with him and that he was twice her age (he had turned forty in April 1823), is instructive. According to her journal, his positive qualities did not escape her: he was "entertaining & interesting," "amiable & amusing," with fine physical features. "He is neither tall nor slight," Emily noted, "but most interesting, dark, hair of a man of genius waving, silky, & black, grey eyes full of varying feeling, & an amiable smile."[42] Along with her mother and sister, she recognized his acute sensitivity: he reads a "sweet little poem on spring" and she feels a tender sadness; he sends "delightful verses" for her birthday and she transcribes them in her autograph book. His frequent appearance at their dinner table provides her with the opportunity to study his character: "How much there is to pity in a man who is too sensitive for the 'rub and scrub' of life! [she writes in Italian]. We ourselves don't do justice to his merit; how then can the world do it? But knowing his exalted feelings, his sensitiveness, it is cruel to look at him with a cold and critical eye." Yet, in spite of this recognition, something about Irving distanced her, discomforted her when, on occasion, she was left alone with him. Clearly, he never aroused in her a lover's quickening of pulse; on the contrary, she often responded—again, against her better judgment—with "fits" of "coldness." At times she even chided herself for not expressing more "gratitude" for his "esteem & regard." She witnessed his despondency, observed his depression, and understood that "that good dear nice" American author could not satisfy her. "Mr. I——," she perceived, "is in want of constant excitement, & support, interest & admiration of his friends seem the very food he lives on[—]he is easily discouraged & excited." Her sister's observation corroborates Emily's: "It should be perhaps remembered," Flora Foster Dawson wrote in her memoir, "that he was particularly sensitive to praise—not from vanity, but *modesty*; that is to say, he constantly needed the encouragement it afforded him, to keep his courage up to the proper height, or else he had not spirits to write."[43] Without this "support" and "praise," in other words, he could not make his pencil rise to the task. His urbanity, sophistication, and charm did not prevent Emily from seeing that he had a tendency to withdraw into himself, and that he depended on others to arouse him from his emotional lethargy. She could not help noticing that, from women especially, he required kindness, sympathy, nurturing. Gifted with a keen intelligence, she had intuited—though her journal never indicates so directly—that though he could appreciate passion in others, and though he was no stranger to sentiment, basically he lacked sexual ardor.

Stanley Williams argues that, at various times in his life, Irving had sexual relations with women: "He was a man," the biographer writes, "and he experienced the varying feelings of a man toward women, from the youthful worship of Matilda to, probably, the occasional free living in certain periods of his life." On this issue however, I would agree with Marcel Heiman, who believed that Irving led a celibate existence. Like Heiman, I can find no record to substantiate Williams's claim; neither a hint nor an allusion, in letter, notebook, or journal, exists to serve as evidence that Irving's involvements with women were anything other than Platonic friendships. Rather, emotionally dependent and sexually inexperienced, he displaced his erotic energy into his writing. In fact, he often described his literary activity in the the same language that men might use to talk about their sexual lives. When inspiration moved him and words flowed from his pen he felt "excitement": "Ever since I have resumed my pen my spirits have revived and my mind is rising into tone." When he was "dejected" or "depressed" and could not produce he suffered a "fit of sterility." "I want rousing up," he said in one such situation, and then immediately followed it with the words, "I am endeavouring to get my pen into exercise." He needed writing the way most men need sex: having "abandoned" his "pen too long and suffered the fire of composition to go out," he wrote to Emily in 1825, he feels "dismantle[d]." "This fire seems necessary to warm and animate me." On another occasion, in his most explicit metaphor, his pen becomes an object of desire: "from long habit," he told his friend Storrow, "my mind requires to mount the pen occasionally as an old huntsman requires to be occasionally on horseback, even though he hunts to no purpose."[44] Here the pen becomes the woman to be mounted; apparently, this was the only way Irving could climb into the saddle, recalling the cowboy's strong attachment to his horse, which was *his* substitute woman. In sum, the satisfaction many men derive from sexual accomplishment he found solely in a good day's output: "I sleep better & feel pleasanter," he said after tossing off several pages. Emily Foster may not have had the benefit of examining Irving's journals or reading his letters, but she obviously recognized that the source of his power was located primarily in his literary instrument.

We must derive an interpretation of the life before we can accurately and fully read the *Tales*. Like her mother, Emily possessed a warm, enthusiastic nature, and it is hardly surprising that men found her attractive. Before Irving arrived in Dresden she had at least three suitors, an Englishman, an Italian, and a German. The latter, attached to the Bavarian legation at the Saxon court, who pursued her with an intensity far greater than anything Irving could muster, succeeded not only in winning her regard, but in eliciting a lover's responses: at one point, after having inadvertently revealed her feelings, she becomes embarrassed and trembles under his stare; a little while later, when she learns that he has been transferred and must leave Dresden, she spends a sleepless night wondering how she will fill her evenings.[45] Compared to Matilda Hoffman, Emily Foster appears mature and worldly. One has only to glance at their portraits and the difference becomes instantly recognizable: at seventeen, Matilda Hoffman was still a girl, with a girl's willingness to adore and be adored; at eighteen, Emily Foster had already become a woman, with a woman's need for the totality of a man's attention. Neither flirtatious nor suggestive, she had outlets for her energies other than men; for one, she possessed deep religious convictions. Clearly, however, she preferred to be a Bavarian official's *amor* rather than an American writer's ideal.[46] Not yet twenty, and with somewhat limited experience, she nevertheless knew that a man "who is too sensitive for the 'rub and scrub' of life" would most likely fail as a husband. Eventually, she married and had five children. Irving, of course, remained a bachelor, and in his later years at Sunnyside was ministered to by a bevy of nieces.

A strange allusion in one of the letters he sent Mrs. Foster on his trip away from Dresden (where he spoke of feeling of "some consequence" in her domestic circle) will clarify the issue here. When the group left the house and "entered the great maze of fashion," he writes, "I was like the poor little duck in the Grossen Garten, and was fain to draw off to a corner."[47] The following gloss on the passage, provided by Irving's nephew, Pierre, helps decode its hidden meaning:

> In a neglected part of the Grossen Garten was a lonely little lake, near a deserted palace. The only vestige left of the gayety once there, was a melancholy swan, pining alone, until a wild duck took pity on its forlorn estate, and kept it company. There, cheered by his gay little friend, they used to sport and play, until, in an evil hour, three more swans were brought to the place. When the little wild duck came, as usual, to seek his old companion, ungrateful as he was, he turned against him, and, puffing out with pride, joined his new acquaintances to drive off his former friend, who still hung about in corners, and tried to follow, with love stronger than life. But if he dared approach, they all united to attack him, till at last, with blows from their beaks, they killed him, faithful to the last.[48]

In the privacy of Mrs. Foster's home the vagabond Irving, the "wild" duck, feels of "some consequence" as he "sports and plays" with the beautiful swan, Emily, undaunted by competition. In fact, even within that home, he sulks when other guests arrive, and competes with all friends for attention. But in society, "the great maze of fashion," the swan meets three others of its own kind (the Englishman Airey, the Italian Allegri, the Bavarian Gumppenberg?), equally graceful, elegant, young . . . and sexual. The wild duck Irving cannot measure up, though he holds on "with love stronger than life," for if he keeps the swan's companionship he can bask in a renewed sense of himself: he may pretend, if only in her presence (and in the midst of her family), that he, too, is a swan. She, of course, prefers her new mates, who make her feel the "pride" of her own attractiveness and desirability. Since he cannot match their prowess he is discarded; when he continues to approach they turn on him, and with their powerful beaks (something he does not possess) peck him to death. The violence of the final image strongly suggests that the allusion originates in sexual anxiety, and underscores the reason why Irving remained "faithful to the last": maintaining his position in the Fosters' home validated his sexual identity. Merely *courting* a young woman made him feel virile. Consciously, he may have believed he was in love with Emily; unconsciously, however, he "loved" her because he needed and wanted the security of the family and the illusion of being a lover.

Until the time of his proposal, the Fosters' house had been a safe, nonthreatening haven. Here Irving could act out the fantasy of husband and father without having to perform any of the duties (especially the sexual ones) that accompanied those roles. In effect, he was neither married nor single. Though he told himself and the world that "fortune by her tardy favours and capricious freaks seems to discourage all my matrimonial resolves,"[49] in truth he actually feared, on a level far below his own ken, that degree of involvement with women. Yet, as we have seen, he also felt deeply apprehensive about remaining single. Once he had thought that he and his adolescent chums, Paulding, Brevoort, and Gouverneur Kemble, would "form a knot of queer, rum old bachelors, at some future day to meet at the corner of Wall street or walk the sunny side of Broadway and kill time together."[50] Such a vision comforted him; there was, after all, safety in numbers. As long as the group remained intact, he would share a common identity, and his disappointment as an unmarried man would be mitigated. But his friends, as most men eventually do, were settling down. "I cannot bear that all my old companions should launch away into the married state and leave me alone to tread this desolate & sterile shore . . . ," he had earlier told Brevoort.[51] The comparison is striking: they were boats launching (which is a masculine word) ahead; he was, once again, cast away near to drowning, feeling unmanly ("sterile") or immature (like a child, in the line from *Paradise Regained*, "gath'ring pebbles on the shore"). While they would "flourish & fructify and be caressed into prosperity," he added on the occasion of his friend's nuptials, he would be "left lonely & forlorn, and blasted by every wind of heaven."[52] Again they are imaged as sexual and fertile; he is "blasted" and barren. "Melancholy" rather than "glad," Irving was chagrined by the news:

> It seemed in a manner to divorce us forever; for marriage is the grave of Bachelors intimacy and after having lived & grown together for many years, so that our habits thoughts & feelings were quite blended & intertwined, a seperation [sic] of this kind is a serious matter—. . . . Though this unknown piece of perfection has completely usurped my place, I bear her no jealousy or ill will; but hope you may long live happily together, and that she may prove as constant & faithful to you as I have been.

The only marriage he had known until now was with men: indeed, the separation, the "divorce," was a "serious matter," since the "constant & faithful" friend had been abandoned. Now, only he and Kemble were still unwed, and soon, he knew, Kemble would join his comrades (though actually he, too, never married). Irving's conflict is painfully evident: marriage is the *sine qua non* of adult male life and yet he was in dread of it.[53] The "grave of Bachelors['] intimacy," it brings with it the fear of death in the form of sexuality, two themes which are linked recurrently in the stories to come. (Ironically, Irving had told Brevoort that after all the "grave advice" he had given him on the subject of marriage, he felt "regret" that his friend had "serious thoughts of the kind," with the word "grave" again suggesting the association with death.) Thus, if he lost the Fosters he would be facing an untenable position, once again emotionally shipwrecked, treading water, barely surviving. Awaiting him lay the "desolate and sterile shore" of himself.

Irving's offer to Emily thus constituted his hopeless attempt to freeze time, to frame the moment: his goal, futile as it may have been, was to escape both a sexual marriage and a sterile bachelorhood. This he could accomplish only by preserving the home he had found with the Fosters. Had she accepted—a possibility difficult to imagine—he surely would have suffered terrible anxiety, though momentarily he might have convinced himself of his good fortune. Her rejection, however, left him without even a fleeting illusion, and propagated a wave of muted hysteria, since it directly involved an issue that he could not confront: the dread of his own sexuality had remained, and would continue to remain, unexamined. For the present, however, confusion prevailed, which undoubtedly was Irving's way of avoiding the true source of his "excited" condition. From Prague he wrote to Mrs. Foster that his "mind" was in "a restless state of strife & indiscision [sic]"; he was afraid "to confess all the wild ideas & impulses that flit across it." Again he felt evil, guilty; he wished to blur consciousness: "I want to be either quite alone," he said, "with my mind in full exercise, or quite in motion; with my imagination kept in excitement by the rapid change of objects—a partial pause at this moment throws me into a state of inquietude, and suffers a thousand fruitless & uncomfortable feelings to come thronging upon me." Like his youth, his feelings were "fruitless" because they were not generative; they produced no actions or results. Within this labyrinth of emotion, however, he understood that returning to Dresden would be psychologically imprisoning. Yet he acted as if he had no control over himself: "You talk of my coming back [he responded to a letter from Mrs. Foster], "I am ashamed to say it I am almost wishing myself back already[.] I ought to be off like your bird but I feel I shall not be able to keep clear of the cage. I wish I liked you all only half as much as I do."[54]

Never again would Irving experience a crisis of such proportions. "I have fifty plans of what I ought to do & only one of what I should really like to do," he cried out to Mrs. Foster. "My ideas have been flying to all points of the compass, and what I shall do in the end, whether go north, south, east or west—stay where I am—or tamely come back to Dresden[—]is what perplexes me." "It is very ridiculous to talk in this way," he said with some degree of self-consciousness, "yet how can I write frankly & not speak from what is uppermost in my mind. . . . If I come back to Dresden . . . I only come back to take a farewell that would be a more uncomfortable one than I will choose to acknowledge—. . . Why then not keep away now I am here[?]" Why not, indeed, except that nothing less than his identity was at stake:

> When I consider how I have trifled with my time, suffered painful vicissitudes of feeling, which for a time damaged both mind and body—when I consider all this, I reproach myself that I did not listen to the first impulse of my mind, and abandon Dresden long since. And yet I think of returning! Why should I come back to Dresden? The very inclination that draws me thither should furnish reasons for my staying away.[55]

The conflict was so traumatic that on the very day Irving wrote this letter he began to experience pain in his face; two days later he felt "feverish."[56] The delirium persisted throughout his absence from Dresden, to where, one month later, in spite of his self-recrimination and -laceration, he returned, resuming, as closely as he might, his "old habits" and intimacy within the inner sanctum of the Fosters' family circle.[57]

Irving entertained no real hope of Emily's reconsidering her former resolve; he wanted only to replay, for whatever time possible, his patriarchal role in the household and to accompany the Fosters when, on July 12, 1823, they left Dresden for England. The trip through the picturesque Harz mountains marked the last occasion he would act as the head of (t)his family. As they departed, the group formed a memorable tableau: Irving and Mrs. Foster, seated in an open carriage, leading the way; Emily, Flora, their brothers, and the boys' tutor, nestled in a "post chaise," following just behind; with several friends, mounted on horseback, serving as an escort.[58] A stranger, viewing the scene from a slight distance, might easily have thought that a handsome English couple and their children were exiting through the gates of the old German city. The journey took several days, during which time Irving maintained his joviality, but when they reached Kassel, the point at which he was to diverge and make his way up the Rhine toward Paris, he faltered; once more he changed his plans and accompanied the Fosters to Rotterdam where, having arrived at land's end, he had to relent. In his journal he recorded the separation sans emotion; beneath the silence, however, he suffered deeply. Superintending the Fosters' affairs one final time, he secured their berths on the steamboat, acting, Flora Foster Dawson said, "like a man expected to be his own executioner." "Mr. Irving," Emily wrote, "accompanied us down the river quite into the sea, when he was put down into the boat, as he looked up to us, so pale & melancholy, I thought I never felt a more painful moment." On this site "I . . . bade them adieu," Irving told his brother Peter, "as if I had been taking leave of my own family; for they had been for nearly eight months past more like relatives than friends to me."[59] But the wrenching, acute as it was, unfortunately did not signal the end of his misery; though the Fosters were gone, the blank page still awaited him.

Alone in his room in Paris he feared, rather than embraced, the opportunity to transform his travels into sketches. A "dread of future evil—of failure in future literary attempts" took hold of him.[60] "I have," he confessed to his brother Peter, "a kind of horror on me, particularly when I wake in the mornings, that incapacitates me for almost any thing." Although this trepidation about "resuming literary pursuits" may, on the surface, have resembled that of previous occasions, it was nevertheless fundamentally different. "I feel like a sailor," he told Peter, "who has once more put to sea, and is reluctant to quit the quiet security of the shore."[61] Here, Irving varies the "castaway" image to indicate that authorship, his former anchor, now appears like a threatening storm on the horizon. The introspection demanded by the composing process meant setting his bark adrift in the dangerous waters of the private self, a voyage for which this seasoned traveler was, at present, manifestly unprepared. Unlike either the death of Matilda Hoffman or the folding of P. and E. Irving, the Dresden affair with Emily Foster involved emotions that could not be filtered through the lens of art. Though he had previously been successful at distancing himself from his anxieties by projecting them onto a persona whom he then could mock, this time Irving needed to suppress them completely. Yet at first he would not yield to his forebodings: in September 1823, he created the delusion that once he got down to work he would "spin . . . out very fluently" his "German localities, manners, characters."[62] But as soon as he started to write his ailments began to plague him: again, he was hobbled by an inflammation of the ankles and "indisposed" by a swelling in his face.[63] Such unmistakably clear signals prompted him to put aside his fragmentary manuscript, to which he did not return until December of that year when, "restless and anxious," he made another unsuccessful attempt at composition. Six more weeks would pass before he could make the ink flow, and even then he remained "full of uneasy thoughts."[64] His nightmare of creative impotence was fast becoming a reality.

Nevertheless, despite his inability to utilize Geoffrey Crayon, as he had in his *Sketch Book* days, to aid in the therapeutic process, Irving did refashion a positive identity. He was able to reclaim his project and eventually finish *Tales of a Traveller* because, while he never truly healed the wound opened by Emily Foster, he found a way to close it and restore order to his damaged psyche. Although he maintained a correspondence with Mrs. Foster and, perhaps, occasionally lapsed into the fantasy of husband/father, he now channeled all of his energies into a different kind of relationship. In effect, the sense of balance that a lover had upset a disciple restored. John Howard Payne, American playwright and ne'er-do-well (remembered, if at all, as the author of the popular song "Home, Sweet Home" and as a rejected suitor of Mary Shelley) reentered Irving's sphere at just the right moment, and the older writer seized the opportunity to play the comfortable, secure roles of master craftsman and financial consultant, with the younger, less-talented, and profligate dramatist taking the part of the literarily eager but fiscally incorrigible tutee. Irving had initially made Payne's acquaintance in New York in 1806 just after the fifteen-year-old prodigy's first play had been produced in February of that year.[65] The friendship was renewed in Paris in 1821, and then, in the fall of 1823, Payne proposed a collaboration: he would translate works from the French theater and Irving, a sophisticated theatergoer, could edit and adapt them for the London stage. Ever in debt, Payne needed funds badly; he also required

Irving's expertise to carry out his plan, since he had little feel for dramatic structure. Irving, too, could use the extra money, for his Dresden trip, coupled with unsound investments in a steamboat venture, had depleted his resources. In addition, to a certain extent he believed, much as Henry James would in later years, that he had "dramatic stuff" within him.[66] Moreover, if, as Irving demanded, Payne submitted the recast plays to the London theater managers under his own name, then he could maintain his anonymity, thereby indulging his new passion without risking his reputation.[67] But beyond these plausible explanations for why he agreed to Payne's proposal lies one that supersedes them all: basically, the partnership served psychological, not literary, ends.

From the time that Irving first knew Payne, the latter had looked to him for counsel, which the former gave freely and enthusiastically. In 1809, for example, while Payne was on a successful acting tour of several eastern cities, Irving advised the teenager that, despite his popularity, he must not remain in any one place for too long: "You cannot gain greater notoriety & applause; but you may cease to be a novelty—curiosity may become satisfied—and the public becoming familiar with you in private as well as in public, will not have the same eagerness to see you perform, on future occasions. There[']s very little flattery in this to be sure, but you will find it invariably the truth—nor need a man be vexed with the world, nor humbled in his own opinion when he perceives it." Sounding very much like a patient father addressing his recalcitrant son, the twenty-six-year-old Irving also warned the erratic young man that, where economic matters were concerned, he should look to the future:

> And now John [he writes almost pontifically] let me conclude with one more short piece of advice . . . take care of the money you make and dont squander it away idly, like a mere boy. Your present sunshine may be but short, yet in that time, with assiduity & good management, you may lay up a little competence that shall place you out of the reach of bad weather all the rest of your life. . . . [P]lay any thing but the idler, the spendthrift & the little great man—I hope you are superior to all of these.[68]

Superior to none of them and, in fact, taking each one to its limit—even to the extent of spending part of the year 1821 in London's Fleet Prison for judgments brought against him by his creditors[69]—Payne was still enacting these roles in 1823 when the two shared an apartment and huddled over their

175

theatrical venture. But that was precisely the point: instructing the hapless playwright both professionally and financially enabled Irving to reconstitute his shattered sense of self since, compared to his apprentice, he felt remarkably in control of his life. Next to the childish and irresponsible Payne, Irving seemed, if to no one other than himself, the paragon of a mature, stable adult, not like the child "gath'ring pebbles on the shore."

Inadequate as prospective husband, he perfectly, if only temporarily, fulfilled the requirements of father and mentor. After overseeing their "dramatic experiments," he sent Payne off to London at the end of October, 1823, directing his movements and dealings through their correspondence. "Do not suffer yourself, under any circumstances, to make a sacrafice [sic] of any of the pieces," Irving writes in late November; "if the theatres make difficulties, withdraw the pieces at once—theyll accept them at some future time—Dont let them think they can beat you down & get bargains out of you." By mid-December, however, he was cautioning the unpredictable Payne not "to get on ill terms with the managers." "Deal with them always coolly [sic] & good-humouredly—it is the most dignified[,] the most advantageous and the most comfortable way." Primarily encouraging his emissary, he occasionally found it necessary to chastise him: "Dont cry out before your [sic] hurt, nor send *conjectural* bad news, for want of real . . . & let us have no suspicions & doubts & constructions." Annoyed with Payne's "groaning & fretting," he preached, in Polonius-like rhythms, about the danger of adopting a negative attitude: "above all things dont doubt & despond without good reason. Remember fortune is an arrant female—and most apt to play false to those who doubt her." And, once again, like an indefatigable patriarch trying to persuade his hopeless scion to change his wasteful ways, he coaxed Payne toward financial respectability, justifying his persistence (as all parents inevitably do) by reference to the caring feeling that had prompted it:

> Let me again and again press on you the importance of management in your expense. . . . You have it in your power to make twice three times as much as you need to spend,—but through a little mismanagement you are continually toiling to make up foregone & needless expenses. I trust you will arrange your affairs better in future & getting yourself once out of the mire[.] . . . I may bore you a little by the iteration of this topic, but I trust you will properly understand the motive which dictates it,—not a love of finding fault or a desire to wound your feelings, but a sincere and earnest wish for your welfare.[70]

176

Payne, however, proved unredeemable, and had to assume, upon his arrival in London, the alias of J. Hayward, Esq., in order to escape his creditors. The older man knew this and yet he persevered, urging the younger to follow his example: "I never suffer myself to be behind in money matters," he said proudly. More than a year later, and months after *Tales of a Traveller* had been published, he was still berating his friend for his carelessness, still celebrating himself, much like an American rancher whose code was "cash on the barrelhead," as being "tenacious in money matters": "I pay down for every thing, and cannot bear to have an account standing against me: much less to be dunned for one."[71] Clearly, Irving could have maintained no genuine hope of reforming the reprobate; his letters, which flowed relatively unabated until May 1826, and in which he continued to outline plans for Payne's financial solvency, were really exercises in self-rehabilitation—a form of therapy by contrast—and self-congratulation. In fact, he may even have been conscious of the process: in January 1825, after Payne had openly acknowledged his literary assistance in a long dedication to the printed version of one of their joint efforts, Irving wrote somewhat mockingly: "Perhaps you might have mentioned among the many important obligations I have conferred upon you, the vast treasury of *excellent advice*, given freely & gratuitously, and which lies by you as a solid capital, untouched."[72] In any case, though Payne's unpaid bills had cost him no end of aggravation—and a not inconsiderable outlay of funds—during their collaboration, Irving treated him generously when, on January 31, 1824, he (Irving) withdrew from the partnership, insisting that whatever profits might accrue from their efforts belonged to the impecunious playwright.[73] True, in absolute terms he may have been sacrificing only a modest sum, but at the time his own financial condition was, to say the least, precarious. However, compared to the true benefit of the relationship, the restoration of his psychological balance, the money was insignificant. By the middle of February 1824, he was back at his desk; having abandoned the idea of another sketchbook, he now took up the plan for a series of interlocking stories that would become *Tales of a Traveller*. Though he did not realize that the fitful sleep accompanying the resumption of his work was a manifestation of his subliminal dread—a deep uneasiness that would not depart, despite the fact that he was no longer committed to producing a sketchbook, with its blatantly autobiographical content—he nevertheless pushed on with the manuscript. Rising early on the morning of February 19, he wrote steadily throughout the day, marking his progress, as he would continue to do over the next several weeks, in his journal: "finish the story by ½ past 3, having written 23 pages since ½ past 9."[74] Working methodically in units of hours, he was getting the job done and, like Nick Adams in Hemingway's "Big Two-Hearted River," also at the verge of collapse, he was holding himself together.

Once again, therefore, as he had in his pre-*Sketch Book* days, Irving triumphed over despair, conquered self-doubt, and regained his equilibrium. But there was a primary difference between the two episodes: with *Tales*, the process of composition brought no release and no aid to self-reflection. From beginning to end the task was an ordeal, one that left him "all the worse for writing."[75] Yet, in spite of every indication to the contrary, he steadfastly clung to a belief in the ultimate success of his literary endeavors. On the day he recommenced, he entered the following note in his journal about beauty arising from disaster:

> Considering the smallness of the globe what a great part of it is uninteresting & almost uninhabitable, consisting of desarts [sic]—flat monotonous plains &c &c. The beautiful parts are but few & limited & these in fact have been made by convulsions, which have broken the even surface of the original world—thrown up mountains—made crags—precipices[,] vallies . . . So also with the moral world—It is the convulsions & revolutions that have made all that is romantic and picturesque in events & manners—what a dull world this would be for poets & painters had there been no deluge or earthquake and no war.[76]

The metaphor extended as well to the psychological realm: for upwards of two years Irving's life had been "convulsed," its "even surface" ruptured by the trauma of his homelessness, Emily Foster's rejection, and his subsequent but unrecognized sexual anxiety. Could he now wrest a "romantic and picturesque" work of literature from such painful "convulsions," such "revolutionary" experience? Apparently he thought he had done just that, for on March 25, 1824, he wrote to his publisher that friends who had read parts of the manuscript "think the work will be the best thing I have written and that it will be very successful with the public—An author is not perhaps the best judge of his productions otherwise I might throw my own opinion into the scale."[77] Sadly, as far as *Tales* was concerned, Irving remained the worst of judges. He could never quite understand why the book he self-deludedly claimed was "written in a freer and happier vein than almost any of my former writings," that contained "more of an artist like touch about it—though this is not a thing to be appreciated by the many," turned out to be nothing less than a critical failure.[78]

II

How is it possible that the man who had such a torturous time finishing *Tales of a Traveller* (who had confided in his journal that he was "all the worse for writing")—who, again in the privacy of his diary, said that he was "distrustful" of his "work"[79]—could tell his best friend that the book was "written in a freer and happier vein" than any of his other and, to be sure, far more successful productions? How could he use the mild phrase "has met with some handling from the press" to categorize the critical response when, in fact, its publication called forth a blast of negative reviews that ranged from describing Geoffrey Crayon as "indisputably feeble, unoriginal, and timorous" to damning the tales as "poor second-hand, second-rate manufactures," to charging their author with the "vulgarism of indelicacy" while condemning parts of his book as "indecent?"[80] Knowing all this, indeed, suffering terribly as a consequence of these attacks—often entering in his journal the words "restless," "uneasy," and "depressed" to describe his current state of being[81]— how could he have said, in this December 1824 letter to Brevoort, that "as I do not read criticism good or bad, I am out of the reach of attack"? (Had he completely forgotten his journal notation, made only two weeks before, which recounted how, at the bookseller Galignani's, he had "met my evil genius . . . who told me the critics were attackg me like the d——l in Engd—Retd home for a short time but could not remain—downhearted—. . . A rainy day tho mild—a Black day to me"?)[82] Clearly, Irving's feelings about his new book were so confused and contradictory that just months after it was published he could not properly sort out events and emotions related to its composition, or its reception. In addition, wounded deeply by this onslaught, he was desperately trying to protect himself in any way he could manage, even if it meant— and surely this was unconscious—engaging in self-delusion. How else to account for the fact that, when it came to discussing the work with friends and relatives, not only did memory fail him, but on at least one occasion he actually lied about its genesis. It seems incredible that he could have told his sister that his current writings "are more true to life; for they are the transcripts of scenes that I have witnessed," when page after page in his journal indicates that friends and acquaintances supplied him with anecdotes and reminiscences that he transmuted into the stories that constituted his disparate collection.[83] Yet, if we take "witnessed" to mean "bearing witness to" or emotionally experiencing, then he is far more accurate than he realizes.

This context of misstatement and misperception calls into question Irving's most widely quoted pronouncement about his fictional practices, which comes, not so surprisingly, in the same 1824 letter to Brevoort: "I fancy much of what I value myself upon in writing, escapes the observation of the great mass of my readers: who are intent more upon the story than the way in which it is told." What he really cares about, he said, is "the play of thought, and sentiment and language; the weaving in of characters, lightly yet expressively delineated; the familiar and faithful exh[i]bition of scenes in common life; and the half-concealed vein of humour that is often playing through the whole." Like his other statements to Brevoort, this one also deflects attention from any personal involvement in his tales; again, Irving evades the issue of responsibility for the more disturbing aspects of his imaginative projections. Certainly his concentration on "execution" should not be ignored, nor should his desire to satirize and thwart the expectations accompanying both sentimental and gothic fiction go unexamined.[84] But formal and generic considerations simply do not account for what remains compelling about Irving's third European work. The fact that, having willingly deceived himself, he remained purposely blind to what he had wrought points toward *Tales* as the revelation of personal truths and sexual anxieties too painful to acknowledge.

In the preface to *Tales*, which is surely the strangest and most deceptive of any Irving ever wrote, Geoffrey Crayon addresses, in good nineteenth-century fashion, the "Worthy and Dear Reader," but after this conventional salutation he strikes several unexpected and alien poses. Bedridden by some unnamed "treacherous malady" in the "old frontier town of Mentz," restless, unable to concentrate on his German lessons, or even to read, Crayon appears on the verge of nervous collapse: "I have worn out every source of amusement. I know the sound of every clock that strikes, and bell that rings, in the place. I know to a second when to listen for the first tap of the Prussian drum, as it summons the garrison to parade, or at what hour to expect the distant sound of the Austrian military band" (p. 11). Sounding like one of Poe's obsessed narrators speaking from within a haunted chamber rather than Irving's familiar persona, Crayon says that he has decided, in order to keep the monotony from driving him crazy, to compile a book from materials he has gathered while traveling. Although these circumstances are hardly the ones under which Irving completed his work, to a certain extent Crayon's emotional imbalance here reflects his creator's during those months of strained composition. And the intensity, exaggerated and heightened for effect, makes Crayon appear misshapen, unrecognizable. The whimsical traveler/observer of *The Sketch Book* is nowhere to be found.

Whatever sincerity the opening paragraphs of the preface contain quickly vanishes in the remaining ones. After stating his intentions, Crayon then proceeds to mock the very enterprise in which he is engaged: "The art of book-making has been made familiar to the meanest capacity. Everybody is an author. The scribbling of a quarto is the mere pastime of the idle." If a young gentleman can toss off a "brace of duodecimos in the intervals of the sporting-season," if a young lady can compose a "set of volumes with the same facility that her great-grandmother worked a set of chair-bottoms," then why should Geoffrey Crayon not arrange his papers for publication? Surely he can be forgiven for his presumption if everyone else shares it. Considering that in 1824 Washington Irving was the most famous American author in the world, this is not just modesty, or even its opposite, satiric parody, but rather an attempt at absolute self-effacement, as if Crayon were blotting out his public image instead of building on it. After all, why should the narrator of *The Sketch Book* have to explain or defend himself? One reason is that, because he feels like a Hemingway hero who has to prove himself with every book, he wants to remove some of the pressure from his performance. And, on an even deeper level, he would like to escape responsibility altogether for that performance.

Having in the space of two pages presented himself as an invalid, a neurotic, and an amateur, Crayon now dons the mask of doctor of morality. Though it may not be apparent at first, each of his tales, he claims, contains a "sound moral," since he is "for curing the world by gentle alteratives, not by violent doses." "The patient," he continues, "should never be conscious that he is taking a dose." (And, to be sure, a "dose" is just what he gets.) Therefore, he has "disguised" his moral by "sweets and spices, so that while the simple reader is listening with open mouth to a ghost or a love story, he may have a bolus of sound morality popped down his throat, and be never the wiser for the fraud." "Fraud" is surely the right word for what takes place here: clearly, there has never been anything didactic about Geoffrey Crayon. In fact, according to the contemporary American author and critic John Neal, rather than hiding morality, these tales "smuggle[d] impurity" into American households. Instead of earning his audience's gratitude, Neal argued, Irving deserved its censure, for he had betrayed the faith placed in him as an "immaculate creature for this profligate age."[85] Something other than a "bolus of morality" was being forced down the throat of the "simple reader."

All this masking suggests that, consciously or not, Crayon (and behind him Irving) wants to evade responsibility for the impressions his tales may create. Thus, toward the end of the preface, he declares that, as "an old traveller," he has "read," "heard," "seen," and "dreamt" more than he can possibly account for. "My brain," he says, "is filled . . . with all kinds of odds and ends." Like items of clothing in an "ill-packed travelling-trunk," these "heterogeneous matters" have become so jumbled in his mind during his journeying that he no longer can separate fact from fiction: "I am always at a loss to know how much to believe of my own stories" (p. 14). In effect, he has called the status of every detail in the collection into question, since he does not remember whether it ultimately derives from a book, or a conversation, or from the fantasies and nightmares to which he is prone. Therefore, no blame can be laid on him for whatever excesses or "impurities" *Tales* may contain: after all, as he has just told us, the source of any image, symbol, or metaphor is undetermined and indeterminate. An elaborate scheme of justification, this argument permits Crayon to withdraw from his own creation, which he proceeds to do by disappearing behind a series of narrators and interpolated tales, from the Nervous Gentleman and other guests at the hunting dinner in Part One, to Buckthorne in Part Two, to the various travelers in Part Three, to Diedrich Knickerbocker in Part Four. With no role to play (except as Buckthorne's auditor) in any of the narratives and without an interpretive function to perform, Crayon becomes superfluous. His final introductory act reinforces his desire for anonymity while underlining his hostility: dating the document "from the Hotel de Darmstadt, *ci-devant* Hotel de Paris, Mentz, otherwise called Mayence," Crayon falsely leads the reader to conclude that the following pieces have some relationship to this German locale. Irving knew that his audience was expecting a "German work," and the preface implies that they will not be disappointed. A subterfuge, especially since it posits a geographical unity that does not exist, the statement functions as another disguise behind which Geoffrey Crayon hides. Moreover, it coalesces an attitude toward the reader which has, up to this point, remained diffused: instead of functioning as an ally, Crayon has become his adversary, frustrating him by creating expectations that he cannot, or will not, satisfy.

Thus, rather than exonerate, the preface actually implicates Crayon/Irving in the matter of his tales: culpability must fall on him precisely because he tries too hard to evade it. And, right from the outset, one sees why: the first three (supposed) ghost stories—"The Adventure of My Uncle," "The Adventure of My Aunt," and "The Bold Dragoon"—slim, ephemeral productions though they may be, nevertheless have a current of innuendo running through them which is composed of more than just sly jokes and risqué humor. These tales manage to suggest what will become manifest before the first section concludes: sexuality, more than just a taboo subject and therefore the secret source of the vitality of much sentimental and gothic fiction, is a subversive and destructive force, and must be avoided or repressed. In "The Adventure of My Uncle," the narrator's uncle encounters the specter of a woman who had been ravaged in the room which he occupies. In "The Adventure of My Aunt," another narrator's aunt is threatened with rape and mutilation by a sword-wielding vagabond who, we are told in Irving's double-edged prose, had "stolen into her chamber to violate her purse, and rifle her strong box, when all the house should be asleep" (p. 51). In "The Bold Dragoon," yet another narrator's grandfather displays such prowess and agility that he manages to visit several rooms of an inn throughout the night (for purposes of seduction and sex, though this is not explicit) and in his own room he literally makes the furniture dance. But what appears to be a celebration of masculine might, albeit couched behind ambiguous language, has an underside to it: the Irish dragoon, who found his way "among the petticoats" better than any man the narrator ever knew, has a sexual appetite that is out of control, the implication being that once he gets going (when "the blood in his veins" runs "in a fever-heat") he will accept anyone—or anything—as a partner. There is, too, something tawdry in the depiction of the dancing furniture: a "coxcombical" leather chair "thrusts out" a claw foot and slides up to a "tarnished" "easy-chair . . . with a hole in its bottom"; a "three-legged stool" tries a hornpipe but is "horribly puzzled by its supernumerary limb" (p. 63). Though one critic finds this scene—which may be nothing more than the dragoon's drunken vision—"appropriately erotic," it is distasteful and, moreover, has an unsavory effect on the reader, as if the sexualizing of inanimate objects actually could provide some form of titillation.[86]

Ghost stories without active ghosts, bothersome interlocutors challenging narrators' authority, inklings of sexual licentiousness which never develop—all these contribute to the tactics of disruption that Irving employs in order to prohibit the reader from imaginatively entering the world of his tales. Additionally, several times within the first three stories a "hatchet-faced" inquisitive gentleman interrupts the narrative as it is building suspense, his physiognonomy a symbol of his power to destroy continuity (a readerly coitus interruptus), thus frustrating both tale-teller and audience. In this opening section, therefore, Irving teases the reader with promises of fulfilling experience, then denies him the pleasure of the anticipated climax. Using a language as suggestive as Irving's (and my own), one contemporary reviewer said that these stories "seem all wanting in those satisfactory conclusions for which we pant so ardently, when our curiosity has been put to the rack, and our sympathies worked to a considerable fermentation." Moreover, he added, "they often break off suddenly, like those broken skeins of incident, of which our dreams are composed." Hedges believes this writer has "miss[ed] the point," which may be true in terms of Irving's conscious intention to parody the techniques of the popular fiction of the day; in another sense, however, he is right on the mark, since he has absorbed, albeit unawares, Irving's unconscious strategy for displacing his own sexual frustrations into the aborted structure of his tales. The problem here is not, as the anonymous reviewer claimed, that he "displays a levity, and sometimes stoops to a vulgarity, which must pain a serious, and disgust a delicate mind," but rather that, in neglecting an opportunity for self-exploration through his Crayonesque persona, Irving exposes himself in a way that surely would have appalled him had he been a witness to his own exhibition.[87]

When he does furnish his readers with a (veiled) glimpse of consummation, it is nothing short of horrifying. The "Adventure of the German Student" (which takes place during the French Revolution) marks the first of three stories that involve a disturbed protagonist's relationship to an ideal or, more precisely, an "idealized" woman. Gottfried Wolfgang, the student of the title—who, it should be noted, carries, like his creator, a last name which is usually a first name—has withdrawn so deeply into the study of "speculative doctrines" that he has ceased to function effectively in the world at large. The consequences of these pursuits are severe: he suffers from impaired health and a "diseased" imagination. Moreover, because he admires women but is too shy to approach them, his reveries focus on "images of loveliness" which far surpass anything reality can offer until, in an oft-repeated dream, he fashions an image of the eternal feminine. A figure of "transcendent beauty," she takes possession of his thoughts in a way similar to that in which Matilda Hoffman haunted Irving's memory. At this point the surface events of the story, though apparently quite clear, are sufficiently ambiguous in their implications to permit multiple interpretations. Late one night Gottfried passes by the guillotine which, Irving carefully informs us, "had that very day been actively employed in the work of carnage," and spies a woman dressed in black slumped by the steps leading up to the scaffold. When he speaks to her she raises her head and he beholds the very face of his dreams. Inquiring if she has a home, he receives the answer "Yes—in the grave!" Whereupon he carries her off to his apartment, literally "support[ing] her faltering steps" through the now quiet streets. When he discovers that she is an "enthusiast" like himself, he confesses his "mysterious dream," conducts a spontaneous marriage ceremony, and swears his allegiance to her forever. She accepts by pledging "I am yours," and they spend the night together. (Irving devotes an entire page of a nine-page story describing this pact.) In the morning Gottfried leaves his "bride" sleeping while he seeks larger quarters, but when he returns he finds her dead body in his bed. A policeman, summoned by the student, recognizes the figure and shouts "how did this woman come here?" He registers shock, naturally enough, because she had been guillotined the previous day, and when (as if to prove the point) he removes a black band from around her neck her head falls to the floor, driving Gottfried first into a mad frenzy and ultimately to an asylum (pp. 66–74).

By using a technique that Hawthorne was to perfect, Irving creates enough uncertainty to allow his reader—and himself—to deny the central, and awful, experience of the story: in his desperate hunger for union with the woman of his dreams, the German student has copulated with a corpse. Since Gottfried has believed from the outset that an "evil genius" has been pursuing him, seeking to "ensure his perdition," and since, as a way of explaining or justifying his necrophilia, he seizes on the idea "that an evil spirit had reanimated the dead body," we can read the "adventure" as a story of supernatural possession (an early version, perhaps, of "The Exorcist"). Or, since the narrator claims to have heard the tale from the student himself, whom he met in a "mad-house" in Paris, we are encouraged to see it as the raving of a deranged soul. Therefore, no event attains the status of "fact"; every occurrence is subject to undecidability and dismissal. There is, secondly, the possibility that the story is nothing more than the projection of a mad narrator who, because his face has a "dilapidated" look, is described as "the old gentleman with the haunted head"; after all, what was he doing in the madhouse with the student? Again, certainty is defied. As Hedges has pointed out about the first of Irving's obstacles to consistent interpretation, but which also holds true for the second, the tale is reduced to a joke.[88] However, though plausible, these explanations overlook many of the carefully placed details of the story and fail to account for whatever power it possesses to compel the reader's attention, which involves the psychology of the student's troubled mind: lonely and isolated, unable to establish a relationship with a woman, he is driven to distraction by his unsatisfied need until, on a night during the "reign of terror," he sees in the dead woman by the guillotine the incarnation of his beloved. She serves as the perfect love object, since she offers no resistance to his idealization of her. She is precisely what he wants her to be: "ravishingly beautiful," alone, and helpless. He then gets to play the role of savior and, once their pact is made, husband and lover. Though his imagination may be "diseased," and though he may have acted in a delirium, he loses his sanity only when he realizes the extent of his sexual perversion. In effect, Irving has concretized and exaggerated his own romantic situation: his first love, Matilda Hoffman, was literally dead, his second, Emily Foster, emotionally dead to him.

To quote Fitzgerald in *The Great Gatsby*, one pays "a high price for living too long with a single dream." Irving, it is safe to say, knew something about obsession, consumed as he was by the future and the hope of marriage and by the past and the heartbreak of loss. Like Gottfried, he had harbored a vision that "haunted his thoughts by day, his slumbers by night." For fifteen years he had been longing for his ideal love, the sweet, gentle, tender Matilda Hoffman; since her death in 1809 she had been a continual presence in his mind. In a passage from an 1817 notebook which apostrophizes her, he recollects their parting scene and recalls his misery:

> Oh Matilda where was the soul-felt devotion—the buoyancy—
> the consciousness of worth & happiness that once seemed to lift
> me from the earth when our eyes interchanged silent but eloquent
> vows of affection . . . how lovely was then my life—How has it
> changed since—what scenes have I gone through since thou hast
> left me—what jarring collisions with the world—what heartless
> pleasures—what sordid pursuits—what gross associations—what
> rude struggles—. . . . The romance of life is past[.] [89]

The "sordid pursuits," "gross associations," and "rude struggles" that Irving endured refer, primarily, to the suffering he knew during the collapse and eventual bankruptcy of the family business—which, to be sure, was genuine and severe—yet his language connotes sexual dissipation or profligacy, as if he had been forced to take to the streets and make his way among whores, prostitutes, and pimps; from another point of view, he could almost be describing the wretched excesses of the French Revolution that Gottfried witnesses in the streets of Paris. It appears as if once the ideal vanishes, and with her the possibility of transcendence ("the consciousness . . . that once seemed to lift me above the earth"), then what remains are the dregs of experience. Yet, in spite of all the "scenes" he had "gone through," Irving never lost his faith in this concept; in 1828, in Madrid, after seeing a woman named Madame Alcañices perform a tableau based on Murillo's version of the Immaculate Conception, he gave verbal expression to the beliefs that, years earlier, had been intimately bound up with his love for Matilda:

> It was more like a vision of Something Spiritual and celestial than a representation of any thing merely mortal; or rather it was a woman, as, *in my romantic days* I have been apt to imagine her, approaching to the Angelic nature. I have frequently admired Madame Alkanisas as a *mere* beautiful woman when I have seen her dressed up in the fantastic finery of the mode; but here I beheld her elevated into a representation of divine purity and grace, exceeding even the *beau ideal* of the painter, for she even Surpassed in beauty the picture of Murillo. I felt as if I could have knelt down and worshiped [sic] her. . . . For my part I am superstitious in my admiration of [women], and like to walk in a perpetual delusion, decking them out as divinities. I thank no one to undecieve [sic] me and to prove that they are *mere* mortals[.] I shall feel quite Sorry when I meet Madame Arkanesas again to find her once more returned from the clouds, a *mere* fashionable lady.[90]

Clearly, Irving prefers women in their "Angelic" state since, like Lily Bart in Edith Wharton's *The House of Mirth*, Madame Alcañices becomes only a "mere beautiful woman" once the tableau has concluded. (Notice that he uses the word "mere" three times to describe her normal state.) Unlike Lawrence Selden, however, he has no desire to approach the being who could, momentarily, create such an image of perfection. By 1828 he had apparently resigned himself to the role of admiring bachelor, an idealist content to keep the object of his adoration at a safe viewing distance, thus protecting himself, his faith in the transcendent, and his memories.

But in 1824, in his "romantic days," it was somewhat different. He was still lamenting Matilda's absence, still keeping her image alive in his imagination, only now he was projecting it onto others:

> She died in the flower of her youth & of mine but she has lived for me ever since in all woman kind. I see her in their eyes and it is the remembrance of her that has given a tender interest in my eyes to every thing that bears the name of woman.[91]

Not only, like Gottfried, does he idealize a dead woman, but in this way he had also tried to spiritualize Emily Foster, to remake her in Matilda Hoffman's image; she constituted his attempt to recapture the "romance of life." In her eyes he saw Matilda's, just as in those of the guillotined woman Gottfried envisioned his dream lover. Irving had dropped his protective guard long enough to offer vows, but Emily had not responded with the words "I am yours." Her rejection cast him adrift in a turmoil of emotions, which the "Adventure of a German Student" mirrors, ranging from despair at never possessing the ideal to horror at what that possession costs, both psychologically and psychosexually.

It is the latter that induces a fear which, in the context of the story, is justified: sexual pursuit brings madness and death. Without a beloved Gottfried remained a melancholy man, distracted by the fixed idea of her loveliness but still sane. However, to have the woman of your dreams, to win, like the student with his "honest earnestness," first her "confidence," then her "heart," and finally her body ("'I am yours,' murmured she, and sank upon his bosom") means leaving the insular and safe world of self-contained fantasy and reverie and entering the dangerous territory of amatory relations. This results in loss of control and psychic disintegration. Yet the fear extends even further to include utter powerlessness and impotence. The guillotine—"horrible engine" of destruction, "dreadful instrument of death"—whose "scaffold was continually running with . . . blood," sickening the student's heart and causing a shudder to ripple through him, looms imposingly in the background and represents sexuality's absolute threat—the dread of discovering that one's masculinity is not intact. It calls to mind the recurring images of "maiming and cutting down" that appear often in Irving's fiction, which, according to Hedges, "carry an unconscious implication of fear of castration."[92] Suggesting, therefore, along with the the decapitated head, the archetypal male "fear," the presence of the guillotine forces us to acknowledge the terror in the souls of both character and creator, who have seen a void where a sexual identity should exist. Both were, to recall the line Irving copied and italicized from *Paradise Regained*, "*Deep verst in books & shallow in himself.*"

If the ideal cannot be possessed, then perhaps it can be preserved, and in "The Story of the Young Italian" we have a protagonist who fiercely dedicates himself to just such a task, ultimately committing an impassioned murder when the woman he chastely adores is stolen from him and abused. The tale, in the hand of the guilt-ridden young Italian, Ottavio, is offered primarily as a way of explaining a mysterious and disturbing picture he had painted, which turns out to be the agonized face of the man he killed. An overly long and inadequately sustained account of his life, the story's real interest involves the sublimation of his sexual feelings into art and his passion for his beloved into idolatry. Shunted off to a monastery from a home in which he had been neglected, he flees, making his way to Genoa where he becomes apprenticed to a painter of great eminence. While under this master's tutelage he first spies the lovely and pure Bianca (the word means "white" in Italian), whom he immediately wants to "worship," just as Irving did with Matilda and Emily (and later, for a moment, Madame Alcañices). She was, he says, "like one of those fictions of poets and painters, when they would express the *beau ideal* that haunts their minds with shapes of indescribable perfection" (p. 112). Already she is a type; thus, naturally, "she seemed too exquisite for earthly use [the word has sexual overtones]; too delicate and exalted for human attainment." Nevertheless, he feels "giddy" in her presence, as if he had been drinking in a "delicious poison." "Violent fires" burst forth from his "soul," though as soon as he acknowledges his passion he represses it. Like the German student, he is too shy, inexperienced, and fearful to act, preferring to let her image dwell in his imagination, where it becomes his "pervading idea of beauty." Thus, he transforms Bianca into muse and model and becomes noted for his "felicity in depicting female loveliness."

The circumstances under which the pair next meet exacerbate the young Italian's conflict which, to be sure, is Irving's writ large: as much as he wants to possess his beloved, he also desperately needs to idealize her, and the more he idealizes her the more unapproachable she becomes. He remains locked in unconscious battle with himself, which accounts for his turbulent emotional responses, especially throughout this part of the story. Both have been taken into the house of the same wealthy nobleman, who has become patron to Ottavio, protector to Bianca. The proximity of his beloved intensifies the Italian's already heated feelings: at the same time she confirms all his "ideal picturings," her "young, and tender, and budding loveliness" sends a "delicious madness" to his brain (p. 117). According to Hedges, "overtones of incest" develop with the suggestion of a brother/sister relationship[93]—the pair do draw closer together—but, if anything, the young man becomes more fearful of approaching his chaste ideal; the instant he feels aroused he suppresses his erotic urges and willfully gazes on her as "something more than mortal." In addition, like Irving during his Dresden days, he bemoans his poverty: without "wealth" or "prospect" he can make no claim on her affections. His confession of his unworthiness echoes Irving's own language in the correspondence: "I am an offcast from my family—a wanderer—a nameless, homeless wanderer—with nothing but poverty for my portion; and yet I have dared to love you—have dared to aspire to your love" (p. 120). When he hears of his brother's death and his father's affliction, and learns that all is forgiven, he waxes ecstatic, since he can now claim the very things Irving himself desired, "a home, a name, rank, wealth."

Despite Ottavio's torment, the story might still have arrived at a conventional ending, whether comic or tragic, had not Irving inserted into this cauldron of emotions a third actor, the count's son Filippo, who, from the time Ottavio first arrives at his father's house, attaches himself to the painter. The young Italian reciprocates the affection and the two become "intimate friends and frequent companions." About the same age, they are like brothers (completing the brother/sister triangle), except for one basic, crucial difference: where Ottavio is passive, gentle, and considerate, Filippo is aggressive, violent, and tyrannical. (Later, when Ottavio slays him—for Filippo's countenance is the one he paints—he says that he fled from the scene "like another Cain,—a hell within my bosom, and a curse upon my head.") With the introduction of this character, Irving externalizes what had heretofore been Ottavio's internal struggle, for Filippo functions, in effect, as a double, the dark sexual aspect of the Italian's nature that he had been keeping under iron control. Not surprisingly, Irving was fascinated by the concept of a divided self, and in 1825 he tried to find the lost play of Calderon de la Barca on this topic, *El Embozado* (the masked or disguised one), especially after he discovered that Byron had planned to write a drama based on the idea. In fact, Irving himself sketched out scenes for a play, in which he describes the "Embozado" as the protagonist Fernando's "Second self." In his version, the hooded figure tries to prevent Fernando's seduction of a village maid and, when he fails, haunts and "molests" him until he throws himself from a precipice and drowns.[94] "The Young Italian" is an earlier, not fully realized, and perhaps only partially conscious variation on the same theme: here the double takes sexual license with the young woman while the protagonist dutifully attends to a dying parent. Having been entrusted with Bianca's care, Filippo suppresses Ottavio's letters, declares his death, marries Bianca, and then "use[s]" her "harshly," exactly what Ottavio, in the same language, had declared must never happen. And it is Filippo who then perishes violently: utterly enraged when he discovers that he has been betrayed, Ottavio stabs his double mercilessly. The extent of his unbridled, unabated anger is shocking: "I sprang upon him with the blood-thirsty feeling of a tiger; redoubled my blows; mangled him in my frenzy, grasped him by the throat, until, with reiterated wounds and strangling convulsions, he expired in my grasp" (p. 135).

An act of "unsated" rage, the slashing of Filippo resonates with meaning beyond Ottavio's punishing him for his perfidy. "Was this beauteous flower snatched from me to be thus trampled upon?" he thinks just before he accosts Filippo, and the question, which rouses him to "madness"—literally causing him to "foam at the mouth"—drives him on to commit his ghastly deed. The heavenly woman of his devotions has been defiled by a being over whom he believed he had established "superiority." Symbolically, his repressed sexuality has broken free of mental control and ravished the ideal he had sacrificed his masculinity to protect. Frustration plays its part here as well, and as the battle within him breaks out into full-scale war he destroys, in what amounts to an act of self-mutilation, that part of him which he could not harmonize with his frantic need to elevate his beloved to a position of stainless innocence. No wonder, then, that he feels such tremendous guilt and remorse since, in effect, he has committed an unnatural act, killing not only a pseudo-brother, but part of himself: "Oh! could I but have cast off this crime that festered in my heart—could I but have regained the innocence that reigned in my breast as I entered the garden at Sestri." Ottavio's desire to preserve the purity of a sexless relationship reminds one of the duck in the Grossen Garten who only wanted to swim in the vicinity of the graceful swan, admiring her beauty, basking in the reflected glory of her perfect form. Another hopeless dream, that, too, ended in symbolic sexual violence. Capable of neither possessing nor preserving the ideal, Irving again directs his anger inward, furious at having found himself in such a psychologically untenable position.

Clearly, something within him broke free of customary restraint during the writing of *Tales*; the sexual urges he could not directly express through action he vented in these violent characters and alter egos. Thus, in the third panel of this symbolic triptych, "The Story of the Young Robber," where he unleashes an outright attack on the ideal itself, he leaves the reader with no choice but to reflect back on the events in his own life that caused such bitterness. The final tale in the section called "The Italian Banditti" (followed only by the conclusion of the frame narrative), the "Young Robber" climaxes Irving's use of sexually suggestive material by making innuendo and undercurrent yield to explictness. The highwaymen, the romanticized "banditti" who terrorize the road between Naples and Rome, earn their fame as sexual outlaws by raping, not once but multiple times, the fair, innocent, and chaste Rosetta, another madonna figure for yet another protagonist who needs an image of saintliness to worship. After the bandit chief ravishes her, lots are drawn and the "help-less girl" is "abandoned to the troop" (p. 414). The cruelest episode in all his fiction, it shocked his contemporary audience; the *United States Literary Gazette*, for example, called the scene "revolting" and complained that it was "unnecessarily forced on the reader's imagination." Questioning Irving's motivation, it fumed over the fact that these "horrors" were the "only *incidents* of the story" that he had invented. "We have heard the tale ourselves," the reviewer added, "the same in every thing but these particulars." [95] But Irving was by no means in control of his creative impulses, and he was unaware that in recycling the story he was using it as an outlet for, while transforming it into an emblem of, his repressed rage over his impotence, psychological as well as physical. The hero here, the unnamed "young robber" of the title, does not actually participate in the sexual savaging of his "fresh" and "tender" love, but as her executioner he "possesses" her in a way that, despite his agony, implicates him in her violation.

Like both the German student and the Italian painter, the young robber is an ardent admirer of women, but unlike these celibate men he has had his share of sexual experience. His "easy success" among the "sunburnt females" of his village, however, has not brought contentment; if anything, it has increased his hunger for virginal purity, which Rosetta satisfies. Unfortunately, her father favors another suitor, a wealthy farmer from a nearby town, whom the young man stilettos in a moment of jealous fury. (Emily Foster rejected Irving partly due to his poverty, or so he believed; again and again he blamed his lack of a steady income for his inability to enter the married state.) Irving seems to have had a particular fondness for this weapon, since it is the same one with which Ottavio kills Filippo and which the robber later uses on Rosetta. A potent instrument of destruction with its long, slender, pointed blade, it pierces its victim easily and brings death instantly. But it also draws a great deal of blood. Thus it suggests, in addition to his prowess, the young man's fierce passion, which intensifies after he joins the bandit gang as a means of seeking refuge from the law. In addition, "stiletto" is related to "stylo" (short for stylograph) and "stylus," two kinds of writing implements (*stylo* in French is the colloquial form of *stylographe*, a fountain pen), and thus may have reminded Irving, on a subconscious level, of the instrument of his own power.

The vengeance that Ottavio wrecked on Filippo the robber will now, in the name of love, commit on Rosetta since, unlike Irving, he refuses to accept either rejection or defeat. He must possess her, which means, in the psychology that rages here, that she has to be destroyed, since possession of the ideal is a logical impossibility. One night when the gang is prowling in the vicinity of her home, he steals off to find her. Like a voyeur, he peers through the vines that line a path where she customarily strolls, growing excited when he spies her just beyond, dressed in white. Thrusting himself forward, he accosts her; when she screams, the other bandits appear and carry her off for purposes of ransom. Still, he pursues his claim, insisting that she be entrusted to his care. His language reveals his frenzied desire: "Her head rested on my shoulder; I felt her breath on my face, and it seemed to fan the flame which devoured me. Oh God! to have this glowing treasure in my arms, and yet to think it was not mine! . . . [My] brain was fevered with the thought that any but myself should enjoy her charms." Sexual jealousy again ends in "impotent rage," which ultimately will be directed toward the beloved herself. But before Rosetta can die, she will have to be ravaged. Lingering over the description of her defilement, Irving seems to take perverse pleasure in the details:

> I beheld the wretched victim [says the young robber], pale, disheveled, her dress torn and disordered. . . . To what a condition was she reduced! she, whom I had once seen the pride of Frosinone, whom but a short time before I had beheld sporting in her father's vineyard, so fresh, and beautiful, and happy! Her teeth were clenched; her eyes fixed on the ground; her form without motion, and in a state of absolute insensibility. I hung over her in an agony of recollection at all that she had been, and of anguish of what I now beheld her. I darted around a look of horror at my companions, who seemed like so many fiends exulting in the downfall of an angel. (pp. 414–15)

But fall the angel must, and when her father refuses to pay the ransom, on the grounds that she has already been "dishonored," the robber insists that he be the one to execute the death sentence. Hastening to "seize upon" his "prey," he at last enjoys "exclusive" possession of his bride. Skillfully "plung[ing]" his knife "into her bosom," he dispatches her in "triumph," a deed that apparently brings him satisfaction: "a painful and concentrated murmur, but without any convulsive movement, accompanied her last sigh." Ironically, but nevertheless aptly, the only image of union in the entire book—and the one true erotic moment in all of Irving's fiction—involves a surrogate sexual act that spells death for the woman. In Irving's male fantasy, the homicide victim has become the ideal partner. A means of purging fear, hostility, and pain, the violence, in addition to its potential for catharsis, also signals Irving's vicarious thrill in the despoiling of the ideal, his only possible victory. Here, in fact, we have the reversal of the Grossen Garten story: the duck has his revenge as the lovely, graceful female gets pecked to death by the horde of male bandits. No wonder Crayon had to disappear from the text. How could Irving's gentle persona have presided over such a desecration?

Paradoxically, *Tales of a Traveller*, Washington Irving's least autobiographical fiction, may well be his most revealing. Desperate to complete the book whose composition caused him no end of aggravation, he nevertheless managed to find stories he could use not only to fill out the two volumes, but also to release potentially crippling anxieties, both psychologically and, if we remember his mysterious ailments, his swelling legs, physically as well. He fashioned the "Adventure of the German Student" from a tale related to him by Thomas Moore; he modeled "The Story of the Young Italian" on Washington Allston's romance, *Monaldi*; he derived "The Story of the Young Robber" from the true account of a kidnapped servant of Lucien Bonaparte.[96] Yet in each case he made alterations and additions that turned the tales into vehicles of personal expression: most significantly, he pushed the violent action to extremes and heightened the stainless purity of the ideal woman. The question of his awareness, therefore, continues to nag: could he really have been oblivious to what had transpired in the writing process? Yet the answer, as far as can be determined, remains yes: neither in the voluminous journals and notebooks that he kept from 1822 through 1826, nor in the many letters he wrote during this period, does there appear one word of private confession or public acknowledgment in regard to the sexual undercurrent of *Tales*, except for one line in a journal entry dated April 8, 1824, which reads "distrustful of my work—particularly Robber Stories," and even that remains ambiguous. Having read the "illnatured fling" at him in the American newspapers and the harsh comments leveled by the English periodicals, he wrote that "It is hard to be stabbd in the back by ones own kin when attacked in front by strangers," but still came no closer to revelation than he had previously.[97] The explanation he offered for the poor notices had nothing to do with the nature of their criticism. He was, he said, "isolated in English literature; without any of the usual aids and influences by which an author[']s popularity is maintained & promoted": "I have no literary coterie to cry me up; no partial review to pat me on the back; the very review of my publisher is hostile to every thing American."[98] (This, of course, was his earlier line and was part of the sentiment that motivated and shaped *The Sketch Book*.) In addition, he never showed any sign of having experienced an emotional breakthrough: though he visited the Fosters in England in July 1824, just at the time he was reading proof for *Tales* and the ordeal of composing was still fresh, he displayed no anger or pain. In fact, the most strident comment he ever made to them concerned the religious practices of Emily and her circle: "I felt out of tune there," he wrote to her a year later, "where you were all wound up to so high a key." And, he added, "I was a little jarred too by the well meant but unskillful and unreasonable handling of some of the professional persons I met there," who would break out into spontaneous prayer."[99] Yet his comments contain signs of hidden jealousy over the fact that Emily was aroused and excited by the evangelists, something he had not succeeded in achieving. If he broached the subject of his former attachment to the family at all, his journals give no indication of this. As far as we know, he said nothing; presumably, he also allowed himself to feel nothing.

The three most powerful stories in *Tales of a Traveller*, therefore, constitute Irving's unconscious howl of protest over the suffering he endured when Emily Foster's rejection silenced his hopes for marriage and heterosexual legitimacy. No personal experience would ever push him so close to the edge of nervous collapse; none would ever again so badly distort his work. But, in addition to those just analyzed, *Tales* contains three other stories which, taken together, suggest that Irving may also have been trying to put this experience into a perspective that would enable him to emerge with a positive recognition of his assets. The "Adventure of the Little Antiquary," "The Devil and Tom Walker," and "Wolfert Webber, or Golden Dreams" are all comic pieces which reverse the focus of the previous grouping to concentrate on the relationship between a protagonist and his own "property." The term as it is used here means, literally, his valuables, be it jewels, money, land, or, finally for Irving, his manuscripts—his literary property—but it also connotes sexual capacity, especially in regard to the little antiquary, a "rusty, musty, old fellow" who, "always groping among ruins," reminds one of Diedrich Knickerbocker and, to a certain extent, Geoffrey Crayon as well. (Like the antiquary, who is yet another bachelor, Irving's personae are more fond of the "crusts and cheese-parings of antiquity" than the "best-conditioned modern palaces"). The story, part of "The Italian Banditti" sequence, locates this seeker after "mouldy and crumbling" buildings in the midst of the Apennines hunting after the "ancient cities of the Pelasgi," supposedly embedded in the "mountains of the Abruzzi." In a note appended to the text, Irving explains how antiquarians love to fancy the existence of the Pelasgian cities and how "strange" it is "that such a virgin soil for research, such an unknown realm of knowledge, should at this day remain in the very centre of hackneyed Italy!" The idea here (which will be taken up again in "Wolfert Webber") involves the futility of searching for buried treasure, whether it be the ruins of an ancient civilization, pirate gold, or one's lost sexuality. All are illusory. Thus, in that same playfully ironic tone that he tends to reserve for those figures who resemble him in some way, he mocks the antiquary for having too high a regard for his precious possessions, which include curious ancient coins "buried deep in a pocket of his little black breeches" and a "set of seals at the end of a steel chain, dangling half-way down to his knees." (The lewd suggestiveness of Irving's imagery once again shocks the modern reader.) But the item he prizes above all, an antique intaglio seal ring with a Venus at its center, which he worships with the "zeal of a voluptuary," is the one by which he leaves his mark. The incongruity of such a "feeble little man" identifying himself with the goddess of love fits perfectly with the mock-heroic tenor of the tale and prepares us for his comeuppance at the hands of the highwaymen whom he encounters in the mountains.

Once the meek antiquary meets the fierce bandits Irving's language becomes weighted with sexual allusions and double entendres. Upon first sighting them the old Doctor "pluck[s] up a stout heart, at least as stout a heart as he could, seeing that he was but a puny little man at the best of times." When he sits down with them to have some wine, the men draw their guns or knives from their belts and lay them on the table; he, naturally, has nothing to put forth and, "eying ruefully the black-muzzled pistols, and cold, naked stilettos," shudders with "fear and trembling." Including him in their merrymaking, they "[push] the bottle bravely, and pl[y] him vigorously," with the word "plying" suggesting preparation for a seduction, whether it be business or sexual. As they sing of their exploits and tell "many ruffian jokes" they mortify the doctor, who feels compelled to laugh at their "cutthroat pleasantries." Gradually, however, the wine works its wonders and the antiquary, forgetting his fears, declares that, were he once again a young man, he too would "turn bandit." But such an act requires the necessary equipment, and the comic absurdity of one so impoverished joining those so endowed is underscored at the conclusion when the outlaws refuse to strip him of any of his possessions. "We know who and what you are," the chief tells him; "you carry all your wealth in your head." Your "ring" is a "counterfeit," your "Venus" a "mere sham."[100] Humiliated, the little antiquary "fire[s] up in vindication of his intaglio," but the robbers will not dispute the matter and, telling him to "value it" as he "please[s]," mount their steeds and ride boldly off into the hills.

Whereupon he hobbles back to the town, failing completely to see the irony of the situation, and thus "indignant that they should have pronounced his Venus an impostor" (pp. 335–38). The contrast between those who have and he who has not, between they who can and he who cannot, is, to say the least, striking.

Irving's broad humor, leaving no doubt about the vulnerability of its target, saves the "Adventure of the Little Antiquary" from mordancy while at the same time suggesting that some good-natured self-mockery is taking place. Reminiscent of the burlesque *History of New York*, the comedy here is directed at the Knickerbocker-like figure of the antiquary not so much because he lacks a powerful, forceful masculinity, but more so because he will not recognize the truth about his "property": what he considers valuable (an antique intaglio ring, a manuscript on the Pelasgian cities) the world has little use for, and what the world considers valuable (firm manhood, offspring) he cannot produce. Clearly, then, any happiness he may achieve will depend on his accepting his limitations while making the most of his talents. Irving—who, interestingly enough, had early on in his career in *Letters of Jonathan Oldstyle* (1802–3) and *Salmagundi* (1807–8) identified with old bachelors—had himself paid a high price for such wisdom, but the emotional outlay in this case returned some literary profit since the final two stories in the volume, "The Devil and Tom Walker" and "Wolfert Webber, or Golden Dreams," incorporate this knowledge, in fact making it their central premise. As part of the fourth section of *Tales* entitled "The Money-Diggers," both belong, like "The Legend of Sleepy Hollow," to the late Diedrich Knickerbocker's cache of "papers" and, therefore, just as the earlier story did in *The Sketch Book*, shift the focus from Europe back to America, specifically to New York and New England. "Tom Walker" and "Wolfert Webber" are the results of Knickerbocker's having "unearthed" a "number of fables" while digging for facts; mirror images of each other—Tom Walker is basically unredeemable and his story appropriately concludes on a dark note; Wolfert Webber is only misguided and his tale thus ends on a light one—they warn that miserliness brings utter misery, greed leads to total loss. But underneath the neat "lesson" lies the protagonists' unruly obsession: Tom Walker and Wolfert Webber drive themselves to the grave (though Wolfert, in good comic fashion, earns a reprieve at the story's finale) because they will not rest easy with the property allotted to them.

In both stories "property" generally means land but, again, it also alludes to sexuality. In "The Devil and Tom Walker" failed masculinity surfaces symbolically through Irving's description of Tom as "meagre," his house as "forlorn," with an "air of starvation" about it and, growing nearby, some "straggling savin-trees, emblems of sterility" (p. 450). In addition, no smoke "curl[s] from its chimney," no traveler "stop[s] at its door." This "land of famine" creates a perfect setting for the barrenness, literally and figuratively, of Tom Walker's marriage: instead of making love Tom and his wife enjoy cheating each other out of "what ought to have been common property." The devil provides an alternative to their sexless relationship and both seek him out to escape—Tom from a termagant wife, Dame Walker from a spiteful husband. While her entrails are eaten alive by a vulture, so that Tom finds "nothing but a heart and liver tied up" in her apron, he strikes a bargain with the devil and becomes a usurer. Though he grows rich he remains poor, since no amount of wealth can compensate for the dryness and sterility within him. In the end, after Irving has satirized the rage for speculation prevalent among his own generation ("everybody . . . dreaming of making sudden fortunes from nothing"), the devil calls for Tom Walker, a fate Tom had postponed but could not prevent; he is last seen, like Ichabod, aboard a horse galloping madly across the fields, only Tom's steed is headed "down into the black hemlock swamp." The man whose hunger for property had raged out of control leaves behind only the emblems of his own spiritual and sexual condition: bonds and mortgages "reduced to cinders"; an iron chest filled not with gold and silver, but with "chips and shavings"; a stable with "two skeletons" instead of horses; a magnificent house "burnt to the ground" (p. 467).

"The Devil and Tom Walker," for all of its fire-and-brimstone imagery, remains a comic piece since Tom, a thoroughly execrable fellow, gets precisely the punishment he deserves. Whatever bitterness Irving might have felt in regard to his own fate and then poured into his character dissolves in the exaggeration of Tom's miserly ways; more than just sexual, his impotence extends outward to become a metaphor for his entire being. Thus his desperate attempt to renege on his promise and resist his master's clutches generates no suspense for the reader, since we know from the outset that a man completely devoid of a life-force is already dead. Along with Irving, we can dismiss him as unworthy of our concern; Wolfert Webber, on the other hand, engages our sympathy since he becomes dissatisfied with his property only when the city, prospering all around, begins to encroach upon it, thereby threatening its ability to produce enough to meet his family's needs. While everyone else's prospects increase, Wolfert's fortunes decrease. Formerly a "rural potentate" swaying the "sceptre of his fathers," this worthy Dutch burgher, a combination of Baltus Van Tassel and Dolph Heyliger (with a daughter who resembles both Katrina and Dolph's mistress), has declined in stature and esteem until his cares "seemed to pinch up the corners of his cocked hat into an expression of anxiety, totally opposite to the tranquil, broad-brimmed, low-crowned beavers of his illustrious progenitors" (p. 474). Once glorious, the Webber line has, to borrow a phrase from Shakespeare, "shrunk to this little measure." The son is not the man his fathers were.

Like all the Webbers preceding him, Wolfert raises cabbages; in fact, the "whole family genius, during several generations, was devoted to the study and development of this one noble vegetable; and to this concentration of intellect may doubtless be ascribed the prodigious renown to which the Webber cabbages attained." Irving's attitude toward his inept hero remains mock-heroic; here he even goes so far as to claim a kinship between the man and the produce of his garden: "had the portraits of this line of tranquil potentates been taken, they would have presented a row of heads marvellously resembling in shape and magnitude the vegetables over which they reigned" (pp. 470–71). But the identification serves a purpose beyond burlesque since Wolfert, after hearing stories of buried pirate gold unearthed on various parts of the island, refuses to accept his land's limitations, insisting that it now offer up more than just the hereditary cabbages. Repudiating his "little realm" and the "narrowness of his destiny," he dreams of discovering "an immense treasure in the centre of his garden." His vision of "hidden wealth" involves, therefore, on a literal level, "ingots and money-bags" and, on a symbolic one, power and reconstituted manhood. Unfortunately, when he excavates his property he uncovers no gold: only a "sandy barrenness" lies beneath the rich topsoil. The more he digs, the poorer he becomes until, finally, he has no crop to "supply . . . his household during the sterility of winter." Like his modern-day counterpart Willy Loman, he has nothing "in the ground." By demanding that the land produce what it cannot give, Wolfert has destroyed the peace and harmony of his home.

The little antiquary's ring holds a "sham Venus"; Tom Walker's treasure chest contains "chips and shavings"; Wolfert Webber's garden yields "sand and gravel": Irving was obviously consumed by the idea that something that should have been bursting with vitality, overflowing with riches, or teeming with productivity turns out to be dry, empty, and lifeless. After reading these three stories it becomes clear that the objects of value his protagonists either cling to or search for represent his masculinity, the sexual self that Emily Foster's rejection caused him, however subliminally, to question and doubt. Yet what he also seems to be striving toward in these tales is a recognition of the futility of that search (a search that he abandoned), accompanied by an acceptance of his gifts, "meagre" though they might be. That is why Wolfert's quest for hidden gold, which occupies the rest of the narrative, must necessarily prove a futile one, since "whether any treasure were ever actually buried at that place" remains merely a "matter of conjecture" (p. 540). Nearly killing himself in the pursuit of something that does not exist, he winds up "bruised in body and sorely beaten down in mind." But Irving rescues his hero from ultimate despair and death by turning things upside down, so that the field he thought worthless acquires sudden value when the city corporation announces its plans "to run a new street through the very centre of his cabbage-garden." Thus, his "waste" land is magically transformed into a fertile one when it comes to be "laid out in streets, and cut up into snug building-lots." Though it never produced gold, it now returns an "abundant crop of rent." Like Dolph Heyliger, therefore, Wolfert finds an "unlooked-for source of wealth" just as Irving's ending supplies an unexpected dimension for the idea of "golden dreams": perhaps it is just a character's wish-fulfillment—and an author's fantasy—that ordinary property, which had once returned but a "paltry crop of cabbages," should now be worth more than he could have imagined in his wildest dreams.

As the concluding story in *Tales*, "Wolfert Webber" emphasizes the importance of this hope, yet it was not until November 1825 that Irving gave any indication of believing at least some version of it. Late that year an economic depression, resulting in the failure of one banking firm and two publishing houses, caused him severe distress, which was manifested, as before, in broken, anxious sleep. A vision from one of these fitful nights reveals that the source of his apprehension was the feared loss of his "literary property":

> Last night dreamt of being in a large old house[—]found it giving way above, escaped and saw it falling to ruins—It took fire—thot. all my property & especially my Mss: were in it—rushed towards the house exclaiming I am now not worth a six pence—Found one room of the house uninjured—my brother E.I. [Ebenezer Irving] in it[,] arranging papers, wiping books &c, told me that he had just managed to save every thing that belonged to us, by putting them into this one room that remained uninjured.[101]

Just as Wolfert finds that his garden is most valuable when the corporation threatens to bulldoze it, Irving, under the cloud of financial disaster—imaged in the collapsing house and the subsequent fire—realizes that his manuscripts are the only valuable property he possesses. Without them he is "not worth a six pence"; that is, he feels worthless. "When I once See a little capital of manuscripts *growing under my hand* I shall feel like another being," he told his friend Storrow in December of that year, obviously both proud and excited (not to mention stimulated) by his production, "and shall be relieved from a thousand cares and anxieties that have haunted my mind for a long time past." Being in the "vein of composition," he said, wards off a "recurrence of all the gloomy thoughts that almost unmanned me."[102] Emily had intuited correctly: his pen was his true—and only—source of phallic power.

Thus, it is not to a dream of buried treasure that he returns in a moment of deepest anxiety, but to a recognition of where his true riches lie. Like the "un-injured" room of the house, the uninjured part of himself harbored whatever had been salvaged from the disaster of his Dresden experience. It is interesting, therefore, especially when remembering how often he complained of bodily aches (the psychosomatic medical problems that were connected to his career), that he chose the word "uninjured" rather than "undamaged" to describe the room that had survived. His body, in fact, was injured; his imagination, however, though it had been out of control, was preserved. It would seem, therefore, that through all the pain, doubt, and despair what remained intact—the only resource left to him—were his creations. Yet, as *Tales of a Traveller* also illustrates, Irving was grappling here with what for him was an impossible paradox: while his books were a source of safety, there was danger in a life devoted to the imagination.

III

The truth that Irving grasped in 1825, however, was not the conviction he held in 1824. In fact, less than a month after the English edition of *Tales* appeared he gave every indication of believing just the opposite. Affected, perhaps, by the negative criticism that was already making its rounds, he began to rail against the same imaginative indulgence that he had previously celebrated (though he had always maintained a recognition of some of the more humorous aspects of such preoccupation). For example, upon hearing that his nephew Isaac had begun to practice law in New York—the same field he had found so repugnant in the days when he was courting Matilda Hoffman—he commented to his sister on what he hoped would be the young man's "steady industry & application," and then seized the opportunity to criticize what he perceived as America's permissive attitude toward the imagination:

I think we are a little to[o] apt, in our country, to overvalue a certain vivacity & quickness of intellect which often shows itself in boyhood; but which seldom ripens to any thing useful. A kind of poetical blossomming [sic] of the mind, which cannot be too greatly distrusted and guarded against[.] When a boy shows early signs of this mental vivacity; which is apt to be the mere flowering forth of the imagination;—care should instantly be taken to cultivate & strengthen the more solid & useful properties of the mind. The imagination will always take care enough of itself; & is too apt, if encouraged in early youth, to over run all the other mental requisites, and make a mere weedy kind of character. . . . The first object should be to produce that habit of application, and that method both in thinking & acting that fit [boys] to become exact men of business, in whatever may be the line of life in which they may eventually engage.[103]

This hardly seems like the Washington Irving who had insisted, both in 1817 and then again in 1819, that he must remain in Europe in order to pursue the avenues of creativity open to him. Nor does the speaker here appear to be the same man who had rebelled against becoming a "useful" citizen under any circumstances other than his country's full acceptance of the importance of the man of letters to its society. Could he really have come to believe that America now "overvalue[d]" the imagination, and that all young boys ought to grow into "exact men of business"? That, in fact, too much reliance on imagination produced a "weedy," sinful character (the reference is to the weeds of sin associated with the Garden of Eden)? What had happened to the author who, aware of his own talents, capacities, and limitations, had created two of the most memorable characters in American literature, both of whom were identified with him and both of whom, with their "insuperable aversion to all kinds of profitable labour," challenged the principle of usefulness? Where was the Irving who had fondly remembered the "sunny realm of boyish imagination," who, in the guise of his lovable persona, had "follow[ed] the bent of his vagrant inclination" and produced the work that brought him international acclaim and his country literary recognition?

Apparently he was in a revisionist mode, especially when it came to counseling his brother Ebenezer's son Pierre, who wanted to pursue a career as a writer. "I hope none of those whose interests & happiness are dear to me will be induced to follow my footsteps and wander into the seductive but treacherous paths of literature," he told his nephew in December 1824; "there is no life more precarious in its profits and fallacious in its enjoyments than that of an author." Echoing the sentiments he had expressed to his sister, he implored him not to "meddle" with "works of the imagination": "Your imagination needs no feeding indeed it is a mental quality that always takes care of itself; and is too apt to interfere with the others." And, in language startling for its unexpected forcefulness and for the explosion of hidden anger, he concluded this tirade by completely repudiating his preoccupations for the last several years of his life: "I have a thousand times regretted with bitterness that ever I was led away by my imagination—. . . the man who earns his bread by the sweat of his brow eats oftener a sweeter morsel, however coarse, than he who procures it by the labor of his brains." The imagery is that of Genesis and God's curse to Adam after his sinful fall; in Irving's mind, workers are sexual men and therefore enjoy the fruits of their physical labor. Thus for himself, he wished that at an early age he had been "imperiously bound down to some regular & useful mode of life and been thoroughly inured to habits of business." For his nephew, he desired nothing more than to hear of his becoming "a valuable practical man of business" and, in order to assist him, offered advice based not on his own achievements (as he had done with John Howard Payne), but on his failures: "Endeavour to make your talents convertible to ready use, prompt for the occasion, and adapted to the ordinary purposes of life—cultivate strength rather than gracefulness—in our country it is the useful not the ornamental that is in demand." [104]

Pierre obviously heeded these words, for his next letter contained the news that he had entered his father's countinghouse, an action which "gratified" Irving. But he also said that he had been "mortified" by his uncle's observations, which he had taken as censure for his past activities. Replying that he had only meant to issue a warning for his nephew's future, Irving again cited himself as an example to be avoided: "I had felt, in my own case, how insensibly a young man gets beguiled away by the imagination, and wanders from the safe *beaten* path of life, to lose himself in the mazes of literature. Scarcely any author ever set forth with the intention or surmise of becoming such; he becomes so by degrees; and I have seen enough of literary life to warn all of those who are dear to me, should I see any danger of their straying into it." [105] (One thinks of Daedalus, the artist/inventor who found his way out of the maze and gave prudent advice about escape to his son Icarus, who ignored it and consequently fell.) These statements, when examined in conjunction with the first stanza of a poem by Robert Wild (1609–79), "Alas poore Scholler! Whither wilt thou go?," which Irving copied into both his journal and his notebook for May 1823, at the most anxious moment of his Dresden sojourn (just after Emily Foster rejected his marriage proposal and he left the city to calm his frazzled nerves), reveal the scenario he settled upon as an explanation for what had happened to him. The only instance in all his journals and notebooks where such a double entry occurs, the poem obviously was meaningful to him:

> In a melancholy study
> None but myself.
> Methought my muse grew muddy;
> After [seven] years reading[,]
> And costly breeding
> I felt, but could find no p[e]lf.
> Into learned rags
> I have rent my plush and sattin
> And now am fit to beg
> In hebrew greek and latin;
> [Instead of Aristotle
> Would I had got a patt[e]n]
> Alas, poor scholar, whither wilt thou go?[106]

What we see is that, like the poor scholar with whom he identifies, Irving believed the seven years (1817–23 inclusive) he had devoted to reading, imagining, and writing had been wasted. He had saved no money, acquired no property ("pelf"), and secured no wife and family to validate his manhood. As he understood it, therefore, he had made a poor investment; having expended his intellectual capital ("plush and sattin") foolishly, all he had to show for his efforts were a handful of manuscripts ("learned rags"), the meager products of his imagination. Once a young man of great promise, he was now alone, a "melancholy" forty-year-old bereft of inspiration. Moreover, by channeling all his energy into literary pursuits he had so distorted himself that he was now unfit for any legitimate occupation, thus incapable of assuming the roles of husband and father. Though he was skilled in the ways of books ("fit to beg/In hebrew greek and latin"), this knowledge served no worldly purpose. Had he only traveled the "beaten path of life," given himself over to "useful" endeavors, espoused the mundane and ordinary (a "patten," an overshoe or sandal) instead of grasping for the transcendent and extraordinary ("Aristotle") or the luxurious (the rhyming word "sattin"), he would no longer be on the road, asking himself "whither wilt thou go?" Rather, he would have all the comforts and amenities of a home.

Through his letters and several of the stories in *Tales of a Traveller* Irving created a livable fiction, which can in turn be interpreted, if seen below the surface, as the fabricated "truth" he needed in order to continue with his life and his career. Only through such a reading does the psychology of his choices become available. Because he could never fathom the underlying reasons for Emily Foster's refusal, could never, that is, come to terms with his romantic and sexual inadequacies, he blamed his devotion to the imagination for the failure of his proposal and his subsequent misery upon parting with her family. If in his youth he had only been "bound down" to some "useful mode of life" rather than wandering through the "mazes of literature" he would have become more "manly," not, like Ichabod, a shifting, "weedy" character but, like Brom, a substantial, respected member of his community, a man with a practical outlook and a steady income. Perhaps if he had even been a little more like Wolfert and, instead of always dreaming about foreign travel, had continually strived for wealth, he might have eventually found a way to turn his own property into profit. Then Emily might have viewed things differently, might have recognized him as properly endowed for the role of husband. Yet, ironically, almost in the same way *Tales* highlights his sexual anxieties and frustrations through its substructure, the poem that he thought so nicely summed up his troubles points to the real dilemma of these years via its imagery. The line "Into learned rags / I have rent my plush and sattin" has a violent sexual connotation, suggesting the rending or tearing of tissues, in particular of a virgin's hymen, and is perhaps an image of rape, yet one where the persona plays both feminine and masculine roles. Moreover, it appears as if the scholar/writer had spent his precious vitality in wasteful, unfulfilling ways, as if, indeed, the imagination were a poor substitute for the real business of life, which is not to produce books, but to "breed" offspring. Moreover, remembering the deeper significance of Wolfert Webber's search for buried treasure, the scholar's inability to find any "pelf" (which in addition to "property" also means "riches") after all his years of labor eerily echoes the plight of Irving's impotent protagonists. To be sure, he could not have read these implications into "Alas poore Scholler!" Nevertheless, like his other "fictions" from this period—his stories, the favorite poems he copied into his notebook, the imagery of his letters, all of which attempt to support his grand illusion about imagination—it reveals the truth even as it tries to conceal it.

The longest story in *Tales of a Traveller*, "Buckthorne, or The Young Man of Great Expectations" (from Part Two, "Buckthorne and His Friends"), conceived and executed before Irving expressed his views on the practical life versus the literary calling, constitutes an earlier, fictionalized version of these same ideas. Shaped in the image of his creator, Buckthorne suffers poverty, loss, and humiliation because he permits his fancy to lead him astray. Basically, his troubles stem—and the narrative generates—from his confusing, at a young age, illusion and reality:

> I used to sit at my desk in the school, on a fine summer's day, and instead of studying the book which lay open before me, my eye was gazing through the windows on the green fields and blue hills. How I envied the happy groups on the tops of stage-coaches, chatting, and joking, and laughing, as they were whirled by the schoolhouse on their way to the metropolis. . . . I fancied to myself what adventures they must experience, and what odd scenes of life they must witness. All this was, doubtless, the poetical temperament working within me, and tempting me forth into a world of its own creation, which I mistook for the world of real life. (p. 207)

The autobiographical strain, which is fairly evident, determines the movement of events, so that the story contains a recognizable, even predictable, pattern: gifted with poetic sensibility, Buckthorne pursues the muse until, "turned adrift upon the world," he becomes an object of some ridicule and scorn. (Again, it is interesting to note how Irving applied the melodramatic language of his personal correspondence to his imaginative work.) Having "indulged in poetry as a pleasure" and suffered for it, he resolves to enter the "republic of letters" as a hack writer. Ultimately, however, disenchanted with the grub-street existence and disinherited from his uncle's estate, he sees the error of his ways, whereupon his fortunes are reversed and his inheritance is restored. It remains only for him to "renounce" the "sin of authorship" by leaving it to the "critics." Irving envisioned a similar conclusion for himself, declaring in several letters from this period (full of words like "evil," "sin," and "tempt") that as soon as he had saved enough money he would abandon the odious task of earning a living through literature. In one example of his own renunciation he told his nephew Pierre that he looked "forward with impatience to the time, when a moderate competency will place me above the necessity of writing for the press." "I have," he added, "long since discovered that it is indeed 'vanity & vexation of spirit.'" In another, he wrote his friend Leslie that "if the public will keep with me a little longer, until I can secure a bare compitency [sic], I feel as if I shall be disposed to throw by the pen; or only to use it as a mere recreation." [107] Of course, he continued to write "for the press" throughout his long life; his promise to sever his ties to the world of letters, however sincere it may have been in the moment of utterance, was one more instance of fiction making. Moreover, his use of such weak, qualified language as "I feel as if I shall be disposed to" instead of the stronger, more assertive "I will" shows that, although he attributed his waywardness to his imaginative propensities, he remained hesitant and insecure about even the *thought* of putting aside a literary career. He understood, albeit on a level below consciousness, that the pen was still his only source of power.

Significantly, "Buckthorne" (like "The Story of the Young Italian") also links imaginative indulgence to sexual failure, only here Irving treats the theme comically; like Wolfert, once the young man of "great expectations" ceases to follow the dictates of his fancy, thereby relinquishing pursuit of his dream—in this case romance and sexual conquest—some version of it materializes. From the outset, when his verses to the squire's daughter (whom he has envisioned as his "Sacharissa") earn him a flogging from the schoolmaster, he is thwarted in every advance he makes to a woman. And when, sometime later, he joins an acting troupe and plays the part of the lover in a traditional pantomime, his comic role perfectly reflects his inability to succeed with the fair sex: "I had merely to pursue the fugitive fair one; to have a door now and then slammed in my face; to run my head occasionally against a post; to tumble and roll about with Pantaloon and the Clown; and to endure the hearty thwacks of Harlequin's wooden sword" (p. 223)—traditionally a phallic symbol. At the university he seduces the shopkeeper's daughter with poetry, arranges an assignation in her chamber, and, relishing the idea of her "ruin," eagerly climbs the side of the house to meet her: "I clambered with a beating heart; I reached the casement; I hoisted my body half into the chamber; and was welcomed, not by the embraces of my expecting fair one, but by the grasp of the crabbed-looking old father in the crisp-curled wig" (p. 250). In the ensuing action he is beaten with a cane by the aged shopkeeper, a humiliating experience to be sure, but the imagery with which his initial capture is portrayed tells an even more devastating story, since it suggests a kind of castration: with his "body half into [her] chamber," he discovers that he is not entwined by his fair young lover at all, but rather caught in the viselike grip of her shriveled old father. As if this were not enough to discourage him, he again suffers a blow to his masculinity when, in the midst of still another poetic pursuit of yet another young lady, his excesses become the object of the town's mockery: "I saw at once the exterminating cloud of ridicule bursting over me. My crest fell. The flame of love went suddenly out, or was extinguished by overwhelming shame."[108] The crest, literally the tuft of feathers on the head of a bird, or the comb of the cock, is associated with male prowess, especially since male birds display their beautiful plumage as a sign of pride or self-confidence. Thus, a fallen crest signifies humiliation—and emasculation. It would be hard to imagine a more graphic image of impotence, especially when we are told that immediately following this moment of shame Buckthorne, his cheeks "tingling" with blushes, limply withdraws or, as he rather lamely states it, "beat[s] a retreat." However, once the cocky poet acknowledges his defeat and repents—that is, abandons his faith in the imagination—Irving lifts him from his crestfallen state and he marries his first love, Sacharissa. Like "Wolfert Webber," "Buckthorne" ends on a note of wish-fulfillment, but this time it was one that Irving was never to realize. In his long and fruitful career he produced many books—seven alone during his European years—but he never took a wife and he fathered no children.

Some of Irving's critics have argued that the rejection of imagination in both his tales and his letters from this period coincides perfectly with early nineteenth-century American skepticism toward fiction and fancy, a distrust that may be traced, ultimately, to the premises of Scottish Common Sense philosophy.[109] *Tales* clearly shows that an "ill-directed" imagination leads a man to misjudge the world and to pursue false or poorly conceived paths of action, perhaps to wander aimlessly, to drift without purpose or goal. Thus, the problem of a vagrant imagination was subsumed under the larger cultural issue of a country expanding too rapidly, of runaway progress obliterating national self-definition. Suspicion of imagination paralleled the fear of discontinuity, the threat to stability inherent in the push toward "boundlessness." If one of the defining characteristics of American society from 1815 to 1832 is mobility; if, according to John Higham, during this time the United States resembled "a bivouac rather than a nation, a grand army moving from the Atlantic to the Pacific, and pitching tents along the way,"[110] then not only does Washington Irving's restlessness reflect that of his countrymen but, in addition, his abiding concern that fiction had permanently unsettled him mirrors America's anxiety that the country had been unloosed from its moorings. *Tales of a Traveller* repeatedly reminds its reader that fantasy is not reality, emphatically warns him that traveling aimlessly—Irving's metaphor for voyaging in the realm of imagination devoid of any moral or spiritual goal—will leave him stranded without a home.

However, to fully understand Irving's hostility toward imagination, which is really more in spirit than in practice (and which later mellowed into ambivalence), one must appreciate how it was linked in his mind to the fear of sexuality; of all the anxieties that plagued him during these years perhaps the deepest, most threatening one was potential loss of control, so that if he surrendered himself to either experience—that is, to imaginative or sexual abandon—he would not only lose his focus but, far worse, he would come unhinged. If, according to the narrator, the story of the young robber "proved to what excess the passions may be carried when escaped from all moral restraint" (p. 416), then Irving's tales of "frustrated artists or young men and women crazed by fiction and imagination" (as Michael Bell puts it) [111] illustrate the outer fringes to which the mind may be driven when following the dictates of an imagination (or a libido) freed from moral constraints and given license to roam unimpeded. On one page of his notebook, Irving copied out consecutively three passages—from Milton's *Comus* (1634) and *Paradise Lost* (1667), and from John Fletcher's *The Faithful Shepherdess* (1609)—that conjoin sexuality and imagination and speak to the necessity of protecting oneself from the dangerous extremities of both. The fact that he himself juxtaposed these pieces implies he was aware of echoes and correspondences among them:

> A thousand fantasies
> Begin to throng into my memory,
> [O]f calling shapes, & beck'ning shadows dire,
> And airy tongues that syllable mens names
> On sands, & shores & desart wildernesses[.] (ll. 205–9)

> IGNIS FATUUS
> Hov'ring and dansing with delusive light,
> Misleads th' amaz'd night-wanderer from his way,
> Through bogs & mires, & oft through pond or pool
> There swallowd up & lost, from succour far. (9:639–42)

> POWER OF CHASTITY
> Yet I have heard (my mother told it me,
> And now I do believe it) if I keep
> My virgin flower uncropt, pure chaste & fair
> No goblin, wood-god, fairy, elfe, or fiend
> Satyr, or other power that haunts the groves,
> Shall hurt my body, or by vain illusion

209

"Ichabod Crane Fleeing the Horseman." (From *Illustrations of "The Legend of Sleepy Hollow,"* etched by Felix O. C. Darley [New York: The American Art-Union, 1849].)

> Draw me to wander after idle fires;
> Or voices calling me in dead of night,
> To make me follow, & so tole me on
> Through mire & standing pools to find my ruin. (1.1. 111–20)[112]

The primary thrust of the three linked stanzas expresses the major underlying motif of Irving's life and work from this era: resistance to sexual allurements. In the lines from *Comus* that he copied (and others from the same section), the "lady," a "lonely Traveller," fears being carried away both by Comus and his followers, who, "In wanton dance . . . praise the bounteous *Pan*," and her own "fantasies." Almost the way a Romantic poet would, Milton makes the outer landscape mirror her inner emotions; darkness prevails because, for the moment, the woman has wavered in her faith to a "Supreme good." Appropriately, the section from book 9 of *Paradise Lost* focuses on Satan's seduction of Eve and her inability to resist his extraordinary luminosity. The Miltonic simile, involving the will-o'-the-wisp (*ignis fatuus*), suggests the devil's intense attraction which, again, "misleads" the "wanderer." Clearly, the speaker in Fletcher's poem struggles with a similar temptation as voices created by the nymphs who populate the forest draw her on "to wander after idle fires." To avoid the beings that would deceive them, each must remain "chaste," though of course Eve, "our credulous Mother," succumbs. But chastity means more than keeping the "virgin flower uncropt," necessary though that may be (and a lesson Irving apparently took to heart); one must be spiritually pure as well, virtuous in mind and soul, which Milton, as a true Puritan, emphasizes in the lines from *Comus* that follow closely upon the ones that Irving jotted into his notebook:

> O welcome pure-ey'd Faith, white-handed Hope,
> Thou hov'ring Angel girt with golden wings,
> And thou unblemish't form of Chastity,
> I see ye visibly, and now believe
> That he, the Supreme good, t' whom all things ill
> Are but as slavish officers of vengeance,
> Would send a glist'ring Guardian, if need were,
> To keep my life and honor unassail'd. (ll. 213–20)

The aspiration after transcendent virtue here may, for Irving, have been the other side of the horror of sexuality. In all three of the stanzas that attracted him there appear remarkable images of sterility which suggest, as the speaker in Fletcher's poem indicates, that to be led down the path of sexual temptation is "to find my ruin." Although for Milton these geographical images mean lust or the stagnation of sin, for Irving they are metaphors of impotence (which is why he is drawn to them). "Sands, & shores & des[e]rt wildernesses," "bogs & mires," and "standing pools" are similar to many such images that have appeared throughout his writings; in fact, in *Tales*, as Hedges noted, the stagnant ponds on Buckthorne's uncle's estate represent "sterility or impotence," and "reflect the fears which at times render Buckthorne ineffectual as a human being."[113] Moreover, to be a "night-wanderer," to be dragged through the mire of sexuality, is also to suffer, again like Buckthorne (with the shopkeeper's daughter), castration anxiety; thus, the only way to keep the "fiend" from "hurt[ing] my body," to avoid being "swallowd up & lost," is to "keep / My virgin flower uncropt." One of Irving's final notebook entries for this period, which suggests that he saw himself as a fading, shriveled flower, reads like a personal gloss on this symbolism: "Behold the sweetness and freshness and fragrance of life is over; what remains is seared and withered, and colourless. If the morning could not yield thee full delight what canst thou expect from the arid and sultry noon or the chill of gloomy evening."[114] Thus, besides other misgivings, Irving also had a sexual-identity problem since he sees himself as rose rather than as sword—though perhaps appropriate in an age when a forty-year-old virgin was usually female not male.

Each of the above three stanzas, however, may also be read—and a romantic sensibility like Irving's would easily have done this—as a commentary on the dangers of the imagination, which leads those who already have a tendency to "wander" even further astray. Interestingly, the "travelers" who are tempted here are all women: Irving identifies with these three figures (notice that it is Eve, not Adam, to whom he likens himself) because, though passive, they all have active imaginations that are easily captured and held in thrall by the spirits of the forest and woods, both the ones actually present and the ones they create. The "Tempter" appeals to Eve, for example, not only because "Hope elevates, and joy / Bright'ns his Crest" (ll. 633–34) into the shape of "Power," but because he conjures up for her imagination a delicious picture of her own transcendent power. The speaker in *Comus* struggles with "calling shapes" and "beck'ning shadows," visions that her memory and fancy dangle before her. The gods that "haunt the groves" through which the faithful shepherdess travels threaten her body by first feeding her mind with illusions. What each woman must do, therefore, and the very thing Eve fails to accomplish, is bring an unruly imagination under control. This, as far as Irving could understand it, was the problem he encountered with *Tales of a Traveller*. And it was something his American readers would also have recognized. "As long as reason holds control over the Imagination," the *Southern Literary Messenger* said some years later, "it is a contributor of good, but when itself predominates, reason runs riot and madness takes the reins." The "difference between a man who abandons himself to a wild imagination and he who brings it to order," Irving wrote in his notebook, "is the same as between he who keeps his seat on a horse that runs away with him & he who brings all the wildness of the animal into subjection."[115] With *Tales*, the horse had definitely run away with the rider.

The mention of horse and rider—especially in this context—recalls the moment in "The Legend of Sleepy Hollow" when Ichabod, truly a man of "unruly imagination," confronts the ghost of the Hessian soldier on his melancholy ride home after Katrina Van Tassel's rejection of his suit. Though he "seemed gathered up in the gloom, like some gigantic monster ready to

"The Headless Horseman," by Barry Moser. (From *Two Tales,* by Washington Irving, copyright © 1984 by Pennyroyal Press, Inc. Reprinted by permission of Harcourt Brace Jovanovich, Inc.)

spring upon the traveller," the apparition, as we all know, is nothing more or less than a cloaked and hooded Brom Bones, mounted on his favorite black steed. This is apparent in an etching that Felix O. C. Darley, Irving's most famous nineteenth-century illustrator, prepared for a special edition of the tale published by the American Art-Union, in which he captures "the shadowy object of alarm" perfectly from the *reader's* point of view, complete with his pumpkin head "carried before him on the pommel of [his] saddle!" (*The Sketch Book*, pp. 292, 293).[116] But what, in fact, does *Ichabod* see that strikes such terror into his heart? Not just a headless goblin, I would maintain— though that in itself would be frightening enough, since headlessness represents yet another manifestation of castration anxiety. Ichabod, however, may very well be "horror struck" because he beholds exactly what Barry Moser, the most recent of Irving's illustrators, has depicted in a brilliantly conceived wood engraving for his own edition of the tale: nothing but the shell of a man, his exterior like that of a human body, his interior a hollowed-out cavity.[117] Thus, the "appalling" figure from whom Ichabod flees in absolute panic is his projection not merely of loss, but of absence. Unconsciously, he fears that, like Moser's "headless horseman," he has no core of being, merely a void where his selfhood—and manhood—should be. Moreover, if (as I have suggested in chapter 3) Ichabod represents a caricatured version of his creator, how uncanny that Katrina's fictional rebuff, which initiates this terrifying episode, should anticipate Emily's real one. And since for Irving sexual insecurity implies artistic insecurity, escape becomes the only option for both author and character.

"My fate," Irving told his friend Thomas Storrow in November 1822, is "to wander; or rather, it is my vocation." "Which way I shall direct my wanderings when I leave this [city] I cannot say," he wrote to Leslie a few weeks later. "I find it is all useless to project plans of tours, as I seldom follow them, but am apt to be driven completely out of my course by whim or circumstance."[118] To "wander," either under his own "direction" or guided by "whim or circumstance," had been Geoffrey Crayon's professed motto; transforming Crayon's observations and "adventures" into literature had been Irving's source of knowledge, pleasure, and success. By the middle of 1825, however, both his tone and outlook had changed. Now he was telling his nephew—ironically, even bitterly—of the dangers of yielding to the roving instinct: "No one should travel unless his fortune be made, or unless his travelling will put him in the way of making his fortune. . . . The knowledge to be gained by a mere ramble through Europe is of all things the most useless & superficial."[119] Apparently, he had altered his agenda from transcendence to acquisition: wealth was the price for a bride; without money one was weak financially, romantically, and sexually. The pilgrim had metamorphosed into the vaga-bond; the voyage to self-discovery had become the road to self-delusion. At the end of 1824 he said good-bye to a year "saddened by disappointments & distrust of the world & of myself; by sleepless nights & joyless days." His fare-well to 1825 found him "doubtful of fortune & full of uncertainties"; it had been "a year very little of which I would willingly live over again."[120] But 1826 brought a major realignment: he had been invited to Madrid to trans-late a masterwork on the voyages of Columbus. Here was a traveler with not just a goal but a lofty calling, a visionary with a grand imagination plus the manly execution of a successful plan. Spain proved to be Irving's Lourdes, for it was in Spain that he replenished his faith in writing, restored his belief in imagination. And it was in Spain that he discovered the Alhambra, one of the great architectural wonders of the world, which became the site of his most important act of imaginative repossession.

S I X

In Reality Imagination Triumphs
The Alhambra

Of the three sketchbooks that grew out of Washington Irving's seventeen-year sojourn in Europe, *The Alhambra* traditionally has been regarded as the least vital. In its own time, while it did not quite rival *The Sketch Book* either in immediate impact or in sustaining interest, it did receive widespread critical reception, which helped to solidify Irving's reputation as the foremost American writer of the nineteenth century. In modern scholarship, both *The Sketch Book* and *Bracebridge Hall* continue to attract some attention and still manage to gather a small though faithful readership; *The Alhambra*, however, has been relegated to the shelf, as at best a literary oddity, at worst an outdated and outmoded guidebook. In 1832, as Irving's biographer has written, a large part of *The Alhambra*'s appeal "lay in its novelty"; Irving was, after all, among the first group of Americans to explore the Moorish palace, which lay far off the usual path of the Grand Tour.[1] Today, neither readers nor critics (nor scholars, for that matter) have much patience with the romantic atmosphere that pervades Irving's last European fiction; indeed, the Moorish legends and tales he transformed from bits and pieces collected around the fort seem, as William Dunlap once observed, "very slight stuff."[2]

The Alhambra, however, is still of interest because of what criticism has overlooked: the nature and dimension of the experience recorded in its pages and the way it encapsulates the conflict between the opposing demands of fiction and reality, a conflict that had been brewing in Irving since *The Sketch Book* years. Like his other fictions, *The Alhambra* is essentially autobiographical in conception (although also like those earlier works it incorporates into its structure the fruits of Irving's antiquarian pursuits), parading before the reader scenes and episodes that can be traced back to the daily events of his life in the late spring of 1829. This autobiographical quality becomes especially

216

important because throughout his stay in Spain the idea of an earthly paradise had taken hold of him and appears as a central theme in both his writings and his own personal search for an extended moment of transcendence.[3] If the ideal woman is truly unattainable, then Irving would strive for an ideal place. No matter where he traveled on the Continent this goal had eluded him until, three-and-a-half years after he entered Spain, this exotic southern land provided him with the culminating moment of his European journey in the form of a privileged residence in one of the most famous structures in all the world. It is an interesting irony of literary history that the book which bears the name of the great Moorish palace should prove to be a critical disappointment when it actually shows Irving to have found what so many of his contemporaries longed for but failed to achieve, the quintessential Romantic experience: a perfect state of timeless existence. The Alhambra, an ideal subject and working environment, yielded *The Alhambra*, a less than immortal work of art.

Irving's years in Spain were among the most delightfully productive of his entire career, yielding several major works including, in addition to *The Alhambra* (1832), the *Life and Voyages of Columbus* (1828) and the *Conquest of Granada* (1829).[4] Within two months of arriving he knew that he had embarked on an entirely new phase of his European journey. "Spain," he said, "equals all my expectations as to the peculiarities of the country and the people." It was "quite unlike the rest of Europe," with "strong characteristic traits" of its own.[5] Yet only a year later he began to feel an intense desire to see America again, and for the first time since his early days in Liverpool, when the drudgery of trying to save the family business nearly broke his spirit, spoke seriously of returning. In part this was due to the attacks on him in the American press and his fear that he had been "cast off" by his countrymen. "I am conscious that my long absence from home has subjected me to unfavorable representations and has been used to my disadvantage," he told Brevoort in 1827; and, as he had done so many times before, he once more assured his friend of his patriotism and loyalty:

> Do not let yourself be persuaded . . . that time or distance has estranged me in thought or feeling from my native country, my native places, or the friends of my youth. The fact is that the longer I remain from home the greater charm it has in my eyes, and all the colouring that the imagination once gave to distant Europe now gathers about the scenes of my native country. I look forward to

217

my return as to the only event of any very desireable [sic] kind that may yet be in store for me. I do not know whether it is the case with other wanderers, but with me, the various shifting scenes through which I have passed in Europe have pushed each other out of place successively and alternately faded away from my mind, while the scenes & friends of my youth alone remain fixed in my memory and my affections with their original strength and freshness.[6]

In part, however, as the latter half of the passage to Brevoort indicates, Irving felt genuinely homesick; in Seville, in 1829, he wrote to his brother Peter that he had a "craving desire to return to America, which has been increasing on me for the two years past, until now it incessantly haunts my mind and occupies all my dreams." Two months later, in the midst of his residence in the Alhambra, when he was luxuriating among scenes of unsurpassing beauty, he again told Peter that he was "full of anxiety to return home." Yet before two more weeks had passed he was claiming that he could not leave the palace: "I am determined to linger here until I get some writings under way connected with the place, and that shall bear the stamp of real intimacy with the charming scenes described."[7] His imagination demanded that he stay close to the source of his renewed creative vigor; his emotional and patriotic loyalty to America insisted that when the opportunity arose for removing to England he seize it as the first giant step toward his permanent departure from Europe.

The tensions manifest in this choice, which involve personal anxieties as well as professional commitments, are embodied in lines Irving copied into an 1825 notebook from Lord Bolingbroke's essay "Reflections upon Exile" (1716): "We love the country in which we [are] born, because we receive particular benefits from it, and because we have particular obligations to it[.] In all other respects a wise man looks on himself as a citizen of the world: and, when you ask him where his country lies, points, like Anaxagoras, with his finger to the heavens."[8] America was his country, and he felt obliged to honor it; the Alhambra was the imaginative heaven that he had been pointing toward all his life, and he did not want to abandon it. Yet leave it he did: when notice of his appointment as secretary of the American Legation at London arrived he packed his bags and left behind the greatest of all dream worlds, heading back to the real one for whose offices he had little regard and no desire. "I confess I feel extremely reluctant to give up my quiet and independent mode of life, and am excessively perplexed," he wrote only ten days before setting out, adding that "my antipathy to the bustle, show, and business of the world incline me to hold back." "I only regret that I had not been left entirely alone, and to dream away life in my own way."[9] But transcendence, as he knew only too well, was temporary: in the end, twenty years in the Catskill Mountains or two and a half months in the Alhambra amounted to the same thing. Like the quintessential American dreamer, he had to go home again. Neither Rip Van Winkle nor Washington Irving could live forever outside the boundaries of America, since neither character nor author could commit himself totally to the imagination, and it was only in imaginative literature that psychological distance from America was possible. *The Alhambra* reflects this truth, says, in fact, precisely what Twain would give far greater resonance to more than fifty years later in *Huckleberry Finn*, and something Irving's nineteenth-century audience well understood: there was no leaving behind the "bustle, show, and business of the world," no getting beyond the realities of American experience, no permanent escape from the rigorous demands of an American identity.

I

Irving's Spanish adventure, climaxed by his stay in the Alhambra, began on January 30, 1826, when he received a letter from Alexander H. Everett, then head of the American Embassy in Spain, inviting him to become a member of the legation at Madrid. Everett, who had met Irving previously both in Paris and The Hague and was aware of his recent immersion in Spanish language and literature, proposed that he make an English translation of a work on Christopher Columbus that was about to be published by the Spanish historian Martin Fernandez de Navarrete.[10] It was especially desirable, Everett believed, that an American undertake the task, and Irving seemed the ideal choice: the only American writer of his time with an international reputation, his association with the project would mean its receiving wide attention; moreover, he was already on the Continent and he was willing to undertake the translation. For his part, Irving was delighted with the news of his appointment, and though Stanley Williams speculates that he would most likely have been drawn to Spain anyway, his first letter after receiving the information expresses amazement at the turn of events that was about to carry him into the promised land: "How little did I dream a week since that Spain, the country I have been so wishing to see, but into which I feared I should never get a peep, should be the very port into which the first whiff of good luck should blow me."[11]

If the events of 1822–26 are placed in the larger context of Irving's life up

219

to that point, a distinct pattern may be discerned: inevitably, each time a serious misfortune occurs, causing severe psychological distress and a consequent loss of stability and self-confidence, it is succeeded by an increased determination and sustained effort, accompanied, paradoxically, by fits of anxiety and temperament. The death of Matilda Hoffman in 1809 brought on the resolve that enabled him to finish *A History of New York*; the collapse in 1818 of the family hardware business led directly to his conviction that literature must become his livelihood, a decision which was responsible for *The Sketch Book*; finally, his intense depression over the failure of *Tales of a Traveller* and the loss of public esteem, in conjunction with a series of financial setbacks,[12] precipitated his study of Spanish language, literature, and history, which permitted him to take advantage of the authorial possibilities that unfolded during his sojourn in Spain. Though he could not have known it at the outset, Spain would come to mean the rebirth of exhausted energy and the revival of a flagging spirit. Initially, it offered just the stimulation required for self-restoration: a rich cultural life, colorful and unique national and local customs, and, much to his delight, unlimited access to a vast wealth of antiquarian material, which would greatly facilitate his transformation into the biographer of Columbus and the historian of Granada.[13] Eventually, Spain would also satisfy, beyond even his expectations, the hunger for romantic experience.

Irving's first response to the new country was precisely what one would expect, since he immediately viewed both the landscape and peasants he encountered through the eyes of a painter: "The Spaniards seem to surpass even the Italians in picturesqueness [he wrote to Leslie]; every mother[']s son of them is a subject for the pencil. It is a continual wish of my brother & myself that we could have you & Newton with us; you might lay up ample materials for your Spanish pictures."[14] But such perceptions, and the urge to transform them into literary "sketches," would have to be postponed in light of what Irving saw as the opportunity to accomplish something significant: to give the world access to the accumulated scholarship of a foremost Spanish historian who had hunted through all the major and minor manuscript repositories in Spain that had never before been open to inspection. But when he sat down to his translation, he discovered that Navarrete's masterwork, *Colección de los viages y descubrimientos, que hicieron por mar los españoles desde fines del siglo XV* ("A Collection of the Sea Voyages and Discoveries made by the Spaniards Since the End of the Fifteenth Century") was not a coherent history at all, but rather a vast collection of letters, documents, and other source materials, including excerpts from Columbus's journals; there were no narrative, no exalted phraseology, no anecdotes or illustrations, and no heightened sense of Columbus's perilous adventures.[15] In other words, Navarrete's volumes in no way approached the book Irving would have written had he himself gathered the disparate materials, since he thought they were "*dry*," by which he meant that, one, the general reader was sure to find the work less than compelling and hence the translation would do little to enhance his reputation, and two, the booksellers were not likely to offer a considerable amount for it, if anything at all.[16] Irving's judgments in these matters had always been keen, and he trusted them now. He knew that to meet the requirements of financial reward (he needed money) and popular success (he wanted to regain public acclaim after *Tales of a Traveller*'s poor reception) that he had imposed on the new work, something else was in order—a book that would utilize the vast amount of resources at his disposal, but one that would be uniquely his own. In addition, he hoped that this work on Columbus, in whom American interest was always great, would silence his detractors, whose antagonism over his prolonged absence was a perennial source of discomfort to him. "I confess it will give me satisfaction," he told Brevoort, "if my present work, by its success, replies to some of the cavilling that has been indulged against me."[17] Out of this complex of needs, demands, and available material came the idea of a full-fledged life of Columbus, and on July 29, 1827, after twenty-one months of the most strenuous literary labor he had known, *A History of the Life and Voyages of Christopher Columbus* was completed.

Irving's *Columbus* concerns us here for the way it reflects his attitude toward his subject, what this attitude reveals about his preoccupations at the time of its composition, and how a knowledge of these things may help us to understand both the genesis and structure of his last major work of fiction, *The Alhambra*. *The Life and Voyages of Columbus* is not really a "life" at all, nor does it precisely qualify as "history." Although he might have done so had he wanted, since he had access to the very manuscripts Navarrete had spent decades collecting, Irving did not add anything new to the standard, though often contradictory, accounts of the life and voyages that preceded his own. These were also at his side as he worked, but neither was it his intention to produce a major work of synthesis, even though he did make ample use of the available information. (He himself thought of his work as a "History combining all that had been related by different historians, as well as the minor but very interesting facts existing in various documents recently discovered.")[18] Irving's *Columbus* qualifies, rather, as a work of the imagination, though in

221

characteristic fashion his imagination does not create its own world. As Williams has pointed out, it is not that Irving invents details or greatly distorts the accepted evidence or facts;[19] instead, he embellishes, heightens, shapes, and colors the events and incidents of his original sources so that at any one moment the mood that prevails is one of either drama, pageantry, or disaster. At times, Irving looks more like the fiction writer than the historian. In fact, as with the fictional sketch, Irving anticipated a uniquely American genre, the nonfiction narrative. Avoiding complex problems of intention or motive and eschewing the questions that more serious scholars would likely have asked—those of an economic, political, social, and even an intellectual nature—he concentrates his energy on the idealized figure of Columbus; and, even though he does not deviate from the conventional structure of the story, by the time one reaches the end of this massive work it is apparent that Columbus's journey across the Atlantic is not, as it had once been considered, a renaissance voyage of discovery, but rather a romantic quest for the unattainable. As Hedges has noted, Irving fills the book with religious allusion—most prominently Columbus's "penchant for donning a monk's habit and going on penitential journeys"—thus recasting the explorer as "a perpetual pilgrim, though what he seeks most of the time is not the Celestial City but a terrestrial paradise."[20] Indeed, in Irving's version of the third voyage, for example, Columbus actually believes that he has reached the outskirts of the blessed kingdom. And as the symbolic coincidences accumulate, his status as a mythic hero on a fated journey solidifies. Principles of evil, therefore, must also exist—Columbus brings the Old World to the New—and thus, as is the case with all Edens, a sense of loss becomes the eventual reality.

In several important ways, Irving's *Columbus* is reminiscent of his previous books: it tends, like them, to reveal at least as much about its author as it does about its subject. To be sure, the major themes of Irving's life and work are there—the search for a more perfect home for the spirit and the inevitable recognition of the mutability of all existence—but beyond that, he seems at times to be straining to identify with his hero: Columbus's voyages to the New World are made to parallel Irving's spiritual quests in the Old. Of course, in the guise of his persona he was inevitably at the center of all his books; technically, however, *Columbus* differs from its predecessors in two significant aspects. For one, all the comic elements that distinguish the other works are eliminated here—there is no mockery, no burlesque, no ironic undercutting. For another, Irving intensifies his usual process of elaboration: in *Columbus*, rhetoric lifts scenes and episodes out of the realm of the ordinary and into the plane of the mythical; an abundance of prophetic signs and visions and a vast amount of sentiment lavished on Columbus's sorrows and sufferings alternately turn the story of his life and voyages into allegory and moral fable. And the ornamental style and highly poetic prose which adorn the entire narrative leave the reader doubtful, in spite of Irving's claim of authoritativeness, as to what is fact and what is fiction. Yet, paradoxically, even though *Columbus* is more romantic in mood and vision than his previous works, Irving maintains a consistent point of view: he does not have to mock Columbus's excesses as he once did Crayon's. This first achievement in Spain indicates the change that was taking place in his fortunes, both literary and worldly; indeed, it sets an important precedent for the other books that germinated during these years, especially since it accomplished the two goals he had set for it: it brought him a handsome sum from his English publisher, John Murray, and it received a highly favorable critical reception.[21] Irving's imagination had taken hold of his Spanish material, and his works became glorifications of the richness of his inner life. In a fundamental way, each appears to be more of a "romance" than the previous one. The problem comes in trying to understand how *The Alhambra*, which constitutes the ultimate romantic experience, both fits and does not fit into the pattern.

While Irving was sifting through the numerous manuscripts and books in Obadiah Rich's library in preparation for his *Columbus*, he discovered many volumes that pertained to the Moorish occupation of southern Spain. He must have immediately recognized the significance of this material, for his journal reveals that he laid *Columbus* aside and began to plan out a new work.[22] The history of the great Moorish city of Granada and its ultimate conquest by the Spaniards was, to say the least, a compelling subject: Granada, he confessed, had been since boyhood a kind of dream,[23] and a book on the Moors and their enchanted city promised the possibility of recapturing that mood. But Irving was too determined to be sidetracked more than just temporarily from his original manuscript, and when that was finished he was far too exhausted to continue his literary labors. It is quite possible, since the completion of the *Columbus* required a curtailed social schedule, that he now would have turned to engagements with his friends and local society to relax his mind and pass the time, but, fortunately, on October 10, 1827, the English artist David Wilkie, an old friend from Irving's Paris days, arrived in Madrid to study the Spanish masters; together they began to explore the wealth of paintings in the museums and churches of the city, with Wilkie playing the role of experienced instructor just as Washington Allston had previously done, both in Rome in 1805 and, together with Leslie and Newton, in London in 1817.[24] Such activity had always served the purpose of sharpening his eye for pictorial detail and, as Irving seems to have been a man prone to ritual behavior, in retrospect it looks as if this was the first step toward the production of another travel sketchbook. In fact, on March 1, 1828, he set out on the first of two memorable journeys to southern Spain. Traveling south and west by older modes and routes he made his way to Cordova; he then headed southwest on horseback for several more days until, on March 9, 1828, he reached the city of Granada. And on March 10, only one day after arriving, he entered the Alhambra for his first glimpse of the famous Moorish palace.[25]

The journey was picturesque and exciting, especially as the threat of encountering highway robbers was a perennial one; as always, Irving traveled with his literary associations in tow, and these enhanced his perceptions of the "wonderfully wild and romantic" moonlight scenery. Yet it is clear from a letter written a few days after his arrival that his first glimpse of the city was in perfect harmony with his fanciful conception of it:

> Granada, *bellissima* Granada! think what must have been our delight, when, after passing the famous bridge of Pinos, the scene of many a bloody encounter between Moor and Christian, and remarkable for having been the place where Columbus was overtaken by the messenger of Isabella, when about to abandon Spain in despair, we turned a promontory of the arid mountains of Elvira, and Granada, with its towers, its Alhambra, and its snowy mountains, burst upon our sight. The evening sun shone gloriously upon its red towers as we approached it, and gave a mellow tone to the rich scenery of the vega. It was like the magic glow which poetry and romance have shed over this enchanting place.

A landscape that could rise to the demands placed upon it by poetry and romance was bound to have its attractions for Irving, but as it turned out, it was not so much the city and its surroundings that took hold of his fancy, though he remained conscious of their immense beauty. Rather, it was the marvelously intricate structure and romantic history of that magnificent legacy of the Moors, the Alhambra, that now captured his imagination. Right from the beginning the fortress was like a symbolic literary work:

> The Alhambra and the Generalife have most excited our enthusiasm. The more I contemplate these places, the more my admira-

tion is awakened of the elegant habits and delicate taste of the Moorish monarchs. The delicately ornamented walls; the aromatic groves, mingling with the freshness and the enlivening sound of fountains and runs of water, the retired baths, bespeaking purity and refinement, the balconies and galleries open to the fresh mountain breeze, and overlooking the loveliest scenery of the valley of the Darro and the magnificent expanse of the vega; it is impossible to contemplate this delicious abode and not feel an admiration of the genius and the poetical spirit of those who first devised this earthly paradise.[26]

His "heart and soul," he said, were "intoxicated" by the scenery, especially the vega, a fertile, lowland plain, rich with sensual suggestiveness. No wonder his feelings were engaged, his curiosity aroused.

As his letters and diaries indicate, his old appetite for exploration, which had vanished for several years, was reawakened. Wandering about the Alhambra he recalled the famous events associated with it. He examined the fountain in the Court of Lions, and the stain beside it, where the remaining members of a great warrior family, the Abencerrages, were massacred. He searched the palace for the gate through which the last king of the Moors, Boabdil el Chico, passed on his way to surrendering the keys of the city to his conquerers, Fernando e Isabel (Ferdinand and Isabella), known in Spanish history as "Los Reyes Católicos" (the Catholic Monarchs). He tried to verify a related anecdote he had come across in an old chronicle: "Boabdil asked of the sovereign . . . that no one might be permitted to enter the Alhambra by the portal at which he had sallied forth. This prayer was granted; the portal was walled up, and has continued so to the present day."[27] At first, no one responded to his inquiries, but then some elderly residents who had passed their entire lives in the Alhambra pointed out a gateway which, according to their recollection, had always been sealed; one of them even "remembered to have heard his parents say it was the gate by which the Moorish king had departed, when he took his last leave of the Alhambra." Irving was delighted, and inspired: "With the keen relish of antiquarian research, I traced the whole route of the Moorish monarch down to the vega, to a small chapel dedicated to St. Sebastian. . . . Here an inscription on the wall designated it as the place where the unfortunate Boabdil met the Catholic sovereigns and surrendered to them his throne." And as he left Granada, he reenacted Boabdil's parting scene from the height of Padul where, overcome by grief, the deposed king wept as he turned to take one last look at his beloved city. At this spot, known to the Spaniards as "*el suspiro del Moro*" ("the last sigh of the Moor"), Irving was shown the hoofprints of Boabdil's horse in the rock on which he stood while his rider gazed back at the red towers of the Alhambra in the distance. As to the veracity of this, the credulous Irving remained skeptical (at least in his letters), but his sentiments naturally turned toward the plight of the melancholy monarch: "As you turn from this scene to pursue the route of the unfortunate king, a dreary waste of naked and sunburnt mountains extends before you. Poor Boabdil may have contemplated it as emblematical of his lot. He had turned his back upon all that was sweet and pleasant in life, and a stern, and rugged, and joyless futurity lay before him."[28] Though his fate had altered from the bleakness of 1824 and 1825, Irving, just as he had previously with Columbus, now identified with the last ruler of the Moors. Boabdil was destined to play an important role in both the *Conquest of Granada* and *The Alhambra*. Like him, Irving, too, would turn his back on the "enchanted palace," forever leaving behind an "oriental dream."[29]

In terms of his literary fortunes, however, by far the most important event of this stay in Granada was his first meeting, on Saturday, March 15, with Mateo Ximenes, one of that group of poor, longtime residents of the palace whose families had lived there from generation to generation ever since the time of the Conquest—*hijo de la Alhambra* ("a son of the Alhambra") as Mateo was later to inform him.[30] Mateo's obvious familiarity with the complex structure of the Alhambra endeared him at once to Irving and he became the latter's guide and constant companion. In this capacity he served two important functions: he introduced Irving to the neglected parts of the Alhambra, including the towers that lay in ruins; and, more importantly, he regaled him with the superstitions and legends that had been circulating time out of mind among the inhabitants of the Alhambra. Irving jotted down these tales and anecdotes, most of which involved the countless treasures the Moors had buried and, as he wrote, "the apparitions of their troubled spirits about the towers and the ruins where their gold lies hidden."[31] The ultimate importance of these stories of subterraneous mounds of wealth and peripatetic ghosts for Irving can only be fully established by examining their function in the context of *The Alhambra*; however, on this occasion Mateo afforded him a privileged, if only partial, glimpse into the imaginative life that lay beyond the magnificent architecture and splendid gardens of the Alhambra—a life that few, if any, visitors had ever encountered.

On March 20, 1828, after having spent ten days in the famed city of Granada, Irving left southern Spain and headed through the Sierra Nevada mountains toward Seville. He had not advanced his *Granada* manuscript much further, but he certainly had gained a better knowledge of the terrain on which the endless battles that he would recount in his history had taken place. It is possible that he may even have begun, as his biographer speculates, the manuscript that was eventually to become *The Alhambra*.[32] But if this is so, then it could only have been *The Alhambra* in its most preliminary and germinal form, for he had not yet discovered the essential wonder of the palace. He may have seen and sensed more than other outsiders, but a transcendent imaginative experience lay beyond his ken. He himself must have intuited this, for in his letter written from within the walls of the fortress he indicated that, despite what he had uncovered, the real spirit of the Alhambra had escaped him: "We talk of realizing past scenes when we tread in the traces of renowned historical events, but I find it impossible to get into the vein of feeling consonant to such a place. The verity of the present checks and chills the imagination in its picturings of the past." The song of an Andalusian girl dissipated the image of Boabdil "passing in regal splendor through these courts"; the chatter of a peasant awakened him from reveries of other Moorish cavaliers "who once filled these halls with the glitter of arms and the splendor of oriental luxury."[33] He could not link the present and the past; the former kept intruding upon the latter, impeding its recovery. The Alhambra, the pleasure palace of the upper classes, was majestic, but in 1828 it remained a showpiece. The scene of historical pageantry and personal despair, of ancient wealth and contemporary poverty, it was essentially a grand artifact, a museum. It did not yet live.

Still, Irving had seen enough of the savage, natural beauty of the Spanish landscape, and the "wild and melancholy grandeur of its naked mountains," to be fervently impressed. Moreover, certain "singular" characters—he described one as having "all the air of one of those predatory rovers who hover like hawks among the Spanish mountains to pounce upon the traveller"— whom he met on his travels were "complete subject[s] for Wilkie's pencil."[34] In fact it was to Wilkie, who had remained behind in Madrid, that he expressed his belief that so much of what he had encountered was prime material for their art:

> The more I see of this country the more I see of rich subjects for the pencil. These southern people are much more characteristic and national than the people about Madrid, and I think when you see a little more of them, you will find your imagination teeming with new ideas for pictures. Had you been with us on our hardy

and picturesque journey among the mountains you would have been continually delighted with the extraordinary Scenes presented by this wild country and its equally wild inhabitants.[35]

But even though he was stimulated by what he had observed, and despite the fact that his journal was filled with notes on Mateo's legends, he did not produce a series of sketches on Spanish customs and manners, undoubtedly because he knew that the Alhambra would have to be at the center of a new sketchbook and that he would have to experience it more intensely to bring this project to fruition. Moreover, according to a letter written in April 1829, he was not yet ready to give himself over to another fiction, which he considered as "some light work in [his] old vein" (i.e., like *The Sketch Book*). He had, he said,

> some things sketched in a rough state, in that vein, but thought it best to hold them back until I had written a work or two of more weight, even though of less immediate popularity. . . . Depend upon it, had I continued to write works merely like the Sketch-book the public would have ceased to read them. One must prose and be tedious at times, to get a name for wisdom with the multitude, that one[']s jokes may afterwards pass current.[36]

This, at least, is how Irving explained delaying his Spanish sketchbook. It is also his attempt to justify the amount of attention he devoted to his manuscript on the conquest of Granada, which he worked on in various residences in and around Seville, finally completing it in the little town of Puerto de Santa Maria, outside of Cadiz, at the very end of August, 1828.

A Chronicle of the Conquest of Granada, even more than *Columbus*, shows Irving straining to satisfy both his need to consider his Spanish material in romantic terms and his recognition that such a work required historical accuracy. Inevitably, because he could not give up either, he had to discover a way of holding them in creative tension, and he derived two means for this: the device of fictitious manuscripts and the use of a narrator modeled, as he said, on "the good old orthodox chroniclers, who recorded with such pious exaltation the united triumphs of the cross and sword."[37] Through these choices he also attempted to shift the responsibility for the liberties taken with his subject—mostly in its form of presentation—away from himself and onto his garrulous historian/narrator, Fray Antonio Agapida. This method, Irving insisted, was the book's main virtue. By extracting from the old chronicles what was useful to him—dates, descriptions of battles, and, in Williams's

228

words, a "phraseology of adventure and conflict"—and applying to this his way with a sentimental tone and romantic detail, which was designed to bring out "characters and incidents in stronger relief than they are to be met with in the old histories"—a process he variously labeled, as if he were speaking about a painting, "colouring," "tinting," or "embellishing"—he believed that he had produced something of real value, a work more significant, in fact, than his original sources.[38] *Granada*, he said, was "an attempt, not at an historical romance, but a romantic history." Besides endeavoring to give it "something of the effect of a work of the imagination," he hoped it would be appreciated as "an entertaining and popular form," a work that, "without sacraficing [sic] the intrinsic truth of history," had presented on a vast panoramic scale the entire scope of the events that had culminated in the Spanish expulsion of the Moors from Granada, "all being dressed up with an eye to the scenery of the country and the customs of the times."[39] Thus, *Granada* was history, romance, and Irvingesque sketch all meshed into one book.

In this respect, Fray Antonio Agapida served as another distancing technique, especially since, like some of Irving's other famous narrators, the friar is presented comically—not, like Crayon, the dupe of his own imaginative projections but, like Knickerbocker, a caricature, drawn in a broad comic style. His presence, Irving believed, allowed him to inject a measure of "romance and satire" into his narrative.[40] Clearly, the "romance" involves the symbolic meaning he attached to the city itself. Irving makes every effort, relies on all the powers of suggestiveness at his command, including his remarkable feel for romantic imagery and exalted, poetic language, to equate the Moors' failure to retain Granada with Adam and Eve's loss of paradise. Unmistakably, Granada was Eden:[41]

> It was a vast garden of delight, refreshed by numerous fountains, and by the silver windings of the Xenil. . . . [The Moors] had wrought up this happy region to a degree of wonderful prosperity, and took a pride in decorating it, as if it had been a favorite mistress. The hills were clothed with orchards and vineyards, the valleys embroidered with gardens, and the wide plains covered with waving grain. Here were seen in profusion the orange, the citron, the fig, and pomegranate, with great plantations of mulberry trees, from which was produced the finest silk. The vine clambered from tree to tree; the grapes hung in rich clusters about the peasant's cottage, and the groves were rejoiced by the perpetual song of the nightingale. In a word, so beautiful was the

earth, so pure the air, and so serene the sky of this delicious region, that the Moors imagined the paradise of their prophet to be situated in that part of the heaven which overhung the kingdom of Granada.[42]

If, for Irving, the city, which he saw mostly from afar, was a lovely woman (a "favorite mistress"), then the Alhambra, which he came to know intimately, was an even more enticing one. Together they signify that once, on earth, a place existed where people could live in perfect self-sufficiency, harmony, order—and, as well, in a kind of sensual "paradise." The endless combats, battles, triumphs, and defeats that are the substance of the book are all tedious, meaningless events unless viewed against the background of the culminating loss of Granada.

Having labored to create such a wonderland, the Moors then surrendered the one place on earth where man could have been content. For their efforts and achievements, they earned Irving's love and respect; he felt they "deserved this beautiful country" which, in his heightened prose, itself becomes a woman of "oriental charm":

> No lover ever delighted more to cherish and adorn a mistress, to heighten and illustrate her charms, and to vindicate and defend her against all the world than did the Moors to embellish, enrich, elevate, and defend their beloved Spain. Everywhere I meet traces of their sagacity, courage, urbanity, high poetical feeling, and elegant taste. The noblest institutions in this part of Spain, the best inventions for comfortable and agreeable living, and all those habitudes and customs which throw a peculiar and oriental charm over the Andalusian mode of living may be traced to the Moors.[43]

In the end, however, they remain morally culpable (and thus subject to some satiric handling) because they allowed their own sense of fulfillment, and the flow of luxuries without toil, to weaken and corrupt them until they were no longer capable of defending their home. Internal struggles, petty jealousies, and excessive avarice, pride, and stubbornness, lead to betrayal and defeat. Paradise is finally lost. But in the midst of this tale of woe, Irving lavishes romantic sentiment on Boabdil, known alternately as "El Chico" ("The Little One") or "El Zogoybi" ("The Unfortunate" or "The Unlucky"). In Irving's version of the story, it is not Boabdil's fault that the city falls to the Christians. He simply finds himself in a world that he cannot set right, not because he acts fearfully or cowardly, but because he suffers from an inability to take a determined course of action: to Irving, he personified "weakness of will."[44] (In the historical version, however, he is weak spiritually and morally: when he cries upon leaving Granada for the last time his mother scornfully tells him not to shed tears like a woman over what he could not defend like a man.) Against his cruel, warriorlike adversaries he had little chance of success, yet Irving renders his downfall with beauty and tenderness. Drawing upon the legends and anecdotes he had accumulated, he concludes his story of the Moorish occupation of Granada with Boabdil's request that the gate in the Alhambra through which he has departed be sealed forever. Then, as the last king of the Moors begins his journey toward exile in Africa, he turns with his men to face the city they can never reenter. Here, at "el suspiro del Moro," the inconsolable Boabdil cries out, "'Allah Achbar! when did misfortunes ever equal mine?'" Fittingly, the final glimpse of Granada justifies the Moors' grief. "Never had it appeared so lovely in their eyes," Irving writes. "The sunshine, so bright in that transparent climate, lit up each tower and minaret, and rested gloriously upon the crowning battlements of the Alhambra; while the vega spread its enamelled bosom of verdure below, glistening with the silver windings of the Xenil. The Moorish cavaliers gazed with silent agony of tenderness and grief upon that delicious abode, the scene of their loves and pleasures."[45] Boabdil and his followers then disappear, but Irving would not forget this king whose fate it was to be expelled from the land of perfection. By this time, the idea of an earthly paradise had become a central theme of his Spanish experience, and within that theme Boabdil's place was secure. It is not surprising, then, that he turns up in *The Alhambra*, where the author must work out his own destiny in the midst of a different sort of Eden that he finds within the walls of the renowned palace.

II

It is nearly impossible to distinguish romance from reality in *The Alhambra*, and this, as much as anything else, has tended to obscure the meaning of Irving's adventures in the ancient fortress. "Care was taken," he wrote in the "Preface to the Revised Edition," "to maintain local coloring and verisimilitude; so that the whole might present a faithful and living picture of that microcosm, that singular little world into which I had been fortuitously thrown; and about which the external world had a very imperfect idea."[46] Yet despite this declaration of "truthfulness," the accuracy of the representation is questionable. The book proper commences, appropriately enough, with a sketch of "The Journey"; but after a matter-of-fact introduction and a few "remarks on Spanish scenery and Spanish travelling," Irving moves off into what appears to be a larger-than-life sojourn through "stern, melancholy country, with rugged mountains, and long sweeping plains, destitute of trees, and indescribably silent and lonesome, partaking of the savage and solitary character of Africa" (p. 3). Ever-present danger is balanced by the wonderful sights and sounds on the road to Granada. Each part of the landscape has its romantic associations: the ruins of a Moorish castle or a crumbling tower of a Roman fortress suggest days of grandeur and "chivalrous contests between Moor and Christian" (p. 14). Villages stage small fiestas for the travelers; beautiful women dance picturesque boleros; peasants parade in native costume. Moreover, dramatic shifts of tension in the narrative, from the wilderness of a desolate mountain pass with its threat of lurking violence to the benevolent hospitality of the gentle villagers, are mirrored in contrasted settings of rough, almost impenetrable exteriors and soft, beautiful, voluptuous interiors. As in ancient romances, the landscape seems more symbolic than real:

> Vast sierras, or chains of mountains, destitute of shrub or tree, and mottled with variegated marbles and granites, elevate their sunburnt summits against a deep-blue sky; yet in their rugged bosoms lie ingulfed verdant and fertile valleys, where the desert and the garden strain for mastery, and the very rock is, as it were, compelled to yield the fig, the orange, and the citron, and to blossom with the myrtle and the rose. (p. 6)

At the end of the wasteland, "this wild and intricate country," lies the city of gold, Granada. Near the city, at the summit of a steep hill, in the midst of sparse mountain terrain, stands the Alhambra. Within the dilapidated, crumbling walls of the fortress, there is a maze of lush interiors, with gardens of delight dedicated to ease, comfort, and pleasure. Irving presents his expedition as a continuation and fulfillment of the romantic visions of *Columbus* and *Granada*—first Columbus, then King Boabdil and the Moors, and now Irving himself, quest after a terrestrial paradise. At one point he likens himself to Don Quixote, a picaresque hero in search of spiritual adventure; his Biscayan guide, consequently, becomes "the renowned Sancho himself" (p. 7).[47] The young man is, of course, familiar with the story of Cervantes' hero; Irving, however, smiles inwardly upon discovering that although the guide knew the Don's life, "like many of the common people of Spain, he firmly believed it to be a true history" (p. 12). Irving appears to have shifted ground here: since the confusion between fact and fiction is so central to the meaning of *Don Quixote*, and since he laughs at the "simple-hearted" guide who takes the novel to be a "true history," he implies that his own history is a fiction. Yet, since he insists on the "truthfulness" of his narrative, and since he offers his impressions of foreign wonders as did the travel diarist reporting back to the New World from the Old, he wants his adventure to be accepted as fact. As it turns out, the latter reading is correct: the heightened contrasts and the explicit (and implied) comparisons symbolize Irving's inner, unstated feelings and beliefs about the significance of his flight.[48] Yet scholarly and critical commentary have failed to recognize this; the assumption always has been, as one critic has stated, that in *The Alhambra* Irving was completely "under the spell of romanticism."[49]

The best evidence that *The Alhambra* records an actual, lived experience is a notebook Irving kept in the summer of 1829, which contains a wealth of information on almost every facet of his stay in this former stronghold of Moorish power. In fact, unlike Irving's other journals, which give only a brief mention of events, this notebook includes a record of his reading (of which many passages are in Spanish), lists of activities and conversations, personal meditations, and fragments of stories which he heard and hurriedly transcribed.[50] Here, too, one finds descriptions of all the picturesque inhabitants of the Alhambra whom Irving studied for his finished sketches. Of this "household," no one member was more important to him than his "ragged philosopher" Mateo Ximenes, whose knowledge of every nook and cranny of the palace, familiarity with its people, and, most importantly, belief in the veracity of his own legends, rekindled Irving's imagination.[51] With his guide he wandered the Alhambra, watching as Mateo pointed out the settings of his tales of treasure and then listening as the legend was spun out before him.[52] Outside the palace the two took exquisite walks; in the orchard of the nearby Generalife they watched a beautiful sunset, and the notebook records both Mateo's rather rapturous outburst and Irving's own quieter, more thoughtful response to the scene.[53] Thus, whether listening to Mateo's stories, or making notes on Spanish peasantry, or watching the "checquered light of the sun thro trees," or bathing in the Court of Myrtles, or wandering in the Court of Lindaraxa, Irving was content. It was, he said of his stay in the Alhambra, "delicious."[54]

Along with the notebook of 1829, which confirms the extensive autobiographical strain in the published work, letters from the period corroborate the significance of this experience in Irving's life. From inside the palace he wrote to Brevoort that he was "nestled in one of the most remarkable, romantic and delicious spots in the world. . . . It absolutely appears to me like a dream." And he told his sister that a good deal of his time was spent idling "among these beautiful and interesting remains of Arabian Magnificence." "I feel as if living in one of the enchanted palaces that we used to read of in the arabian nights [sic]." So remarkable was the Alhambra that, years later, he still vividly remembered the time he spent withdrawn from the world and its cares: "It was a dreamy sojourn, during which I lived, as it were, in the midst of an Arabian tale, and shut my eyes as much as possible to every thing that should call me back to every day life. If there is any country in Europe where one can do so, it is among these magnificent but semi-barbaric ruins of poor, wild, legendary, romantic Spain."[55] The voyager from the New World was in the process of discovering one of the hidden secrets of the Old: the Alhambra invited those outsiders of sufficient sensibility and curiosity to penetrate its mystery, for within the unpromising, fortified exterior of the pile lay scenes of unsurpassable Oriental charm.

According to Oleg Grabar, the palace is in the tradition of city-citadels. Since its purpose was to provide "a setting for . . . the life of princes," its site and fortified appearance were intended to separate the aristocratic world of the royalty from the bourgeois and popular world of the city below. In addition, seen from the outside, Islamic palaces give no indication of their interior riches. If one looks at sections of the building or at the external frame of the complexes of the Lions or the Myrtles, then one may see that their "visible shells hardly suggest the brilliance or even the actual forms of the interiors." The "deeper meaning of a palace-citadel or a palace-fort," therefore, is "that it possesses a secret which construction seeks to defend."[56] Irving must have intuited this, for his actions and movements were all designed to bring him closer to what he sensed lay in the depths of the structure. The protected "treasure" held him in thrall.

Upon entering the fortress, one felt immediately the "early associations of Arabian romance" and could expect at any moment "to see the white arm of some mysterious princess beckoning from the gallery, or some dark eye sparkling through the lattice." Imaginary women are everywhere—so much better than real ones. For Irving, "the abode of beauty [was] here, as if it had been inhabited but yesterday" (pp. 32–33). The overwhelming sensations were, paradoxically, ones of immediacy and vividness combined with a feeling of luxurious ease, of sensuous drifting, of having entered a realm where everyday reality was inverted, where the imaginary had become the actual. Water, brought from the mountains by old Moorish aqueducts and circulating throughout the palace, induced, through its endless flow, a dream-like state:

> While the city below pants with the noontide heat, and the parched Vega trembles to the eye, the delicate airs from the Sierra Nevada play through these lofty halls, bringing with them the sweetness of the surrounding gardens. Every thing invites to that indolent repose, the bliss of southern climes; and while the half-shut eye looks out from shaded balconies upon the glittering landscape, the ear is lulled by the rustling of groves, and the murmur of running streams. (p. 33)

Again and again, in notebook and correspondence, Irving mentions being lulled into a hypnotic state by the sound of water. As Grabar explains, water and its surrounding gardens "represented paradise, at times a specifically Islamic holy paradise, . . . at other times a more sensuous paradise of physical well-being whose possible mystical associations should not overshadow occasional orgiastic connotations."[57]

Irving had always loved the lazy, borderline state of consciousness signifed by the "half-shut eye," which he associated with the territory that lies somewhere between fact and fiction, between reality and fantasy.[58] Its call was an irresistible summons which he could not refuse. Only a few days after his arrival, on May 12, 1829, to be exact, he and his traveling companion, Prince Dmitri Dolgorouki, attaché to the Russian legation at Madrid, happily accepted the invitation of the governor of the Alhambra to occupy the royal apartment in the palace, which was a suite of empty chambers, quite modern in style, located in the front part of the fortress.[59] Shortly thereafter fate began to take its course as situation and circumstance conspired to make Irving the lone sojourner in the vast fortress. Having been summoned back to Madrid, the prince took his leave, and his departure was soon followed by that of Irving's nephew Edgar, who had arrived unexpectedly on the first day of his occupancy of the Alhambra. Suddenly, Irving was alone and for the next several months, surrounded solely by Spaniards, he would speak and read and muse about nothing but the language, the literature, and the romantic history of this southern land. At this very point in the narrative, just when he is left to his own caprices and thrown back upon himself, he alters his style significantly by switching almost exclusively to the use of the present tense. Such formal manipulation as the shifting of tenses is, of course, a way of indicating that time, or more exactly, Irving's sense of time, is altering, as if he had slipped into a suspended present or an eternal now. And accompanying a change in tense is a change in consciousness, a release of tension: as Irving said, he lived "quietly, snugly, and without any restraint, elevated above the world and its troubles." "I question," he continued, "if ever poor Chico el Zogoyby [Boabdil] was as comfortable in his palace."[60]

Moving about the labyrinthine structure, Irving discovers a multitude of lavish, sensual interiors which stimulate and then overpower the senses; moreover, with the help of Mateo, he learns that every haunt, every part of the palace, each surrounding area has its associations for the people who reside there. These "sons of the Alhambra" are representative of the poorest classes of Spain and are practiced in the art of doing nothing. To them, life is one long holiday amidst the ruins of the magnificent Moorish palace. As with the grandfather of Mateo Ximenes, their "whole living, moving, thinking, and acting . . . had thus been bounded by the walls of the Alhambra; within them [they] had been born, within them [they] lived, breathed, and had [their] being" (p. 38). Like Bracebridge Hall, the Alhambra is an insular world where traditional lore had not died. But where the life of the English ancestral mansion was threatened and eventually destroyed by economic forces in the social and political world beyond its boundaries, existence inside the Alhambra remains unaltered. Having no pragmatic concerns, the inhabitants of the Alhambra have no work week, yet "are as observant of all holy days and saints' days as the most laborious artisan." In addition, "they attend all fêtes and dancings in Granada and its vicinity, light bonfires on the hills on St. John's eve, and dance away the moonlight nights on the harvest-home of a small field within the precincts of the fortress, which yield a few bushels of wheat" (p. 42). Thus, the main difference between the Alhambra and Bracebridge Hall is that life in the former has not lost its authentic quality. Unlike Squire Bracebridge's domain, the scene at the Alhambra is not an artificial restoration of a mode of life which had already passed away. Here, the outside world did not impose its limitations; there is little to remind one of other, more demanding realities. Precisely because of this, within their given area the "hijos de la Alhambra" lead a rich, imaginative existence, which often inverts the accepted order of the external world. Thus, Irving, a longtime friend to anglers, and an admirer of Izaak Walton,[61] marvels at the Alhambran version of this pastime: "aerial fisherm[e]n" place themselves on the tops of the battlements and bastions to ensnare the swallows and martlets that breed in and sport about its towers. Using hooks baited with flies, these "arrant idlers" entrap the birds in "their giddy circlings"; by adapting the usual and practical methods of worldly fishermen to suit their particular and unusual circumstances, the "sons of the Alhambra" have "invented the art of angling in the sky" (p. 42).

Having glimpsed the strange, compelling beauty of the palace and the highly original, bizarre, but imaginative character of its inhabitants, Irving began to feel discontented with the formal royal suite he was occupying; there was a mystery here which seemed to hover just beyond his grasp, and to pursue it he believed he must "ensconce [him]self in the very heart of the building." In "The Mysterious Chambers," he makes just the discovery that will allow him to realize his ambitions. When, "in a remote gallery," he comes upon a locked door, he immediately senses that here lies the mystical experience he has been seeking. This surely was the "haunted wing of the castle" (p. 56). Given that "every unit [of the monument] was an intentionally 'interiorized' creation to be seen, appreciated, and used from the inside," it is perfectly understandable that he desires to move toward the center of the building. As Grabar writes, the artists who designed the Alhambra "*invited and still invite a unique search for the inner principle or the single unit which makes the whole possible*."[62] Irving was again responding, acutely and sensitively, to the deliberate construction and design of the monument. He sought the core, surrounded by its mysteries and defenses.

Thus, the overpowering urge to explore the chambers compels him to uncover a fanciful suite of rooms bordering on the Court of Lindaraxa, a "charming little secluded garden, where an alabaster fountain sparkled among rose and myrtles, and was surrounded by orange and citron trees" (p. 56). The apartment, elegant and sequestered, is pleasing, but it is the sense of history about the place that really stimulates and fascinates him: the rooms had once been occupied by Elizabeth, queen to Philip V of Spain, and the garden had been named for the Moorish beauty who had flourished in the court of Muhamed the Left-Handed. Once again, the "dilapidations of time" hold the New World pilgrim in thrall:

> Four centuries had elapsed since the fair Lindaraxa passed away, yet how much of the fragile beauty of the scenes she inhabited remained! The garden still bloomed in which she delighted; the fountain still presented the crystal mirror in which her charms may once have been reflected; the alabaster, it is true, had lost its whiteness; the basin beneath, overrun with weeds, had become the lurking-place of the lizard, but there was something in the very

decay that enhanced the interest of the scene, speaking as it did of that mutability, the irrevocable lot of man and all his works. (pp. 57–58)

In the Alhambra, even the moles become beauty marks. The shadow of the past hovered nearby; "mutability," as it had been in *The Sketch Book*, was once more the unavoidable theme. Yet this time the feeling of loss, though still accompanied by awe and dread, fails to drive Irving into some form of satiric or burlesque humor; remaining undisturbed, he is not ultimately forced into comic irony by the absence of historical order. Here, he is closer than ever before to being in touch with its spirit; so that despite the room's "forlorn, remote and solitary" location, and even though it forebodes "frightful loneliness," Irving insists on moving in: "That," he declares, "would indeed be living in the Alhambra, surrounded by its gardens and fountains, as in the time of the Moorish sovereigns" (p. 58).

In the ensuing sequence, the quest to "live in the Alhambra" takes on the shape of a story of initiation, with Irving undergoing a rite of passage by spending a solitary night in his forsaken quarters, achieving, in effect, union with the building. In a way, of course, the extraordinary coherence the seemingly disparate events assume is due to the fictional form of their presentation. However, the form does not impose a pattern of meaning on the experience; that pattern, on the contrary, is inherent in it from the beginning. The sketch form only allows Irving to see the pattern and to explore and realize its meaning. Thus, it is not the fear of unwelcome visitors, which is the main concern of Irving's Alhambra friends, that affects him most on his initial trial of courage. The first night in these quarters is "inexpressibly dreary" because Irving is apprehensive about "the character of the place itself, with all its strange associations: the deeds of violence committed there; the tragical ends of many of those who had once reigned there in splendor" (p. 58). It is as if "the place itself" were testing him, trying to determine how intensely he could saturate himself in its history, and thereby weighing his worthiness to know its secrets. Accordingly, separated from the others, he must brave the workings of his imagination as it conjures up images from the long history of first the Moorish, and then the Christian occupation of the Alhambra—the haunted chambers of his own mind, he seems to be saying, are more threatening than any dangers imposed from without. Within this mirrored setting, he feels like the hero of a hobgoblin story, "left to accomplish the adventure of an enchanted house." But as in those tales of terror, the heroism resides not in doing battle with visible apparitions but rather in proving that the mind is strong enough to overcome itself.

Every anxiety that now plagues him, significantly enough, correlates precisely with a particular aspect of the place: "phantoms of the memory" (of past events which had occurred there), rustling noises as if spirits of the departed had returned, "the grotesque faces carved in high relief in the cedar ceiling," the eerie sound of rushing water coming from the Hall of the Abencerrages, reminding him of the dismal stories to which it had given rise. Taking lamp in hand, he faces the challenge by touring the palace, "traversing scenes fraught with dismal recollections": "One dark passage led down to the mosque where Yusef, the Moorish monarch, the finisher of the Alhambra, had been basely murdered. In another place [was] the gallery where another monarch had been struck down by the poniard of a relative whom he had thwarted in his love" (p. 60). While there are some comic overtones to this passage—again, there is the suggestion of Irving as a Quixote-like figure doing battle with spiritual windmills—on the whole he takes the ordeal quite seriously. Like the true hero, his quest to know overcomes his fear of the unknown, and the reward is illumination:

> In the course of a few evenings a thorough change took place in the scene and its associations. The moon, which when I took possession of my new apartments was invisible, gradually gained each evening upon the darkness of the night, and at length rolled in full splendor above the towers, pouring a flood of tempered light into every court and hall. The garden beneath my window, before wrapped in gloom, was gently lighted up, the orange and citron trees were tipped with silver; the fountain sparkled in the moonbeams, and even the blush of the rose was faintly visible.
>
> I now felt the poetic merit of the Arabic inscription on the walls: "How beauteous is this garden; where the flowers of the earth vie with the stars of heaven. What can compare with the vase of yon alabaster fountain filled with crystal water? nothing but the moon in her fulness, shining in the midst of an unclouded sky!" (pp. 60–61)

In addition, with the repetition of moon and moonbeams, fountains and images of water, Irving calls upon female symbols almost as D. H. Lawrence does, in a compulsive, obsessive way. Mentions of the moon conjure up visions of Diana, the virgin goddess; and of course, images of vessels and water suggest both sexual and fetal comfort.

239

Occurring only about one-fourth of the way through the book, this scene actually climaxes the narrative sequence (which means that the structure comes close to reproducing the pace and flow of the original experience: the space allotted in the book to the sequence of events leading up to the shift in residence almost directly parallels the time sequence of Irving's actual stay in the Alhambra.)[63] After this test of his will and his desire to penetrate to its secrets, the Alhambra no longer appears to Irving as a formidable mystery; it is now, like a lover, open and yielding. Inside the fortress the boundaries of time are completely obliterated: the elegant memorials that dimly shadow forth the "checkered fortunes" of those who passed through these corridors are no longer opaque and distant. Unlike other monuments of a historical and romantic past, the Alhambra does not promise, yet ultimately withhold, the glories of bygone days. Enclosed within its walls, hidden from the world's ken, the past is not only preserved; it is, as Irving discovered, imminently present:

> Sometimes, when all was quiet, and the clock from the distant ca-
> thedral of Granada struck the midnight hour, I have sallied out on
> another tour and wandered over the whole building; but how dif-
> ferent from my first tour! No longer dark and mysterious; no
> longer peopled with shadowly foes; no longer recalling scenes of
> violence and murder; all was open, spacious, beautiful; every
> thing called up pleasing and romantic fancies; Lindaraxa once
> more walked in her garden; the gay chivalry of Moslem Granada
> once more glittered about the Court of Lions! (p. 61)

The effort involved in trying to comprehend the Alhambra's myriad courts, arches, passageways, and towers, "cast[s] a sort of spell, evoking real or imaginary events and emotions that find their place inside its walls."[64] Moreover, under the silvery, transforming beams of moonlight, as if a symbolic woman were overlooking the scene, another realm of experience "between the Actual and the Imaginary" becomes available, one that Irving already had, in fact, dismissed from possibility:

> Who can do justice to a moonlight night in such a climate and
> such a place? The temperature of a summer midnight in Andalusia
> is perfectly ethereal. We seem lifted up into a purer atmosphere;
> we feel a serenity of soul, a buoyancy of spirits, an elasticity of
> frame, which render mere existence happiness. But when moon-
> light is added to all this, the effect is like enchantment. Under its

plastic sway the Alhambra seems to regain its pristine glories. Every rent and chasm of time, every mouldering tint and weather-stain is gone; the marble resumes its original whiteness; the long colonnades brighten in the moonbeams; the halls are illuminated with a softened radiance—we tread the enchanted palace of an Arabian tale! (p. 61)

Allowing for the accustomed heightening of language, and even for the hyperbole occasioned (at the time of writing) by the memory of such beauty, Irving is still describing a realized ideal. Here, his imagination could extend itself into its surroundings and, instead of being repulsed or brought up short, could meet with its own reflections. This indeed was a paradise, a place—to borrow Fitzgerald's words from *Gatsby*—"commensurate to his capacity for wonder." Or, to put it another way, the Alhambra, owing to the secret of its construction, was "a world elsewhere": its fascination, its lure, lay in the fact that it could induce and sustain illusions. "The peculiar charm of this old dreamy palace," Irving wrote, "is its power of calling up vague reveries and picturings of the past, and thus clothing naked realities with the illusions of the memory and the imagination" (p. 79). Architecturally, therefore, the Alhambra was the perfect embodiment of the ideal, sensuous state of being that he had always sought. According to Grabar, "the overwhelming objective of the Alhambra's elevation lies in its seeking to provide what may be called illusions, that is, impressions and effects which are different from the architectural or decorative means used to create them." From various points of analysis, one may discover "a consistent attempt to give the impression that things are not quite what they seem to be." Other "syntactic devices" heighten these impressions, so that a mood is created which makes it seem as if all activities inside the monument are taking place "outside time and space."[65] Irving had achieved a state of transcendence.

The world had always destroyed the fantasies and projections of Geoffrey Crayon, but here, much to Irving's delight, it was rather a different story. Each room is, in effect, another tale; thus, the imaginative associations that he carries with him, and which inform all his perceptions, are for once perfectly congruous with the structure of his environment. In "The Court of Lions," for example, he feels so close to the "mementos of the past" that with just a slight exertion of the fancy, pictures of ancient scenes come floating across his sight. Here, in the "presence of Ferdinand and Isabella, and their triumphant court, the pompous ceremonial of high mass, on taking possession of the Al-

241

hambra," was performed. For Irving, the moment, in all its vividness, is once again alive:

> I picture to myself the scene when this place was filled with the conquering host, that mixture of mitred prelate and shaven monk, and steel-clad knight and silken courtier; when crosses and crosiers and religious standards were mingled with proud armorial ensigns and the banners of the haughty chiefs of Spain, and flaunted in triumph through these Moslem halls. I picture to myself Columbus, the future discoverer of a world, taking his modest stand in a remote corner, the humble and neglected spectator of the pageant. I see in imagination the Catholic sovereigns prostrating themselves before the altar, and pouring forth thanks for their victory; while the vaults resound with sacred minstrelsy, and the deep-toned Te Deum. (p. 80)

While it may appear at first as if Irving is revealing a carefully harbored admiration for the Catholic church, this is rather the eucharistic imagination freed from the demands of institutional affiliation, admiring rite and symbolism, not dogma. Irving's vision encompasses a scene of pure ceremony, full of regal splendor, a ritual of thanksgiving uncorrupted and untainted by the machinations of the court. As pure form, the mass exists outside of any "true" historical context. In fact, it is itself an Alhambra, a replaying in the recurrent present of the past events of the Last Supper and the Crucifixion. When the priest repeats Christ's words "This is my body" then the bread *at that instant* transubstantiates into Christ's body. For these reasons, therefore, there is no need for Irving to trouble himself about the social, political, or religious implications of the victory of the Catholic sovereigns over his beloved Moors. For a brief period, the world was his imagination, and his imagination was the world. The union was delightfully—and unthreateningly—sensual.

III

Unlike "Westminster Abbey" (in *The Sketch Book*), where he also communed with figures from the past, "The Court of Lions," even in darkness, does not hold a "potential trap for the imagination."[66] Though it is a place in the Alhambra (and, like the abbey, it gives its name to one of the sketches) "favorable to this phantasmagoria of the mind," and though the "transient illusion" it calls forth may soon disappear, Irving does not respond as if the ancient relics and ruins of the court signify, as they did in the abbey, his own alienation either from the past (because it is only a series of fragments, virtually unknowable) or from the present (because in seeking out the past he risks losing himself forever to his own contemplations). The threat fails to materialize for one primary reason: besides having experienced the essential mystery of the Moorish monument, Irving also touched the wonderful imaginative spirit of its inhabitants. The poetic quality of their existence—they live on the borderline between the fantasies of their own daydreaming and the realities of their historical setting—is underscored by the legends of the Alhambra that they share and offer up to Irving, both as explanations of the strange symbols and constructions found among the fortress and as romantic adjuncts to a textbook rendering of the Moorish and Christian occupation of the Alhambra. What do, for instance, the figures of the key and the hand over the Gate of Justice symbolize? Why is the weathercock on top of one of the royal palaces in the form of a bronze warrior on horseback? And why is it considered a portentous talisman? The legends of the Alhambra provide romantic meanings for these phenomena; they also tell of buried treasure, of enchanted Moorish warriors doomed to suffer, in vaults and caverns below and beyond the Alhambra, the Christian occupation of their palace. Like the legendary people of Sleepy Hollow, the inhabitants of the Alhambra lead lives which mediate between the past and present, the strange and the familiar, lives infused with excitement and mystery. In the Alhambra as Irving found it, reality and fantasy interpenetrated. This is the state of mind that he embraced; living there for a time in a mood and atmosphere akin to romance, he was not concerned about being cut off from the outside world. Thus, he achieved here what he could not accomplish in "Westminster Abbey," in "The Boar's Head Tavern, East Cheap," or in *Bracebridge Hall*: for almost three months he reveled in illusions of the past without some representative of the present materializing in order to mock his foolish (and "unmanly") literary preoccupations. That he then took the multitude of traditional stories and legends that he had heard and pieced them together to form coherent narratives is, in its way, a symbolic act, signifying his acceptance of the "improbable truths of the Alhambra" (p. 192). He knew the country too well to be "deluded by its romance"; nor did he allow himself to regard these legendary marvels too seriously.[67] Yet such recognitions did not prevent him from assimilating the knowledge that in the Alhambra the past is always present—not the original experience, which was often commonplace and even, at times, sordid, but the past as it was romantically re-created in legend and myth. His own rewriting of the stories of Mateo Ximenes and the other "sons of the Alhambra" indicates a tacit acknowledgment of this "improbable truth."

No wonder Irving felt that he would never again "meet on earth with an abode so much to my taste, or so suited to my habits and pursuits."[68] The long Spanish adventure had led to his fortress; the search for the terrestrial paradise, in fiction and in reality, culminated in this garden. Nowhere does Irving make it clearer as to why his quarters in the Alhambra were the perfect setting for a "spectator" such as himself than in a letter he wrote from the Alhambra to Prince Dolgorouki; finally, he had found the perfect physical emblem of a truly imaginative existence:

> I never had such a delicious abode. One of my windows looks into the little Garden of Lindaraxa, the citron trees are full of blossoms and perfume the air, and the fountain throws up a beautiful jet of water; on the opposite side of the garden is a window open into the Saloon of las dos Hermanas; through which I have a view of the fountain of Lions, and a distant peep into the gloomy hall of the Abencerrages. Another window of my room looks out upon the deep valley of the Darro, and commands a fine view of the Generalife. I am so in love with this apartment that I can hardly force myself from it, to take my promenades. I sit by my window until late of night, enjoying the moonlight, and listening to the Sound of the fountains, and the Singing of the nightingales; and I have walked up and down the Chateaubriand Gallery until midnight. There is something so completely solitary and tranquil in thus being shut up in the centre of this great deserted palace.[69]

Irving has fallen in love with a romantic palace, which enfolds him in womblike shelter. Not surprisingly, the description is of a completely passive existence; Irving is inhabiting the Alhambra precisely the way he lives in the imagination. Absolutely nothing threatens the perfection of the moment: the mutable world, with its cares and anxieties, remains visible through the windows but shut out; like Eden, the Alhambra has walls beyond which penetration is not possible. And if Eden is ultimately no more than a state of mind, a consciousness of continual satisfaction, how interesting that the picture Irving has painted here seems to suggest both what it would look like and how it would feel to view the world solely from within the mind's eye, protected from actually having to participate in the flux and therefore undisturbed by all the factors that distort ordinary perception. A few years earlier he had copied into his notebook a passage from one of Milton's letters in which the blind poet speaks of the richness of his internal vision: "Why should I not submit with complacency to the loss of sight, which seems only withdrawn from the body without, to increase the sight of the mind within," he had written to the scholar Emeric Bigot.[70] Now Irving knew what Milton had experienced, understood how much he had gained from the loss of ordinary, external sight. Or, to adopt a more literary analogy, the Alhambra was Irving's "house of fiction" from whose windows he peered out and gazed upon the world, isolated, yet held in thrall by the illusions and projections of his own imagination.

By its very nature, Eden was a circumscribed experience; so, too, was the Alhambra, for like the original version of the Garden, this one also contained the seeds of its own destruction. To his brother Peter, Irving wrote that

> the effect of the climate, the air, the serenity and sweetness of the place is almost as seductive as that of the castle of Indolence, and I feel at times an impossibility of working, or of doing anything but yielding to a mere voluptuousness of sensation. I found, therefore, that, like the Knight of Industry, it was necessary to break the charm and escape.[71]

Lines from the "Castle of Indolence" had formed the epigraph to "Sleepy Hollow" as the poem presented a state of mind which he found attractive and compelling, even seductive, begging him to yield. Having experienced it within the walls of the Alhambra, he pursued it, yet he could never wholly rid himself of the fear that, if he lingered too long in his reveries, he would forever abandon himself to the pleasing sensations of his imaginative wanderings and thus forsake the reality below. "Extreme enjoyment of the climate while the imagination is excited to pleasant dream & reveries," he jotted in his notebook. "[T]here is such a disinclination to exertion[,] such a delicious indolence creeps over one—we love to loiter on the grass or crumbling wall and do nothing."[72] Like Sleepy Hollow, therefore, the Alhambra was a world in which the dreamer flourished, but in this respect, and especially in terms of Irving's ambivalent view of the status of a fiction writer, it is worth emphasizing that Sleepy Hollow was an imaginative place. The Alhambra, that other "castle of Indolence," was real. Where before he could always set aside his fiction to traverse the path from his study to society, inside the Alhambra he remained enclosed within his own mind. He felt, he told Brevoort, as if he were "spell bound in some fairy palace"; later he voiced the same concern to his sister: "The delightful tranquility and beauty of the place have combined to fix me here as with a Spell."[73] For the peripatetic Irving to be "fixed" was a new sensation but, gradually, the extreme opposites of traveling and stasis

245

came to seem more like polarities of the same experience. In either case—whether as a wanderer on the Continent or as a captive in the Moorish palace—he had not yet found his home.

In "The Author's Farewell to Granada," Irving wonders how he will ever leave his "Moslem elysium" to "mingle once more in the bustle and business of the dusty world." "How was I to encounter its toils and turmoils," he asks, "after such a life of repose and reverie! How was I to endure its commonplace, after the poetry of the Alhambra!" (p. 274). Yet the very next line—"But little preparation was necessary for my departure"—reveals how important and, once he had decided to depart, how untraumatic separation actually was for him (and therefore betrays the primarily rhetorical function of the previous questions). Passing at a point north of the Alhambra where the road wound into the mountains, "El Rey Chico the second," like his predecessor, bade adieu to the paradise he was leaving behind. The hill on which he stood "commanded a glorious view of the city, the Vega, and the surrounding mountains," but it was "at an opposite point of the compass from *La cuesta de las lagrimas* (the hill of tears) noted for 'the last sigh of the Moor,'" opposite because Boabdil had traveled southward toward Africa, the place from which his people had originally departed. Irving, too, was heading back to where his odyssey had begun and where the English people originated. The finale was just what the sense of an ending demanded, for it reinforced what he had always suspected and even known but which he was now only experiencing for the first time: a worldly paradise, of whatever form and shape, must be lost.

With this farewell, Irving completed the process of identification with the the Moorish king that had begun on his first trip to Granada in 1828. Like Boabdil, he was neither fearful nor cowardly, but suffered from "weakness of will." Or, perhaps, given his tendency to project his consciousness onto the world, he had from the beginning fashioned Boabdil in his own image. In either case, he left the palace because he could not make up his mind to stay. When an unexpected letter arrived offering him a diplomatic appointment as secretary of the U.S. Embassy in London, he neither seized the opportunity nor refused it; he simply took it as a sign that it was time to extricate himself and move on:

> I have [he wrote to his brother Peter, using language that he would later incorporate into *The Alhambra*] a thorough indifference to all official honors, and a disinclination for the turmoil of the world; yet having no reasons of stronger purport for declining, I am disposed to accord with what appears to be the wishes of

my friends. My only horror is the bustle and turmoil of the world—how shall I stand it after the delicious quiet and repose of the Alhambra? I had intended, however, to quit this place before long, and, indeed, was almost reproaching myself for protracting my sojourn, having little better than sheer self-indulgence to plead for it.[74]

"My brothers and my most particular friends," he told Everett, "have all written to me urging me so strongly to accept [the appointment] that I have yielded to their wishes, in opposition to my own." Preferring, at least in part, to see himself as driven about "at the mercy of chance and circumstance," Irving embraced the idea that just as he had been "blown" into Spain, so he was blown out again: "So goes this mad world; honors and offices are taken from those who seek them and are fitted for them, and bestowed on those who have no relish for them."[75] In effect, by identifying with Boabdil he continued his own self-mythologizing: the melancholy, unfortunate "El Zogoybi" was Washington Irving's alter ego, destined to suffer in a disordered world that requires far more strength than he possesses to set it right. Just as Boabdil loses everything, Irving understood that loss had been the predominant pattern of his own life—Matilda, Emily, his home, his moorings—and his psyche gravitated toward images and figures that reflected this self-conception. It was, moreover, a pattern recognizable to his American readers. By 1832 they had said good-bye to the Founding Fathers and, as the *New-England Magazine* had lamented (in 1831), to the Republic as well. Not even the then president, Andrew Jackson, the personification of "will" itself, and thus as a leader the very antithesis of Boabdil, could recover the original vision.

"Thus ended one of the pleasantest dreams of a life," Irving wrote by way of concluding *The Alhambra*, "which the reader perhaps may think has been too much made up of dreams" (p. 276). Here, in his last sketchbook, and his last important fiction, he sums up both his great pleasure and his great anxiety in living a life of the imagination. Had he felt imaginative pursuits to be more valid, he might have rephrased his parting line to read "thus ended one of the pleasantest 'fictions' of a life." But his mind-set would not allow for such an exalted view of fiction, or perhaps it was too early in the history of America's literary development for the use of a metaphor which has as its underlying premise the quite contemporary idea that life is, in effect, composed of a series of stories that are told in order to make sense of experience. Yet since repeated narrative references to the states of mind denoted by "dream," "sleep," and "reverie" establish the fictional ground for his tales,[76] somewhere in his consciousness the dichotomy that existed was that of dream and reality, with "dream" having a whole range of associations, all the way from illusion to imaginative wholeness. The experience Irving lived and portrayed in *The Alhambra* was for him a "dream," but it suggests a more profound state of being where life burns with the flame of creative intensity. Such a state might eventually be self-consuming, especially for one as divided as Irving, a man who fretted over the fact that in nineteenth-century America creating fictions was not considered a "serious" occupation; had he been able to sustain his imaginative reverie, however, he might have produced a work in which the power of the original experience is maintained throughout its fictional re-creation. The fact, as his biographer argued, that he would have written a better, truer book had he stayed was not ultimately the major consideration in his decision to leave.[77] He did not want to go, but as he (consciously) understood it, to remain would have been "self-indulgent." (He even had the illusion of a love life there.) His anxiety over facing the "bustle and turmoil of the world" is honest. Yet to an equal if not greater extent he feared that by giving himself over to his creations he would lose that very world he at times found so abhorrent.

"I assure you," Irving wrote to Brevoort from beyond the walls of the fortress, "when I took my last look at the Alhambra from the mountain road of Granada, I felt like a sailor who has just left a tranquil port to launch upon a stormy and treacherous sea." Once more the pilgrim was "cast out"; yet again the traveler was set adrift in the mutable world. Only by now the too familiar image has lost some of its power to convey the deep-rooted personal and cultural conflicts involved in Irving's decision to accept the appointment in spite of his reservations. In terms of cultural pressures, although he said that he doubted "whether I should not serve my country, my friends and myself better by continuing on in the tranquil and retired career of literature," he saw the post offered to him by his government, "without any view to party purposes, and without any solicitation by me or my friends," as a "mark of respect." Proof of the "good will" of his countrymen, it was the sign he had been looking for, and he was genuinely "flattered." But more so, he felt realigned: now the "link" to America could not be denied.[78] In terms of personal pressures, the Alhambra finally threatened him because he perceived its charm as sexually alluring and therefore dangerous. What he had implied to his brother by the phrase "yielding to a mere voluptuousness of sensation" he made explicit in commenting to Everett that "there is a Seductive voluptuousness in this climate, when tempered by these marble halls, and gushing fountains and shady bowers, that tempts one to more indolent enjoyment." It was not simply that the Puritan in him worried about being "incapacitated" for work, but that he feared being sexually aroused, as if he had been lured into a bordello and evil lurked everywhere. Like Adam in Eden, Irving in the Alhambra was not free from temptation. "The sole fault was that the Softness of the climate, the Silence and Serenity of the place[,] the odour of flowers and the murmur of fountains," he started to explain to Brevoort his reason for leaving, and then began to complete the thought with the words "induced me to yield to," but cancelled them, and instead repeated the phrase about feeling like the Knight of Industry when enthralled in the Castle of Indolence (which itself has sexual overtones).[79] Because he never could fully "yield to" either sexual or imaginative experience, he left the Alhambra. He had had his moment of transcendence; it was more than he had hoped for and all that he could handle.

If Irving never quite lost the world—indeed, on his return home to and subsequent residence in America, he gained not only a measure of fame and celebrity but became its adored literary hero—he did, in his last sketchbook, relinquish the persona he had created to protect him from the real world. Almost from the outset, even more noticeably than in *Tales of a Traveller*, the anxious, whimsical, self-mocking Geoffrey Crayon disappears from its pages. Having discovered this joyous paradox—the history of the Moorish occupation of the Alhambra is the history of paradise lost, yet nowhere else on earth was such a rich imaginative existence possible—Irving felt comfortable enough to jettison Crayon. The revised version of the book makes this clear: besides eliminating the vestiges of comic irony and a certain playfulness of tone, the 1848 edition removed Crayon's name from the title page. *The Alhambra* now appeared with Irving as its author while the other fictions were still listed as the works of Geoffrey Crayon.[80] It was not a terribly daring move, for the adoption of the Crayon guise hardly seemed necessary anyway: the book was less a work of personality, as *The Sketch Book* and, to a lesser extent, *Bracebridge Hall* had been, than one of mood, feeling, and atmosphere. An accurate perception of its central experience is vital to a proper understanding of what the book is about, but over the years few have read it with such an interest in mind. Moreover, the experience is in itself quite un-Crayonesque, if that descriptive term is defined according to the tenor and tone of loss that mark the previous fiction. Having gained some imaginative control over his immediate environment, Irving found that Geoffrey Crayon was expendable. Without him, however, a good deal of the comic vitality of the earlier fiction was gone; perhaps, though, that was the price exacted for a transcendent moment in reality.

When Irving left the Alhambra on July 29, 1829, the Spanish adventure was over. As it turned out, it was more than just the end of "one of the pleasantest dreams of a life," for after *The Alhambra* he no longer dwelt in the house of fiction. Instead, he returned home to an America that had chided and taunted him for having dallied so long in foreign territory. Over the next several decades, however, he did publish more books, which include three accounts of the expansion and development of his country, and which expose many of the ironies and deceptions of western exploration and settlement. It has been suggested that with these works he was "paying his debts"—having lived outside the prescribed limits of American experience, he had sinned—and that America was eager to receive them.[81] There is some truth to this assertion; in a letter to his brother Peter in 1829 he shows signs of yielding to the pressure to produce "American" books, and thus, in effect, lays the groundwork for *A Tour on the Prairies* (1835), *Astoria* (1836), and *The Adventures of Captain Bonneville* (1837): "I feel the importance, . . . and I may say the duty, of producing some writings relating to our own country which would be of a decidedly national character. It is greatly desired by my friends in america [sic], and would be at the same time very gratifying to my feelings and advantageous to my literary character at home."[82] Nevertheless, in spite of what appears to be mere submission to the demands of a popular audience, the frontier narratives contain depths that criticism has yet to fathom; in its way "the West" was as fertile a territory for his imagination as the Old World had been. Moreover, his three-volume work on George Washington's life, written at the very end of his own, remains a most interesting attempt to validate America on the eve of the Civil War and in the face of its undeniable failures. Though in the last third of his career he wrote no more sketchbooks, his creative impulses remained strong. America called its wandering son home and the prodigal returned: having traveled and imagined for seventeen years in the Old World, it appeared as if he had finally come back to roost in the New. But Washington Irving did not vegetate on the land he claimed for himself near Tarrytown. Though his expatriate years were behind him, he had a good deal more to say about the ambiguities of American identity. Long before Henry James, he understood the "complex fate" of being an American.

C O D A
Washington Irving and the House of Fiction

In a sense, Washington Irving was our first great "escape" artist: literature was his way of avoiding the difficult tasks that the commonplace, workaday world demanded of its citizens. From the time of his earliest ramblings in Sleepy Hollow country and his youthful jottings in his notebooks, imagining and writing were his means of transcending the mundane. "I trace many of my best feelings and best thots [thoughts] to their first burst while wandering on the banks of the Hudson," he wrote in an 1825 notebook. "It was there the world dawned upon me as a fairy land; and though checquerd and sad experience have thrown many a cloud on it, yet still I look back beyond these all to the sunny realm of boyish imagination." Later, he would settle permanently in Tarrytown on the Hudson, amidst the lovely landscapes that "swell[ed]" his "heart" and refreshed his "feelings." "The man who retires to the scenes of his child hood—like a battle worn soldier[—]Scarred all over with the conflicts of the world," reads another entry in that same notebook, almost as if it were an unconscious prediction of his own future, or as if he were plotting his own fate.[1] The physical withdrawal from the "bustling disputatious" society that had "scarred" him to the highlands where he could "commune with heaven" and with himself marked the concrete manifestation of a mental journey he had made often during his years abroad; again and again, when actualities disappointed him, he retreated to his imagination to recapture the "sunny realm" of boyhood fancies, either along the timeless shores of his beloved American river or within the time-drenched interiors of his revered English institutions. Only in the Alhambra, where he truly *lived* an imaginative existence, did he find in reality what Richard Poirier referred to as an "environment of 'freedom'" that all Americans at one time or another have longed to inhabit.[2]

For Irving, then, as for so many other American writers who followed him, imagination was an escape, "a world elsewhere," but, in another metaphorical direction, it also represented an anchor, the means by which he stayed and defended himself against the cares and burdens that plagued him. Whenever he felt undone by occurrences beyond his control—metaphorically "tossed on the sea in a storm"—he gathered his resolve and recovered his strength by cloistering himself from the world and turning his attention to literary pursuits. When, for example, in 1825 one of the most important banking firms in London failed, signifying a financial crisis that threatened American businessmen and jeopardized his investments, Irving followed this healing ritual; whereas others would take to their beds, he "took" to his "pen":

> As the pittance I possess in the world is all in America, and at the mercy of events, I felt for a time like one who has his all tossing on the sea in a Storm, and could not sleep at night for fancying a thousand evils. At length I took to my pen as a resource and went doggedly to work; by dint of perseverance I turned my thoughts into a literary channel, and have continued to occupy myself ever since. I find my mind greatly relieved in consequence, and trust I may be able to turn my labour to profitable account hereafter.[3]

No matter how successful he became, no matter what position of eminence he occupied, he continually imaged himself, especially in his intimate correspondence (as this study has copiously illustrated), as a man blown about by precipitous winds, thrown completely off course, "at the mercy of events" anywhere around the globe. It is not surprising, therefore, as the letters show, that he was attracted to families with a strong sense of unity, and that the houses and institutions he sketched were bastions of order defying the entropic decay of all earthly things. Barely managing to tread water, this pilgrim clung to literature as he would to a life raft; it was his method of keeping himself afloat, the only means he could envision for stabilizing himself in the midst of the tempest that was usually blustering about him. "One rub or other continues to keep me in dubious circumstances, notwithstanding the sale of my late work [*Columbus*]," he wrote to his friend Storrow in 1828, employing the appropriate Shakespearean word "rub," probably with *Hamlet* in mind (one of his favorite of the bard's plays); "but I trust by further exercise of my pen at length to get ahead of the world and its Sordid cares."[4] Like the melancholy prince he felt burdened by the "cares" of that world; fortunately, however, his task was not to set it right, merely to stay slightly "ahead" of it.

Of these two uses of imagination (as "escape," as "anchor") Irving was cognizant; what he did not know, could not understand (and probably would have denied had the idea been suggested to him) was that the home he continually sought in the external terrain could only be found in the interior landscape. "Home" for Irving meant, above all (as we have seen again and again in his writings), a secure harbor, a place free of conflict and stress, a way of shielding himself from the operations of chance and circumstance, a stay against disorder and confusion. During his European years he found no dry ground, no refuge from the vicissitudes of the human condition:

> I am sorry to find by your letters [he wrote to Brevoort in 1828, again with *Hamlet* in mind] that you have had your share of the rubs and cares of the times; I had hoped you were safe in port and out of reach of Storms and disasters; but so it is; we are none of us completely sheltered from misfortune. If we do not put to sea, the sea overflows its bounds and drowns us on the land. For my own part, with all my exertions, I seem always to keep about up to my chin in troubled water, while the world, I suppose, thinks I am sailing smoothly, with wind and tide in my favour.[5]

The buildings he chose to explore and to possess—Westminster Abbey, the Boar's head Tavern, Bracebridge Hall—all have the weight of the past, of memory and tradition, attached to them. But, ironically, the immersion into time did not provide what he sought; the past proved too threatening when it did exist, although more often than not, as he discovered about the stable life of the English ancestral mansion, the old order had long since faded from view. And when he did find the perfect house—the Alhambra, a royal palace built to sustain projections and illusions—he could neither prolong his stay nor extract from his experience a belief in imagination as the only true home for the wandering soul.

"American books are often written," Poirier has said, "as if historical forces cannot possibly provide [the desired] environment, as if history can give no life to 'freedom,' and as if only language can create the liberated place."[6] Irving would have found this concept an alien one; Henry James and his "house of fiction" were still many years into the future. Moreover, as Tony Tanner has argued, our writers would not truly accept this idea of the "city of words" until the twentieth century.[7] From Irving to James demarcates a considerable artistic development, and American literature would acquire a great deal of self-consciousness and self-reflexiveness along the route. But however much Irving resisted the notion of imagination as the ultimate reality, he does signal the beginning of an American tradition; thus, years before he chronicled the development of the West, he was himself a pioneer, resembling those for whom house building was an act of appropriation as they carved out a territory of their own in America's wilderness. After 1832 Irving lost much of his interest in innovative fictional structures but, appropriately enough, he became preoccupied with the real home he designed for himself which he called, significantly, Sunnyside: he had created a totem to keep the storms away. Having eschewed fictional houses, he instead built a literal one, and when his notebooks were empty (as they were, for example, when he returned from his ministry in Spain in 1846) and no imaginative work forthcoming, he added more sections to his house, as if each new wing would anchor him a little more solidly in the hard American soil. Though in the 1840s he repudiated his current life in fiction—"I have," he said of his slight magazine pieces, "as great a contempt for these things as anybody, though I have to stoop to them occasionally for the sake of a livelihood"[8]—it was not before he had moved American writing in a direction that would culminate with the great Romantics. Before that literature could come of age, however, a reclusive dreamer would spend twelve years in a real house in Salem and a supreme artisan would labor just as long over the construction of a many-windowed figurative one in the land of imagination. In the light of this unfolding cultural history, Sunnyside stands as a reminder that prior to the American writer staking his claim and building his house in the New World of timeless interior space, there were those literary sojourners like Irving who sought in the Old World of historically shaped exterior landscapes something nurturing both to themselves and their art.

All art demands sacrifice of and provides compensation for its creator. Irving's was no different, and though the extent of each is often impossible to determine, it seems fair to say that in his case writing filled the void of a vacant sexuality. In addition to all its other functions, imagination provided him with the excitement and release that men usually find through erotic experience. The Alhambra was voluptuous precisely because its charms aroused, while its soft, dreamlike environment caressed, his imagination. When, in 1827, he felt anxiety about *Columbus* because his publisher had neither acknowledged its receipt nor informed him of its publication date, he wrote to his agent in London that he would like to have "a word or two of intelligence as to the work. . . . You are a parent and must know what a parent feels when a child is about to be launched into the world."[9] But of course he was and would remain without progeny; by 1829 he was finally able to acknowledge overtly what had been true covertly for many years: "I begin to grow hard-ened & shameless in the matter [i.e., "gradually increasing in the belt"—get-ting fat], and have for some time past given up all gallanting, and declared myself an absolute old Bachelor," he told his confidante Brevoort.[10] For the wifeless, childless Irving, creativity was procreativity; art produced life. One looks in vain for a Flaubert-like statement to this effect, for an outright cham-pioning of fiction's domain, which of course would have been a form of heresy in early-nineteenth-century America. Nevertheless it remained true—and this is several years before Poe wrote any of his critical manifestos, more than a half-century before Henry James codified the life of his art—that his books were his children and his imagination was his home.

N O T E S

PREFACE

1. See *The Standard Edition of the Complete Psychological Works of Sigmund Freud*, trans. James Strachey (London: Hogarth Press, 1959), 20:132.

2. Erikson, *Childhood and Society*, 2d ed. (New York: Norton, 1963), p. 406.

3. Wilentz, *Chants Democratic: New York City & the Rise of the American Working Class, 1788–1850* (New York: Oxford University Press, 1984), p. 72.

4. Wilentz, pp. 16–17. Wilentz further notes that in periods of "social fear" New Yorkers "returned to class issues and to class identities and allegiances to defend their interests, and those of the democratic Republic itself, as they saw them."

5. Wilentz, p. 14. For the interdependent concepts of republican thought see the work of J. G. A. Pocock, "Virtue and Commerce in the Eighteenth Century," *Journal of Interdisciplinary History* 3 (1972):119–34, and *The Machiavellian Moment: Florentine Political Thought and the Atlantic Republican Tradition* (Princeton: Princeton University Press, 1975).

INTRODUCTION

1. For the former classification, see George Dangerfield, *The Era of Good Feelings* (New York: Harcourt, Brace, and World, 1952), pp. 95–196; Dangerfield sees the "era" lasting from 1817 through 1819. For the latter, see William R. Taylor, *Cavalier and Yankee: The Old South and American National Character* (New York: Braziller, 1961), pp. 95–141; Taylor does not locate parameters for the "age," but his discussion covers the years from 1821 through the early 1830s. (I further examine the topic of American anxiety in conjunction with my analysis of *The Sketch Book* in chapter 2). All labels such as "age of anxiety" are, in effect, arbitrarily assigned, and certainly may be used to connote various kinds of cultural tensions. Writing from a different perspective—that of "the fall of man from familial security into a deceptive and competitive social world"—Jay Fliegelman, *Prodigals and Pilgrims: The American Revolution against Patriarchal Authority, 1750–1800* (Cambridge: Cambridge University Press, 1982), points to the 1790s as the beginning of the "modern age of anxiety," ushered in by the French Revolution (pp. 241, 243).

2. Adams to Jefferson, Quincy, November 3, 1815; Jefferson to Adams, Monticello, April 8, 1816, in *The Adams-Jefferson Letters*, ed. Lester J. Cappon (Chapel Hill: University of North Carolina Press, 1959), 2:456, 467; R. A. Yoder, "The First Romantics and the Last Revolution, *Studies in Romanticism* 15 (1976):493.

3. Jefferson, *Notes on the State of Virginia*, ed. William Peden (Chapel Hill: University of North Carolina Press, 1955), p. 161; Charles Sydnor, *Gentlemen Freeholders: Political Practices in Washington's Virginia* (Chapel Hill: University of North Carolina Press, 1952), p. 9; see also Taylor, pp. 31–32.

4. Jefferson to Edward Coles, Monticello, August 25, 1814, in *Thomas Jefferson: Writings* (New York: Library of America, 1984), p. 1345; Sydnor, p. 9.

5. Webster, "Second Speech on Foot's Resolution" (January 26, 1830), in *The Works of Daniel Webster*, 10th ed. (Boston: Little, Brown, 1857), 3:316, 342; Taylor, pp. 109–15.

6. Irving to Henry Brevoort, Ship Mexico, Sandy Hook, May 25, 1815, in Washington Irving, *Letters: Volume 1, 1802–1823*, ed. Ralph M. Aderman et al. (Boston: Twayne, 1978), p. 394. See also Stanley T. Williams, *The Life of Washington Irving* (New York: Oxford University Press, 1935), 1:130–31, 143–44.

7. Irving to Henry Brevoort, Birmingham, July 5, 1815, in *Letters*, 1:399. England, he said, "delighted" him.

8. In *Home as Found: Authority and Genealogy in Nineteenth-Century American Literature* (Baltimore: Johns Hopkins University Press, 1979), Eric Sundquist sees the family as a metaphor for "unsettled social and political institutions" (p. xv). In pursuing the idea of "home" in nineteenth-century America—a pursuit he likewise conducts in psychological, emotional, and cultural terms—Sundquist focuses on a major text by each of four writers—Cooper, Thoreau, Hawthorne, and Melville—who, he argues, made their careers "representative" of their culture. It should be clear, however, that although I have applied this designation to Irving, he never envisioned himself in this way; though he may not have been any less culturally stable than his successors, he was too personally insecure and too uncertain about the efficacy of a literary vocation to equate his anxieties with his country's.

9. John Higham, *From Boundlessness to Consolidation: The Transformation of American Culture, 1848–1860* (Ann Arbor: William L. Clements Library, 1969), pp. 6–15. Higham applies the term "age of boundlessness" to the years 1815–48. See also George B. Forgie, *Patricide in the House Divided: A Psychological Interpretation of Lincoln and His Age* (New York: Norton, 1979), pp. 96–97.

10. Channing, "The Present Age" (May 11, 1841), in *The Works of William Ellery Channing* (Boston: American Unitarian Association, 1903), 6:150–54; Higham, p. 6.

11. Rowland T. Berthoff, *An Unsettled People: Social Order and Disorder in American History* (New York: Harper and Row, 1971), p. 203. As Berthoff puts it, "one of the hinges of the old American society had been broken." In an earlier study Berthoff argued that 1815 marked an important turning point in American civilization, when a relatively homogeneous, unified, and stable agrarian society began to come apart and the values and beliefs that had lasted for two hundred years began to give way to the

restlessness and insecurity which characterized the nineteenth century. See "The American Social Order: A Conservative Hypothesis," *American Historical Review* 65 (1960):495–514.

12. "Notes 1815–1821," in Washington Irving, *Journals and Notebooks: Volume 2, 1807–1822*, ed. Walter A. Reichart and Lillian Schlissel (Boston: Twayne, 1981), p. 65.

13. Both Higham (p. 8) and Forgie (p. 96) warn that it would be a grievous error to assume that traditionalist attitudes disappeared during this time. The point is rather that the radical quality of the age's crucial issues can only be fully comprehended in the context of "boundlessness."

14. Alexis de Tocqueville, *Democracy in America*, ed. Phillips Bradley (New York: Knopf, 1945), 2:99.

15. Berthoff, *An Unsettled People*, p. 219.

16. Forgie, p. 7; Lincoln, "Eulogy on Henry Clay" (July 6, 1852), in *The Collected Works of Abraham Lincoln*, ed. Roy P. Basler (New Brunswick, N.J.: Rutgers University Press, 1953), 2:121. In his stimulating book, Forgie chronicles the complex changes in the psychological relationship of a second generation of Americans to the first, from the years after 1815 through the beginning of the Civil War. My study concentrates on the 1815–32 period and, therefore, does not examine the tensions of this relationship—the "recurring rediscoveries of sin" in the Fathers—once slavery becomes the primary issue in the late 1830s, 1840s, and 1850s. (For that focus see, in addition to Forgie, Eric J. Sundquist, "Slavery, Revolution, and the American Renaissance," in *The American Renaissance Reconsidered: Selected Papers from the English Institute*, ed. Walter Benn Michaels and Donald Pease [Baltimore: Johns Hopkins University Press, 1985], pp. 1–33, esp. 3–9.) However, I do range beyond my seventeen-year focus for examples and illustrations: tensions which became manifest after 1832 were often present in a latent form in prior years. I have constructed at least part of my argument in this section on the foundation of Forgie's work, and I am indebted to him for leading me to much fascinating material.

17. "Declaration of Independence," *Casket* 7 (1832):50; see also Forgie, p. 8. As Fliegelman has so persuasively demonstrated, the Founding Fathers were supremely concerned with their parental role; in the Republic, a true father forms his child's character as part of a proper education so that he may "participate in society" (see chapter 1, "Educational Theory and Moral Independence," pp. 9–35).

18. Webster, "On the Education of Youth in America," in *Essays on Education in the Early Republic*, ed. Frederick Rudolph (Cambridge, Mass.: Harvard University Press/Belknap Press, 1965), pp. 45, 64–65; see also Forgie, pp. 14–19. Forgie uses the classifications "heroic" and "postheroic" for the generations of the Fathers and the sons, respectively.

19. "Thoughts upon the Character of the Age," *United States Literary Gazette*, 1 (1824):42.

20. D[avid] H[atch] B[arlow], "American Literature," *Graham's Magazine* 38 (1851):328.

21. "Thoughts upon the Character of the Age," pp. 30, 42; original italics.

22. Webster, "Adams and Jefferson" (August 2, 1826), in *Works*, 1:147. The continuity of the virtuous Republic depended upon whether the actions of Americans would be governed by gratitude toward its rulers, since, as Fliegelman puts it, "gratitude was the barometer of a republican people's virtue" (p. 214).

23. Webster, "Adams and Jefferson," in *Works*, 1:115; Choate, "On the Political Topics Now Prominent before the Country" (October 28, 1856), in *The Works of Rufus Choate*, ed. Samuel Gilman Brown (Boston: Little, Brown, 1862), 2:414; my italics; "Oration before the Young Men's Democratic Club, in Tremont Temple," Boston *Daily Advertiser*, July 7, 1858, quoted in Forgie, p. 19.

24. Webster, "The Character of Washington" (February 22, 1832), in *Works*, 1:229.

25. *Annals*, 18 Cong., 1 Sess., House, 855. December 22, 1823; quoted in Paul C. Nagel, *One Nation Indivisible: The Union in American Thought, 1776–1861* (New York: Oxford University Press, 1964), p. 50. In his 1832 commemoration speech, Webster used almost the identical words when he spoke of Washington conjuring the American people to regard the Union as "the very palladium of their prosperity and safety, and the security of liberty itself."

26. For the development in the latter half of the eighteenth century of a new understanding of parental responsibility and filial freedom—the "antipatriarchal revolution"—based on Locke's *Education* treatise, see Fliegelman, esp. part 1 (pp. 1–89). The "problems of family government," which were the primary concerns of the fiction and the pedagogy of the age—problems such as "balancing authority with liberty," "maintaining a social order while encouraging individual growth"—were a microcosm of larger political issues with which Americans grappled (p. 5). A man's relationship to his society could be understood in terms of the "obligations parents and children owed one another" (p. 26). In *Rites of Passage: Adolescence in America, 1790 to the Present* (New York: Basic Books, 1977), Joseph Kett calls attention to the renewed interest in writing about the home after 1820 (he refers to it as a "fervor"), and stresses how important family ideology was in the nineteenth century (p. 79).

27. Yoder, pp. 495–96. "The real literary monuments of American Romanticism are dedicated to 'the perfect whole' [Emerson, "Each and All"], the 'transcendental Union' [Whitman, "Thou Mother with Thy Equal Brood"], or 'the mysterious federation' [Melville, *Mardi*, chap. 163] that is a replica of organic nature."

28. Still, there were connections to the Republican era. In "Sentimental Power: *Uncle Tom's Cabin* and the Politics of Literary History," *Glyph* 8 (1981):79–102, Jane P. Tompkins shows that Stowe sought to return economic and social power to an older way of life, the "rural communities . . . practic[ing] the reciprocity and mutual supportiveness that characterize the Quaker community in [her] novel" (p. 97). In "Modernization and the American Fall into Slavery in *Uncle Tom's Cabin*," *New England Quarterly* 54 (1981):499–518, esp. 506–10, Theodore P. Hovet analyzes Stowe's criticism of the intrusion of modern business into the organic world of the farm.

29. Stephen Innes, *Labor in a New Land: Economy and Society in Seventeenth-Century Springfield* (Princeton: Princeton University Press, 1983); William Cronon, *Changes in the Land: Indians, Colonists, and the Ecology of New England* (New York: Hill

and Wang, 1983), esp. pp. 74–77, 139–41. The earlier historians, whose conclusions about the cohesiveness and equality of some American farming centers Innes and Cronon question the generality of, are Kenneth A. Lockridge, *A New England Town, The First Hundred Years: Dedham, Massachusetts, 1636–1736* (New York: Norton, 1970); Philip J. Greven, Jr., *Four Generations: Population, Land and Family in Colonial Andover, Massachusetts* (Ithaca, N.Y.: Cornell University Press, 1970); John Demos, *A Little Commonwealth: Family Life in Plymouth Colony* (New York: Oxford University Press, 1970); Michael Zuckerman, *Peaceable Kingdoms: New England Towns in the Eighteenth Century* (New York: Knopf, 1970).

30. Innes, pp. xvii, 122, 149.

31. Lincoln, "'A House Divided': Speech at Springfield, Illinois" (June 16, 1858), and "First Debate with Stephen A. Douglas at Ottawa, Illinois" (August 21, 1858), in *Works*, 2:461, 3:18 (according to Forgie, in the earlier speech Lincoln was referring not to the South's possible secession from the Union, but to its dominance of it [pp. 273–75]; he also analyzes Lincoln's repeated mention of house imagery [pp. 271–72]); Webster, "Reception at Buffalo" (May 22, 1851), in *Works*, 2:546. In his book, *Faulkner: The House Divided* (Baltimore: Johns Hopkins University Press, 1983), Eric Sundquist anticipates my interest in the language that Lincoln (and others) used to categorize the extraordinary tensions in American society in the middle of the nineteenth century. Although Sundquist's primary concern is with Faulkner, his study originates with an analysis of the racial issues of the period 1820–60 (as well as the Lincoln-Douglas debates), and, as with his earlier book, I have benefited from his scholarship.

32. "It is by a constant recurrence to the first principles of our government, and the upright character of her earlier statesmen, that our glorious Union is to be nurtured and preserved" (Notice of *Memoirs of the Life of William Wirt . . . ,* by John P. Kennedy, *United States Magazine and Democratic Review* 26 [1850]:191); see also Forgie, p. 8.

33. Washington, "First Inaugural Address" (April 30, 1789), in *A Compilation of the Messages and Papers of the Presidents, 1789–1897,* ed. James D. Richardson (Washington, D. C.: Government Printing Office, 1896), 1:52.

34. Mason Locke Weems, *The Life of Washington,* ed. Marcus Cunliffe (Cambridge, Mass.: Harvard University Press/Belknap Press, 1962), p. 4; original italics. According to Cunliffe's introduction, the *Life* first appeared in book form in 1809; by 1829 it had gone through at least twenty-nine editions.

35. Review of *The Writings of George Washington,* ed. Jared Sparks, *Southern Literary Messenger* 1 (1835):592.

36. "To Whom Does Washington's Glory Belong?" *Southern Literary Messenger* 9 (1843):589. Forgie and Fliegelman differ in their interpretations of this mythologizing of Washington as the preeminent Father. Where Forgie emphasizes the postheroic generation chafing under the oppressiveness of the virtuous example of the founders, Fliegelman sees in their response not a betrayal of Revolutionary ideology but a solidifying of the antipatriarchal values that compose this ideology. For the latter, it is not that Washington is celebrated as America's father, but rather "what kind of father he is described as being" (p. 199). He is the parent Britain failed to become, the ideal ex-

ample of a "virtuous and independent man." My own concerns here mediate between these two views; primarily, I am interested in the postRevolutionary generation's sense—perhaps unconscious—that the failure to uphold republican values meant the loss of the home Washington had built.

37. [Henry T. Tuckerman], "The Character of Washington" (Review of *Life of George Washington*, by Washington Irving), *North American Review* 83 (1856):29.

38. "Mount Vernon," *Casket* 4 (1829):505.

39. "Where Are We?" *Southern Literary Messenger* 19 (1853):237; Forgie, pp. 186–88.

40. Everett, "The Character of Washington" (February 22, 1856), in *Orations and Speeches on Various Occasions* (Boston: Little, Brown, 1868), 4:45.

41. Weems, p. 123; original italics.

42. In fact, the White House, the oldest public building in Washington (its cornerstone was laid in 1792), was constructed on a site chosen by George Washington, though John Adams was the first president to live there (1800). Designated "the Palace" in the original plans, it actually acquired its popular name years before the building was restored and painted white. (It had been burned by British troops in 1814.) The name became official when Theodore Roosevelt had it engraved upon his stationery (*The New Columbia Encyclopedia*, ed. William H. Harris and Judith S. Levey, 4th ed. [New York: Columbia University Press, 1975], p. 2970, col. 3).

43. From Washington's death in 1799 until the mid-1850s, when a campaign was undertaken to purchase and restore his home, Mount Vernon existed in a terrible state of disrepair. According to Van Wyck Brooks, "travellers noted for forty years the shocking neglect and decay of the house and tomb of Washington at Mount Vernon" (*The World of Washington Irving* [New York: Dutton, 1944], p. 158n).

44. Everett, "Circular" of the Bunker Hill Monument Association (September 20, 1824), in George Washington Warren, *The History of the Bunker Hill Monument Association during the First Century of the United States of America* (Boston: James R. Osgood, 1877), p. 112; also quoted, in part, by Forgie, p. 50.

45. "Henry Clay as an Orator," *Putnam's Monthly* 3 (1854):495.

46. Lincoln, "Address before the Young Men's Lyceum of Springfield, Illinois" (January 27, 1838), in *Works*, 1:115.

47. Adams, "Inaugural Address" (March 4, 1825), in *Messages and Papers of the Presidents*, 2:294.

48. Edward Everett, "Eulogy on Adams and Jefferson" (August 1, 1826), in *Orations and Speeches*, 1:131.

49. Webster, "Adams and Jefferson," in *Works*, 1:114, 146, 147.

50. "Charles Carroll, of Carrollton," *Casket* 5 (1830):457.

51. Knapp, "Eulogy, Pronounced at Boston, Massachusetts" (August 2, 1826), in *A Selection of Eulogies, Pronounced in the Several States, in Honor of Those Illustrious Patriots and Statesmen, John Adams and Thomas Jefferson* (Hartford, Conn.: D. F. Robinson and Norton & Russell, 1826), p. 190; see also Forgie, pp. 52–53.

52. Lincoln, "Lyceum Address," in *Works*, 1:115; original italics.

53. "The Perilous Condition of the Republic," *New-England Magazine* 1 (1831):

281–89 (quotations on pp. 282, 281, 282, 283, 288, 289). A year later, the *Casket* concluded its article on the Declaration of Independence (see n. 17) by referring to the "sickening scene of modern degeneracy" (p. 51).

54. Wirt, *A Discourse on the Lives and Characters of Thomas Jefferson and John Adams, Who Both Died on the Fourth of July, 1826* (Washington, D.C.: Printed by Gales and Seaton, 1826), pp. 24–25.

55. "Lucian and His Age," *United States Magazine and Democratic Review* 11 (1842):225; "Thomas's Reminiscences" (Review of *Reminiscences of the Last Sixty-Five Years* . . . , by E. S. Thomas), *United States Magazine and Democratic Review* 8 (1840):227.

56. Wayne Franklin has argued convincingly for this interpretation of the "settlement" narratives; see *The New World of James Fenimore Cooper* (Chicago: University of Chicago Press, 1982), esp. pp. 1–38. Franklin does not discuss *The Spy*.

57. According to James D. Hart, *The Popular Book: A History of America's Literary Taste* (1950; rpt. Berkeley: University of California Press, 1962), p. 304, and Frank Luther Mott, *Golden Multitudes: The Story of the Best Sellers in the United States* (New York: Macmillan, 1947), p. 305, *The Spy* was far and away the most widely read American book in the year it was published, rivaling two of Walter Scott's works, *Kenilworth* and *The Pirate*, in its popularity. In fact, Mott claims that Cooper's novel was the most successful book in American literature up to its time (p. 74).

58. Three of the historians I have relied upon for both source material and interpretations of the 1820s also discuss Cooper's novel—Forgie (pp. 218–25), Taylor (pp. 101–6), and Yoder (pp. 513–17). My analysis has benefited from, and occasionally approaches, theirs in its emphasis on Cooper's concern with contemporary American dilemmas.

59. James Fenimore Cooper, *The Spy, The Works of James Fenimore Cooper*, Red Rover Edition (New York: Putnam's, n.d.), 26:12. Future references to this edition will be found in the text.

60. Forgie, p. 221.

61. Yoder, pp. 514–15.

62. Taylor, p. 106.

63. Susan Fenimore Cooper, "A Glance Backward," *Atlantic Monthly* 59 (1887):205.

64. Glenda Gates Riley, "The Subtle Subversion: Changes in the Traditionalist Image of the American Woman," *Historian* 32 (1970):214; original italics.

65. Sarah J. Hale, "Walter Wilson," in *Sketches of American Character*, 4th ed. (Boston: Freeman Hunt, 1831), p. 8. Future references to this edition will be found in the text.

66. Taylor argues that home was important for Hale because it was here, and not at schools and colleges, and certainly not in the workplace, where character was formed; and "nothing is . . . more important to the future of the country than the formation of a stable American character" (p. 127).

67. Sarah J. Hale, *Northwood* (New York: H. Long and Brother, 1852), p. 341. Future references to this edition will be found in the text.

68. Cf. "The Springs": "This trifling away of time when there is so much to be done, so many improvements necessary in our country, is inconsistent with that principle of being useful, which every republican ought to cherish" (*Sketches*, p. 193).

69. Taylor, p. 138.

70. "Tour in Scotland 1817," in *Journals and Notebooks*, 2:124.

71. "Tour in Scotland 1817," in *Journals and Notebooks*, 2:133–34. The editors of the Twayne edition speculate that Irving copied the passage in which these lines appear from his reading. However, there is no evidence that the words are not his own; however, even if they are a transcription, they certainly reveal his mood during this period of his life. Cf., also from "Tour in Scotland 1817": "My companions & friends have gone into the land of forgetfulness—I am a lonely melancholy man[—]a stranger & sojourner in a foregn [sic] land—no one cares for me on earth but I trust that there are gentle spirits that look down on me from heaven—that watch over my slumbers and shed comfort on my path—" (pp. 127–28).

72. "Tour in Scotland 1817," in *Journals and Notebooks*, 2:116.

73. "Notes While Preparing Sketch Book &C. 1817," in *Journals and Notebooks*, 2:183.

74. Irving to Henry Brevoort, Birmingham, March 15, 1816, in *Letters*, 1:433; original italics.

75. "Notebook 1818, Number 1," in *Journals and Notebooks*, 2:264.

76. "Notebook 1818, Number 1," in *Journals and Notebooks*, 2:268. "I longed," says Geoffrey Crayon in his introductory remarks to *The Sketch Book*, "to escape . . . from the commonplace realities of the present, and lose myself among the shadowy grandeurs of the past" ("The Author's Account of Himself," in *The Sketch Book of Geoffrey Crayon, Gent.*, ed. Haskell Springer [Boston: Twayne, 1978], p. 9. I have dealt with this idea of the "past" in relation to Irving's imaginative exploration of England in "The Value of Storytelling: 'Rip Van Winkle' and 'The Legend of Sleepy Hollow' in the Context of *The Sketch Book*," *Modern Philology* 82 (1984):394–98.

77. "Notes While Preparing Sketch Book &C. 1817," in *Journals and Notebooks*, 2:179, 183, 188, 187, 185–86.

78. Yoder, pp. 495–96; Paulding to Washington Irving, [Washington] January 20, 1820, in *The Letters of James Kirke Paulding*, ed. Ralph M. Aderman (Madison: University of Wisconsin Press, 1962), pp. 61–62; M. A. Weatherspoon [Bowden], "1815–1819: Prelude to Irving's *Sketch Book*," *American Literature* 41 (1970):571.

79. Review of Everett's *Orations, New-York Review* 1 (1825):333–41 (quotations on pp. 337, 338–39, 340, 341). Benjamin T. Spencer has chronicled the pursuit of a national literature in *The Quest for Nationality: An American Literary Campaign* (Syracuse, N.Y.: Syracuse University Press, 1957). The *New-York Review* article focuses on a primary issue of this campaign.

80. In 1817 Irving filled an entire notebook with extracts from (mostly) late-eighteenth-century travel literature about America; see "Extracts from Travels 1817," in *Journals and Notebooks*, 2:203–53. In 1825 he planned to take a Tocquevillian look at America by covering such topics as "American Character," "American Scenery," "Manners in America," etc. The notes that remain indicate that Irving was not fully engaged with his material and, therefore, it is not surprising that he abandoned the

project. For a discussion of Irving's intentions and reproductions of his working notes, see Richard Dilworth Rust, "Washington Irving's 'American Essays,'" *Resources for American Literary Study* 10 (1980):3–27.

81. Hedges, "The Theme of Americanism in Irving's Writings," in *Washington Irving: A Tribute*, ed. Andrew B. Myers (Tarrytown, N.Y.: Sleepy Hollow Restorations, 1972), p. 31.

82. Irving to Henry Brevoort, Paris, March 10, 1821, in *Letters*, 1:614.

83. "Notebook 1818, Number 2," in *Journals and Notebooks*, 2:282. This notation occurs years before he conceived of his biography of Washington.

84. "Notes While Preparing Sketch Book &C. 1817," in *Journals and Notebooks*, 2:182.

CHAPTER ONE

1. Washington Irving, "The Author's Account of Himself," *The Sketch Book of Geoffrey Crayon, Gent.*, ed. Haskell Springer (Boston: Twayne, 1978), pp. 10, 9; future references to this edition will be cited in parentheses in the text.

2. Van Wyck Brooks, *The World of Washington Irving* (New York: Dutton, 1944), p. 159; William L. Hedges, "Washington Irving: *The Sketch Book of Geoffrey Crayon, Gent.*," in *Landmarks of American Writing*, ed. Hennig Cohen (New York: Basic Books, 1969), p. 59.

3. In part this is because the equivalent of the "authorized biography," the heavily edited version of Irving's life and letters prepared shortly after his death by his nephew, Pierre M. Irving (*The Life and Letters of Washington Irving*, 4 vols. [New York: Putnam, 1862–64]), while not inaccurate, failed to present the multidimensional aspect of the man. Irving's modern-day biographer, Stanley Williams, called Pierre Irving's biography "protective" (*The Life of Washington Irving* [New York: Oxford University Press, 1935], 1:475, n. 76), and documented several instances where he suppressed passages of letters that tended to cast an unfavorable light on his uncle. (See, for example, 1:479, n. 138.) In its own way, this biography set the tone for future studies of Irving much like Rufus Griswold's did for Poe.

4. Two examples of the Irving mythos at work must suffice here. The reader of these volumes is "conscious of having been in the company of a singularly charming, cultured, mellow human being," William P. Trent and George S. Hellman claim in the introduction to their edition of *The Journals of Washington Irving (From July, 1815 to July, 1842)* (Boston: The Bibliophile Society, 1919), 1:xviii. Irving "was always and everywhere the genial, kindly gentleman we naturally suppose the author of 'The Sketch Book' and the friend of Sir Walter Scott to have been" (p. xxv). Henry Seidel Canby's evaluation is similar: "A delightful temperament, a pleasing play of sentiment and humor upon fortunate themes, and a triumph of style—this was the current estimate of 'The Sketch Book.' And it remains our estimate, except that the 'sob stories,' as they would be called in the modern vernacular, can no longer be regarded as fortunate" (*Classic Americans: A Study of Eminent American Writers from Irving to Whitman* [New York: Harcourt, Brace, 1931], p. 90).

5. Hedges, "*The Sketch Book of Geoffrey Crayon, Gent.*," p. 62. Hedges also writes

that Crayon's "tour of England gradually reveals itself as an unconscious quest for order and stability" (p. 61).

6. The irony here is illuminated by Haskell Springer's comment in his introduction to the Twayne edition that "[t]he history of *The Sketch Book*'s reputation in England and America had one common denominator which was unaltered by time": "Nearly everyone, no matter what his opinions on the literary worth of the book in whole or in part, was captivated by the personality of its author as it lay revealed on the printed page." No one, it seems, could penetrate the surface of the text to fathom Irving's complex use of the Crayon persona, so that "in the reviews of 1850 no less than in those of 1820 his geniality, humanity, warmth of character and moral strength were repeatedly noted and admired" (p. xxxi). Springer might just have easily referred to the commentary of 1950, for as I have already indicated, this critical attitude lasted well into our own century.

7. These words appear in the Conclusion to the manuscript of *Walden*, located at the Henry E. Huntington Library in San Marino, California. The entire paragraph, which includes other mentions of failure, was cancelled by Thoreau.

8. Williams, 1:145–67. As Williams indicates, and Irving's letters from the period corroborate, he had no choice but to become deeply entangled in the affairs of P. and E. Irving, his brothers' Liverpool importing establishment, since Ebenezer was located in New York and Peter, who was with him in Liverpool, was too ill to run the business.

9. Irving to Mrs. Amelia Foster [Dresden, April-May 1823], in Washington Irving, *Letters: Volume 1, 1802–1823*, ed. Ralph M. Aderman et al. (Boston: Twayne, 1978), p. 742. Although Irving was only a nominal partner in his brothers' firm, he believed that when it finally collapsed in 1818 he shared, in Williams's words, "their notoriety" (1:151).

10. Williams, 1:153.

11. Williams, 1:154–55.

12. Williams, 1:155. Irving's statement of purpose may be found in his letter to Mrs. Amelia Foster (*Letters*, 1:743).

13. "My own individual interests are nothing," he continued. "The merest pittance would content me if I could crawl out from among these troubles and see my connections safe around me" (Irving to William Irving, Liverpool, Fall? 1816, in *Letters*, 1:457).

14. Irving to Henry Brevoort, Birmingham, July 16, 1816; Irving to ?, Liverpool, January 9, 1816, in *Letters*, 1:449, 432.

15. Irving to Henry Brevoort, Birmingham, July 16, 1816, in *Letters*, 1:449, 450. By "disordered times" Irving is also alluding to the economic troubles that plagued England after a brief period of prosperity at the close of the Napoleonic Wars.

16. Irving to Henry Brevoort, Birmingham, December 9, 1816, in *Letters*, 1:462, 463.

17. Irving to Henry Brevoort, Liverpool, July 11, 1817, in *Letters*, 1:486; my italics.

18. "Notes While Preparing Sketch Book &C. 1817," in Washington Irving, *Jour-

nals and Notebooks: Volume 2, 1807–1822, ed. Walter A. Reichart and Lillian Schlissel (Boston: Twayne, 1981), p. 174. According to Williams (1:158, 168), by the end of August, 1817, "nine sketches lay unfinished in Irving's portfolio."

19. Irving to Mrs. Amelia Foster, in *Letters*, 1:743; original italics.

20. Quoted in Williams, 1:150.

21. "Notes While Preparing Sketch Book &C. 1817," in *Journals and Notebooks*, 2:186.

22. Irving to Henry Brevoort, Liverpool, May 9, 1816, in *Letters*, 1:446.

23. Irving to Henry Brevoort, Birmingham, March 15, 1816, in *Letters*, 1:435; original italics.

24. Irving to Henry Brevoort, Birmingham, July 16, 1816, in *Letters*, 1:449. This complaint runs like a motif through almost all of Irving's correspondence with Brevoort during the period of business failure.

25. Irving to Henry Brevoort, Birmingham, November 6, 1816, in *Letters*, 1:457.

26. Irving to Henry Brevoort, Liverpool, July 11, 1817, in *Letters*, 1:487.

27. Irving to William Irving, Jr., Liverpool, December 23, 1817, in *Letters*, 1:515. (In the July 11 letter to Brevoort, Irving speaks of being "reconciled to the features of adversity" in England; here he writes that "in protracting my stay in Europe I certainly do not contemplate pleasure, for I look forward to a life of loneliness and of parsimonious and almost painful economy.")

28. Irving to Henry Brevoort, Birmingham, July 16, 1816; Irving to Henry Brevoort, Liverpool, October 10, 1817, in *Letters*, 1:450, 509. To his brother William he wrote that all his "views," "wishes," "ambition," and "affections" were centered in America, but he had to follow his own plan (Irving to William Irving, Liverpool, December 23, 1817, in *Letters*, 1:515).

29. Irving to Ebenezer Irving, London, March 3, 1819, in *Letters*, 1:540–41.

30. Irving to Henry Brevoort, Paris, March 10, 1821, in *Letters*, 1:614.

31. Irving to Henry Brevoort, Paris, March 10, 1821, in *Letters*, 1:614.

32. *Edinburgh Review* 33 (1820):79.

33. Review of *Salmagundi*, *Monthly Review* 2d ser., 65 (1811):419.

34. Review of *The Sketch Book*, *Edinburgh Review* 34 (1820):160.

35. Review of *The Sketch Book of Geoffrey Crayon, Gent.*, *Quarterly Review* 25 (1821):51–53.

36. "Specimens of American Literature," *Edinburgh Magazine and Literary Miscellany* new ser., 4 (1819):207; original italics.

37. Williams, 1:190.

38. "American Literature," *Retrospective Review* 9 (1824):316.

39. So declared the *Quarterly Review*, which went on to say that Irving "seems to have studied our language—where alone it can be studied in all its strength and perfection—in the writings of our old sterling authors; and in working these precious mines of literature, he has refined for himself the ore which there so richly abounds" (p. 67). In the *Edinburgh Monthly Review* he was compared to the authors of *The Tatler* and *The Spectator* (4 [1820]:304), and the *Monthly Review* recognized him as an aspiring young imitator of British models (2d ser., 93 [1820]:198–207). "He is not *na-*

tional, but English" was how the *Retrospective Review* put it (p. 316; original italics), and in a column entitled "New Books Published in October," the *Monthly Magazine* said *The Sketch Book* "bids fair to rank high among the best classical writings of our own country" (50 [1820]:362).

40. Edward Everett, Review of *Bracebridge Hall*, *North American Review* 15 (1822):209. Ostensibly a review of Irving's second European sketchbook (1822), the essay devotes substantial space to *The Sketch Book*.

41. Everett, pp. 213–15.

42. Review of *The Sketch Book of Geoffrey Crayon, Gent.*, *North American Review* 9 (1819):348.

43. Dana, p. 348; original italics.

44. For the clearest statement, see Katherine Glowes, "Devices of Repetition in Irving's 'The Wife,'" in *Washington Irving Reconsidered: A Symposium*, ed. Ralph M. Aderman (Hartford: Transcendental Books, 1969), p. 65.

45. Glowes, p. 65.

46. "Notes While Preparing Sketch Book &C. 1817," in *Journals and Notebooks*, 2:199.

47. Hedges has written on this aspect of the sketch in *Washington Irving: An American Study, 1802–1832* (Baltimore: Johns Hopkins University Press, 1965), p. 132.

48. In his notes to the Twayne edition, Springer points out that some of Roscoe's friends bought a fraction of his library at the auction, but when they tried to return the books he declined the offer (p. 307). Irving was unaware of this, and it is probably safe to say that had he known, he would have modified his tone, since gestures of friendship always touched him. Nevertheless, the latent hostility in the sketch is genuine.

49. Hedges, *Washington Irving*, p. 137.

50. The sexual imagery in both stories has been noted and discussed. See, for example, Marcel Heiman, "Rip Van Winkle: A Psychoanalytic Note on the Story and Its Author," *American Imago* 16 (1959):3–47; Philip Young, "Fallen from Time: The Mythic Rip Van Winkle," *Kenyon Review* 22 (1960):547–73; Terence Martin, "Rip, Ichabod, and the American Imagination," *American Literature* 31 (1959):143–44; and Hedges, *Washington Irving*, pp. 137–43.

51. Joy S. Kasson, *Artistic Voyagers: Europe and the American Imagination in the Works of Irving, Allston, Cole, Cooper, and Hawthorne*, Contributions in American Studies, Number 60 (Westport, Conn.: Greenwood Press, 1982), pp. 26–28.

52. The most strident of his contemporary critics, Hazlitt wrote that Irving "gives us very good American copies of our British Essayists and Novelists. . . . [H]is writings are literary *anachronisms*" (*The Spirit of the Age: or Contemporary Portraits* [2d ed.; London: Henry Colburn, 1825], p. 405; original italics). The difference between Hazlitt and the reviewers who noted Irving's "Englishness" was that they had complimented what he criticized .

53. Williams, 1:177. *Urn-Burial* was first published in 1658, *Meditations and Contemplations* in 1746–47.

54. Kasson sees Irving's concern over the issue of "imitation" in a slightly different

way. In order to achieve professional status, Irving needed literary models; subsequently, he worried that he had "followed those models too closely" (p. 37).

55. See my essay in *Early American Literature* 21 (Winter 86/87):226–47, "Washington Irving and the Genesis of the Fictional Sketch," for a discussion of the characteristics and the development of Irving's literary form.

56. Pattee, *The Development of the American Short Story: An Historical Survey* (New York: Harper, 1923), p. 6; original italics.

57. When Irving wrote to Walter Scott, at the time of *The Sketch Book*'s first appearance in America, declining the latter's offer of the editorship of an Edinburgh periodical, he also portrayed himself as incapable of sustained literary production: "I have no command over my talents such as they are; am apt to be deserted by them when I most want their assistance & have to watch the veerings of my mind as I would those of a weather cock. . . . I must therefore keep on pretty much as I have begun, writing when I can & not when I would. I shall occasionally shift my residence, and trust to the excitement of various scenes & objects to furnish me with materials; though I hope as I gain experience & confidence to be more copious & methodical" (Irving to Walter Scott, London, November 20, 1819, in *Letters*, 1:570).

58. According to Walter Graham, these writers preferred to issue their work in periodical form; then, if it proved a critical and financial success, they proceeded until they had enough for a book-length publication (*English Literary Periodicals* [New York: Nelson, 1930], p. 127).

59. As W. B. Gates notes, "in *The Sketch Book*, as in no other work by Irving, Shakespeare not only colored the style and manner but even helped to shape the spirit of Irving's imagination" ("Shakespearean Elements in Irving's *Sketch Book*," *American Literature* 30 [1959]:450).

60. Although I label Crayon a "persona" and describe his function in *The Sketch Book* as that of Irving's surrogate, I do not wish to engage here in the theoretical debate on the validity of the concept for critical interpretation. I am aware of the pros and cons of using "persona," but see little advantage to pursuing them extensively in this context. For the positive side of the argument, see George T. Wright's analysis of the historical changes in the design and function of poetic personae in "The Faces of the Poet," the first chapter of his *The Poet in the Poem: The Personae of Eliot, Yeats, and Pound* (Berkeley: University of California Press, 1960), pp. 1–59, and Robert C. Elliott's extended explanation and defense of critics' continued reliance upon the term in *The Literary Persona* (Chicago: University of Chicago Press, 1982), esp. pp. 35–103. The negative view is most cogently and forcefully articulated by Irvin Ehrenpreis in his essay "Personae," in *Restoration and Eighteenth-Century Literature: Studies in Honor of Alan Dugald McKillop*, ed. Carroll Camden (Chicago: University of Chicago Press, 1963), pp. 25–37; rpt. in Ehrenpreis, *Literary Meaning and Augustan Values* (Charlottesville: University Press of Virginia, 1974), pp. 49–60, and in the dialogue between Vincent Buckley and Robert Wilson in "Persona: the Empty Mask," *Quadrant* (Australia) 19 (November 1975):81–96. (Elliott's book called my attention to the existence of this discussion.)

I find that "persona" applies well to Irving's methods in *The Sketch Book*, though I grant that its use is not entirely justified in all instances. As Ehrenpreis notes, in eliminating the author from his work and replacing him with a speaker (or persona), we run the risk of obliterating historical connections and destroying "historical truth" (*Literary Meaning*, pp. 51–52; see also Elliott, pp. 67–68).

61. Wright, p. 9.

62. Thackeray to Mrs. Elliot and Kate Perry, Vevey (Switzerland), July 28–31, 1853, in *The Letters and Private Papers of William Makepeace Thackeray*, ed. Gordon N. Ray (Cambridge, Mass.: Harvard University Press, 1946), 4:436. Elliott quotes this passage (from the London edition of Thackeray's letters) on p. 114 of *The Literary Persona*.

63. Elliott cites Christopher Isherwood as a good example of an author who writes "ambiguously autobiographical works" that play with the reader's expectations about what kind of "truth" the book will reveal. Isherwood purposefully mixes novelistic and autobiographical techniques. "If the autobiography *Lions and Shadows* reads like a novel," Elliott writes, "Isherwood's novels read very like autobiography." In several of these books the main character is identified as "Christopher Isherwood," "whose progress in searching out his own identity casts him into a close but complex relationship with the author of the same name" (p. 72). There are striking similarities here to the Crayon/Irving fusion, though in terms of willfully mixing genres Irving was a far less self-conscious writer than Isherwood.

64. Irving's notebooks indicate that there were scattered moments when he was genuinely infused with a romantic spirit. Such feelings, however, usually occur only at the outset of a particular excursion or exploration, before any discovery or encounter takes place. See, for example, "Tour in Scotland 1817" (in *Journals and Notebooks*, 2:97), where Irving remarks on the "picturesque & romantic . . . general appearance" of Edinburgh as he is about to undertake his first ramble about the city. The preconceptions are quickly diffused.

65. Brooks, p. 159. Notice, again, how critics only paid attention to the smooth surface of Irving's prose.

66. In discussing Swift's use of the persona in *A Tale of A Tub*, Elliott writes: "The basic rule is that although the persona need not be a consistent character, the personation must be consistently maintained" (p. 128). In *Bracebridge Hall* and *The Alhambra*, Irving allows his own voice to overtake Crayon's, so that Crayon all but ceases to function in the capacity of a persona.

CHAPTER TWO

1. Hedges, "Washington Irving: *The Sketch Book of Geoffrey Crayon, Gent.*," in *Landmarks of American Writing*, ed. Hennig Cohen (New York: Basic Books, 1969), p. 59.

2. Jeffrey, Review of *The Sketch Book*, *Edinburgh Review* 34 (1820):160; Frank Luther Mott, *Golden Multitudes: The Story of the Best Sellers in the United States* (New York: Macmillan, 1947), p. 72; James D. Hart, *The Popular Book: A History of America's Literary Taste* (1950; rpt. Berkeley: University of California Press, 1963), p. 83. Both Mott and Hart note that the public quickly bought up the first printing of two thousand copies of part 1 (in about three months) and continued to buy future issues as they appeared, even calling for more editions. (The sales of *The Sketch Book* did not

taper off until the 1840s when, according to Mott, the flood of "cheap reprints of English works apparently drove Irving's books out of the American market" [p. 71].) This is even more significant when the cost is taken into consideration—seventy-five cents for a pamphlet of about seventy pages or so (for the first edition) was a steep price in Irving's time.

3. Stanley Williams, *The Life of Washington Irving* (New York: Oxford University Press, 1935), 1:xiv.

4. Hart, p. 83.

5. *The Sketch Book of Geoffrey Crayon, Gent.*, ed Haskell Springer (Boston: Twayne, 1978), p. 9; future references to this edition are included in the text.

6. *The American Image of the Old World* (New York: Harper and Row, 1963), p. 76.

7. Strout, pp. 76, 80. Strout believes that such writers as Irving and Longfellow were able to achieve a "reconciliation of the American myth of the New World with their affection for the Old World" with little personal tension largely because they saw Europe in such a complimentary way. To a certain extent (though not entirely) this is true of the Irving of *The Sketch Book* (1819–20), though he would show soon in *Bracebridge Hall* (1822) the virtual collapse of the old aristocratic order. Strout is right to emphasize that it was precisely because America "had defined itself as a fresh start in history" that it "produced such nostalgic hungers for a Europe made enchanted by the traces of an ancient past" (p. 83). Yet as I intend to argue, the American imagination was propelled toward European borders by a greater motivating force than romantic nostalgia.

8. Irving's accounts of his experiences in England, in both fictional and journal form, largely ignore the social and political acrimony that existed in the country just after the War of 1812 ended in 1815. The English people knew some troubled times then: there were bad harvests in 1816 and 1817; the "Corn Law" of 1815 and a severe famine made life even more unpleasant for the poor; in 1819 there were riots and laws were passed restricting civil liberties. Irving did not openly acknowledge this confusion (though he briefly alluded to it in his sketches of "John Bull" and "Little Britain"), nor did he refer to the poverty and other unfortunate social conditions created by industrialization in Liverpool, where he spent a good many of his earlier days in England attending to the family business. He never saw children working in the factories and the coalpits, mostly because he did not visit the sweatshops and the collieries. (For some of the responses of English writers to these uneasy social conditions, including the tensions and hatreds among the classes, see Carl H. Woodring, "The British Literary Scene in the 1820s," in *Washington Irving: A Tribute*, ed. Andrew B. Myers [Tarrytown, N.Y.: Sleepy Hollow Restorations, 1972], pp. 37–41.)

9. Strout, p. 79. Strout does not say exactly that Americans were "escaping" from their own lives, but that is the implication of his argument. And in terms of this argument, it is interesting to note again the extent to which Americans openly championed the present and disavowed the past *within* their own society. The lack of respect they showed for their monuments is a case in point. "It is the common remark of travellers," wrote the American expatriate painter (and illustrator of Irving's works) C. R. Leslie, "that in America there are no antiquities,—no objects of veneration belonging

to times past. Americans themselves feel this, and yet they make little effort to preserve or secure those they might. To the stranger visiting Philadelphia, how interesting it would be to be shown the houses of Penn and Franklin" (*Autobiographical Recollections*, ed. Tom Taylor [Boston: Ticknor and Fields, 1860], p. 122). Perhaps the caretaking and preservation of these sites would have been too powerful a reminder to Americans that their society no longer embodied the values for which these men stood nor any longer was actively dedicated to the goals for which they had fought.

10. Somkin, *Unquiet Eagle: Memory and Desire in the Idea of American Freedom, 1815–1860* (Ithaca, N.Y.: Cornell University Press, 1967), pp. 3–4.

11. Somkin, pp. 34, 7; see also Charles L. Sanford, *The Quest for Paradise: Europe and the American Moral Imagination* (Urbana: University of Illinois Press, 1961), p. 110.

12. See, for example, Herbert Croly, *The Promise of American Life*, ed. Arthur M. Schlesinger, Jr. (1909; rpt. Cambridge, Mass.: Belknap/Harvard University Press, 1965), p. 454.

13. Wood, *The Creation of the American Republic, 1776–1787* (Chapel Hill: University of North Carolina Press, 1969), p. 47; see also William Hedges, "The Myth of the Republic and the Theory of American Literature," *Prospects* 4 (1979):108.

14. Santayana, "Materialism and Idealism in American Life," in his *Character and Opinion in the United States* (New York: Scribner's, 1920), p. 168.

15. Franklin, "Information to Those Who Would Remove to America," in *The Writings of Benjamin Franklin*, ed. Albert Henry Smyth (New York: Macmillan, 1905–7), 8:614; see also Sanford, *Quest for Paradise*, pp. 125, 133–34.

16. Willard, *An Address to . . . the Legislature of New York Proposing a Plan for Improving Female Education* (Albany, 1819), rpt. in Charles L. Sanford, ed., *Quest for America, 1810–24*, Documents in American Civilization (New York: New York University Press, 1964), doc. 58.

17. Baldwin, *Considerations for the American Patriot: A Sermon delivered on the occasion of the annual Thanksgiving, December 12, 1827* (New York, 1828), quoted in Somkin, p. 17.

18. Beecher, "The Gospel the Only Security for Eminent and Abiding National Prosperity," *National Preacher* 3 (1829):147.

19. "Notebook 1818, Number 2," in Washington Irving, *Journals and Notebooks: Volume 2, 1807–1822*, ed. Walter A. Reichart and Lillian Schlissel (Boston: Twayne, 1981), p. 294.

20. "Notes and Extracts, 1825," in Washington Irving, *Journals and Notebooks: Volume 3, 1819–1827*, ed. Walter A. Reichart (Madison: University of Wisconsin Press, 1970), pp. 668, 669. For excerpts on "virtue," see, for example, pp. 672–73.

21. Unpublished "Memoranda" notebook in the Berg Collection, New York Public Library, quoted in Richard D. Rust, "Washington Irving's 'American Essays,'" *Resources for American Literary Study* 10 (1980):8. Although the notebook is undated, through internal evidence Rust has determined its year as 1825.

22. "'A Time of Unexampled Prosperity,'" in Washington Irving, *Wolfert's Roost*, ed. Roberta Rosenberg (Boston: Twayne, 1979), pp. 95–96. The essay was one of several Irving collected in 1855.

23. *The Journals and Miscellaneous Notebooks of Ralph Waldo Emerson*, ed. William H. Gilman et al. (Cambridge, Mass.: Belknap/Harvard University Press, 1960–), 4:257. The entry is dated January 21, 1834.

24. *Journals and Miscellaneous Notebooks*, 4:344 (November 26, 1834).

25. William Charvat makes this point in his discussion of Emerson's responses to the economic panic of the late 1830s in "American Romanticism and the Depression of 1837," *Science and Society* 2 (1937):78–79.

26. *Journals and Miscellaneous Notebooks*, 5:23 (March 23, 1835). Emerson also used this material in "The Senses and the Soul," *The Dial* 2 (1842):378–79.

27. *Journals and Miscellaneous Notebooks*, 7:431–32 (April 20, 1841).

28. *Journals and Miscellaneous Notebooks*, 7:268 (October 11, 1839).

29. *Journals and Miscellaneous Notebooks*, 5:332 (May 21, 1837). This was the year of the great depression and economic panic, and Emerson has these "black times" in mind as he records thoughts in his journal.

30. [James Russell Lowell], "Self-Possession vs. Prepossession," *Atlantic Monthly* 8 (1861):763; see also George B. Forgie, *Patricide in the House Divided: A Psychological Interpretation of Lincoln and His Age* (New York: Norton, 1979), pp. 73–76.

31. "The Kansas Question," *Putnam's Monthly* 6 (1855):431–32.

32. I quote Donald Weber's description of the Revolution from his essay-review of Michael Colacurcio's *The Province of Piety: Moral History in Hawthorne's Early Tales*; see "A True Sight of History: Hawthorne and the Sense of the Past," *The New England Quarterly* 58 (1985):97.

33. Robert H. Woodward, "Dating the Action of 'Rip Van Winkle,'" *New York Folklore Quarterly* 15 (1959):70; original italics.

34. Barry Gross, "Washington Irving: The Territory Behind," *Markham Review* 10 (1981):5. Gross writes that, "myth aside, it is his own voice he hears, his own desire for permanent escape."

35. See Sanford, ed., *Quest for America*, docs. 18, 19, 20, 21, 26, 71.

36. "Tour in Scotland 1817," in *Journals and Notebooks*, 2:153–54.

37. Lorman A. Ratner, "American Nationalism Fifty Years after the Revolution," in *Washington Irving: A Tribute*, p. 45.

38. Adams, *The Diary of John Quincy Adams, 1794–1845*, ed. Allan Nevins (New York: Longmans, Green, 1928), p. 360.

39. Webster, "Adams and Jefferson" (August 2, 1826), in *The Works of Daniel Webster*, 10th ed. (Boston: Little, Brown, 1857), 1:115; see also L. H. Butterfield, "The Jubilee of Independence, July 4, 1826," *Virginia Magazine of History and Biography* 61 (1953):136.

40. Wirt, *A Discourse on the Lives and Characters of Thomas Jefferson and John Adams* . . . (Washington, D.C.: Gales and Seaton, 1826), pp. 63–64.

41. Ann C. Loveland, *Emblem of Liberty: The Image of Lafayette in the American Mind* (Baton Rouge: Louisiana State University Press, 1971), pp. 17–18, 43–44; Somkin, pp. 149–51.

42. Ticknor, "Lafayette" (Review of *Mémoires pour servir à la Vie du Général Lafayette* . . ., by M. Regnault-Warin, and *Memoirs of the Life of Gilbert Motier Lafayette*, by Gen. H. L. Villaume Ducoudray Holstein), *North American Review* 20 (1825):179.

43. Loveland, p. 49; Smkin, p. 163, Ticknor, "Lafayette in America" (Review of *Lafayette en Amérique en 1824 et 1825 . . .*, by A. Levasseur), *North American Review* 30 (1830):220.

44. Niles, Editorial: "La Fayette," *Niles' Weekly Register* 26 (August 28, 1824):426; original italics; also quoted in Somkin, p. 134, and Loveland, p. 40.

45. Wayne Franklin, *The New World of James Fenimore Cooper* (Chicago: University of Chicago Press, 1982), p. 44. Franklin makes some acute observations on what Lafayette's tour meant to America in the context of discussing Cooper's response to the general's New York visit in September 1824.

46. Franklin to Joseph Galloway, London, February 25, 1775, in *The Papers of Benjamin Franklin*, ed. Leonard W. Labaree et al. (New Haven: Yale University Press, 1959–), 21:509; Jefferson, "First Inaugural Address" (1801), in *A Compilation of the Messages and Papers of the Presidents, 1789–1897*, ed. James D. Richardson (Washington, D.C.: Government Printing Office, 1896), 1:323; see also Sanford, *Quest for Paradise*, pp. 120–21, 126–27.

47. Lewis Leary, "Washington Irving: An End and a New Beginning," in his *Soundings: Some Early American Writers* (Athens: University of Georgia Press, 1975), p. 308.

48. Hedges, "Washington Irving: *The Sketch Book of Geoffrey Crayon, Gent.*," p. 63.

49. In *The American in England during the First Half Century of Independence* (New York: Holt, 1926), Robert E. Spiller has suggested that Irving's explorations were for a "true England," which might sooner be found in her "quiet eddies" than in the busier, more populated areas of the country. He also notes that "the heart of the city was not in the rush of traffic on the Strand, but rather in the Templar's Chapel or in the shadow of St. Paul's, the 'Little Britain' where Franklin had stayed" (p. 298). But he is misleading when he claims that the England Irving described never really existed "outside the storehouse of his own whimsical imagination" (p. 291). In fact, Irving's notebooks and journals reveal that he saw and experienced most of what Crayon sketches. Spiller fails to understand that in re-creating this England, Irving heightened and intensified the tone, feeling, and texture of his material in order to highlight the significance of Crayon's adventures. The England delineated in *The Sketch Book* was real; what Crayon wants to locate within it, however, exists only in his conceptualizing imagination.

50. The inscription on the title page of *The Sketch Book* (from Burton's *Anatomy of Melancholy*) reads, "I have no wife nor children, good or bad, to provide for. A mere spectator of other men's fortunes and adventures, and how they play their parts; which methinks are diversely presented to me, as from a common theatre or scene." While Irving may have thought of himself as a homeless wanderer during the years he was writing *The Sketch Book*, Crayon is not nearly as detached a figure as the "spectator" characterization would imply.

51. Interestingly enough, "Little Britain" is the only sketch other than "John Bull" in which Crayon alludes to occurrences that were a source of trouble and disruption to contemporary England. (See Springer's explanatory notes to "Little Britain" in the Twayne edition [pp. 328–29] for a detailed list of the "sinister events" Crayon has in

mind. Among them are radical meetings in support of reform issues and a conspiracy plot against the memb:rs of the English cabinet.) Perhaps by alluding to so many unfortunate and disturbing events here, Crayon was making a connection between the decline of "John Bullism" and the rise in instances of unrest and dissension in the country. However, since this is Crayon's only real recognition of what might be deemed a "troubled" England (mentioned in just a single paragraph of the sketch), it in no way can be construed as typical of his attitude toward the mother country, nor does it discount the admiration he expressed on other occasions.

52. Hedges, "Washington Irving: *The Sketch Book of Geoffrey Crayon, Gent.*," p. 63.

53. Both Donald A. Ringe, in *The Pictorial Mode: Space and Time in the Art of Bryant, Irving and Cooper* (Lexington: University Press of Kentucky, 1971), pp. 102–3, and William Hedges, in *Washington Irving: An American Study, 1802–1832* (Baltimore: Johns Hopkins University Press, 1965), p. 133, discuss the effect of changing light in "Westminster Abbey."

54. Cf. Hedges, who writes that in the abbey Crayon "begins to sense the past as also a potential trap for the imagination" (*Washington Irving*, p. 133).

55. "Notebook 1818, Number 1," in *Journals and Notebooks*, 2:255.

56. See, for example, the essays by Terence Martin, "Rip, Ichabod, and the American Imagination" (*American Literature* 31 [1959]:137–49), Robert A. Bone, "Irving's Headless Hessian: Prosperity and the Inner Life" (*American Quarterly* 15 [1963]:167–75), Donald A. Ringe, "New York and New England: Irving's Criticism of American Society" (*American Literature* 38 [1967]:455–67), and William P. Dawson, "'Rip Van Winkle' as Bawdy Satire: The Rascal and the Revolution" (*ESQ* 27 [1981]:198–206).

57. "Traits of Indian Character" appeared in *Analectic Magazine* 3 (1814): 145–56; "Philip of Pokanoket" was published in the same volume ("Traits" in February, "Philip" in June), pp. 502–15. According to Haskell Springer's Textual Commentary in the Twayne edition (pp. 360–64), both essays were heavily revised for inclusion in *The Sketch Book*. Significantly, Irving deleted some of his more virulent attacks on the white man's cruelty to the Indians, while at the same time he added passages which, in Springer's words, "prais[ed] the Indians for their prime virtues." Also, it is clear that the narrative voice of these piece. is Irving's own; there is no painful personal experience to distance himself from and thus no need for his Crayon persona.

58. Analogously, Walter Channing, in his "Essay on American Language and Literature" (*North American Review* 1 [1815]:307–14), pointed to the native tongue of the Indian as the source of an original American literary expression. Channing especially appreciated the uniqueness and boldness of the Indian's language, which "was made to express his emotions during his observance of nature," and, in contrast to Americans, who were too enamored of and dependent upon foreign writings, the Indian's contentment with his "literary condition."

59. Hedges, "Washington Irving: *The Sketch Book of Geoffrey Crayon, Gent.*," p. 60.

60. In *Our Old Home*, ed. Claude M. Simpson (Columbus: Ohio State University Press, 1970), p. 7. *Our Old Home* was originally published in 1863.

CHAPTER THREE

1. The other full-fledged tale (as opposed to the autobiographical/fictional sketches) in the collection, "The Spectre Bridegroom," also does not belong to Crayon outright; he has picked it up at a country inn and is merely repeating verbatim what he has overheard. This is yet another way that Irving maintains *The Sketch Book*'s unity.

2. Hedges, "Irving, Hawthorne, and the Image of the Wife," in *Washington Irving Reconsidered: A Symposium*, ed. Ralph M. Aderman (Hartford, Conn.: Transcendental Books, 1969), p. 25; original italics. Hedges has suggested that as a "unity of interest and feeling" develops in *The Sketch Book*, it does so to the extent "that one finally wants to read 'Rip Van Winkle' and 'The Legend of Sleepy Hollow,' if not as stories told by Crayon instead of Knickerbocker, then at least as stories that have touched Crayon almost personally" ("Washington Irving: *The Sketch Book of Geoffrey Crayon, Gent.*," in *Landmarks of American Writing*, ed. Hennig Cohen [New York: Basic Books, 1969], p. 60).

3. Washington Irving, "Rip Van Winkle" and "The Legend of Sleepy Hollow," in *The Sketch Book of Geoffrey Crayon, Gent.*, ed. Haskell Springer (Boston: Twayne, 1978), pp. 30–31, 272. All future references to this edition will be cited in parentheses in the text.

4. Hedges has seen (but not pursued the idea) that both "Rip" and "Sleepy Hollow" are tales about "a home and a way of settling down" (*Washington Irving: An American Study, 1802–1832* [Baltimore: Johns Hopkins University Press, 1965], p. 141).

5. William R. Taylor, *Cavalier and Yankee: The Old South and American National Character* (New York: Braziller, 1961), p. 135.

6. Hale, "The Springs," in *Sketches of American Character*, 4th ed. (Boston: Freeman Hunt, 1831), p. 193; also quoted in Taylor, p. 136.

7. Irving to Moses Thomas [Liverpool? March 3, 1818]; Irving to Henry Brevoort, London, September 9, 1819, in Washington Irving, *Letters: Volume 1, 1802–1823*, ed. Ralph M. Aderman et al. (Boston: Twayne, 1978), pp. 520, 560. Irving's second statement here is ambiguous, for he may also mean that since he considers *The Sketch Book* the result of "irregular and precarious" work habits, he hopes that he can produce a finer work of literature under more favorable emotional circumstances.

8. Robert A. Bone, "Irving's Headless Hessian: Prosperity and the Inner Life," *American Quarterly* 15 (1963):172.

9. Irving to Henry Brevoort, Liverpool, July 11, 1817; Irving to Ebenezer Irving, London, March 3, 1819, in *Letters*, 1:486, 541.

10. Irving to Walter Scott, London, November 20, 1819, in *Letters*, 1:570.

11. Bone views the tensions I am sketching here in a slightly different way as the "pressure" or "threat" of a commercial society to "the artistic process as such" (p. 169). However, we disagree significantly in our interpretation of Ichabod's character and actions, especially his barely controlled appetite.

12. Martin, "Rip, Ichabod, and the American Imagination," *American Literature* 31 (1959):138–39.

13. Irving to Henry Brevoort, Paris, March 10, 1821, in *Letters*, 1:614; original italics.

14. "Notes and Extracts, 1825," in Washington Irving, *Journals and Notebooks: Volume 3, 1819–1827*, ed. Walter A. Reichart (Madison: University of Wisconsin Press, 1970), p. 665.

15. Notes and Extracts, 1825," in *Journals and Notebooks*, 3:660.

16. Irving to Henry Brevoort, London, August 15, 1820, in *Letters*, 1:593.

17. Springer, "Creative Contradictions in Irving," in *Washington Irving Reconsidered*, pp. 14–15. Springer argues that both "Rip Van Winkle" and "The Legend of Sleepy Hollow" belong to that middle ground "'between fact and fiction,' partaking of both to produce something better than either" (p. 15). For Irving, therefore, imaginative experience existed "on the borderline between two states of mind." While this is generally accurate, it is important to see that "Rip" and "Sleepy Hollow" actually occupy different levels of imaginative terrain because the "realities" they express correspond to extremely divergent psychological states ("Rip" is a form of realism, while "Sleepy Hollow" is "make-believe") and therefore demand on Irving's part and, by extension, the reader's, different imaginative conceptions.

18. Springer suggests something along these lines (but does not pursue it) when he writes that "the achievement of truth, though its importance is primarily literary, has personal and societal implications as well" (p. 15).

19. Hedges, *Washington Irving*, p. 140.

20. See, e.g., Martin, p. 142; Hedges, *Washington Irving*, p. 140; and Springer, p. 16.

21. Both Hedges (*Washington Irving*, p. 140) and Springer (p. 16) note this, though neither explores the full significance of the transformation.

22. Hedges, *Washington Irving*, p. 139.

23. John Lynen, *The Design of the Present: Essays on Time and Form in American Literature* (New Haven: Yale University Press, 1969), p. 157.

24. Lynen, p. 159.

25. Lynen, p. 159.

26. Ringe, *The Pictorial Mode: Space and Time in the Art of Bryant, Irving and Cooper* (Lexington: University of Kentucky Press, 1971), pp. 164 ff., discusses the commitment of Irving, Bryant, and Cooper to the idea of continuity, either through a cyclical development or a providential ordering of things to some divine plan.

27. Springer, p. 16.

28. See the definition of "legend" in *Dictionary of World Literary Terms*, ed. Joseph T. Shipley, 3d ed. (Boston: The Writer, 1970), pp. 174–75.

29. In "The Spell of Nature in Irving's Famous Stories" (*Washington Irving Reconsidered*, pp. 18–21), Herbert F. Smith gives an unusual reading of "Rip" and "Sleepy Hollow" in the context of the "relationship between literature as a cultural force and the history of the conservation movement in America" (p. 18). In this way he is able to illuminate the special links between the characters and events of Irving's two tales and their natural settings. Accordingly, the concept of time in Sleepy Hollow is organic because the only sense of temporal movement in this "sleepy region" is the change of seasons (p. 20).

30. Springer, p. 17; Martin, p. 144. Smith, on the other hand, refers to Ichabod as an "anti-conservationist principle" (p. 20).

31. Smith, p. 21.

32. In "New York and New England: Irving's Criticism of American Society," *American Literature* 38 (1967):462, Donald Ringe also sees Ichabod as a "threat" to the Hollow, interpreting his actions in the context of regional conflict.

33. Hedges, "Irving, Hawthorne, and the Image of the Wife," p. 25. For Hedges, this is symbolic of Ichabod's wanting "permanent occupancy of the maternal womb." Sleepy Hollow, a safe, secluded place, is the material equivalent of that fantasy. However, the problem here is that such a fantasy includes more than simply residing there. Ichabod, the outsider, desires not just to inhabit the Hollow but to ravage it, while those who live there by right of birth preserve what sustains them.

34. Springer, p. 17. These explanations are in accord with Springer's overall thesis that, since everything in the story can be rationally accounted for, the title uses the word "legend" and not "history" or "fact" because Irving was employing a purposely self-contradictory technique to leave the reader (as he also does in "Rip") somewhere between a real and a fabulous world. Again, while this is true, it does not go far enough in making distinctions between the qualities of the two imagined worlds.

35. As Springer argues, there is no need for "striving after logic and rational explanation for that which legitimately exists in another realm" (p. 17).

36. This reading of the old man as a converted Ichabod was suggested to me by my UCLA colleague, Susan Brienza, who maintains an interest in Irving's stories. If Ichabod had risen to some prominence in New York, he could have been attending the city council meeting. Although there is no way to test the truth of this hypothesis, the ironies are fascinating to consider.

37. "Notes and Extracts, 1825," in *Journals and Notebooks*, 3:690.

38. "Mountjoy," in Washington Irving, *Wolfert's Roost*, ed. Roberta Rosenberg (Boston: Twayne, 1979), p. 36. The story first appeared in the November and December 1839 issues of *Knickerbocker Magazine* and was one of several pieces Irving collected in 1855; however, he first began making notes for it during the *Sketch Book* years. (See "Tour in Scotland 1817," in Washington Irving, *Journals and Notebooks: Volume 2, 1807–1822*, ed. Walter A. Reichart and Lillian Schlissel [Boston: Twayne, 1981], pp. 119–20 and passim.)

39. Joy Kasson, *Artistic Voyagers: Europe and the American Imagination in the Works of Irving, Allston, Cole, Cooper, and Hawthorne*, Contributions in American Studies, Number 60 (Westport, Conn.: Greenwood Press, 1982), p. 37.

CHAPTER FOUR

1. Washington Irving, *Bracebridge Hall or The Humourists. A Medley by Geoffrey Crayon, Gent.*, ed. Herbert F. Smith (Boston: Twayne, 1977), p. 6; all future references to this edition will be cited in parentheses in the text.

2. Guttmann, *The Conservative Tradition in America* (New York: Oxford University Press, 1967), p. 48.

3. Hedges, *Washington Irving: An American Study, 1802–1832* (Baltimore: Johns Hopkins University Press, 1965), p. 176. The subsequent problem as Irving saw it and Crayon discussed it in the sketch is that the upper classes are prone to "absen-

teeism" and "lavish expenditure." (These ideas are examined in more detail later in this chapter.)

4. Guttmann, pp. 49, 51.

5. Stanley Williams, *The Life of Washington Irving* (New York: Oxford University Press, 1935), 1:202. See also Ben Harris McClary, *Washington Irving and the House of Murray* (Knoxville: University of Tennessee Press, 1969), p. 35. Hedges also accepts this explanation (p. 165). Moore's comment to Irving may be found in his *Memoirs, Journals, and Correspondence*, ed. Lord John Russell (London: Longman, Brown, Green, and Longman, 1853), 3:211.

6. Eugene Current-Garcia, "Irving Sets the Pattern: Notes on Professionalism and the Art of the Short Story," *Studies in Short Fiction* 10 (1973):329.

7. See "Notes While Preparing Sketch Book &C 1817," "Notebook 1818, Number 1," and "Haddon Hall Notebook 1821," in Washington Irving, *Journals and Notebooks: Volume 2, 1807–1822*, ed. Walter A. Reichart and Lillian Schlissel (Boston: Twayne, 1981), pp. 183, 200, 266–67, 334–56, 371–84.

8. Washington Irving, *The Sketch Book of Geoffrey Crayon, Gent.*, ed. Haskell Springer (Boston: Twayne, 1978), p. 159; all future references to this edition will be cited in parentheses in the text.

9. See, for example, Jefferson to John Adams, Monticello, January 21, 1812, in *The Adams-Jefferson Letters*, ed. Lester J. Cappon (Chapel Hill: University of North Carolina Press, 1959), 2:291. See also Charles L. Sanford's comments on Jefferson in *The Quest for Paradise: Europe and the American Moral Imagination* (Urbana: University of Illinois Press, 1961), pp. 127–34.

10. Hedges, *Washington Irving*, pp. 168–69.

11. Ringe, *The Pictorial Mode: Space and Time in the Art of Bryant, Irving and Cooper* (Lexington: University Press of Kentucky, 1971), p. 191.

12. Irving to Henry Brevoort, Birmingham, December 9, 1816, in Washington Irving, *Letters: Volume 1, 1802–1823*, ed. Ralph M. Aderman et al. (Boston: Twayne, 1978), pp. 464–65.

13. *Monthly Magazine* 3 (1797):74. For excellent brief histories of the corn laws and poor laws, see *The New Columbia Encyclopedia*, ed. William H. Harris and Judith S. Levey, 4th ed. (New York: Columbia University Press, 1975), pp. 658, col. 2; 2190, col. 3.

14. See the entries for Thursday, January 3, 1822, and Wednesday, October 11, 1826, in William Cobbett, *Rural Rides* (London: Dent-Everyman, 1912), 1:59–62, 2:147–49.

15. Hedges believes that Irving satirizes Faddy for his "excessive earnestness and Puritanism" (*Washington Irving*, p. 177).

16. Hedges also notes the use of the word "hobby," though he does not see the allusion to *Tristram Shandy* (*Washington Irving*, p. 172, n. 10). Elsewhere he has written that Squire Bracebridge appears as a "hobbyhorse-riding anachronism in a way that to a degree recalls the mocking of the old bachelors of *Salmagundi* with their whim-whams and whalebone habits" ("Washington Irving: Nonsense, the Fat of the Land and the Dream of Indolence," in *The Chief Glory of Every People: Essays on Classic*

American Writers, ed. Matthew J. Bruccoli [Carbondale: Southern Illinois University Press, 1973], p. 155).

17. *Washington Irving*, p. 180. Hedges sees the satire of the gentry in this sketch, but does not trace it back to its origins in "Forest Trees."

18. *Washington Irving*, pp. 176, 182.

19. Marvin Meyers, *The Jacksonian Persuasion: Politics and Belief* (Stanford: Stanford University Press, 1957), p. 8.

20. Hofstadter, *The Age of Reform: From Bryan to F.D.R.* (New York: Knopf, 1955), p. 23.

21. This especially held in America, as Rowland Berthoff explains: "The citizens of the true republic were self-reliant but disinterested property owners, attached above all to the common good, armed against the threat of tyranny, deferential to the special virtues of those of both higher and lower rank, but none among them rich or powerful enough to reduce others to dependence" ("Independence and Attachment, Virtue and Interest: From Republican Citizen to Free Enterpriser, 1787–1837," in *Uprooted Americans: Essays to Honor Oscar Handlin*, ed. Richard Bushman et al. [Boston: Little, Brown, 1979], p. 100).

22. Irving transferred his own familiarity with antiquarian texts, some of which originally appeared in "black letter," to the Squire. For instance, in "The School" (pp. 184–86), Crayon drops the names of three classical authors: Joseph Strutt (1749–1802), whose *Sports and Pastimes of the People of England* (1801) was often reprinted; Roger Ascham, whose *Schoolmaster* (1570) stressed learning through the gentle handling of children, a maxim which the Squire continually preaches; and Henry Peacham (1576?–1643?), whose *The Compleat Gentleman* (1622) condemns, as Crayon says, "the favourite method of making boys wise by flagellation."

23. "Notes and Extracts, 1825," in Washington Irving, *Journals and Notebooks: Volume 3, 1819–1827*, ed. Walter A. Reichart (Madison: University of Wisconsin Press, 1970), pp. 676, 685; original brackets.

24. Chester E. Eisinger, "The Freehold Concept in Eighteenth-Century American Letters," *William and Mary Quarterly*, 3d ser., 4 (1947):42–43, 45–46; A. Whitney Griswold, *Farming and Democracy* (New Haven: Yale University Press, 1948), pp. 50–54. "Landowning [in England] was now 'mainly an aristocratic business,'" says Griswold, "a far cry from the agrarian democracy on the American frontier."

25. Eisinger, p. 44. He notes that "freehold tenure" shares characteristics with the more common term "agrarianism." In fact, the "basis of all agrarian movements in the United States has been freehold tenure of the land."

26. "Notes and Extracts, 1825," in *Journals and Notebooks*, 3:670.

27. "Where Are We?" *Southern Literary Messenger* 19 (1853):237. Farming, Washington once told the leading agricultural writer of his time, Arthur Young, "has ever been amongst the most favourite amusements of my life . . ." (Washington to Arthur Young, Mount Vernon, August 6, 1786, in *The Writings of George Washington*, ed. John C. Fitzpatrick [Washington, D.C.: United States Government Printing Office, 1931–44], 28:510).

28. J. Hector St. John de Crèvecoeur, *Letters from an American Farmer* (New York:

Dutton, 1957), p. 12. See also James L. Machor, "The Garden City in America: Crève-coeur's *Letters* and the Urban Pastoral Context," *American Studies* 23 (1982):74.

29. Eisinger, p. 48.

30. Franklin to Mrs. Catherine Greene, Philadelphia, March 2, 1789, in *The Writings of Benjamin Franklin*, ed. Albert Henry Smyth (New York: Macmillan, 1905–7), 10:3. For Franklin, American farmers were keepers of its "glorious public virtue," the noble "Cultivators of the Earth." He once wrote that agriculture is "the only *honest way*" for a nation to acquire wealth, "wherein man receives a real increase of the seed thrown into the ground, in a kind of continual miracle, wrought by the hand of God in his favour, as a reward for his innocent life and virtuous industry" ("Propositions to Be Examined, Concerning National Wealth" [April 4, 1769], in *Writings*, 5:202; original italics). See also Sanford, pp. 118–21, and Hofstadter, p. 27.

31. Crèvecoeur, p. 20.

32. Jefferson to John Adams, Monticello, April 25, 1794, in *Adams-Jefferson Letters*, 1:253–54.

33. Griswold, pp. 14–15.

34. Jefferson, *Notes on the State of Virginia*, ed. William Peden (Chapel Hill: University of North Carolina Press, 1955), pp. 164–65.

35. Jefferson to John Jay, Paris, August 23, 1785, in *The Papers of Thomas Jefferson*, ed. Julian P. Boyd (Princeton: Princeton University Press, 1950–), 8:426.

36. *Notes on the State of Virginia*, p. 165; Jefferson to John Adams, Monticello, October 28, 1813, in *Adams-Jefferson Letters*, 2:391

37. Jefferson to James Madison, Fontainebleau, October 28, 1785; Jefferson to James Madison, Paris, December 20, 1787, in *Papers*, 8:682, 12:442; Joyce Appleby, "What Is Still American in the Political Philosophy of Thomas Jefferson?" *William and Mary Quarterly*, 3d ser., 39 (1982):295; Jefferson to James Jay, Monticello, April 7, 1809, in *The Writings of Thomas Jefferson*, ed. Andrew Lipscomb and Albert Ellery Bergh (Washington, D.C.: Thomas Jefferson Memorial Association, 1905), 12:271.

38. Jefferson to Benjamin Austin, Monticello, January 9, 1816, in *Writings*, 14:392.

39. *Notes on the State of Virginia*, p. 165; Jefferson to William B. Giles, Monticello, December 26, 1825, in *Writings*, 16:149–50. See also Samuel Rezneck, "The Rise and Early Development of Industrial Consciousness in the United States, 1760–1830," *Journal of Economic and Business History* 4 (1932):799.

40. Irving to Peter Irving, Washington, June 16, 1832, in Washington Irving, *Letters: Volume 2, 1823–1838*, ed. Ralph M. Aderman et al. (Boston: Twayne, 1979), p. 705; original italics.

41. Andrew Jackson, "Seventh Annual Message" (December 7, 1835), in *A Compilation of the Messages and Papers of the Presidents, 1789–1897*, ed. James D. Richardson (Washington, D.C.: United States Government Printing Office, 1896), 3:166.

42. Jackson, "Seventh Annual Message," "Veto Message" (December 4, 1833), in *Messages and Papers of the Presidents*, 3:162, 68.

43. Jackson, "Farewell Address" (March 4, 1837), in *Messages and Papers of the Presidents*, 3:305.

44. Meyers, p. 15.

45. Jackson, "Sixth Annual Message" (December 1, 1834), in *Messages and Papers of the Presidents*, 3 : 111; Meyers, pp. 21, 23, 18.

46. "Notes and Extracts, 1825," in *Journals and Notebooks*, 3 : 666.

47. "Notes and Extracts, 1825," in *Journals and Notebooks*, 3 : 666. Three times here Irving drops the "e" from the ending of the past participle.

48. Rezneck, p. 800.

49. Hofstadter, pp. 41–42.

50. Emerson, "Farming," in *Society and Solitude, The Complete Works of Ralph Waldo Emerson*, ed. Edward W. Emerson (Boston: Houghton Mifflin, 1904), 7 : 137. See also Douglas C. Stenerson, "Emerson and the Agrarian Tradition," *Journal of the History of Ideas* 14 (1953):95–115. For the American agrarian tradition in general, see Henry Nash Smith, *Virgin Land: The American West as Symbol and Myth* (Cambridge: Harvard University Press, 1950), and three additional essays by Chester E. Eisinger: "Land and Loyalty: Literary Expressions of Agrarian Nationalism in the Seventeenth and Eighteenth Centuries," *American Literature* 21 (1949):160–78; "The Farmer in the Eighteenth Century Almanac," *Agricultural History* 28 (1954):107–12; "The Influence of Natural Rights and Physiocratic Doctrines on American Agrarian Thought during the Revolutionary Period," *Agricultural History* 21 (1947):13–23.

51. See Smith, pp. 123–54.

52. Appleby, "Commercial Farming and the 'Agrarian Myth' in the Early Republic," *The Journal of American History* 68 (1982):844–45. Appleby adds that "[i]t was exactly the promise of progressive agricultural development that fueled his hopes that ordinary men might escape the tyranny of their social superiors both as employers and magistrates." In "What Is Still American in the Political Philosophy of Thomas Jefferson?", Appleby writes that "Jefferson was an early advocate of the commercial exploitation of American agriculture"; he was involved in "long-range programs for expanding international free trade in basic farm commodities" (p. 295).

53. Wood, *The Creation of the American Republic, 1776–1787* (Chapel Hill: University of North Carolina Press, 1969), p. 53.

54. Berthoff, p. 102.

55. Wood, pp. 54, 59.

56. *New-England Farmer* (Boston), January 20, 1826, quoted in Berthoff, p. 106.

57. James A. Henretta, "Families and Farms: *Mentalité* in Pre-Industrial America," *William and Mary Quarterly*, 3d ser., 35 (1978):19, 25–27, 30–32.

58. "Notebook 1818, Number 2," in *Journals and Notebooks*, 2 : 289.

59. Irving to Henry Brevoort, Liverpool, October 10, 1817, in *Letters*, 1 : 509.

60. Hedges, *Washington Irving*, p. 188. Hedges's analysis of the story (pp. 183–89) includes a full summary of its events, which I will not repeat.

61. See Williams, 2 : 280–86, for a list and discussion of all the works on which Irving relied for information.

CHAPTER FIVE

1. Stanley T. Williams, *The Life of Washington Irving* (New York: Oxford University Press, 1935), 1 : 218.

2. Irving to Peter Irving, Dresden, March 10, 1823, in Washington Irving, *Letters: Volume 1, 1802–1823*, ed. Ralph M. Aderman et al. (Boston: Twayne, 1978), p. 731; original italics.

3. Irving to Sarah Van Wart, Aix-la-Chapelle, August 2, 1822; Irving to Susan Storrow, Vienna, November 10, 1822, in *Letters*, 1:694, 721. "The Continent," he noted in his journal, "continually present[s] pictures of customs & manners such as formerly prevailed in England" ("German and Austrian Journal, 1822–1823," in Washington Irving, *Journals and Notebooks: Volume 3, 1819–1827*, ed. Walter A. Reichart (Madison: University of Wisconsin Press, 1970), p. 121. The entry is dated January 25, 1823.

4. John Murray II to Irving [London], November 8, 1823, in Pierre M. Irving, *The Life and Letters of Washington Irving* (New York: Putnam, 1862–64), 2:177. For Irving's anxiety about renewed literary endeavors see, for example, Irving to Peter Irving [Paris, August 20, 1823], in Washington Irving, *Letters: Volume 2, 1823–1838*, ed. Ralph M. Aderman et al. (Boston: Twayne, 1979), p. 4.

5. Irving to John Murray II, Paris, December 22, 1823, in *Letters*, 2:26. The editors of the *Letters* conclude incorrectly that what Irving had in mind by additional volumes of "the Sketch Book" were the stories that compose *Tales of a Traveller* (2:27, n. 3). Proof of their mistake comes in a March 1824 letter to Murray, in which Irving says that he has "turned aside" from his "idea of preparing two more volumes of the Sketch Book as I think I have run into a plan & thrown off writings which will be more novel and attractive" (*Letters*, 2:41). These were the pieces he eventually collected in *Tales*.

6. Irving to Charles R. Leslie, Paris, February 8, 1824, in *Letters*, 2:37, 38.

7. "Notes and Extracts, 1819–1823," in *Journals and Notebooks*, 3:584.

8. "Notes and Extracts, 1825," in *Journals and Notebooks*, 3:686. The passage comes from "Hints for an Essay on the Drama," a piece Burke wrote sometime before 1765 but did not further develop.

9. Washington Irving, *Tales of a Traveller, by Geoffrey Crayon, Gent.*, Author's Revised Edition (New York: Putnam's, 1865), title page; future references to this edition will be cited in the text. (At the time of this writing, *Tales* is not available in the Twayne edition of Irving's works.) The quotation comes from the play *Cynthia's Revels*. I am indebted to my UCLA colleague A. R. Braunmuller for help in locating Jonson's lines and for the Renaissance perception of the traveler as a figure to be scorned and mocked.

10. The epigraph to the first section of the book, "Strange Stories by a Nervous Gentleman," from Fletcher's *Wife for a Month*, reinforces the idea of distortion—in fact, violently so—and contains specific mention of a "monstrous lie" (p. [17]).

11. Hedges, *Washington Irving: An American Study, 1802–1832* (Baltimore: Johns Hopkins University Press, 1965), p. 207.

12. "Notes and Extracts, 1819–1823," in *Journals and Notebooks*, 3:584.

13. Irving to Catherine Paris, Surrey, June 21, 1822, in *Letters*, 1:684.

14. I discuss the structure of *Tales* in more detail in the second section of this chapter.

15. Michael D. Bell, *The Development of American Romance: The Sacrifice of Relation* (Chicago: University of Chicago Press, 1980), p. 12. Bell devotes a chapter to *Tales of a Traveller*, examining it in the context of nineteenth-century attitudes toward imagination, fiction and, especially, the romance (pp. 62–85). See also G. Harrison Orians, "Censure of Fiction in American Reviews and Magazines, 1789–1810," *PMLA* 52 (1937):195–214.

16. See, for example, Irving to Henry Brevoort, London, June 11, 1822, in *Letters*, 1:677.

17. Irving to Catherine Paris, Surrey, June 21, 1822, in *Letters*, 1:682.

18. In addition to the letters of June 11 and June 21 cited immediately above, see Irving to Sarah Van Wart, Heidelberg, September 18, 1822, in *Letters*, 1:706, 707.

19. Irving to Sarah Van Wart, Aix-la-Chapelle, August 2, 1822, in *Letters*, 1:695.

20. Irving to Sarah Van Wart, Mayence, September 2, 1822, in *Letters*, 1:703.

21. The phrase "tormenting malady" appears in Irving to Sarah Van Wart, Wiesbaden, August 19 [August 20], 1822, in *Letters*, 1:696.

22. Irving to James K. Paulding, London, May 27, 1820, in *Letters*, 1:585.

23. "German and Austrian Journal, 1822–1823," in *Journals and Notebooks*, 3:22.

24. Irving to Sarah Van Wart, Mayence, September 2, 1822; Irving to Thomas W. Storrow, Vienna, November 16, 1822; Irving to Charles R. Leslie, Dresden, March 15, 1823; Irving to Charles R. Leslie, Dresden, December 2, 1822; Irving to Sarah Van Wart, Vienna, October 27 [November 10], 1822, in *Letters*, 1:703, 724, 736, 725, 719.

25. "German and Austrian Journal, 1822–1823," in *Journals and Notebooks*, 3:18.

26. Pierre M. Irving, 4:339–40. Reminiscences from Flora Foster Dawson and Emily Foster Fuller are printed as an appendix to *The Life and Letters*.

27. Pierre M. Irving, 4:340.

28. Irving to Sarah Van Wart, Vienna, October 27 [November 10], 1822, in *Letters*, 1:719.

29. Irving entered Dresden on November 28, 1822 ("German and Austrian Journal, 1822–1823," in *Journals and Notebooks*, 3:88). Early in December, according to Flora Foster Dawson, he sought and obtained an introduction to the Fosters in their opera box, whereupon, much to the family's surprise, he made inquiries based upon information he had gathered from Mrs. Foster's letter (Pierre M. Irving, 4:338–41).

30. See Williams, 1:236–54; Walter A. Reichart, *Washington Irving and Germany* (Ann Arbor: University of Michigan Press, 1957), pp. 81–102; Marcel Heiman, "Rip Van Winkle: A Psychoanalytic Note on the Story and Its Author," *American Imago* 16 (1959):26–31; and Philip McFarland, *Sojourners* (New York: Atheneum, 1979), pp. 207–15, 222–31. McFarland, who paints a portrait of Irving's life primarily as it intersects with those of other famous nineteenth-century figures—John Brown, Aaron Burr, Walter Scott, Mary Shelley, and John Jacob Astor—tells the entire story of his encounter with the Fosters, but offers no interpretation of the events he records. Williams, Reichart, and Heiman, on the other hand, analyze the significance of this involvement, especially as it exacerbated Irving's inability to work. No one, however, has traced its effect on *Tales of a Traveller*. Hedges mentions the importance

of the attachment and, especially, Irving's affection for Emily Foster (*Washington Irving*, pp. 191, 226–27), but stops short of making connections between the life and the work.

31. Irving to Mrs. Amelia Foster, Prague, June 1, 1823, in *Letters*, 1:759.

32. Pierre M. Irving, 4:346; original italics.

33. Irving to Mrs. Amelia Foster, Hirschberg, May 23 [1823], in *Letters*, 1:751–52.

34. Irving to Peter Irving [Paris(?), July(?), 1823], in *Letters*, 1:768.

35. Irving to Mrs. Amelia Foster, Prague, [June] 8, 1823, in *Letters*, 1:763.

36. Irving to Mrs. Amelia Foster [Dresden, April-May 1823], in *Letters*, 1:737.

37. Pierre M. Irving, 4:358.

38. Williams, 1:253.

39. As Williams points out when discussing Emily Foster's possible influence on Irving's writings, his "silence" concerning her "in his books and manuscripts would seem to indicate that she did not become for long an essential part of him" (1:251).

40. Irving to Emily [Foster] Fuller, Sunnyside, July 2, 1856, in Washington Irving, *Letters: Volume 4, 1846–1859*, ed. Ralph M. Aderman et al. (Boston: Twayne, 1982), p. 590. Irving was responding to Mrs. Fuller's inquiry about opportunities for her son in America. He said that upon opening her letter "a thousand reccollections [sic] broke at once upon my mind of Emily Foster, as I had known her at Dresden, young and fair and bright and beautiful . . ." (p. 589).

41. Irving to Mrs. Amelia Foster: Hirschberg, May 23 [1823]; Prague, June 1, 1823; Prague, [June] 8, 1823, in *Letters*, 1:751, 757, 764.

42. *The Journal of Emily Foster*, ed. Stanley T. Williams and Leonard B. Beach (New York: Oxford University Press, 1938), pp. 116, 126, 111.

43. *Journal of Emily Foster*, pp. 126, 130–31, 134, 126, 158, 118 (editors' translation from the Italian); Pierre M. Irving, p. 340; original italics.

44. Williams, 1:251; Heiman, p. 18; "French Journal, 1823–1826," in *Journals and Notebooks*, 3:541, 547, 555 (the entries are dated November 11 and 26, and December 25, 1825); Irving to Charles R. Leslie, Paris, February 8, 1824; Irving to Thomas W. Storrow, Bordeaux, October 31, 1825; Irving to Emily Foster, Paris, August 23, 1825; Irving to Thomas W. Storrow, Bordeaux, December 25, 1825, in *Letters*, 2:37, 146, 129, 156–57.

45. *Journal of Emily Foster*, pp. 84, 85–86. He is "*going the day after tomorrow*," she notes with emphasis in her journal.

46. Williams recognized the sexual side of her character: "She is not a coquette, as she protests more than once, but she finds it exciting to watch the mercurial Italian compete for her favors with the exuberant, open-hearted Bavarian" (1:245). For likenesses of Matilda and Emily, see the first volume of Williams's biography, opposite pp. 102 and 238.

47. Irving to Mrs. Amelia Foster, Hirschberg, May 23 [1823], in *Letters*, 1:752.

48. Pierre M. Irving, 4:389.

49. Irving to Henry Brevoort, Birmingham, December 9, 1816, in *Letters*, 1:463.

50. Irving to James K. Paulding, London, May 27, 1820, in *Letters*, 1:585.

51. Irving to Henry Brevoort, Birmingham, December 9, 1816, in *Letters*, 1:463.

52. Irving to Henry Brevoort, Liverpool, October 10, 1817, in *Letters*, 1:508.

53. Interesting in this regard are the many images in his writings of dried-up old bachelors. Hedges has noted this; see, for example, his comments on Master Simon and the parson in *Bracebridge Hall* (*Washington Irving*, pp. 168–69). Furthermore, he has recognized Irving's deep ambivalence toward marriage, observing that Crayon exhibits a tendency both in *The Sketch Book* and the later miscellanies to "pull away from wife and marriage, toward an association with fellow bachelors." "Is it merely accidental," he asks, "that 'The Wife' is immediately followed in *The Sketch Book* by Rip Van Winkle's flight from a bad marriage, his fraternization with a group of little old men in a womb-like glen, his twenty years' sleep through the prime of life (and his wife's death) into old age, and his return to the motherly custody of his daughter?" ("Irving, Hawthorne, and the Image of the Wife," in *Washington Irving Reconsidered: A Symposium*, ed. Ralph M. Aderman [Hartford, Conn.: Transcendental Books, 1969], p. 25). One thinks of Irving returning to America and setting up house at Sunnyside with his nieces acting as his caretakers and custodians.

54. Irving to Mrs. Amelia Foster, Prague: May 28, 1823; [June] 8, 182[3]; [June 19(?), 1823], in *Letters*, 1:754, 764, 755, 766.

55. Irving to Mrs. Amelia Foster: Prague, May 28, 1823; Hirschberg, May 23 [1823], in *Letters*, 1:754–55, 752.

56. "German and Austrian Journal, 1822–1823," in *Journals and Notebooks*, 3:166–67.

57. According to Flora Foster Dawson, Irving continued to read to the Fosters from his books and manuscripts, insisting, just as he did previously, that "no visitor should be admitted till the last word had been read, and the whole praised or criticised, as the case may be" (Pierre M. Irving, 4:364–65). Of course, as Mrs. Dawson notes, the Fosters rarely offered negative comment, "as a slight word would put him out of conceit with a whole work."

58. Irving to Peter Irving [Paris(?), July(?) 1823], in *Letters*, 1:768. Interestingly, Mrs. Dawson recalls the scene differently. According to her, the three women rode in the "light English barouche," with Irving seated on the coach box; behind them, in a German traveling carriage, were her two brothers and their German tutor (Pierre M. Irving, 4:365–66). Both Williams (1:243) and Reichart (p. 102) accept her version. If Irving has misremembered the details of the departure from Dresden, it may have been because he wanted to envision it in a particular way. His recollection emphasizes his role as surrogate husband, father, protector, rather than suitor to the eldest daughter.

59. "French Journal, 1823–1826," in *Journals and Notebooks*, 3:200 (the entry is dated July 30, 1823); Pierre M. Irving, 4:376; *Journal of Emily Foster*, p. 167; Irving to Peter Irving [Paris, August 5, 1823], in *Letters*, 2:3.

60. "French Journal, 1823–1826," in *Journals and Notebooks*, 3:209; the entry is dated August 11, 1823.

61. Irving to Peter Irving [Paris, August 20, 1823], in *Letters*, 2:4.

62. Irving to Peter Irving [Paris], September 4, 1823, in *Letters*, 2:6.

63. "French Journal, 1823–1826," in *Journals and Notebooks*, 3:221 (the entries are dated September 15, 16, 17, 1823); Irving to Henry Brevoort, Le Havre, September 26, 1823; Irving to John Howard Payne, Le Havre, September 27, 1823, in *Letters*, 2:7, 9. In his letter to Payne Irving wrote that he was "troubled with a return of my old complaint in the ancles [sic] . . . it was that job of writing that brought it on."

64. "French Journal, 1823–1826," in *Journals and Notebooks*, 3:254, 255, 256, 257, 258, 289; the entries are dated December 8 through December 17, 1823, and February 16, 1824. On December 13, Irving confessed to his "doubts as to literary prospects"; all his attempts to write were "in vain." Four days later, "depressed & despond[ent]," he decided "to arrange the Mss. on hand so as to make 2 vols of Sketch Book," an idea which did not motivate him and which he eventually had to abandon.

65. Grace Overmyer, *America's First Hamlet* (New York: New York University Press, 1957), p. 54; McFarland, pp. 234–35.

66. Irving to John Howard Payne, Paris, November 22, 1823, in *Letters*, 2:17. Earlier in the year, when he was staging amateur theatricals with the Fosters in Dresden, he had written to Leslie, somewhat playfully, that he "had no idea of this fund of Dramatic talent lurking" within him (Irving to Charles R. Leslie, Dresden, March 15, 1823, in *Letters*, 1:736).

67. Reichart, p. 125.

68. Irving to John Howard Payne, Philadelphia, November 2, 1809, in *Letters*, 1:276–77.

69. Overmyer, p. 190; McFarland, p. 238.

70. Irving to John Howard Payne, Paris: November 12, 1823; November 26, 1823; December 17, 1823; November 22, 1823; [January 17, 1824], in *Letters*, 2:14, 19, 25, 17 (original italics), 18, 30–31.

71. Irving to John Howard Payne, Paris: November 26, 1823; January 20, 1825, in *Letters*, 2:20, 98.

72. Irving to John Howard Payne, Bordeaux, January 3, 182[6], in *Letters*, 2:160; original italics.

73. Irving to John Howard Payne, Paris, January 31, 1824, in *Letters*, 2:34. "If . . . the experiment should produce any material benefit to you," Irving wrote, "I shall feel highly satisfied at having made it."

74. "French Journal, 1823–1826," in *Journals and Notebooks*, 3:292.

75. "French Journal, 1823–1826," in *Journals and Notebooks*, 3:295; the entry is dated February 24, 1824.

76. "French Journal, 1823–1826," in *Journals and Notebooks*, 3:290; the entry is dated February 16, 1824.

77. Irving to John Murray II, Paris, March [25], 1824, in *Letters*, 2:41–42. "For my own part," he told his sister after *Tales* had been published, echoing his lines to Murray, "I think there are in it some of the best things I have ever written" (Irving to Catharine Paris, Paris, September 20, 1824, in *Letters*, 2:76).

78. Irving to Henry Brevoort, Paris, December 11, 1824, in *Letters*, 2:90. The contemporary reviews, almost unremittingly bad, have been summarized by Williams (2:294–96) and Reichart (pp. 157–64). In the notes to his chapter on *Tales*, Hedges provides a runnning commentary on the critical reception, often pointing out how, in

his opinion, a particular reviewer misunderstood Irving's point in failing to bring his tales, especially his ghost stories, to expected, and therefore satisfactory, conclusions (*Washington Irving*, pp. 191–235).

79. "French Journal, 1823–1826," in *Journals and Notebooks*, 3:317; the entry is dated April 8, 1824. Other entries also fail to support Irving's assertion: April 22: "wrote alterations on Wolfert Webber—but did not feel much in the vein"; April 23: "Wrote at Wolfert Webber makg alterations—no excitement"; April 24: "Wrote a little at Wolfert—but was not in good mood"; April 25: "Tried to write this morng—but could not get on" (pp. 322, 323).

80. Review of *Tales of a Traveller*, *Westminster Review* 2 (1824):340; "Letters of Timothy Tickler, Esq. to Eminent Literary Characters: No. XVIII," *Blackwood's Edinburgh Magazine* 16 (1824):295; Review of *Tales of a Traveller*, *United States Literary Gazette* 1 (1824):229.

81. Among many others during the Fall of 1824 are the entries dated September 5: "woke early in morng. restless & uneasy—full of doubts of Success of work"; September 9: "Woke several times in the night—restless & uneasy"; November 7: "awoke very early: depressed, dubious of myself & public"; November 21: "A restless night—broken sleep & uneasy thoughts" ("French Journal, 1823–1826," in *Journals and Notebooks*, 3:392, 393, 421, 427).

82. "French Journal, 1823–1826," in *Journals and Notebooks*, 3:428; the entry is dated November 23, 1824. Two days later he recorded an anecdote about the Duke of Wellington reading the "papers which attack him & laugh[ing] to himself" (p. 429). Undoubtedly Irving envied the duke his equanimity.

83. Irving to Catharine Paris, Paris, September 20, 1824, in *Letters*, 2:76. For Irving's efforts at gathering scraps and residues of tales, see, for example, the entries dated February 16, February 29, April 7, and May 3, 1824, in "French Journal, 1823–1826," in *Journals and Notebooks*, 3:290, 298, 316, 326. *Blackwood's* said that the ghost stories are "old, and familiar to everybody conversant in that sort of line," adding that they are "not improved by their new dress" and warning Irving that he should be "excessively scrupulous" before he "sets to work upon anything he hears" (pp. 294, 295). If by "transcripts of scenes that I have witnessed," however, Irving meant that on his travels he had actually passed through the landscape in which his tales are set (rather than that he had observed the events and incidents about which he writes), then he certainly brings no fresh perspective to bear on either the culture or the scenery he describes. (In "Irving's Use of His Italian Experiences in *Tales of a Traveller*: The Beginning of an American Tradition," *American Literature* 31 [1959]:192, Nathalia Wright has shown that of the nine tales in the collection that have Italian settings, "all but one are laid in cities or regions which Irving had visited.") Stressing location as unity may also have been a way of avoiding the real underlying vein of loss, frustration, and impotence.

84. Hedges has thoroughly analyzed Irving's storytelling techniques in *Tales*, including his use of frame narratives, multiple narrators, and, in general, his self-consciousness as a writer of fiction (*Washington Irving*, pp. 191–235). G. R. Thompson studies Irving's experiments with "point of view, narrative frames, and Gothic modes,"

primarily in the first section of *Tales*, "Strange Stories by a Nervous Gentleman" ("Washington Irving and the American Ghost Story," in *The Haunted Dusk: American Supernatural Fiction, 1820–1920*, ed. Howard Kerr et al. [Athens: University of Georgia Press, 1983], pp. 13–36). Donald Ringe charts Irving's contributions to the tradition of Gothic fiction, emphasizing how he focused on imagination as the source of "faulty perception" (*American Gothic: Imagination and Reason in Nineteenth-Century Fiction* [Lexington: University of Kentucky Press, 1982], pp. 80–101). All of this fine critical exegesis notwithstanding, the tales for the most part remain tedious and unanimated, except where Irving's obsessions break through their mundane surfaces.

85. "American Writers: No. IV," *Blackwood's Edinburgh Magazine* 17 (1825):67.

86. Thompson, p. 26. Other critics have noted the sexual imagery in individual pieces, but have not related it to an overall pattern operative in Irving's *Tales*. This is true for nearly every story I discuss. Moreover, since both Hedges and Mary Weatherspoon Bowden (*Washington Irving* [Boston: Twayne, 1981], pp. 96–110) have independently summarized the events of all the important stories in the collection, I will not repeat them.

87. Review of *Tales of a Traveller*, *Eclectic Review* 24 (1825):65–66, 74; Hedges, *Washington Irving*, p. 197. In concluding, the reviewer stops just short of of accusing Irving of "coarseness" and "profaneness" and wonders whether he now "thinks worse of the public" or has himself been "*worsened* by his travels" (p. 74; original italics).

88. Hedges, *Washington Irving*, p. 199. Hedges accepts the ghost theory, seeing the woman as a "revitalized female corpse." Ringe sees the tale as the "mental projection of a mad protagonist" (p. 97). Thompson stresses the "essential epistemological ambiguity" of the story (p. 29). Both John Clendenning ("Irving and the Gothic Tradition," *Bucknell Review* 12 [1964]:98) and Kelley Griffith, Jr. ("Ambiguity and Gloom in Irving's 'Adventure of the German Student,'" *CEA Critic* 38 [1975]:11) believe that Gottfried has made love to the cadaver, imposing his "fantasy" upon it. James E. Devlin ("Irving's 'Adventure of the German Student,'" *Studies in American Fiction* 7 [1979]:93–94), on the other hand, argues unconvincingly that the story concerns the student's self-abuse, so that he enjoys not "necrophilial passion," but "final surrender to sexual satisfaction *in solo*."

89. "Notes While Preparing Sketch Book &C. 1817," in *Journals and Notebooks: Volume 2, 1807–1822*, ed. Walter A. Reichart and Lillian Schlissel (Boston: Twayne, 1981), pp. 185–86.

90. Irving to Prince Dmitri Dolgorouki, Madrid, January 22, 1828, in *Letters*, 2:265; my italics. While Irving genuinely appreciates Madame Alcañices's beauty, he seems to have some trouble spelling her name correctly.

91. "French Journal, 1823–1826," in *Journals and Notebooks*, 3:281. The precise date of this entry cannot be determined. It appears on the bottom of the page for February 1, 1824, but upside down and therefore most likely inserted at a later time.

92. *Washington Irving*, p. 201, n. 20.

93. *Washington Irving*, p. 210.

94. "French Journal, 1823–1826," in *Journals and Notebooks*, 3:465, 519–21.

Irving first recorded his interest in *El Embozado* on March 16, 1825. He then outlined his play on single sheets of paper which he inserted between the entries for September 19 and September 20, 1825. Byron's friend Captain Medwin gave him the notes he had collected on Byron's own version of the drama, which Irving copied into his notebook. See "Notes and Extracts, 1824–1827," in *Journals and Notebooks*, 3:710–12. Williams, Hedges, and others have discussed the connections between Irving's interest in the double figure and Poe's, especially where the story "William Wilson" is concerned (Williams, 1:466–67, n. 8; Hedges, *Washington Irving*, p. 211, n. 32).

95. *United States Literary Gazette* 1 (1824):229; original italics.

96. "French Journal, 1823–1826," in *Journals and Notebooks*, 3:353–54 (the entries are dated June 23 and 24, 1824); Michael Clark, "A Source for Irving's 'The Young Italian,'" *American Literature* 52 (1980):111–14; *United States Literary Gazette*, p. 229.

97. "French Journal, 1823–1826," in *Journals and Notebooks*, 3:480; the entry is dated April 28, 1825. "My countrymen," he added, "may regret some day or other that they turnd from me with such caprice, the moment foes abroad assailed me." Obviously, he had been wounded by the critical response to *Tales*.

98. Irving to Charles R. Leslie, Paris, December 8, 1824, in *Letters*, 2:87–88. John Murray published the *Quarterly Review*, which had no kind words for American literature.

99. Irving to Emily Foster, Paris, August 23, 1825, in *Letters*, 2:130. See also "French Journal, 1823–1826," in *Journals and Notebooks*, 3:361; the entry is dated July 10, 1824.

100. Hedges calls attention to this line, but without the context of Irving's own anxieties it loses a good deal of its resonance (*Washington Irving*, p. 222).

101. "French Journal, 1823–1826," in *Journals and Notebooks*, 3:546; the entry is dated November 25, 1825. Irving adds that the "dream was doubtless occasioned by my letter to E. I. written yesterday requesting him in case of difficulty to place my literary property &c in the hands of Brevoort or J.T.I. [his brother, John Treat Irving]." Interestingly, Irving sees only a direct and practical impetus for the dream; he offers no deeper analysis.

102. Irving to Thomas W. Storrow, Bordeaux, December 2, 1825, in *Letters*, 2:151.

103. Irving to Catharine Paris, Paris, September 20, 1824, in *Letters*, 2:79, 80.

104. Irving to Pierre Paris Irving, Paris, December 7, 1824, in *Letters*, 2:84, 85.

105. Irving to Pierre Paris Irving, Paris, March 29, 1825, in *Letters*, 2:106; original italics.

106. "German and Austrian Journal, 1822–1823," "Notes and Extracts, 1823," in *Journals and Notebooks*, 3:157, 632. In the journal, the passage is one of several miscellaneous entries that occur between those for May 19 and May 20, 1823. The thirteen lines form the first of eight stanzas of Wild's poem, though the text, spelling, and punctuation vary from the the the original (3:157, n. 175). Irving circled and crossed out the bracketed lines, but they have been recovered by the editors.

107. Irving to Pierre Paris Irving, Paris, December 7, 1824; Irving to Charles R.

Leslie, Paris, December 8, 1824, in *Letters*, 2 : 84, 88. The quoted phrase in the letter to his nephew comes from one of Irving's favorite books of the Bible, in fact the one he most often references, Ecclesiastes (1 : 14).

108. Michael Bell calls attention to these lines as "suggestive," but does not draw out their full implication (p. 68).

109. On Irving's relationship to the Common Sense philosophers, see Bell, pp. 64, 72, and Ringe, pp. 83–85.

110. Higham, *From Boundlessness to Consolidation: The Transformation of American Culture, 1848–1860* (Ann Arbor: William L. Clements Library, 1969), p. 10. Higham quotes here from an unnamed observer.

111. Bell, p. 65.

112. "Notes and Extracts, 1819–1823," in *Journals and Notebooks*, 3 : 569.

113. Hedges, *Washington Irving*, p. 217.

114. "Notes and Extracts, 1824–1827," in *Journals and Notebooks*, 3 : 743.

115. "The Imagination; Its Seat, Its Disposition, Its Pleasures, Its Pains, Its Powers," *Southern Literary Messenger* 21 (1855):226; "Notes and Extracts, 1824–1827," in *Journals and Notebooks*, 3 : 748.

116. *Illustrations of The Legend of Sleepy Hollow, designed and etched by Felix O. C. Darley for the members of the American Art-Union* (New York: The American Art Union, 1849).

117. *Two Tales: Rip Van Winkle and The Legend of Sleepy Hollow* (San Diego: Harcourt Brace Jovanovich, 1986).

118. Irving to Thomas W. Storrow, Vienna, November 16, 1822; Irving to Charles R. Leslie, Dresden, December 2, 1822, in *Letters*, 1 : 724, 725.

119. Irving to Pierre Paris Irving, Paris, August 29, 1825, in *Letters*, 2 : 132.

120. "French Journal, 1823–1826," in *Journals and Notebooks*, 3 : 442, 557; the entries are dated December 31, 1824, and December 31, 1825.

CHAPTER SIX

1. Stanley T. Williams, *The Life of Washington Irving* (New York: Oxford University Press, 1935), 1 : 376. Scholars previously have argued that whatever place *The Alhambra* enjoys in the history of American literature is due to a note of exoticism that it introduced into that literature. For example, Henry A. Pochmann, in his introduction to *Washington Irving: Representative Selections* (New York: American Book Company, 1934), states unequivocally that "the chief importance of the volume is that it is one of the few examples of Oriental Gothic in this country" (pp. lxviii–lxix).

2. Quoted in Williams, 1 : 376.

3. For this idea in relation to Irving's *Life and Voyages of Columbus* and the *Conquest of Granada*, see Williams Hedges, *Washington Irving: An American Study, 1802–1832* (Baltimore: Johns Hopkins University Press, 1965), pp. 236–67.

4. A fourth book, *Voyages and Discoveries of the Companions of Columbus*, appeared in 1831. Irving also collected a great many notes on Spanish history, some of which he published independently as magazine articles, others in part 3 of *The Crayon Miscellany* (1835) under the general title "Legends of the Conquest of Spain." Moreover,

during these years he began gathering material on Mahomet, which he revised on his second stay in Spain in the 1840s, and which he finally brought out as *Mahomet and His Successors* (1850).

5. Irving to Thomas W. Storrow, Madrid, March 30, 1826, in *Letters*, 2:190.

6. Irving to Henry Brevoort, Madrid, April 4, 1827, in *Letters*, 2:225, 226. Later he confessed to Brevoort that "the idea that the kindness of my countrymen towards me, was withering, caused me for a long time the most dreary depression of Spirits, and disheartened me from making any literary exertions (Irving to Henry Brevoort, Madrid, February 23, 1828, in *Letters*, 2:275).

7. Irving to Peter Irving: Seville, March 3, 1829; Alhambra, May 30, 1829; Alhambra, June 13, 1829, in *Letters*, 2:387, 434, 436.

8. "Notes and Extracts, 1825," in Washington Irving, *Journals and Notebooks: Volume 3, 1819–1827*, ed. Walter A. Reichart (Madison: University of Wisconsin Press, 1970), p. 657.

9. Irving to John Wetherell, Alhambra, June 18, 1829, in *Letters*, 2:448.

10. Alexander Hill Everett, editor and diplomat, served at The Hague from 1818 until 1824. In 1825 he was appointed minister to Spain. The older brother of the well-known *North American Review* essayist, Edward Everett, he also wrote for the *Review*. As Hedges suggests, a factor in Irving's accepting the appointment and undertaking the translation was that he trusted Everett's literary judgment as to the importance of Navarrete's book (p. 237)

11. Williams, 1:297; Irving to Thomas W. Storrow, Bordeaux, February 3, 1826, in Washington Irving, *Letters: Volume 2, 1823–1838*, ed. Ralph M. Aderman et al. (Boston: Twayne, 1979), p. 172.

12. In 1825, Irving's interest in several business schemes depleted the store of capital that he had accumulated. Chief among these were investments in a Rouen steamboat line and a Bolivian copper mine. There was, in addition, the failure of a London bank, which meant the loss of two thousand pounds. In response to these disasters, he wrote to his friend Storrow that "it seems as if all my attempts to strike a little ahead are defeated." A little later on he confided: "I find there is nothing to be gained in looking beyond the pen" (Irving to Thomas W. Storrow: Beycheville, October 17, 1825; Bordeaux, October 31, 1825, in *Letters*, 2:141, 146).

13. When Irving came to Madrid he was introduced by Everett to the American book collector and bibliographer Obadiah Rich, who gave him permission to work in his personal library, which contained important and rare documents. According to Williams, "Rich owned probably the finest private collection of Hispano-Americana in Europe" (1:304).

14. Irving to Charles R. Leslie, Madrid, February 23, 1826, in *Letters*, 2:178. The Newton Irving mentions is the artist Gilbert Stuart Newton, with whom he had been on intimate terms in London.

15. See Williams, 1:305–7 for a further description of the contents of this work and of the labor involved in putting it together. The first two volumes of Navarrete's massive collection had been published in 1825; the third did not appear until 1829; the last two saw print in 1837. (All translations from the Spanish are my own.)

16. Irving to Thomas W. Storrow, Madrid, March 15, 1826, in *Letters*, 2:187;

original italics. "None but an historiographer," he added, "would have appetite to devour or Stomach to digest" such a work.

17. Irving to Henry Brevoort, Madrid, February 23, 1828, in *Letters*, 2:275. "But," he added, "I fear I can never regain that delightful confidence which I once enjoyed of, not the good opinion, but the *good will* of my countrymen"; original italics.

18. Irving to Alexander H. Everett, Seville, April 23, 1828, in *Letters*, 2:305. For a discussion of the myriad sources of the *Life and Voyages*, and the manner in which Irving assimilated them, see Williams, 2:296–302, and Hedges, pp. 242–45.

19. Williams, 2:310.

20. Hedges, p. 240.

21. For the contemporary response and a history of the critical opinion on *Columbus*, see Williams, 2:302–8.

22. "Spanish Journal, 1826–1827," in Washington Irving, *Journals and Notebooks: Volume 4, 1826–1829*, ed. Wayne R. Kime and Andrew B. Myers (Boston: Twayne, 1984), pp. 48–58; the entries are dated from September 1 through November 16, 1826.

23. In one of the beginning sketches in *The Alhambra* Irving had written: "From earliest boyhood, when, on the banks of the Hudson, I first pored over the pages of old Gines Perez de Hytas's apocryphal but chivalresque history of the civil wars of Granada, and the feuds of its gallant cavaliers, the Zegries and Abencerrages, that city has ever been a subject of my waking dreams; and often have I trod in fancy the romantic halls of the Alhambra" (*The Alhambra*, ed. William T. Lenehan and Andrew B. Myers [Boston: Twayne, 1983], p. 39; future references to this edition will be cited in the text).

24. "Spanish Journal, 1827–1828," in *Journals and Notebooks*, 4:104–5; the entries are dated October 10 and 11, 1827.

25. "Spanish Journal and Notebook, 1828," in *Journals and Notebooks*, 4:134–44.

26. Irving to Antoinette Bolviller, Granada, March 15, 1828, in *Letters*, 2:281–82; original italics. See also "Spanish Journal and Notebook, 1828," in *Journals and Notebooks*, 4:144; entry dated March 9, 1828. The Darro River runs through the center of Granada; above it, on a high slope, stands the Alhambra. The Generalife is a small Moorish palace adjacent to the Alhambra. It, too, has beautiful gardens and fountains, but is neither as immense nor as complex a construction as the Alhambra.

27. Irving to Antoinette Bolviller, Granada, March 15, 1828, in *Letters*, 2:283. See also "Spanish Journal and Notebook, 1828," in *Journals and Notebooks*, 4:145; entry dated March 11, 1828.

28. Irving to Antoinette Bolviller, Malaga, April 2, 1828, in *Letters*, 2:292. In the "Spanish Journal and Notebook," 1828," Irving noted this anecdote and next to it sketched the "Suspiro del Moro" (*Journals and Notebooks*, 4:156 and opposite 56. Although he constantly records scenes, people, and places—in fact, almost everything that will appear in future sketches—the only object that elicits a response is a picture of Boabdil, which impressed him greatly (p. 152). To Irving, the picture is a confirmation of all the melancholy feelings that the plight of the last Moorish monarch had inspired.

29. Irving to Peter Irving, Alhambra, July 4, 1829; Irving to Henry Brevoort, Valencia, August 10, 1829, in *Letters*, 2:446, 461.

30. "Spanish Notebook and Journal, 1828," in *Journals and Notebooks*, 4:147. Born in the Alhambra, Mateo had always lived there except during the years that the French occupied the fortress (1810–12 and 1820–22).

31. Irving to Antoinette Bolviller, Granada, March 15, 1828, in *Letters*, 2:284.

32. Williams, 1:330.

33. Irving to Antoinette Bolviller, Granada, March 15, 1828, in *Letters*, 2:283.

34. Irving to Prince Dmitri Dolgorouki, Malaga, March 29, 1828; Irving to Antoinette Bolviller, Malaga, April 2, 1828, in *Letters*, 2:289, 293.

35. Irving to David Wilkie, Malaga, April 2, 1828, in *Letters*, 2:297.

36. Irving to Colonel Thomas Aspinwall, Seville, April 4, 1829, in *Letters*, 2:396.

37. Introduction, in *The Conquest of Granada*, Author's Revised Edition (New York: Putnam, 1850), p. [lxiii]. (At the time of this writing, *Granada* is not available in the Twayne edition of Irving's works.)

38. Williams, 1:346, 344; Irving to Prince Dmitri Dolgorouki, Seville, December 13, 1828, in *Letters*, 2:361. Just as he had with *Columbus*, Irving was composing by accretion, and in the same letter to Dolgorouki he described *Granada* as "a kind of chronicle, made up from all the old chronicles & histories; printed or in manuscript, that I could meet with."

39. Irving to Colonel Thomas Aspinwall, Cadiz, August 31, 1828; Irving to Thomas W. Storrow, Puerto de Santa Maria, October 22, 1828, in *Letters*, 2:330–31, 349.

40. Irving to John Murray, Granada, May 9, 1829, in *Letters*, 2:414–15.

41. Hedges also believes Irving sees Granada this way. He writes that "the chief significance of the book" is Irving's effort "to turn the fall of Granada into an emblem of mutability" (p. 254).

42. *Conquest of Granada*, pp. 19–20.

43. Irving to Antoinette Bolviller, Seville, May 28, 1828, in *Letters*, 2:315.

44. Hedges points out that Irving wrote an anonymous review of his own book in the *Quarterly Review* (43 [1830]), in which he noted that his interpretation of Boabdil differs widely from the accepted view of the Moorish king as a cowardly and cruel leader (p. 255).

45. *Conquest of Granada*, pp. 526, 525.

46. Washington Irving, *The Alhambra*, Author's Revised Edition (New York: Putnam, 1851), p. viii. (For some reason unknown to me, the editors of the Twayne edition of Irving's works, although they adopt the Author's Revised Edition of 1851 as copy text, omit the Preface.) Irving inserted this statement in part to counteract the sense that the first readers of *The Alhambra* had gotten that the book was a romance. However, this was largely his own fault, since the original edition was ill-conceived and did not achieve the effect of "verisimilitude" he had wanted.

47. Both Hedges (p. 263) and Williams (1:360) have pointed to Irving's identification of himself with the hero of Cervantes's epic.

48. Irving later recalled that everything in the work relating to himself was "unexaggerated fact"; see Irving to S. Austin Allibone, Sunnyside, November 2, 1857, in Washington Irving, *Letters: Volume 4, 1846–1859*, ed. Ralph M. Aderman et al. (Boston: Twayne, 1982), p. 639.

49. Pochmann, *Representative Selections*, p. lxviii. Evidence of Irving's having "follow[ed] the full stream of Spanish romance" can be found, Pochmann says, in the tales which he developed from the local traditions and legends of Granada, and whose "frank supernaturalism rests on magic hidden in the bowels of the earth by the Moors, demon steeds, flying carpets . . . and phantom armies that emerge from the heart of the mountains" (p. lxviii). While Pochmann's assessment is accurate, he is only talking about approximately one-half of the book. He never asks what possible relationship exists between the fantastic legends Irving collected and then embroidered into tales and what he himself has to say about the time he spent in the Alhambra. He assumes, almost a priori, that the romantic air about the book derives solely from Irving's contrivance as sentimental romanticizer.

50. "Spanish Journal and Notebook, 1829" in *Journals and Notebooks*, 4:260–99. Many of the autobiographical passages in *The Alhambra* have their origins in this 1829 notebook, and almost all the material for such sketches as "Public Fetes of Granada" and "The Veteran" (whom Irving describes as one of the "curious acquaintances" he made on his rambles about the fortress) may also be found here.

51. "Spanish Journal and Notebook, 1829," in *Journals and Notebooks*, 4:267, 268, 271. Cf. *The Alhambra*, pp. 36–39, 40–42. In *The Alhambra*, Irving applies several appellations to his guide, most often "gossiping squire" and "historiographic squire" (pp. 37, 41, for example).

52. In his 1829 notebook Irving recounts a tale Mateo told of a bricklayer who, while blindfolded, assisted a clergyman in burying four huge jars of gold (*Journals and Notebooks*, 4:272–73). Irving expands this anecdote in *The Alhambra* into "The Adventure of the Mason," pp. 76–78. In introducing the tale (p. 75), he relates almost exactly the circumstances in which he first heard it from Mateo.

53. "Spanish Journal and Notebook, 1829," in *Journals and Notebooks*, 4:268–70. In "A Ramble Among the Hills," Irving tells of this experience and repeats, almost verbatim, Mateo's response to the star of the Sierras (*The Alhambra*, pp. 154–55).

54. "Spanish Journal and Notebook, 1829," in *Journals and Notebooks*, 4:275, 270.

55. Irving to Henry Brevoort [Alhambra, May 23, 1829]; Irving to Catharine Paris, Alhambra, June 16, 1829, in *Letters*, 2:424, 441–42; "Recollections of the Alhambra," in *Wolfert's Roost*, ed. Roberta Rosenberg (Boston: Twayne, 1979), p. 230. The essay was originally published in the *Knickerbocker* for June 1839.

56. Grabar, *The Alhambra* (Cambridge: Harvard University Press, 1978), pp. 113–14, 167, 114–15. The Alhambra, erected and occupied by the Moors four hundred years before Irving's time, had fallen to the Spaniards, under the leadership of Ferdinand and Isabella, in 1492.

57. See, for example, "Spanish Journal and Notebook, 1829," in *Journals and Notebooks*, 4:277 (entry dated July 11, 1829); Irving to Peter Irving, Alhambra, June 13, 1829, in *Letters*, 2:436; Grabar, p. 120.

58. Cf. the epigraph to "The Legend of Sleepy Hollow" (*The Sketch Book*, ed. Haskell Springer [Boston: Twayne, 1978], p. 272):

> A pleasing land of drowsy head it was,
> Of dreams that wave before the half-shut eye;
> And of gay castles in the clouds that pass,
> Forever flushing round a summer sky.
> "Castle of Indolence"

In both "Sleepy Hollow" and *The Alhambra*, interestingly enough, legend plays an important part in the lives of the people, lives which are characterized by a propensity for imaginative activity.

59. In *The Alhambra*, Irving's account of the offer occurs in "Important Negotiations—The Author Succeeds to the Throne of Boabdil" (pp. 35–36). The sketch is the beginning of Irving's identification with the last Moorish ruler of Granada, often referred to as "El Rey Chico" ("The Little King").

60. Irving to Peter Irving, Alhambra, May 13, 1829, in *Letters*, 2:419.

61. Cf. Irving's sketch of "The Angler," where Geoffrey Crayon expresses his fondness for the pastoral vision as it appears in "the seductive pages of honest Izaak Walton" (*The Sketch Book*, pp. 264–71).

62. Grabar, p. 208; my italics.

63. Even though there is some discrepancy as to the date Irving changed his quarters—Pierre Irving has it as June 12, 1829 (*The Life and Letters of Washington Irving* [New York: Putnam, 1862–64], 2:390); Stanley Williams, however, establishes the date as May 29, 1829 (1:366)—the two choices are near enough to each other to say that after about one-fourth to one-third of his total stay in the Alhambra (he took up his residence there on May 12 and departed on July 29), he changed his quarters to the "mysterious chambers" where he remained for the duration of his visit.

64. Grabar, pp. 209–10.

65. Grabar, pp. 185–86.

66. This is how Hedges (p. 133) describes the threat imposed by the abbey.

67. Stanley T. Williams, *The Spanish Background of American Literature* (New Haven: Yale University Press, 1955), 2:45.

68. Irving to Henry Brevoort, Valencia, August 10, 1829, in *Letters*, 2:461.

69. Irving to Prince Dmitri Dolgorouki, Alhambra, June 15, 1829, in *Letters*, 2:438–39.

70. "Notes and Extracts, 1825," in *Journals and Notebooks*, 3:674. Milton's letter is dated March 24, 1656.

71. Irving to Peter Irving, Alhambra, July 18, 1829, in *Letters*, 2:447.

72. "Spanish Journal and Notebook, 1829," in *Journals and Notebooks*, 4:277. Of course this anxiety had beset Irving before, most notably in connection with *Tales of a Traveller*, but also in *The Sketch Book* in "Westminster Abbey" (although it was present even in the initial sketch of "The Voyage").

73. Irving to Henry Brevoort [Alhambra, May 23, 1829]; Irving to Catharine Paris, Alhambra, June 16, 1829, in *Letters*, 2:424, 442.

74. Irving to Peter Irving, Alhambra, July 18, 1829, in *Letters*, 2:447.

75. Irving to Alexander H. Everett, Alhambra, July 22, 1829; Irving to Thomas W. Storrow, Bordeaux, February 3, 1826; Irving to John Wetherell, Alhambra, July 18, 1829, in *Letters*, 2:450, 172, 448.

76. Haskell Springer, "Creative Contradictions in Irving," in *Washington Irving Reconsidered: A Symposium*, ed. Ralph M. Aderman (Hartford: Transcendental Books, 1969), p. 14.

77. Williams takes Irving severely to task for choosing the appointment over what would have been best for his writing (1:368–69). As he argues, it is extremely important for the overall effect of the book that the structure be right, and both the British and American first editions have numerous flaws in this area. Different legends are associated with and grow out of Irving's contact with different parts of the Alhambra; each legend should be placed immediately after the sketch of the particular court or hall or tower to which it makes reference. But in the two-volume 1832 edition, the sketches appear mostly in the first, the legends in the second. The book definitely loses something this way—most emphatically, the sense of the interpenetration of reality and fantasy which was an integral part of the experience. Also, "The Author's Farewell to Granada," where Irving makes his identification with Boabdil most explicit, was not included in the first edition; neither were many passages which heighten the mystery and sense of discovery that surround the Alhambra.

78. Irving to Henry Brevoort, Valencia, August 10, 1829; Irving to Ebenezer Irving, Alhambra, July 22, 1829; Irving to John Wetherell, Alhambra, July 27, 1829; Irving to Peter Irving, Alhambra, July 25, 1829, in *Letters*, 2:460, 451, 456, 454.

79. Irving to Alexander H. Everett, Alhambra, July 22, 1829; Irving to Henry Brevoort, Valencia, August 10, 1829, in *Letters*, 2:450, 461.

80. Hedges also notes this (p. 265n).

81. Professor Robert Ferguson of the University of Chicago, in a conversation with the present writer, expressed his feeling that much of Irving's later work was a form of "paying his debts" to America by celebrating its vigorous westward expansion.

82. Irving to Peter Irving, Granada, May 9, 1829, in *Letters*, 2:412.

CODA

1. "Notes and Extracts, 1825," in Washington Irving, *Journals and Notebooks: Volume 3, 1819–1827*, ed. Walter A. Reichart (Madison: University of Wisconsin Press, 1970), pp. 660, 661.

2. Poirier, *A World Elsewhere: The Place of Style in American Literature* (New York: Oxford University Press, 1966), p. 5.

3. Irving to Thomas W. Storrow, Bordeaux, December 2, 1825, in Washington Irving, *Letters: Volume 2, 1823–1838*, ed. Ralph M. Aderman et al. (Boston: Twayne, 1979), p. 151. Cf. "French Journal, 1823–1826," in *Journals and Notebooks*, 3:544, 546, 547; entries dated November 16, 24, and 26, 1825.

4. Irving to Thomas W. Storrow, Madrid, February 23, 1828, in *Letters*, 2:278.

5. Irving to Henry Brevoort, Madrid, February 23, 1828, in *Letters*, 2:275.

6. Poirier, p. 5.

7. See Tanner, *City of Words: American Fiction 1950–1970* (New York: Harper & Row, 1971), esp. the Introduction, pp. 15–31.

8. Irving to Helen Dodge Irving, Sunnyside, April 30, 1847, in Washington Irving, *Letters: Volume 4, 1846–1859*, ed Ralph M. Aderman et al. (Boston: Twayne, 1982), p. 131.

9. Irving to Colonel Thomas Aspinwall, Madrid, November 27, 1827, in *Letters*, 2:255.

10. Irving to Henry Brevoort [Alhambra, May 23, 1829], in *Letters*, 2:425.

INDEX

Adams, John, 1, 7, 145; death of, 12–15, 25, 77–78. *See also* Founding fathers, perceptions of
Adams, John Quincy, 12–13, 78
Addison, Joseph, 32, 65
Agrarian virtue, 141, 143–51, 154. *See also* Republican ideology
Alhambra, The. See Irving, Washington, works
Allston, Washington, 223; *Monaldi,* 194
American anxiety, xiii, xv–xviii, 1–31, 76–77, 99, 100, 122, 146, 148, 154, 159, 208
American Institute (American Society), 148
American literature. British/European attitudes toward, 59, 65; creation of, 30, 40, 65, 254; American Renaissance, xiii
American Revolution, 1, 3, 9, 79, 149
Analectic Magazine, 29, 95
Anxiety, defined, xvi–xvii
Appleby, Joyce, 148
Arabian Nights, The, 156

Baldwin, Elihu W., 70
Barca, Calderon, de la, *El Embozado,* 190
Beecher, Lyman, 70
Belknap, Jeremy, *The History of New Hampshire,* 143
Bell, Michael Davitt, 209
Berthoff, Rowland, 5
Bloom, Harold, 54
Bolingbroke, Henry St. John, Viscount, "Reflections Upon Exile," 218
Bracebridge Hall. See Irving, Washington, works

Brevoort, Henry, 2, 27, 30, 34–35, 36, 37, 38, 104, 108, 110, 131, 151, 170, 171, 179, 180, 217, 218, 221, 245, 248, 249, 253, 255
Brooks, Van Wyck, 64
Burke, Edmund, 157
Byron, George Gordon, Lord, 190

Carlyle, Thomas, 34
Carroll, Charles, 13
"Castle of Indolence," 245
Channing, William Ellery, 3–4
Chaucer, Geoffrey, 137
Choate, Rufus, 7
Clay, Henry, 5
Cobbett, William, 133
Common Sense philosophy, 208
Constitution, United States, 9
Cooper, James Fenimore, xviii, 2, 15, 19–20, 26, 30; *The Crater,* 15; *The Pioneers,* 15; *The Spy,* 15–20, 26; *Wept of Wish-Ton-Wish,* 15, 16; *Wyandotté,* 15
Cooper, Susan Fenimore, 19–20
Crèvecoeur, J. Hector St. John de, 142, 147; *Letters from an American Farmer,* 144
Cronon, William, 9

Dana, Richard Henry, Sr., 41
Darley, Felix O. C., 214
Democratic party, xvii
Demos, John, 9
Dolgorouki, Dmitri, Prince, 235, 244
Dunlap, William, 216

299